FAITH, POWER AND TERRITORY
A Handbook of British Islam

PATRICK SOOKHDEO

Faith, Power and Territory: A Handbook of British Islam

Published in the United States of America by Isaac Publishing
6729 Curran Street
McLean VA 22101

ISBN 978-0-9547835-8-7 (pbk)   ISBN 978-0-9787141-3-0 (hbk)

Printed in the United Kingdom by Cromwell Press Limited, Trowbridge, Wiltshire.

Contents

FOREWORD

In his latest book, Dr Sookhdeo sets out to raise awareness among the general public in Britain of key issues relating to the relationship between British Islam and the state. This is an important task, and the approach taken in this study is to be commended in wide-ranging ways.

Due recognition is given to the great diversity among Muslims in Britain, with an acknowledgement that the majority of British Muslims are decent and law-abiding. At the same time, Dr Sookhdeo notes that certain elements within the faith system of Islam serve to unite these disparate groups. Moreover, a process of gradual radicalisation is taking place, fuelled by certain theological doctrines as well as influences from other Muslim communities around the world.

Islam is much more than a set of religious beliefs and practices, relegated to one day per week for the faithful. Rather it is a blueprint for life in all its detail, covering diverse aspects of human living: faith, law, financial structures, social mores and much more. So the outworkings of the Muslim presence in Britain affect multiple dimensions of state and society. Dr Sookhdeo sets out to trace the nature of this complex Muslim presence in an accessible manner.

The relationship between Muslims and non-Muslims has been highly variable in recent years. On one level there has been great tension, resulting from and fuelled by the public transport attacks by Islamist radicals in July 2005 and similar abortive attacks more recently. On another level there has been some coming together of certain Muslims and non-Muslims, in an attempt to bridge bridges rather than walls.

Commentators have tended to focus on one or other of those levels, highlighting either the problems or the successes in inter-community relationships. This present book manages to bridge the two in a way which is most helpful. There are causes for optimism in some ways regarding the relationship between Muslims and non-Muslims in Britain. At the same time, there are clear causes for concern, especially given the continuing threat to British society from Islamist radicals, accompanied by a subtle but discernible process of Islamisation taking place in certain segments of British education, law, media and so forth.

At this time there is a very clear struggle taking place within the British Muslim community to shape the future direction of the community. The participants in this struggle are summarised expertly in this book, with its focus on leading Muslim organisations and individuals, from diverse ideological and institutional streams.

The resolution of this struggle is vital for the future well-being of British society. I strongly affirm Dr Sookhdeo's two-fold call: first to the British government and establishment not to engage in appeasement as a solution to inter-community problems; and second, to peaceful and progressive Muslims to take a strong and public stand against radicals, and to push for reform and reinterpretation of the fundamental ingredients of their faith to address any doctrines or teachings which provide sustenance to radical ideologies.

Professor Peter G. Riddell
London School of Theology
September 2007

PREFACE

The July 2005 London bombings awakened many to the reality of the growing threat of Islamic inspired terrorism in the United Kingdom, perpetrated by British Muslims. Many are confused as to why this should be happening and wonder from where the radical ideologies driving the terrorists emanate.

This book aims to give the general public a working understanding of Islam in Britain. It seeks to cover mainstream Islamic beliefs and practices as well as key opinion-formers and organisational and institutional structures. It highlights the variant ideologies and groups which are particulary important in the UK, and this includes radical Islamist organisations and ideologies. The book shows that modern radicalism, as seen in the UK, is rooted in an intolerant strand of early and classical Islam that has been carried through over the centuries in various forms. It has been strengthened in recent decades by the current global resurgence of Islam and in the UK by the development of multiculturalism amongst other factors.

Islam regards itself as not only a religious faith but also a political power. It has the tenets and practices of a faith, but these are inseparable from structural and institutional power in society. The title "Faith, Power and Territory" is intended to sum up the Muslim concept of their own religion and its application to the UK.

There is a dramatic numerical growth of Muslims in Britain, and their strong religious commitment is evident. How will this reshape a British society based originally on Judaeo-Christian foundations? Britain has evolved into a society shaped by civic institutions and in which great value is placed on the autonomy of the individual. As a result, the idea of a religion such as Islam shaping the structures of society is incredible and almost unintelligible to most indigenous Britons. Nevertheless some would see this development as positive in that, for the first time in centuries, religion is at the centre of society again. However the question of the effect of the presence of zealous Muslims in the UK needs very careful thought. This is particularly true at a time when Christianity is not only increasingly marginalised by pluralism, neutralised by secular humanism and riven by internal conflict but also in a state of serious decline in numbers and influence. The future character of the United Kingdom is uncertain. The dramatic changes that are taking place in culture and religion need to be noted. It is hoped that this handbook will help to give a degree of understanding of the situation and point to some of the issues which need to be addressed.

It is not the author's intention to encourage or incite antipathy or hatred of any kind, but rather to promote understanding through knowledge.

INTRODUCTION

This handbook is intended to provide a framework of basic information on certain aspects of the Muslim community in the United Kingdom. On this can be hung the ever-changing controversies, issues, rhetoric and debates which engage both Muslims and non-Muslims at present. Although most Muslims in the UK are decent, law-abiding individuals whose primary focus is providing for their families, and who follow a traditional version of Islam, they are becoming subject to a process of radicalisation. This radicalisation is a worldwide phenomenon, as Islam increasingly returns to its roots in the form of classical Islam with its concomitant political dimensions. A main focus in this book will be contemporary ideologies, in particular those coming under the heading "radical" because it is radical Islam which has the greatest impact on the lives and situation of non-Muslims. However, it must always be recognised that there is a great diversity in British Islam, and that many Muslims have made very valuable contributions to British society, for example, in the fields of science, medicine, literature, architecture, economics and sport to name but a few. The government has rightly recognised some of these contributions through the award of honours.

Why being a minority poses problems for Muslims

Islam is unique among major world religions in its emphasis on state structures and governance, which are considered to be of as much importance as private belief and morality (if not more). Much of Islamic teaching is concerned with how to rule and

1

organise society within an Islamic state and how that Islamic state should relate to other states.

The late Dr Zaki Badawi, president of the Muslim College in London, commented:

> Muslims, from the start, lived under their own law. Muslim theologians naturally produced a theology with this in view – it is a theology of the majority. Being a minority was not seriously considered or even contemplated... Muslim theology offers, up to the present, no systematic formulation of the status of being a minority.[1]

Islam, which developed in a historical context of political and military dominance, has not evolved a theology of how Muslims should live as a minority i.e. in a society which is not ruled according to Islamic law. It is small wonder that British Islam is in a state of flux and internal discord as Muslims debate how they should live and behave in a non-Muslim society. While this debate obviously applies in many non-Muslim countries, it is particularly vigorous in the UK. In 1997 Abu'l A'la Mawdudi's famous work, *Jihad fi Sabilillah (Jihad in Islam)*, which has shaped much of contemporary Islam, was re-printed in a fresh edition by the UK Islamic Mission Dawah Centre. It contains this paragraph about what will happen when Islam takes power in a non-Muslim nation:

> as soon as the Ummah of Islam seizes state power, it will outlaw all forms of business transacted on the basis of usury or interest; it will not permit gambling; it will curb all forms of business and financial dealings which contravene Islamic Law; it will shut down all brothels and other dens of vice; it will make it obligatory for non-Muslim women to observe the minimum standards of modesty in dress as required by Islamic Law, and forbid them to go about displaying their beauty as in the Days of Ignorance; it will impose censorship on the film industry. With a view to ensuring the general welfare of the public and for reasons of self-defence, the Islamic government will not permit such cultural activities as may be permissible in non-Muslim systems but which Islam regards as detrimental and even fatal to moral fibre.[2]

What unites Muslims

Most Muslims would agree on the following three items as essential components of their Muslim identity.

1. *Creed*
   The Islamic creed runs: "There is no god but Allah, and Muhammad is his messenger." This is understood to mean that Muhammad is the last and final messenger. It is usually recited in Arabic and is known as the *shahada* or *kalimatu shahada*. It is the first duty of every Muslim to affirm their faith with the words of the creed. Some Muslims believe that the mere recitation of these words is sufficient to convert a non-Muslim to Islam, even if there is no belief.

2. *Shari'a (Islamic law)*
   Using the Qur'an and traditions (*ahadith*) of the life of Muhammad, early Islamic theologians and jurists produced detailed regulations to govern not only the private lives of individual Muslims but also the conduct of politics, economics, warfare, criminal justice, inheritance and family law, and many other aspects of communal life. The term *shari'a* (literally "way" or "path") is used to refer to this body of law. Most Muslims agree on the need to follow *shari'a*.

3. *Umma*
   The *umma* is the Islamic nation i.e. whole community of Islam, comprising all Muslim people. No matter how great the differences between Muslims, there is a virtually universal belief that they must support each other against non-Muslims.

What divides Muslims

Much of this handbook is devoted to describing different groups within Islam. Here are some broad categories.

Ethnic

Even in the days of Muhammad there was discrimination on the basis of birthplace and tribe, with his Meccan-born followers considered superior to those born in Medina, and his own tribe, the Quraish, the most dominant of all. Inter-ethnic conflict has continued throughout Islamic history, with Arab, Turk and Persian fighting each other. A phenomenon of our own times is the increasing dominance of Arab Islam over non-Arab Islam, for example, in Indonesia and Central Asia. The same can be seen in the UK where the Asian majority within the Muslim community is increasingly being influenced by the Arab minority. Tensions exist between Asians, Arabs, Africans, Caribbean converts and white converts. Mosques tend to become dominated by one particular ethnic group, although there are a few which are able to maintain an ethnic diversity.

Sectarian

Within twenty years of Muhammad's death there was a huge and bloody leadership conflict which split the Muslim community into three groups. Two of these survive today as the Sunni and Shi'a streams of Islam – still at war with each other in certain parts of the world. The conflict was rooted in theological differences about how the succession to the caliphate should be organised and who were therefore the legitimate successors to Muhammad's authority.

Theology is the source of a surprisingly high proportion of the differences within Islam today. Even the unifying factors cited above can also be dividing factors:

- There are some sects who are not accepted as Islamic by other Muslims. One such is the Ahmadiyya, who were founded in the Punjab in 1889 by Mirza Ghulam Ahmad. They suffer severe persecution in Pakistan because of their belief in an ongoing prophethood after the death of Muhammad i.e. that Muhammad was not the **final** messenger of God (see page 179). The Ahmadiyya are of particular importance in the UK as they are very active here in proselytising.

4

- *Shariʻa* causes division because several competing versions of *shariʻa* exist, devised by different scholars of the eighth and ninth centuries AD. In the UK, where the majority of Muslims have roots in the Indian sub-continent, the most popular would be the Hanafi school of *shariʻa*. Another cause of division is the fact that the *shariʻa* has little to say about many modern situations in which Muslims may be unsure how to conduct themselves. Perplexed Muslims must turn to their twenty-first century leaders for guidance, and those leaders give a variety of different instructions, thus causing futher divisions.

It must be remembered that there is a growing number of completely secular Muslims, who do not practise their faith at all, and are Muslim only in culture. They are a hidden minority within the community and often unrepresented in discussions and debates.

Radical-traditional-liberal

This theological divide spans all the formal sects and groups within Islam. The question of how literally to take the original teachings of Islam is arguably the main subject of debate for British Muslims today. It is definitely an important Islamic issue for British non-Muslims.

Liberal Muslims are happy to adapt their faith to fit modern Western standards of human rights. (They are distinct from secular Muslims in that liberal Muslims do have a faith and will doubtless pray and observe various other religious practices.) **Traditionalists** accept Islam as it developed over its first centuries and became fixed by the schools of law. They do not accept innovations or new interpretations, and many may practise "folk Islam" and Sufism. Most reject secularism and Western culture. **Radicals** (also called Islamists, fundamentalists or extremists) consider themselves reformers who have returned to the basic teachings of Islam as it was in its pure, original form. They seek political domination of society and some are willing to use violence if necessary to achieve this. They reject secularism and Western culture even more forcefully than do the traditionalists.

- Loyalty to the *umma* becomes a divisive issue when it competes with loyalty to the UK as a citizen or resident. British Muslims are debating which of these two loyalties should be paramount.

Islam is the world's second largest religion, with around 1.2 billion adherents worldwide.

Over 50 countries in the world are Muslim-majority, many acknowledging Islam as their state religion and the basis of their legal systems.

In the UK there are now some 3 million Muslims. This compares to 3 million in Germany and 5 million each in the United States and in France.

London has around 1 million Muslim residents. The next largest community is in Birmingham, which has approximately 150,000 Muslims. Over 50% of British Muslims were born in the UK.

The UK has over 5,000 Muslim millionaires.

The UK has at least:
    1700 mosques (many with *madrassas* attached)
    100 Muslim schools
    1200 Muslim organisations

---

1 MUHAMMAD AND THE ORIGINS OF ISLAM

To understand British Islam, it is necessary to know what British Muslims believe. The traditional Muslim view of early Islamic history is based exclusively on Muslim sources, uncorroborated by any other evidence. The earliest of these Muslim sources were written some 150 years after the events they describe.

The following history of Muhammad and early Islam represents what *Muslims believe about their early history* as based on Muslim source texts. Western scholars hold a variety of opinions as to how accurate this is likely to be. The most important aspect of this era in Islamic history is that Muslims, through the centuries since, have always looked back on Muhammad as the perfect model of a human being and the Islamic state he founded in Medina as the perfect model of a state. Muhammad is seen as an example to be followed by Muslims today, and many Muslims would also seek to recreate an Islamic state as similar to his as possible. The time of the first four caliphs, Muhammad's immediate successors as rulers of the Islamic state, is also particularly important in terms of providing a model for later Muslims to emulate. These four are known as the "rightly guided caliphs" and the period of their rule is seen as an early golden age of Islam.

In order to set the stage for what Muslims believe about their history, it is useful to look at the context of the Arabian Peninsula just before the advent of Islam. The Arabic-speaking tribes worshipped numerous gods. Honour and vengeance were important tribal values, and poetry was the main artistic accomplishment.

In Mecca, Muhammad's home town, there was an important pagan shrine, the *ka'ba,* a cube-shaped building that was said to house 360 idols of tribal patron deities. Built into the eastern corner of the *ka'ba* was the "Black Stone", said to have fallen from heaven. This was the site of an annual pilgrimage for tribes from all over Arabia.

There were several Jewish communities in Arabia as well as Christians. Pagan Arabs could thus gain some knowledge of Jewish and Christian scriptures and doctrines.

Arabia was situated between the two super-powers of the time, the Christian Byzantine Empire and the Zoroastrian Persian Empire, which were engaged in a long-running armed conflict with each other.

In later Muslim opinion, this pre-Islamic era was called the age of ignorance (*jahiliyya),* a byword for barbarism, immorality and idolatry. For most Muslims, "true" history begins with the advent of Islam, and they have little interest in anything that happened before.

MUHAMMAD (570–632 AD)

According to Muslim sources, Muhammad was born around 570 AD in the prosperous trading town of Mecca to a poor family of the respected Quraish tribe that had custody of the *ka'ba.* His father had died before his birth and his mother when he was six, leaving him in the care of his grandfather who died two years later. Muhammad was then brought up by an uncle who took him on long trading caravan trips to Syria.

As a young man Muhammad found employment with a rich widow, Khadija, who was fifteen years his senior. They were married when he was 25. They had seven children, but all three of their sons died young. Of the daughters who survived, Fatima is the most famous. She married Muhammad's cousin Ali. After 25 years of marriage, Khadija died and Muhammad subsequently married a further twelve wives.

The birth of Islam

Muhammad used to spend time meditating in a mountain cave near Mecca. At the age of 40, while on such a retreat, Muslims believe that he had a vision of the angel Gabriel, who gave Muhammad the first in a long series of messages which he was commanded to preach to mankind. These messages were later collected by his followers as the Qur'an. Khadija became his first disciple and set aside any doubts he had as to the authenticity of the visions. However, most Meccans rejected his teaching, and their growing hostility led to a violent persecution of the small band of Muslims. In 622 Muhammad and his followers moved to the city of Yathrib (later called Medina) whose inhabitants were more favourably disposed to his message. The migration to Medina is called the *hijra*, and serves as an important paradigm for some Muslims today in their relations with non-Muslims.

Muhammad was able to unite the various factions in Medina and lead them in battle against his Meccan enemies. In Medina he was no longer a mere preacher, but became the head of state – its ruler, lawgiver, supreme judge and military commander. After much fighting, the Meccans eventually surrendered to the Muslims and Muhammad entered Mecca victoriously, destroyed the idols in the *ka'ba,* and turned it into the centre of his new religion, Islam. (Muslims, of course, believe that theirs is not a new religion but a continuation of the revelations given to Adam, Abraham and Jesus.)

The Prophet Muhammad (PBUH)

Because of the great respect and veneration Muslims bear Muhammad, Muslims always refer to him as the "Prophet Muhammad". 'Peace be Upon Him', abbreviated as (PBUH), normally follows any mention of him in English. Sometimes SAS or SAW is added instead, being the abbreviation for the equivalent Arabic phrase (*sala Allah 'alayhi wa sallam,* literally "God prayed over him and gave him peace"). Sometimes this is written in Arabic even if the rest of the text is in English.

Controversies with Jews and Christians

Muhammad had initially recognised the validity of Judaism and Christianity. After moving to Medina, he gradually turned against his Jewish allies who would not accept his claims to being a prophet of the one true God nor practise the new religious customs he initiated. This friction with Jews, and later with various Christian communities, confirmed to him the absolute superiority of Islam. Muhammad fought the Jewish tribes, massacred many of their men, enslaved many of their women and children, and expelled others from their lands. His hardening of attitude to Jews and Christians is clearly seen within the Qur'an, whose earlier verses are much more peaceable than its later verses.

MUHAMMAD'S DEATH AND THE EARLY EXPANSION OF ISLAM

By the time Muhammad died in 632 virtually the whole of the Arabian peninsula was under at least some degree of Islamic control. Under Muhammad's successor, Caliph Abu Bakr, control of the peninsula was consolidated and Muhammad's plans to conquer the neighbouring lands of the Byzantine Empire were implemented. After Abu Bakr the same pattern continued, as large parts of both the Byzantine Empire and the Persian Empire were subdued in what the Muslims called holy war, *jihad*. There was also a large-scale emigration of Arab Muslims into the newly conquered regions, following Muhammad's example of migration to Medina and in order to facilitate political domination.

The four "rightly-guided" caliphs

Abu Bakr 632–634 (died of natural causes)

'Umar 634–644 (assassinated)

'Uthman 644–656 (assassinated)

'Ali 656–661 (assassinated)

CIVIL WAR AND DIVISION

Although the four "rightly guided" caliphs were all trusted friends of Muhammad, there was very far from being a consensus within the Muslim community about their right to succeed him as supreme leader. Some claimed that Muhammad had designated only 'Ali, his cousin and son-in-law, to be his successor. By 656 tensions came to a head in a civil war within the *umma*. The war continued until 661 when 'Ali was assassinated and Mu'awiya (head of 'Uthman's clan, the Umayyads) was established as caliph with his capital in Damascus. The *umma* was split and remains so to this day.

The Shi'a

The Shi'a, who today comprise 10–20% of all Muslims, believe that 'Ali and his male descendants are the legal successors to Muhammad who should rule the Muslim world.

'Ali's son Hussein attempted to regain the caliphate from Mu'awiya's son Yazid. However he and his small band of followers were killed by Yazid's army near Karbala in Iraq in 680. The martyrdom of Hussein became a dominant theme in Shi'a doctrine, and Karbala a place of pilgrimage.

The Shi'a today constitute the majority in Iran, Iraq, Azerbaijan and Bahrain. They form significant minorities in Yemen, Lebanon, the Gulf, and the Indian subcontinent. Since the initial break from the rest of the Muslim community, Shi'as have continued to splinter into ever more groups over the question of legitimate succession between various eligible brothers. The largest group are the Twelvers (or Imamites), dominant in Iran and numerous in Iraq, Lebanon, the Gulf and Pakistan. They recognise twelve Imams of the house of 'Ali, the last one having disappeared in the ninth century. Twelvers believe that this last Imam, the Hidden Imam, will return one day as the saviour (*mahdi*) to establish God's kingdom on earth. Other groups are the Zaydis (Fivers) who ruled Yemen for many centuries, and the Isma'ilis (Seveners) who established the Fatimid Empire in Egypt, but are now a scattered minority led mainly by the Agha Khan. In Turkey there is a significant Shi'a minority, the Alevis, comprising some 25% of the Turkish population, who revere 'Ali as an incarnation of God.

The Kharijis

The Kharijis rejected both Sunni and Shi'a claims, arguing that the position of caliph should be open to any suitable Muslim who was pious enough, irrespective of his (or her) lineage. They believed that those who opposed them were not true Muslims and therefore had to be fought and killed. It was a Khariji who assassinated Caliph 'Ali. The Kharijis rebelled against the Sunni majority almost constantly for two centuries and were finally exterminated. Tiny remnants, now peaceful and called the Ibadis, have survived in Oman, east Africa and southern Algeria.

The Sunnis

The main body of Muslims – those who did not split away to become Shi'as or Kharijis – are now known as Sunnis. They constitute at least 80% of the Muslim community today. The Sunnis accept the historical sequence of the first four caliphs and their successors as legitimate. Their position was that any suitable person from the Quraish tribe could be elected as caliph. Sunni empires and states have dominated the Muslim world throughout its history.

FURTHER EXPANSION AND CONQUEST

Notwithstanding this internal conflict, the Islamic conquest of the non-Muslim world continued. By 750 the Muslim empire stretched from Spain and Morocco in the west to India and the borders of China in the east. Many who would not accept Islam were killed or enslaved and huge tracts of land confiscated for the Islamic state and the Arab settlers. The success of this early *jihad* is considered by Muslims to be miraculous, confirming that God had destined Islam to rule the world.

The conquered subjects entered a long period of Muslim domination. As non-Muslims they had reduced rights within the Islamic state, and this led gradually to large-scale conversions to Islam, which eventually became the majority religion. In Palestine, Syria, Iraq and North Africa there was also a parallel process of Arabisation, as local ethnic and linguistic identities (Coptic, Syriac, Berber) were submerged into an overarching Arabic identity.

For further information

For further information on early Islam, the reader is referred to:

Bernard Lewis, *The Middle East: 2,000 Years of History from the Rise of Christianity to the Present Day* new edition (London: Orion Publishing, 2001)

Bat Ye'or, *The Dhimmi: Jews and Christians Under Islam*, revised and enlarged edition (London: Associated University Presses, 1985)

Bat Ye'or, *The Decline of Eastern Christianity under Islam: From Islam to Dhimmitude* (Cranbury, New Jersey / London: Fairleigh Dickinson University Press and Associated University Presses, 1996)

Patrick Sookhdeo, *Global Jihad: The Future in the Face of Militant Islam* (McLean, Virginia: Isaac Publishing, 2007)

---

2   BEING A MUSLIM

This chapter aims to help the non-Muslim reader understand something of how a British Muslim might live out his or her faith. There is a vast range of beliefs, interpretations and levels of zeal, not to mention ethnic differences, but in spite of that there is a basic core of beliefs and practices which all Muslims (bar the most secular) would acknowledge as intrinsic to their faith. Having examined the common threads of belief and practice, the chapter goes on to look at three variations on this theme which are particularly relevant in the UK. It ends with the problem of loyalty, one of the main dilemmas facing Muslims living in the UK today.

BASIC CORE OF ISLAMIC BELIEFS AND PRACTICE

Islam demands faith in its doctrines and practice of its rituals. It is based on several powerfully unifying core elements, which would be accepted by all Muslims in the UK, as well as around the world. The most important among these are:

- One God
- One final prophet – Muhammad
- One final revelation – the Qur'an
- One law for all – the *shari'a*
- One perfect model – Muhammad
- One people of God – the *umma*

More formally, Islam lists six articles of faith and five (or six) obligatory duties.

Six articles of faith

1. **God:** Muslims believe in the absolute unity of God who has no partners or associates, is all powerful and beyond man's understanding.
2. **Angels:** God's supernatural messengers, who watch over humans and record their good and bad deeds.
3. **Holy books:** The Torah, the Psalms, the Gospels and the Qur'an. Muslims believe the first three have been changed and distorted by Jews and Christians so only the Qur'an is reliable and binding.
4. **Prophets:** Muslims revere a vast range of prophets, incouding Abraham, Moses and Jesus. Muhammad, however, is the greatest prophet, the last and the best. He is the perfect example for humanity to follow.
5. **The day of judgement and the resurrection:** Following catastrophic signs, there will be a resurrection and a final day of judgement in which God will send the wicked to hell and the good to paradise. (See box on Islamic eschatology, page 16.)
6. **Predestination:** God in his sovereignty has decreed all things. Man's duty is to submit to God's will.

Five obligatory duties ("pillars of religion")

1. Frequent recitation of the basic creed (*shahada* or *kalimatu shahada*): "There is no God but Allah and Muhammad is his messenger."
2. Ritual prayers (*salat*) at the five appointed daily times, accompanied by ceremonial washings and postures.
3. Fasting (*sawm*) daily from sunrise to sunset during the month of Ramadan. During the fast Muslims abstain from food, drink, sexual relations and smoking.
4. The giving of alms (*zakat*) to the poor in proportion to one's wealth. (For a full description of what *zakat* can be used for, see the glossary entry on *zakat*.)
5. The pilgrimage (*haj*) to Mecca at least once in a lifetime for those in good health who can afford it.

Some Muslims add holy war (*jihad*) as a sixth pillar.

Islamic eschatology

Classical Islamic eschatology predicted a period of great cosmic conflict preceding the final judgement. This tribulation period is characterised by natural catastrophes as well as terrible wars. An Antichrist figure (*Dajjal*) appears who causes corruption and oppression all over the world, deceiving many by his miracles and false teachings. A heaven-sent saviour, the *mahdi* then appears to fight the forces of Satan, restore Islam to its original perfection and glory, and set up God's kingdom on earth. Muslims in all traditions await the *mahdi* deliverer, but the *mahdi* concept is especially important for the Shi'a. They believe that their last Imam did not die, but is now in a supernatural state of occultation (i.e. hidden) from which he will return as the *mahdi* to initiate a period of universal peace, justice and prosperity in which all humanity accepts Islam. In the meantime, believers undergo a period of trials and testing in which they are called to watch for the "signs of the times" as revealed in the apocalyptic prophecies.

Self-proclaimed *mahdis* have arisen all over the Muslim world throughout its history, posing a danger to established rulers who tended to suppress them as causing *fitna* (civil unrest). Self-proclaimed *mahdis* also led resistance movements to Western imperialism in the nineteenth century. Mahdism is thus a concept with great mobilising powers for Muslims at all times, but especially in times of crisis and weakness.

Da'wa (Islamic mission)

Islam is a missionary religion and all Muslims have a God-given duty to witness to their faith and win converts.[3] Shamim A. Siddiqi sets out in *Methodology of Dawah Ilallah in American Perspective* some detailed guidance on how to engage in *da'wa* in the USA. For example, he describes how to use interfaith dialogue as a stage towards the conversion of the non-Muslim participants in the dialogue.

> Through Contacts with Churches, Synagagues, Colleges and Universities ... The I.M.O.A. [Islamic Movement of America] will open dialogues with dignitaries of the religious institutions, presenting Islam as the common legacy of Judeo-Christian religions and as the only Guidance now available to mankind in its most perfect form for its Falah (Deliverance and Salvation). ... The religious dignitaries and learned teachers of Universities and colleges will also be invited to speak in the arranged open Dawah programme of the Movement on various issues and topics of common interest. ... This will give an opportunity to the Da'ee to thrash out the issue and bring the dicsussion to the desired conclusion. These dialogues, speeches and discussions will pave the way in reducing their hard-line stand against Islam.[4]

Islamic *da'wa* (literally "call") however goes beyond merely proclaiming the Islamic faith and gaining individual converts. It is seen as a communal responsibility aimed at extending the political and legal domain of Islam at the expense of all "unbelievers" (*kuffar*). In this respect it is linked to *jihad*. A recent document produced by the Dutch intelligence service recognises the link between *da'wa* and *jihad*.[5] It is also instructive to see how Muslim charitable giving can go to finance *jihad* and *da'wa* as well as helping the poor. (See glossary entry on *zakat* for the Qur'anic basis of this.)

Da'wa is often misunderstood in the West, being viewed as equivalent to Christian evangelism. But it is important to realise that it is a means by which the Islamic state is created. *Da'wa* includes the academic, financial, legal and all other aspects of society. It aims not only to save the soul but to save the society as well. For many of the *da'wa* organisations (including Islamic aid agencies) which are not necessarily regarded as extremist, the aim of creating an Islamic state is nevertheless central to their philosophy and they continue to seek to fulfil this agenda. Many Muslim activities have a *da'wa* element, for example the annual open day at the Madina Mosque, Keighley, West Yorkshire, which

17

the whole town is invited to attend.[6] Likewise the annual national Islam Awareness Week, whose stated aim is "to raise awareness and remove misconceptions surrounding Britain's second largest faith group" provides a non-threatening way of spreading the message of Islam to non-Muslims.[7]

The Qur'an

The Qur'an is believed to be the literal word of God, revealed to Muhammad in stages over a period of 23 years by the angel Gabriel. It is considered an exact copy of the heavenly, uncreated original inscribed on a tablet in heaven. The Qur'an is seen as incomparable to any human writing, a divine miracle. Most Muslims accept this view of the divine origin and perfection of the Qur'an and react with anger at any criticism of it. It is treated with great reverence, and is memorised and recited by many. Most Muslims refuse to countenance any kind of historical, contextual, archaeological or literary analysis of their holy book, so the Qur'an is rarely given the same rigorous scholarly treatment as the Bible gets. This approach (which is enforced by law in some Muslim countries) is generally followed by non-Muslim academics and media in the UK as well; this results in the Qur'an being effectively immune from criticism or any critical analysis, in stark contrast to the way the Bible is treated.

The Qur'an is written in poetic form. It contains 114 chapters (*suras*) which are not arranged chronologically but mainly in order of length. It contains many contradictions which Islamic scholars cope with by applying the principle of abrogation. In its commonest form this principle states that where two texts conflict, the later-dated one abrogates (cancels) the earlier one.

There was no definitive version of the Qur'an when Muhammad died, but the various parts were gradually collected and collated in different places resulting in several different versions. Most variations were destroyed at the promulgation of an official version in the 650s during Caliph 'Uthman's reign. This fact is not widely known by Muslims, most of whom believe that there has only ever been one version of the Qur'an.

English translations of the Qur'an

There are a growing number of Qur'an translations in English (and other languages) to meet the needs of the 80% of Muslims who do not understand Arabic and for the propagation of Islam. Because Muslims view the Arabic original as the only revealed word of God, translations are viewed as merely attempts to give the meaning of the original, without the possibility of attaining to its perfection.

One of the complications when studying the Qur'an in English is that the numbering of the verses can vary slightly from one translation to another. So a certain phrase found in sura (chapter) 8 verse 60 in one translation might be found at, say, 8:59 or 8:62 in another translation.

While a few translators attempt an exact objective translation of the original, this is a very difficult task because of the ambiguity of the original Arabic. It is perhaps hardly surprising that many translators use interpolations in the text (shown in parentheses), footnotes, introductions and appendices to explain the meaning. This methodology can be used to convey a particular sectarian interpretation as well as include the interpretation of orthodox medieval scholars. Translations funded by Saudi Arabia are especially prone to inserting ideological and political annotations.

Example: The Saudi-financed translation, *Interpretation of the Meanings of The Noble Qur'an in the English Language: A summarized Version of At-Tabari, Al-Qurtubi and Ibn Kathir with comments from Sahih Al-Bukhari* by Dr Muhammad Taqi ud-Din al-Hilali and Dr Muhammad Muhsin Khan, 15th edition, Riyadh: Darussalam Publishers, 1996.

This Sunni translation is meant to replace the popular translation by the Shi'a Muslim A. Yusuf Ali and has been approved by both the University of Medina and the Saudi Dar al-Ifta (Centre for *shari'a*-based decrees). It is now the most widely disseminated English Qur'an. Its doctrinal interpretation is based on the commentaries of al-Tabari (d. 932), al-Qurtubi (d. 1273), Ibn Kathir (d.1372) and al-Bukhari (d. 870) as well as on a strict Wahhabi-Salafi worldview.

Many of its interpolations have an anti-Christian and anti-Semitic tendency. One clear example of this occurs in the first sura which is recited seventeen times a day by all Muslims who pray five times a day.

Surah Al-Fatihah
1. In the Name of Allâh, the Most Beneficent, the Most Merciful.
2. All the praises and thanks be to Allâh, the Lord of the 'Alamîn (mankind, *jinn* and all that exists).
3. The Most Beneficent, the Most Merciful.
4. The Only Owner (and the Only Ruling Judge) of the Day of Recompense (i.e. the Day of Resurrection)
5. You (Alone) we worship, and You (Alone) we ask for help (for each and everything).
6. Guide us to the Straight Way
7. The Way of those on whom You have bestowed Your Grace, not (the way) of those who earned Your Anger (such as the Jews) nor of those who went astray (such as the Christians).

The sections of text in brackets are interpolations which do not occur in the original Arabic, but have been derived from the *hadith*. Note how the additions to verse 7 serve to reinforce a negative attitude towards Jews and Christians.

A footnote to 2:190 explains that *jihad* is a "pillar" of Islam, i.e. an obligatory duty (see pages 15–16), although this is not by any means a universal understanding within Islam. The footnote also makes clear that *jihad* means physical fighting and warfare, although the term *jihad* includes at least three other meanings accepted by most Muslims.

> *Al-Jihad* (holy fighting) in Allah's Cause (with full force of numbers and weaponry) is given the utmost importance in Islam and is one of its pillars (on which it stands). By *Jihad* Islam is established, Allah's Word is made superior, (his Word being *La ilaha illalah* which means none has the right to be worshipped but Allah), and his religion (Islam) is propagated. By abandoning *Jihad* (may Allah protect us from that) Islam is destroyed and the Muslims fall into an inferior position; their honour is lost, their lands are stolen, their rule and authority vanish. *Jihad* is an obligatory

duty on every Muslim, and he who tries to escape from this duty, or does not in his innermost heart wish to fulfil this duty, dies with one of the qualities of a hypocrite.

Some editions of this version also have an appendix about *jihad* written by the Chief Justice of Saudi Arabia, Sheikh 'Abdullah bin Muhammad bin Humaid. This appendix glorifies *jihad* in its traditional understanding as a holy war for the supremacy of Islam.[8]

Hadith

Various collections have also been made of traditions (*ahadith*, singular *hadith*) recording what Muhammad said and did i.e. his way of life (*sunna*). They were preserved verbally for some generations, each with its own chain of names who had passed the tradition on from one to another, and later written down. According to Sunni Muslims, six such collections are considered authoritative, and are viewed as a revelation second only to the Qur'an as a source of divine guidance. These are the collections of Bukhari, Muslim, Ibn Majah, Abu Da'ud, Tirmidhi and Nasa'i. In addition, the Shi'a have their own collections which include sayings of their imams in addition to those of Muhammad. Four canonical Shi'a *hadith* collections are Muhammad ibn Ya'qub al-Kulayni (d. 490), *Usul al-Kafi fi 'ilm al-din*; Ibn Babawayh al-Qummi (d. 991), *Man la yahduruhu'l faqih*; and Muhammad al-Tusi (d. 1068) (two collections) 1. *Tahdib al-ahkam*, 2. *al-istibsar*.

Because the *ahadith* are often easier to understand than the Qur'an, they have played a very important role in establishing the rules of how Muslims should live, based on the model of Muhammad. For example, the Qur'an enjoins Muslims to pray, but it is from the *ahadith* that Muslims know how often they must pray, what times of day to pray, and in what manner to pray.

Islamic law (shari'a)

Islam includes a body of detailed legislation called the *shari'a* which provides instructions for Muslims in every aspect of private and public life. It is like the constitution of the Muslim community, as well as an identity marker separating Muslims from non-Muslims. For most Muslims, *shari'a* is the embodiment of God's will. Most Sunni Muslims believe that it can never be changed from what was agreed in the tenth century AD.

The *shari'a* tries to describe in detail all possible human activities, dividing them into permissible (*halal*) and prohibited (*haram*), and subdividing them into various degrees of good or evil such as obligatory, recommended, neutral, objectionable or forbidden. *Shari'a* regulates in detail all matters of devotional life, ritual purity, marriage and inheritance, criminal offences, commerce and the governing of the Islamic state. It also regulates relations to non-Muslims within the Muslim state as well as to enemies outside it.

The *shari'a* is derived from the Qur'an and *hadith*. Using the same sources, different medieval scholars and jurists came up with slightly different versions and these were enshrined in the various schools of law. The Sunni schools of law are named after their founders: the Hanafi, Shafi'i, Maliki and Hanbali. The Twelver Shi'a have their own school of law. As an example, all schools of *shari'a* agree that a sane adult male Muslim who leaves the faith should be killed (unless he repents) but they differ in what should happen to an apostate woman or child. (See table on page 24.)

Some of the implications of the *shari'a* for life in the UK are discussed in chapter 4.

The veneration of Muhammad

Most Muslims affirm that Muhammad was simply a human channel for God's revelation. At the same time, Muhammad's figure towers over Islam not just as its founder, but as the perfect man who was divinely inspired not only in his Qur'anic recitations, but in all his sayings and deeds (which included leading his people into battle).

Shari'a, fiqh, ijtihad and fatwas

Shari'a is seen as the divinely ordained law of Islam. It is God's revealed will for human conduct, the fundamental basic legal code, the heavenly ideal. In this sense *shari'a* is eternally valid and unchangeable.

Fiqh is Islamic jurisprudence, the human activity of interpreting and applying *shari'a* in specific cases. *Fiqh* is therefore open to some change and adaptation to changing contexts.

Ijtihad is the process of logical deduction in which an individual scholar engages in order to produce a new legal opinion. In orthodox Sunni Islam this process has been forbidden since the tenth century, when it was ruled that all necessary *ijtihad* had been completed. Some reformers assert that *ijtihad* is now possible again.

A **fatwa** is an authoritative legal opinion given by a *mufti* (legal scholar authorised to issue *fatwas*), usually in response to questions posed by individuals or courts. The degree of authority of the *fatwa* is based on the *mufti's* status and reputation.

He is the beloved of God who serves as the supreme example which all Muslims are obliged to emulate in every small detail. Muhammad is also seen as the intercessor with God who can change the divine decrees and admit to paradise those for whom he intercedes.

Love for Muhammad (and his family) is deeply inculcated into most Muslims in childhood. Protecting his honour from any assault is an obligation on all. This is why any suspected denigration of Muhammad immediately creates disturbances and riots in many Muslim countries and communities. It is classed as blasphemy and deserves the death sentence, as Salman Rushdie experienced after his book *The Satanic Verses* was published.

The elevation of Muhammad to what is effectively a position of sinless infallibility has served to turn his human weaknesses into virtues to be imitated. This remains one of the unresolved problems of Islam.

The punishment of apostates from Islam, according to the five main schools of *shari'a*

School of law	Hanafi (Sunni)	Shafi'i (Sunni)	Maliki (Sunni)	Hanbali (Sunni)	Ja'fari (Shi'a)
Sane adult male	Death	Death	Death	Death	Death
Sane adult female	Imprisoned until she repents.	Death	Death	Death	Imprisoned and beaten with rods until she repents or dies.
Child	Imprisoned until of age, then killed.	Imprisoned	Killed on reaching maturity.	Killed on reaching maturity.	Apostasy does not apply to children.
Period for repentance	Three days	Three days	Three days	Three days	Born Muslims must repent immediately, converts to Islam are given time to repent.
Apostasy a *hadd* offence?	Yes	Yes	No	No	Yes
Must apostasy be spoken to incur penalty?	Yes	No - inward apostasy is punishable.	No - inward apostasy is punishable.	No - inward apostasy is punishable.	
Establishing guilt	Two witnesses required.	Even words spoken in jest are counted as apostasy. Two witnesses required.	Ascertain whether the individual was previously a true practising Muslim.		Confession and two truthful male witnesses. Words spoken in anger, jest, and unintentionally do not count.
Other features	Desirable to explain the Islamic faith to the apostate, in hope that he or she will repent.			Emphasis on three-day period for repentance.	

Muhammad veneration is particularly marked amongst South Asian Muslims and therefore is also a major feature of the Muslim community in the UK as most British Muslims have roots in the Indian sub-continent.

SOME VARIATIONS

Islamic mysticism (Sufism)

Sufism is the mystical stream of Islam which arose as a reaction to the rigid legalism of the early religious establishment and as a protest at the growing worldliness and wealth of the expanding Muslim empire. Sufis searched for a personal experience of God and his love. They hoped to achieve this by finding secret hidden (*batini*) meanings in the Qur'an and by disciplines of fasting, prayer, repetition of God's names, breath control, meditation and trance.

Founders of Sufi orders and their successors are venerated as saints who possess powers of intercession and blessing (*baraka*). Their tombs serve as centres of pilgrimage. Sufi saints are known as *sheikhs* in the Arab world and as *pirs* in the Iranian, Turkic and Indian worlds.

The *sheikh* of each order, as the successor of the original founder, teaches his disciples and performs with them the Sufi rituals. His help is sought for matters such as exorcism and healing.

Sufi concepts permeate Islam and were important in the development of Muslim culture and in *da'wa*, helping spread Islam into areas such as Central Asia, sub-Saharan Africa and South-East Asia. An important Sufi contribution to Muslim culture was a rich poetry in Arabic, Persian, Turkish, and many local languages like Urdu, Sindi, Pashto and Punjabi. Most folk-culture in Muslim countries, including local music, is still Sufi-based.

Sufi brotherhoods (*tariqas*) were formed by disciples gathering around a master founder who was revered as a saint and seen as an indispensable guide on the spiritual path. There are hundreds of orders and they are an important religious and political force found amongst both Sunnis and Shi'a. The orders established trade and craft guilds and provided lodges (*zawiyas*) for travellers and

Some of the main Sufi orders

Order	Location	Background
Qadiri	A very widespread order, found all over the Middle East, Turkey, India, the Balkans, and Central Asia	The oldest Sufi order. Founded in the eleventh century, it is considered more orthodox than some other Sufi orders, and is sometimes tolerated by Muslims who oppose Sufism in general. Qadiri *sheikhs* have led resistance to colonialism in Algeria against the French, and in Chechnya against the Russians.
Naqshbandi	Throughout the Muslim World, especially Central Asia	Founded in the fourteenth century, the Naqshbandi focuses particularly upon internal development and meditation. The Naqshbandi order has been a source of opposition to Russian colonialism in the Caucasus and Central Asia.
Chishti	Indian subcontinent and Central Asia	Takes its name from the town of Chisht where it began, which is now in Afghanistan. Emphasis on devotional music, dancing and mysticism. Is regarded as being further from orthodox Islam than the Qadiri or Naqshbandi. The most influential order in the Indian subcontinent.
Shadhili	North Africa, also common in the Middle East	This order, founded in the thirteenth century in Alexandria, has produced an unusual number of suborders. It is the most important Sufi order in North Africa.
Khalwati	Turkey, Middle East	This order gained prominence under the rule of the Ottomans and spread to all parts of their Empire.

merchants along the great trade routes. Orders received endowments from sympathetic rulers and rich citizens and some became very wealthy.

Sufi orders were active in the resistance to colonialism in the nineteenth and early twentieth centuries in various parts of the Muslim world: the Sanussiyya in Libya, the Mahdi movement in Sudan, and Shamil's resistance in the Caucasus.

In the last decades, Sufism has become prevalent in Western countries. Many Western converts to Islam were first attracted to Sufism through their interest in mysticism and spirituality. In the UK, many white converts to Islam are Sufis.

Folk Islam (popular Islam)

Linked to Sufism is folk Islam, widespread among the poor but impacting all levels of Muslim society. It is based on Qur'anic and *hadith* passages about evil spiritual powers, and incorporates local pre-Islamic beliefs and superstitions into Islam. In this worldview the supernatural is accepted as impinging on everyday life. The fear of evil powers such as *jinn* and the evil eye is the driving force behind folk Islam – dangers lurk everywhere, and people need protection from evil forces and intercessors who will plead their case. Fate, angels and evil spirits play an active role in determining what happens to people, and dreams and visions have meaning as messages from beyond. It is vitally important to protect oneself from these powerful forces or try to influence them and manipulate them in one's favour. Magic provides some of the tools and techniques to achieve this. Amulets, vows and invocations, Qur'anic verses on the wall or under the pillow, and invoking God's name are some of the techniques used. So are ceremonies of exorcism, placating spirits and curses. Specialists are often paid to do the job.

God is viewed as being far away and unknowable, while saints are seen as accessible protectors from evil, intercessors with God, and sources of supernatural power and *baraka* centred on their tombs. *Baraka* is imagined as an invisible substance surrounding the grave that is communicated by touch. People visit the shrines of famous saints to ask for their protection from evil powers, for help in the problems of daily life, for the saint's special *baraka,* for healing, and for solutions to all problems of life.

Wahhabism

This puritanical and militant Sunni reform movement began in eighteenth century Arabia, based on a strict and literalist interpretation of Muslim sources and the Hanbali school of law. Its founder, al-Wahhab, considered the Islam of his time to be a degenerate version of true Islam, corrupted by blind imitation of clerics, the Shi'a elevation of imams to the role of mediators, and popular folk religious and Sufi practices such as saint-worship and tomb visitation, which he condemned as idolatry. He compared the Arabian society of his time to the pagan pre-Islamic period of ignorance, and declared Muslim opponents to be non-Muslims or apostates, thus justifying holy war (*jihad*) against them. (See also page 37.)

LOYALTIES

Muslims living in the UK are much exercised over whether they are British Muslims or Muslim Britons, and about what degree of loyalty they should accord to the UK. To this should be added the question of where those who were born in a different country see their first loyalty. A survey conducted by face-to-face interviews with 500 Muslims in Britain during the period 11 February to 28 March 2005 found that only 5% identified themselves as British first and then Muslim. There were also 3% who identified themselves only as British. A total of 55% identified themselves as Muslim first, and then British, while 8% identified themselves as only Muslim. Twenty-five per cent felt that their identity was equally Muslim and British.[9] Unfortunately the survey was not broken down by ethnic group or age, but it does appear that both factors tend to influence the attitude to loyalty. Older South Asian Muslims tend to identify either with their country of origin or with Britain whilst younger Muslims often identify with global Islam and the *umma* as a whole rather than with any country.

Titles for Muslim leaders

Amir   Commander, leader, prince.

Ayatollah Term of honour for leader in Shi'a Islam; literally "Sign of Allah".

Caliph   Literally "successor" i.e. successor to Muhammad as leader of the *umma*. The title used by Sunnis for the supreme spiritual and political leader of the whole Muslim community. (Shi'as use the word "imam" for this supreme leader.)

Imam   This has two distinct meanings. In Sunni Islam it is the prayer leader of a mosque, similar to a Christian parish priest or church minister. In Shi'a Islam "imam" is the term used for the supreme ruler of the Muslim community (equivalent to the Sunni caliph).

Mufti   A Sunni scholar who is an interpreter and expounder of *shari'a*, one who is authorised to issue *fatwas*. The title "Grand Mufti" refers to the highest official of religious law in a Sunni Muslim country.

Mullah   A religious teacher. The term is more common in Iran, India and Pakistan.

Muezzin   The one who gives the call to prayer from the mosque.

Murshid   See *pir*.

Pir   A Persian term for a Sufi "saint" or spiritual guide. May also be known as a *murshid* or a *sheikh*.

Sheikh   Literally "old man" or "elder", this title has a range of different meanings. It can be given to heads of religious orders, Quranic scholars, jurists, those who preach and lead prayers in the mosque, and to Sufi saints. It is also used for a village elder or tribal chief.

Asylum-seekers who have found refuge in the UK are often more willing to conform to the requirements of mainstream society than those born here, though they may be highly critical of British foreign policy as regards, for example, Palestine and Iraq.

Imtiaz Ahmed Hussain, who is a graduate of Al-Azhar University, Cairo and Co-ordinator for the Manchester Islamic Schools Trust, encourages Muslims in the UK to learn from the example of a group of about a hundred early Muslims who fled from persecution in Mecca to find freedom of religion in the Christian kingdom of Abyssinia. This *hijra* pre-dated the classic *hijra* to Medina by eight years, and Hussain sees it as a model of a Muslim minority actively participating in the wider non-Muslim society and giving loyalty to the ruler of the state in which they were living.

> There was good will between Muslim and non-Muslim communities. The predominant Christian community granted freedom and support to the Muslim community. The Muslims for their part recognised that this freedom in turn deserved loyalty to the ruler. The most important dynamic in this relationship was the fact that there was religious freedom... In the same way the Muslim community in Britain should be willing to take an active participatory role in both the local non-Muslim community and the wider society.[10]

By contrast there are many Muslims for whom loyalty to the *umma* overrides loyalty to the UK. For some it overrides loyalty to any nation state. Some consider themselves simply Muslims and leave out all reference to their country of residence or citizenship. Salman Sayyid, a lecturer at Salford University and a member of the Executive Committee of the Association of Muslim Social Scientists, expresses this viewpoint in an article which focuses on the necessity for political involvement.

> The primary political question is always who are our friends and who are our enemies... It is through answering this question that we come to a sense of ourselves. Without enemies there can be no value to being a friend. A world in which we cannot distinguish between friends and enemies is a world without the political. A

world without the political is a world in which existing power relations are considered to be natural and uncontested, a world without the political is also a world in which we cannot dream of something different let alone something better.

The assertion of an Islamicate political identity means that being Muslim begins to mean something other than observing the rituals and practices of Islam. It means that one tries to read from being a Muslim, one's social and political obligations. Being a Muslim requires an engagement with the rest of the ummah; it would be difficult to imagine how one could be a Muslim without regard to the rest of the ummah. This ummatic component of Muslim identity is precisely where Muslims come into contact with authorities of the Westphalian state – since a Muslim identity transcends the boundaries of the nation-state.[11]

In the orthodox view, politics is the means of advancing the cause of the whole worldwide Muslim community, of expanding Muslim control over as much territory as possible and governing it according to *shari'a*. According to this view, the primary duty of Muslims living in non-Muslim states is to help Islamise their host societies.

Any Muslim who leaves Islam is considered a traitor to the *umma* and under *shari'a* would be liable to the death penalty (see page 24).

Muslims in the armed forces

There is debate among British Muslims as to whether they can serve in the armed forces of the UK. Some Muslims in the armed forces feel that their first loyalty is to the *umma*, not to the UK. A Muslim RAF reservist refused to serve in Iraq in 2003 because of this. A Muslim army captain has commented, "I don't know how I'd feel about firing on Muslims." Others however are convinced that their loyalty to the UK means that they cannot accept injunctions by Muslim scholars to refuse to fight in theatres of conflict where they might have to fire on a fellow Muslim. Similar issues have arisen in the American military.

Several contradicting *fatwas* have been issued by Muslim scholars on this subject. Following the September 11 atrocity in 2001, and a question put to Islamic scholars by the most senior Muslim chaplain in the American Armed forces, the prominent Muslim scholar Yusuf al-Qaradawi, Taha Jabir al-Alawani (President of the Fiqh Council of the North America) and several other scholars issued a *fatwa* which stated that it was permissible for Muslim American military personnel to partake in the upcoming battles, against whomever their country decides has perpetrated terrorism against them. The Muslim soldier has to do this despite possible feelings of unease at fighting other Muslims. This *fatwa* is justified by referring to the *shari'a* principles of necessity (*darura*) and the greater public good (*maslaha*).[12]

However a month later, there were reports that these very same clerics had abrogated their position with a new *fatwa* which invalidated the former one and prohibited the participation of Muslim soldiers in the US armed forces in the war in Afghanistan.[13]

Following the American-led invasion of Iraq in 2003, Qaradawi with some other scholars issued a *fatwa* in August 2004 permitting the abduction and killing of American civilians in Iraq.[14]

Because of such attitudes, some Muslim soldiers both in the US and the UK are concerned about the possiblity of retaliation from elements of the Muslim community on their families or themselves because of their profession.

Muslim police officers

The police have gone to considerable lengths to encourage Muslims to serve as police officers. Some police stations have prayer rooms for Muslims, and *halal* food is served at the New Scotland Yard canteen. In 2001 the Metropolitan Police gave women officers the option of wearing a *hijab* instead of the uniform cap. Two years later they agreed to a request from the Association of Muslim Police to allow male officers to wear turbans. It is interesting to note that a female Muslim police officer in Philadelphia, USA, was refused the right to wear a *hijab* when she requested permission to do so.[15] What is even more interesting is that in Muslim-majority countries it is normal for police to wear Western-style uniforms and head gear.

Overtly Muslim dress options for Muslim officers send an implicit message to the Muslim community that loyalty to Islamic norms is more important than their duty as a police officer. For example, a turban is a symbol of religious authority. This unspoken message would become important in cases such as a young Muslim woman fleeing from a forced marriage or from violence in the home due to her Western lifestyle. Such a woman would not feel at ease in sharing her problems with a police officer dressed in Islamic clothing; she would not expect her viewpoint to be accepted. Furthermore, how might non-Muslims needing help respond to a religiously dressed police officer in Muslim-majority areas where non-Muslims experience discrimination and violence? Will this erode confidence in the police force and its impartiality?

Such impartiality is already being called into question by incidents such as the decision of the West Midlands police to investigate a 2007 television documentary called "Undercover Mosque".[16] Having been requested by various viewers to investigate the Muslim preachers who had been shown in the programme apparently preaching hatred and violence, the police announced that they had done so, brought no charges against them, and then had investigated the programme itself for allegedly stirring up racial hatred.[17] This kind of apparent bias towards Islam causes serious concern if not fear to moderate Muslims and non-Muslim Britons, in particular to non-Muslim ethnic minorities. If any such wanted to report their concerns over the words or behaviour of radical Muslims which could have security implications, they might hesitate to do so in case the police turned on them and investigated them for anti-Islamic activity.

While most Muslim police officers serve diligently and dutifully, special problems have sometimes cropped up. One officer in the Metropolitan force's Diplomatic Protection Force refused to guard the Israeli Embassy during the 2006 Israel-Hizbullah war because he disagreed with the Israeli attack on Lebanon.[18]

British police are generally diffident about raiding mosques in search of suspects, and would find it difficult to use Muslim officers in such raids. On 16 January 2007, a terror suspect who broke his control order evaded the police by entering a mosque for shelter, and escaped by a back door while the officers were discussing the matter with the local community and mosque officials.[19]

Muslim immigration officers

Many Muslim immigration officers are involved in making decisions about asylum-seekers. Others may serve as translators or interpreters. An issue arises when individuals are seeking asylum from some aspect of an Islamic society. For example, they may have fled because of threats to their life due to their conversion from Islam to another faith. While many Muslim immigration officers are able to keep their faith separate from the performance of their job, for some Muslims it could be difficult to set aside their own personal convictions on such matters and to make a judgement purely in accordance with British law. Such asylum-seekers would – rightly or wrongly – be fearful that their details might be passed to hostile members of the Muslim community. Also there have been incidents reported of translators in such cases who allow their own opinions to affect their work and may not give accurate and unbiased translations.[20]

3   RADICAL ISLAM (ISLAMISM)

One of the most important aspects of contemporary Islam is radicalism and the violence which often accompanies it. The issue of British involvement in Iraq and Afghanistan and in the "war on terror" has led many Muslims, in particular young people, to identify with the global *umma* and to become critical of British government foreign policy. Exacerbated by the view that Muslims are being brutalised in such places as Palestine and Chechnya, this has led some to become actively involved in jihadist causes and others to give support through other means.

Though the number of radical Muslims (Islamists) in the UK is thought to be only a small percentage of the community, their militant actions are approved by many more and financed by some. Whilst many British Muslims have denounced "terrorism" they often do not include within this term the actions of jihadists, which they consider either defensive or justifiable for other reasons.

All Islamists share the aim of establishing an Islamic state under *shari'a,* first in individual states, then expanded to one universal caliphate. Following the model of Muhammad's *hijra,* they see this as a staged process, but differ in what stages are envisaged.

Those who might be termed "gradualists" seek firstly to islamise society by *da'wa,* meanwhile infiltrating the state and its institutions, until they are able to take power legally and establish an Islamic state with *shari'a.*

Those termed "jihadists" work by recruiting to form secret cells, which are trained and armed. These fighters engage in terrorism, rebellion and coups in order to remove from power the existing governments and establish in their place Islamic states under *shariʻa*.

The radical and Islamist understanding of jihad

Both Qur'an and *hadith* include many passages commending *jihad*. Muslims interpret *jihad* in a variety of ways including the personal struggle against sin and temptation. However, to the early Muslims and to Muhammad himself, physical warfare to conquer non-Muslims was clearly the most important interpretation. As such it is physical warfare against non-Muslims which is emphasised by radical and reformist Muslims who seek to return to the roots of their faith.

The call for violent *jihad* has been increasing in intensity with the growth of the Islamist movement. Reinstating *jihad* is seen as God's method of reviving Muslim power and of establishing the political domination of Islam over the world. Jews and Christians are seen as eternal enemies of Islam, always plotting its destruction, and therefore must be fought by *jihad* until they submit to Islamic dominance. Secular Muslim regimes are regarded as infidel for not fully implementing *shariʻa* and are therefore to be likewise fought against by *jihad* until they are replaced by properly Islamic governments.

With the globalisation of *jihad,* Western states have also become targets of *jihad* activity. The 11 September 2001 attacks as well as the 2004 Madrid and 2005 London bombings are proof of the widening scope of *jihad*, with recruits now coming not only from Muslim countries but also from Muslim communities in the West.

In order to provide a framework for understanding radical Islam in the UK, it is necessary to overview the rise of radical Islam worldwide in the last 200 years. Any such overview, analysis or classification of the various movements within radical Islam is complicated by the fact that there is no consensus on how to define certain key terms such as "Wahhabism" or "Salafism". It is also very difficult to draw hard-and-fast lines to distinguish between different categories given the inter-relationships, networking and influence of individuals and groups on others. Many of the terms used below are therefore fairly fluid and may be used by other authors with somewhat different meanings.

THE DEVELOPMENT OF RADICAL ISLAM

Western colonialism

The Western colonial movement brought almost all Muslim countries under Western rule, and imposed on them arbitrary borders, Western systems of law and education, and a culture based on Judaeo-Christian and secular principles. While at first some Muslims responded with admiration to Western power and culture, by the 1970s attempts by Muslim states at copying Western modes of liberalism, nationalism, socialism and capitalism all seemed to have failed.

The humiliation of being on the receiving end of colonial rule was a severe trial to Muslims, whose theology had taught them that political power was their God-given right. Various Islamic reform movements arose which tried to discover the reasons for Muslim political weakness. Most concluded that their weakness was due to deviation from the right path of original Islam. Reformers called for a purification of Islam by a return to the original sources of Qur'an and *hadith,* adapting *shari'a* for the modern context.

Wahhabism (see also page 28)

One of the most enduring of these reform movements was Wahhabism, founded in the Arabian peninsula by Muhammad 'Abd al-Wahhab (1703–1792). Al-Wahhab ensured the survival of his movement by an alliance with the tribal leader Muhammad Ibn-Saud, and Wahhabism is the state religion of modern Saudi Arabia. It rejects both Shi'a Islam and Sufism as heresies and persecutes their followers.

Wahhabism is a strictly puritanical and militant form of Islam. Al-Wahhab revived the Khariji practice of *takfir*, the process of judging Muslims (individuals, regimes, societies and states) to be apostates and infidels if they did not wholly conform to the *shari'a*. This condemnation justifies *jihad* against them.

The main reason why Wahhabism is of such significance today is the worldwide influence it wields, thanks to the oil money of its homeland, Saudi Arabia. This financial power has transformed a marginal sect into one of the most dominant types of Islam today. With Saudi money, thousands of Wahhabi preachers are sent out, millions of copies of Wahhabi Qur'ans[21] and other literature are distributed, and countless Wahhabi mosques and *madrassas* founded all over the world. Wahhabi influence is also assisted by the fact that Mecca, the site of the obligatory Muslim pilgrimage, is situated in Saudi Arabia. The Organisation of the Islamic Conference (OIC), a body which links over 55 Muslim countries also has its headquarters in Saudi Arabia, where it was founded.

The modern reform movement

The modern reform movement was initiated in India by Sir Syed Ahmad Khan (1817–1898) and in the Arab world by Jamal al-Din al-Afghani (1839–1897) and Muhammad Abduh (1849–1905). The reformers combined traditional Islam with modern concepts and instilled in Muslims a pride in their past glory, renewed their confidence and restored their shattered sense of identity. They stressed the compatibility of Islamic revelation with reason and science and that Islam could adapt to the modern world. They distinguished between the unchanging core of Islamic worship and social externals which could change.

The Salafi movement (also called neo-Wahhabism)

The modern reform movement gave birth to the Salafi movement founded by Rashid Rida (1865–1935), a Syrian based in Egypt. Compared with Afghani and Abduh he was more influenced by Wahhabism and stressed the importance of returning to the pure Islam practised by the *salaf* (pious ancestors i.e. Muhammad, his companions and the first four caliphs). Like Wahhabism, it engaged in *takfir* against secular Muslim societies and rulers. It also rejected the standard schools of law, which had been developed by Muslim scholars in the centuries after the *salaf* lived, and advocated a direct and literal interpretation of the Qur'an and *hadith*. Rida held that Islam did not need to imitate the West, and that *shari'a* could only be properly implemented under a truly Islamic government.

Although the terms "Salafism" and "Wahhabism" are sometimes used interchangeably, contemporary Salafis see themselves as taking the purification of Islam further than Wahhabis, so are better described as neo-Wahhabis. Salafis enforce a rigid code for dress and personal appearance of both men and women. Most ban modern technology such as photography, though some consider television and radio acceptable if used to propagate Salafi doctrine. Most disapprove of music, conventional banking and elections.

There are various streams within Salafism:

- Traditionalist (*taqlidi*) Salafism. The traditionalists follow *sheikhs* like the late Muhammad Nasirudin al-Albani, the late Saudi Grand Mufti Abdel-Aziz Ibn Baz, Sheikh Muhammad Ibn Saleh al-'Uthaymin and Abu Bakr al-Jaza'iri. They are generally hostile to Islamist political activism, adhering to the injunction of obedience even to an unjust Muslim ruler. They oppose the political activism of the Muslim Brotherhood and call all jihadists "Qutbists" (for Qutb, see pages 40, 83–86).
- Violent (*jihadi*) Salafism. The *jihadis* arose in opposition to the traditionalists with the preaching of Abu Muhammad Al-Maqdisi from 1992 onward that emphasised the need to overthrow "impious" regimes through violent means. This is sometimes called neo-Salafism.[22]
- Reformist (*islahi*) Salafism. In 1995–1996 Salafis of a political bent who rejected the use of violence established the reformist branch, espousing peaceful opposition to the secular regimes in Jordan and elsewhere.

From the early Salafi movement developed modern Islamism.

The Muslim Brotherhood

The Muslim Brotherhood was founded in Egypt in 1928 by Hassan al-Banna (1906–1949). Emerging from the Salafi movement, it was the first of the plethora of radical Islamic organisations which exist today, those which are often called "fundamentalist" or – as their followers prefer – "Islamist". Al-Banna aimed to seize political power by a gradual process which began with education, recruitment and training.

The main ideologue of the Muslim Brotherhood was Sayyid Qutb (1906–1966) whose writings became an important reference for many radical Islamic movements, especially with regard to how to assess the Islamic credentials of societies and governments. He took the term *hijra* (emigration) and developed its meaning from a simple description of Muhammad's migration to an ideological goal in the staged process of developing true Islamic societies. He held that all Muslim societies had reverted to pre-Islamic paganism (*jahiliyya*), so that true Muslims were living in a context similar to that of Muhammad in his early career i.e. surrounded by idolatry. Qutb saw three definite stages in the *hijra* process:

1. Peaceful proclamation (*da'wa*) of the message to *jahili* society. This is what Muhammad did in Mecca.
2. Separation (*mufassala*) from unbelievers and all *jahili* society. This parallels Muhammad's migration to Medina to organise the new Muslim community. This stage Qutb conceived of not as total physical separation, but as a spiritual separation while remaining in society to proclaim, recruit and organise.
3. Finally the fight (*jihad*) to implement God's new society on earth, similar to Muhammad's victorious return to Mecca. *Jihad* is aimed first at Islamising Muslim societies, toppling apostate Muslim rulers and establishing Islamic states under *shari'a*; these Islamic states are then able to extend *jihad* to the whole world.

In its early years the Brotherhood worked for evolutionary change through institutional renewal. During the 1930s, however, it developed an ideology of belligerent *jihad* directed against colonialism, cultural modernity and the Jewish presence in Palestine.

Al-Banna glorified *jihad* and the physical act of self-sacrifice:

> Jehad has been made obligatory on every Muslim by Allah. He has laid great stress on Jehad and has promised limitless recompense for martyrs and fighters . . . There is no system in the world which places so much emphasis on jehad and fighting; use of power; mutual discipline and unity; and defence of rights, as in Islam . . . the verses of the Quran and the traditions of the Holy Prophet (S.A.W.) are full of these high teachings. They, in clearest terms, invite towards jehad, fighting and art of fighting and draw attention towards all means of land and sea fighting.[23]

By the 1940s the Brotherhood had established a special secret paramilitary branch, al Tanzim al Khas, which initiated a campaign of terror against the pro-Western Egyptian government and assassinated a number of political personalities, including two prime ministers.

Abdullah 'Azzam (1941–1989), Osama bin Laden's mentor during the Afghan *jihad* (i.e. the Afghan war against Soviet occupation, 1979–89) was a member of the Muslim Brotherhood. 'Azzam was active in recruiting Arab *mujahidin* for the *jihad* in Afghanistan and he was the main promoter of the internationalisation of *jihad* which led to the creation of al-Qaeda and to the Salafi-Jihadi movement.

It is evident that the Muslim Brotherhood, like many other Islamist movements, presents itself to the broad public and to governments as wholly committed to peaceful evolutionary gradualism within the limits of the democratic process. However, it is not averse to using violence when it seems suitable to its goals and appropriate to the situation it finds itself in. The key question is: at what time will it see itself as having arrived at the final stage of the *hijra* model, when violence is called for to deliver the *coup de grace* to the infidel system and replace it by an Islamic state under *shari'a*?

Although outlawed in Egypt, the Muslim Brotherhood won a substantial number of parliamentary seats in the 2005 elections (they ran as independents). Part of its popularity in Egypt is due to its welfare work among the poor.

Most violent Islamist groups today were born out of the Muslim Brotherhood as reinterpreted by Qutb. The Brotherhood itself has become globalised and is very influential in Europe including the UK.

Since the end of the Second World War, and especially following their persecution in Nasser's Egypt, members of the Muslim Brotherhood have settled in Europe. They founded student organisations in most European countries and established a network of mosques, research centres, think tanks, charities and schools. Thanks to their activism and to financial support from Saudi Arabia and other oil-rich Gulf countries, their institutions became prominent representatives of local Muslim communities. With the creation of the supra-national jurisprudential European Council for Fatwa and Research, the Muslim Brotherhood has taken a first cautious step toward introducing *shari'a* within the Muslim communities of Europe.[24]

Yusuf al-Qaradawi, who is president of the European Council for Fatwa and Research and much fêted by the Mayor of London Ken Livingstone, has stated that:

> Islam will return to Europe as a conqueror and victor, after being expelled from it twice, . . . I maintain that the conquest this time will not be by the sword but by preaching and ideology.[25]

The European Muslim Brotherhood network, under the cover of various civil rights groups and Islamic organisations, is in the vanguard of this peaceful conquest. The international Muslim Brotherhood is now better defined as a flexible international network of linked organisations whose members are kept together by ideological affinity.[26]

In 1961 Sa'id Ramadan, formerly al-Banna's secretary, founded the Islamic Centre of Geneva. He persuaded eminent Islamic scholars, including Indian Deobandi and Tablighi scholars like Mohammed Hamidullah and Abdul Hassan Ali Nadwi to join its founding board. It became one of the main headquarters of the Muslim Brotherhood in Europe, and was the first of a score that Ramadan set up throughout Europe with financial aid from Saudi Arabia.

Deoband

This reform movement, like so many, developed as a reaction to Western colonialism, in this case specifically as a reaction to the putting down of the Indian Mutiny (1857) against the British in the North West Frontier. It taught a complete rejection of Western values and advocated a return to classical, conservative Islam. The movement, which accepts a reformed type of Sufism, became very influential in Pakistan, Afghanistan and India, and by 1967 had over 9,000 *madrassas* across South Asia. Each *madrassa* included a "*fatwa* centre" whose scholars could issue *fatwas* on any aspect of daily life, to help contemporary Muslims live in accordance with the Hanafi school of *shari'a*. Based on these *fatwas*, Deobandis developed a system to enable them to live "Islamically" whatever their political or social context.

While some Deobandis are pietistic and politically passive, the majority are politically active and seek to get their own understanding of Islam incorporated in the legislation of their respective states. In Pakistan they are in the forefront of those lobbying the state to implement *shari'a* in national legislation.

In the last quarter of a century the Deobandis have become more radicalised than formerly, and have developed a militancy which the movement did not originally have.[27] This characteristic began with the *jihad* in Afghanistan against the Soviet Union in the 1980s, as Deobandis sought to defend their fellow-Muslims whose land had been occupied by non-Muslims. The Deobandi movement is closely linked with the Taliban of Afghanistan and has given rise to many militant offshoot groups who engage in violence.

Jama'at-i Islami

After Hassan al-Banna founded the Muslim Brotherhood in Egypt in 1928, Abu'l A'la Mawdudi (1903–1979) initiated a reform movement in British India, founding the Jama'at-i Islami in 1941. Its ideology was similar to that of the Muslim Brotherhood but it was more elitist than the very inclusive grassroots Brotherhood. Mawdudi considered that all Muslims should be active in politics and seek to gain political power in their country so that an Islamic state can be set up, with the ultimate aim of a single universal Islamic state worldwide, ruled by *shari'a*.

Post-colonialism

In the post-colonial era, Muslims found to their dismay that independence enabled only very few Muslim-majority states to prosper. The West, though corrupt, godless and non-Muslim, continued to dominate the world economically, militarily, politically and culturally, and was therefore increasingly hated and resented by Muslims.

Conspiracy theories have proliferated, which see the "Crusading Christian West" and Judaism as the main enemies of Islam, plotting its destruction. In return Islamists plot the destruction of the Western way of life, which they seek to replace with Islam. While many Muslims oppose the use of violence and terror to achieve such aims, they often accept the anti-Western, especially anti-American, attitude that fuels the violence.

The oil-rich Muslim states, especially Saudi Arabia and the Gulf states, have achieved enormous economic power and wealth since the 1970s, and oil money has fuelled the resurgence of Islam worldwide in its puritanical anti-Western Wahhabi and Islamist forms.

Islamic terrorism

Movements advocating terrorism as a tool for implementing Islamist goals emerged out of mainstream Islamism. They were impatient with the gradualist approach and demanded immediate violent action to attain an Islamic state.

In the 1970s and 1980s, most such groups focused their violent activities on destablising and destroying the governments of their own states, which they deemed to be governing in an insufficiently Islamic manner. Thus revolution and military coups brought radicals to power in Iran (1979) and Sudan (1989) and destabilised many other Muslim governments.

The 1990s saw a shift towards violence against non-Muslims, starting in places such as Indonesia and Nigeria. An important impetus for this violence was events in Afghanistan in the 1980s when thousands of volunteers from across the Muslim world joined the Afghan forces in their *jihad* against Soviet occupation. After Afghanistan, Muslim fighters of many nationalities moved to other flashpoints where they felt Muslims were under attack from non-Muslims such as Kashmir, Bosnia, Chechnya, Kosovo and the Philippines.

THE DOCTRINE OF SACRED SPACE

The doctrine of sacred space is a key motivation of radical Muslims. Islam is a territorial religion, very conscious of whether or not an area is under Islamic control. Areas under Islamic rule are called *Dar al-Islam* (the House of Islam) and the rest of the world is *Dar al-Harb* (the House of War). The alarming title for territory under non-Muslim control reflects the classical Islamic teaching that such territory must be subjugated by Muslim military might, one of the original meanings of *jihad*.

> The Islamic state, whose principal function was to put God's law into practice, sought to establish Islam as the dominant reigning ideology over the entire world... The jihad, reflecting the normal war relations existing between Muslims and non-Muslims, was the state's instrument for transforming the dar al-harb into the dar al-Islam.[28]

Only one place on earth can be called the home of Islam (*dar-al-Islam*), and that is the place where the Islamic state is established and the *Shari'ah* is enforced and Allah's limits are observed, and where all Muslims administer the affairs of the community with mutual consultation. The rest of the world is the home of hostility (*dar-al-harb*). A Muslim can have only two possible relations with *dar-al-harb*: peace with a contractual agreement, or war.[29]

Any space once gained is considered sacred. Whatever has been won for Islam is dedicated to Allah, and belongs to the *umma* for ever. Non-Muslims could at best be tenants on their former property. Any lost sacred space must be regained – even by force if necessary. So Islam can only be expected to expand its territory, never to move, exchange or yield anything it has already gained in the UK. (See also pages 175–176.)

The origins of this theological position lie in certain Qur'anic texts and in the example of Muhammad's flight from Mecca to Medina. According to the Qur'an, the whole earth belongs to Allah and he has given it to Muslims. Some parts they already possess, while others are theirs in theory and will eventually become theirs in reality. Some passages which support this doctrine are:

> Allâh has promised those among you who believe and do righteous good deeds, that He will certainly grant them succession (to the present rulers) in the land, as He granted it to those before them, and that He will grant them the authority to practise their religion which He has chosen for them (i.e. Islâm). And He will surely give them in exchange a safe security after their fear (provided) they (believers) worship Me and do not associate anything (in worship) with Me. But whoever disbelieved after this, they are the *Fâsiqûn* (rebellious, disobedient to Allâh). (Q 24:55)

> Mûsâ (Moses) said to his people: "Seek help in Allâh and be patient. Verily, the earth is Allâh's. He gives it as a heritage to whom He wills of His slaves; and the (blessed) end is for the *Muttaqûn* (the pious). (Q 7:128)[30]

The Islamic scholar Ibn Taymiyya (1263–1328) was an extremist of his time, who believed that when non-Muslims were conquered by Muslims those lands were being restored by Allah to their rightful owners, the Muslims.

> These possessions received the name of *fay*[31] since Allah had taken them away from the infidels in order to *restore* (*afa'a, radda*) them to the Muslims. In principle, Allah has created the things of this world only in order that they may contribute to serving Him, since He created man only in order to be ministered to. Consequently, the infidels forfeit their persons and their belongings which they do not use in Allah's service to the faithful believers who serve Allah and unto whom Allah restitutes what is theirs; thus is restored to a man the inheritance of which he was deprived, even if he had never before gained possession.[32]

A relevant concept here is that of *waqf*, defined as a religious endowment. Typically it means dedicating a building or plot of land for religious purposes, whose management and revenues will then be regulated by *shari'a*.

The model of the hijra

As we have seen, many Muslims view the *hijra* as a paradigmatic model to be followed in all times. It is held to be a stage in the political quest for the establishment of the Islamic state modelled on Muhammad's practice. They argue that the first Muslim community developed in clearly defined stages that must be emulated today. First came the stage of weakness in which the message of Islam was proclaimed (*da'wa*) to an unbelieving society, then separation from the unbelievers and migration (*hijra*) to a safe place where Muslim strength could be built up, and finally the sacred fight (*jihad*) to reconquer lost space, victoriously extend Muslim political dominion and implement God's ideal state on earth.

Muhammad's treatment of the conquered Jewish lands at the Khaibar oasis served as a paradigm for future treatment of conquered lands. These lands were divided as spoil among the

Muslim fighters, with a fifth going to Muhammad. The former owners were left as tenants paying the *kharaj* tax, but at the mercy of the Muslim rulers who could expel them at any time. This is described in a *hadith*:

Narrated by Ibn Umar

Umar bin Al-Khattab expelled all the Jews and Christians from the land of Hijaz. Allah's Apostle after conquering Khaibar, thought of expelling the Jews from the land which, after he conquered it belonged to Allah, Allah's Apostle and the Muslims. But the Jews requested Allah's Apostle to leave them there on the condition that they would do the labour and get half of the fruits (the land would yield). Allah's Apostle said, "We shall keep you on these terms as long as we wish." Thus they stayed till the time of 'Umar's Caliphate when he expelled them to Taima and Ariha. (Sahih Al-Bukhari, Hadith 4.380).

This model was followed by the early caliphs in the conquest of Egypt and many other non-Muslim lands.[33] At that time conquered lands became the property of the Muslim community as a whole, rather than of the individual warriors.[34]

Variations

Muslim scholars expended considerable effort elaborating the basic concept of *Dar al-Harb* into a detailed classification of types of Muslim territory. The Arabian peninsula included extra holy parts (the Hijaz) and the holiest parts of all (the Haram, i.e. Mecca and Medina). *Dar al-Harb* was also subdivided according to a number of factors, such as whether its original non-Muslim owners had been conquered or had converted to Islam.[35] The classical jurist al-Mawardi (972–1058) wrote what is effectively an instruction manual for Islamic rulers in which he classified land gained from non-Muslims into three types: that taken by force, that acquired because the residents fled in fear, and that gained by treaties of various kinds.[36] Ibn Rushd (also known as Averroes, 1226–98) reports disagreement between the main schools of Islam on whether conquered land can be divided or must stay as a *waqf*.[37]

Contemporary Muslim scholars

Yusuf al-Qaradawi states that lands once held by Muslims may never be given up to non-Muslims. Should the lands be lost in war, it is the duty of all Muslims to retake them, even if this process lasts until the end of the world:

> No Muslim, be he in authority or not, is allowed to abandon any of the lands of Muslims. The land of the Islamic world is not the property of any president, prince, minister or group of people. It is not up to anyone therefore to relinquish it under any circumstances.

> Conversely, it is the duty of individuals and groups to strive hard to liberate occupied territories and retrieve usurped land. The entire nation is jointly responsible for that and it is not up to the ruler or his subjects to choose to give up the land. If a particular generation lapses in idleness or is incapable of shouldering the responsibility, it has no right to force its idleness or incapacity on all the coming generations up till Judgement Day, by giving up what it has no right to. Therefore, I have issued a Fatwa indicating that it is unlawful for all homeless Palestinian refugees to accept damages in return for their lost land, even if they amount to billions. The land of Islam is not for sale; it is not to be relinquished, and no damages can possibly make up for its loss.[38]

For Qaradawi, *jihad* is focused on the retrieval of Muslim lands, and he quotes the Muslim Brotherhood founder, Hasan al-Banna, as saying:

> Our efforts and our *jihad* are focussed on two main axes – Islamic ideology and the Muslim land.[39]

Many Muslims agree that lands once possessed by Islam, if subsequently lost to an invader, remain holy to Islam and must be restored to its rule.

> For Muslims, no piece of land once added to the realm of Islam can ever be finally renounced.[40]

Isma'il Raji al-Faruqi (1921–1986), an influential Palestinian scholar who taught at several North American universities, defines the Islamic state as universal and all pervasive, aiming at controlling the whole earth in terms of territory and all human beings in terms of population. Even outer space should be under its control:

> Islam asserts that the territory of the Islamic state is the whole earth or, better, the whole cosmos since the possibility of space travel [is] not too remote. Part of the earth may be under direct rule of the Islamic state and the rest may yet have to be included; the Islamic state exists and functions regardless. Indeed its territory is ever expansive. So is its citizenry, for its aim is to include all humankind. If the Islamic state is at any time restricted to a few of the world's population, it does not matter as long as it wills to comprehend humanity.[41]

Kalim Siddiqui of the Muslim Parliament of Great Britain advocated emulating Muhammad's transition from Mecca to Medina as a necessary stage in the unification of the whole Muslim *umma* worldwide. Every Muslim enclave becomes a potential base for further expansion of Muslim rule. In this struggle, Islam recognises no borders as it strives to unite all Muslim enclaves everywhere to achieve the ultimate goal:

> The Islamic movement recognises no frontiers in the *Ummah*. The struggle for the liberation of any one part of the *Ummah* can be carried out from any other part of the *Ummah*. Every part of the *Ummah* is a potential asset for all other parts. This means that every obstacle in the path of the Islamic movement in one part of the *Ummah* is also an obstacle for the entire Islamic movement. Every Muslim engaged in the struggle in any part of the world, however remote or isolated, is engaged in a global struggle. Every group that is engaged in the struggle, however small or remote, is also part of the global struggle between Islam and *kufr*.[42]

Implications of "lost lands"

Lands which were formerly under Islamic rule include Israel, Spain, the Balkans and Chechnya to name but a few. It is the Islamic doctrine of sacred space and the consequent compulsion to regain lost lands which fuels many of today's conflicts. The reason that the more extreme Palestinian movements insist on the obliteration of the state of Israel is that the land was once under Muslim rule and must therefore be returned once more to Muslim rule. Palestine is considered by such groups to be a holy *waqf* for all Muslims until the end of time, which can never be transferred to non-Muslims. This is stated in the founding charter of Hamas.

PART III STRATEGIES AND METHODS

The Strategy of Hamas: Palestine is an Islamic Waqf

Article Eleven

The Islamic Resistance Movement believes that the land of Palestine has been an Islamic Waqf throughout the generations and until the Day of Resurrection, no one can renounce it or part of it, or abandon it or part of it. No Arab country nor the aggregate of all Arab countries, and no Arab King or President nor all of them in the aggregate, have that right, nor has that right any organisation or the aggregate of all organisations, be they Palestinian or Arab, because Palestine is an Islamic Waqf throughout all generations and to the Day of Resurrection. Who can presume to speak for all Islamic generations to the Day of Resurrection? This is the status [of the land] in Islamic shari'a, and it is similar to all lands conquered by Islam by force, and made thereby Waqf lands upon their conquest, for all generations of Muslims until the Day of Resurrection. This [norm] has prevailed since the commanders of the Muslim armies completed the conquest of Syria and Iraq, and they asked the Caliph of Muslims, 'Umar ibn al-khattab, for his view of the conquered land, whether it should be partitioned between the troops or left in the possession of its population, or otherwise. Following discussions and consultations between the Caliph of Islam, 'Umar ibn al-khattab, and the Companions of the Messenger of Allah, be peace and prayer upon him, they decided that the land should remain in the hands of its owners to benefit from it and from its wealth; but the control of the land and the land itself ought to be endowed as a Waqf [in perpetuity] for all generations of Muslims until the Day of Resurrection. The ownership of the land by its owners is only one of usufruct, and this Waqf will endure as long as heaven and earth last. Any demarche in violation of this law of Islam, with regard to Palestine, is baseless and reflects on its perpetrators.[43]

Sacralising territory for Islam in the UK

New lands settled by Muslims are being added to the sacred space of Islam. Migrant Muslim communities in the West are constantly engaged in sacralising new areas. While first generation Muslim migrants sacralised the inner private spaces of their homes and mosques through the Islamic rituals performed there, the second generation took to the public sphere by organising processions, whether in honour of Muhammad's birthday or Sufi celebrations in honour of specific *pirs*. In Birmingham a *julus* march was undertaken by Sufis in which the marchers transcribe the name of Allah on the space they cover and call on Muslims in the area to return to their faith.[44] Local place names have been changed in the London Borough of Tower Hamlets in response to the requests of Muslims living there who objected to saints' names and other Christian-sounding names for their parks, electoral wards etc. In some strongly Muslim areas, advertisers have been forced to remove their publicity from hoardings because Muslims have objected, for example, to pictures of scantily clad women.

As in many other parts of the world there appears to be a mosque-building programme in the UK, with huge buildings being erected even where the Muslim population is too small to need such large places of worship. Much of the finance for these mosques comes from abroad, particularly Saudi Arabia. The sacredness of mosques is paramount and they can never be given up or demolished.[45] This should be borne in mind by those involved in granting planning permission and also by church ministers who kindly allow their buildings to be used by Muslim groups for worship. It is also relevant to a proposal announced by the prime minister in August 2005 to close down mosques linked to extremism.

The marked tendency of many British Muslims to live close together and create what are effectively Muslim enclaves can be easily understood in the light of the doctrine of sacred space. According to anecdotal evidence,[46] non-Muslims are already being squeezed out of some Muslim-majority areas by various devices. For example dog-owners have been told to get rid of their pets or the animals will be killed, thus forcing the family to move. (Dogs are considered unclean by Muslims.) Christians and Hindus living in Muslim-majority areas have been threatened and intimidated. In some places Muslim housing officers have apparently used their influence to develop purely Muslim areas. A BBC1 Panorama programme has highlighted the issue of "white flight" in Blackburn.[47] There are some incidents of specifically anti-Christian violence (see pages 73–74). It is likely that before long Islamist voices will be demanding some form of semi-autonomy and the application of *shari'a* principles in these enclaves instead of British law.

ISLAMIC FINANCE

The spectacular growth in Islamic finance and banking which has occurred in the last two decades is a consequence of the growth of radical Islam. First developed and promoted by Islamist movements as part of their ideology that Islam should dominate every area of life, Islamic finance has now become a powerful force in the Muslim world. Thus Western financial institutions and governments who encourage the provision of Islamic financial products are unwittingly encouraging the rise of radical Islam.

Islamic finance is defined by the strict and literal interpretation of Islamic source texts on matters of trade and financial transactions. However, there is controversy within the Muslim world regarding how to interpret the Qur'anic prohibition of *riba* (interest).[48] Some (including Islamists) consider this means that any kind of interest is forbidden.[49] Others take it to be a ban on extortionate interest only, such as the ancient Arabian custom that borrowers had their debts doubled if they defaulted and doubled again if they defaulted again.[50]

Al-Azhar, the main Sunni centre of religious studies located in Cairo, has long argued that *riba* means exorbitant and oppressive interest, and has proclaimed moderate fixed interest as permissible.[51] As a result, in Egypt, most banks pay fixed interest and the government issues interest-bearing bonds. The well known Pakistani reformer and scholar Fazlur Rahman took a stand similar to that of the Egyptian scholars.

However, the interpretation that considers all interest prohibited has now become dominant. Permitted finance is based on profit-sharing rather than interest. Islamists have transformed the various scattered *shari'a* injunctions on economic transactions into a comprehensive quasi-scientific economic system including detailed institutional and organisational procedures. Thus, rather than going back to what was practised in traditional Islam, they have created a different modern system.[52] This view is promoted by Islamist movements such as Jama'at-i-Islami and the Muslim Brotherhood, and has been adopted by a number of Muslim states, apparently to appease Islamist groups and gain greater control over the economy. The European Council for Fatwa and Research, which has links with both these organisations, has taken the same stance, condemning any bank interest as usury and therefore forbidden.

The development of Islamic finance

It was Abu'l A'la Mawdudi, founder of the Pakistani militant Islamist movement Jama'at-i Islami, who originated the modern call for an interest-free Islamic economic system. His disciple Khurshid Ahmad, who was sent to the UK to found the European arm of the Jama'at-i Islami, the Islamic Foundation, continued to work for this goal and established Islamic economics as an academic discipline. As an economist, Ahmad wove the theme of

Some main principles of Islamic banking

- The giving or receiving of interest is forbidden. Shared profits replace interest.
- Money cannot be traded for money.
- Money can be used to buy goods and services which can then be sold at a profit.
- Money must be invested in *shari'a*-compliant ethical industries (no gambling, no pork, only *halal* foods, no alcohol, etc.)
- Trading is permitted but usury is forbidden.

Some main financial tools developed

- **Murabaha** – sale at an agreed mark-up over seller's costs
- **Bay bithamin ajil (BBA)** – the sale of goods on deferred payment basis, similar to *murabaha* but with payment on a deferred basis
- **Ijara** – a leasing agreement, whereby the bank buys an item for a customer and then leases it back over a specific period
- **Ijara-wa-iqtina** – similar to *ijara*, except that the customer is able to buy the item at the end of the contract
- **Mudaraba** – a specialist investment by a financial expert in which the bank and the customer share any profits
- **Musharaka** – an investment partnership in which profit sharing terms are agreed in advance, and losses re-pegged to the amount invested (similar to private equity)
- **Bay al-salam** – payment in advance for deferred delivery of a commodity
- **Bay al-sarf** – rules on the exchange of money for money
- **Istisna** – payment in advance for goods that are manufactured and delivered at a later date
- **Takaful** – Islamic insurance based on pooling resources to help the needy

an Islamic economy into the discourse of the Islamist struggle to weaken the West in preparation for the ultimate phase of establishing Muslim political hegemony in the world.[53]

Ahmad is a prominent intellectual, politician, and economist, one of the main leaders of the Jama'at-i Islami in Pakistan. He holds a BA in Law and Jurisprudence, a Master's degree in Economics and Islamic Studies, and an honorary PhD in Education. Ahmad served as Professor of Economics at the University of Karachi (1955–1968), Federal Minister of Planning and Development in the government of Pakistan (1978–79), and was a member of the Pakistani Senate (1985–1997). He has also served as Vice-President of the Jama'at-i Islami Pakistan. Ahmad was a research scholar at the University of Leicester, UK, and has held academic positions in Pakistan and Saudi Arabia, as well as serving on many associations, committees, and advisory councils across the world. He has written, translated and edited over 50 books on Islam, economics, education and law, both in English and in Urdu. Ahmad was elected first president of the International Association for Islamic Economics founded in 1986.

The spread of Islamic finance

At first Islamic economics were a theoretical exercise, but the oil wealth generated in the 1970s was the impetus for implementing its ideals in practice, for example, in Pakistan, Malaysia, the Gulf and Iran. Islamic banking was pioneered by conglomerates that include the Islamic Development Bank, Dar Al-Maal al-Islami (headquarters in Geneva), and Al-Baraka (headquarters in Jeddah). As well as the ban on interest, Islamic finance eschews investment in un-Islamic industries such as alcohol, gambling or pornography. A whole new elite of Islamic scholars, experts in the new science of Islamic finance, has arisen, employed by the financial institutions to ensure that the company's products comply with their strict interpretation of *shari'a*. A number of prestigious experts appear on many such boards. Some of them are linked to Islamist movements such as the Muslim Brotherhood, Wahhabis, Salafis, Jama'at-i Islami and Deobandis.

Islamic finance is now booming, with some 270 Islamic banks and financial institutions in over 25 countries. The Islamic financial services industry turnover increased ten-fold in the decade to 2005 by which time it amounted to over $400 billion annually. Some statistics forecast that by 2015 Islamic banks will account for 40% of the total savings of the Muslim population worldwide.[54]

4   BRITISH ISLAM

Muslims in Britain are a large and growing community composed of a mosaic of different ethnic, linguistic, cultural, sectarian and geographical backgrounds. The majority of British Muslims have their roots in South Asia, and have brought with them to the UK the traditions and groupings of the Indian subcontinent. A significant portion within each community originates in a fairly specific and small area of their former country: Mirpur in Azad Kashmir for the Pakistanis, Sylhet for Bangladeshis, and Gujarat for Indians. Thus, in Bradford for instance, Mirpuris comprise 80% of the Pakistani population. British Muslims are mainly Sunnis and broadly divided into two groups: the relatively passive Barelwis with their emphasis on the mystical veneration of Muhammad, and the more vocal, more puritanical Deobandis. In addition there are substantial minorities of Arabs from the Middle East and North Africa, Iranians, Africans and Turks, as well as smaller minorities of other Muslims.

Demography

Muslims in Britain now number some three million and their numbers are growing fast due to rapid biological growth, immigration from abroad and some conversions. The population of Leicester and Dewsbury is 33% Muslim. In Birmingham Muslims make up 15% of the population, while in London they represent 10% of the population. As there is a trend for Muslims to live near each other, in many inner city areas Muslim populations represent over half of the total population.[55] Given that parts of some British cities already have Muslim-majority populations it is likely that in ten to fifteen years some of these areas will come under local Muslim political control.

Ethnic composition determines types of organisation

The ethnic composition of Muslim communities in the West determines to some extent the type of Muslim organisations present in each country. Most UK Muslims are of Indian sub-continent origin, so organisations of the type prevalent in Pakistan, Bangladesh and India predominate. At the same time, there are several large Islamist movements that actively seek to gain adherents in all Muslim communities worldwide and appear in almost all Western countries. These include the Muslim Brotherhood and its affiliates, Hizb ut-Tahrir, Wahhabi–Salafi organisations and Tablighi Jama'at.

Separatism – parallel alternative society and institutions

Because of Islam's long history of political dominance and its doctrine of power, Muslims have difficulties adapting to life as minorities in a non-Muslim environment. Traditionalists develop strategies to help Muslims maintain their Muslim identity and resist secular temptations. These tend to push Muslims into physical and spiritual "ghettos". Some more liberal Muslim scholars argue that proper interpretations of Islamic law allow Muslims to live as minorities outside the abode of Islam, as long as they have the freedom to practise and propagate their faith. Islamists on the other hand warn them to reject integration into secular society, while using its freedoms to propagate Islam and set up radical networks that aim at incorporating Britain into *Dar al-Islam*.

Various Muslim leaders recommend that Muslims seek to live in physical proximity to each other, creating areas of Muslim concentration that can bear the infrastructure of mosques and institutions and the autonomy needed to guarantee the survival of a separate and clearly identifiable Muslim community. However, the community must at the same time engage in *da'wa* to the non-Muslim society around it. Its aim should be to grow constantly until it becomes the majority community.[56]

The institutionalisation of Islam in the UK

According to classical Islam, wherever Muslims gather, it is a duty for them to be organised. This is based on several *hadith* that require that even if only two Muslims go on a journey, they should choose one of them as an *amir* (commander, prince). This has been interpreted as an obligation on Muslims always to organise themselves as a separate viable community, able to establish its mosques and schools and represent its members before the authorities. For many Muslims, assimilation into the non-Muslim majority represents a danger they must avoid at all costs. Good communal organisation is a form of defence against the corrupting influences and enticements of non-Muslim society.[57]

The Muslim community in Britain has established thousands of mosques, institutions and organisations, not to mention the many networks linking those with shared ideologies. Some of the groups, especially the more extreme ones, operate under a variety of names.

It is important to note that the mosque has become more than simply a place where Muslims can gather for communal prayer. It has taken on a social, cultural and political function, which is reflected in the growing importance of the "mosque association". Such associations tend to be dominated by first generation immigrants and therefore often enforce traditional views and practice and hamper the spread of new ideas or interpretations. The British mosque is in effect a multi-function community centre, with a wider role than mosques in the countries of origin.[58] Many also have associated *madrassas* (schools where the Qur'an and rudiments of Islam are taught). In the early years of immigration, when there were relatively few mosques in the UK, mosque congregations were multi-ethnic and multi-sectarian. By 2007 there were an estimated 1,700 mosques in the UK, most with a very specific ideological and ethnic basis.[59]

Most Muslims consider that it is profoundly wrong to separate religion and state. In Muslim countries, the state is intimately involved in religious affairs, often controlling the mosques (which can be centres of political agitation and intrigue) and the clerical establishment as well as the Muslim charitable foundations. Many Muslim states hold that the role of a Muslim government is to protect Islam and the *umma* wherever they are to be found. They are therefore active in funding Islamic missionary work worldwide; they also maintain direct links with their respective minorities living in the UK, seeking to strengthen them. Thus British Islamic organisations often combine both religious and political activities and may have financial and other links with Islamic organisations and governments overseas.

Shari'a courts and councils

Many Muslims claim they have the right as a religious minority to follow their own customs and laws. For many Muslims, British law lacks legitimacy and moral standing especially in the realm of family law. These attitudes have given rise to a *de facto* parallel Islamic legal system in Britain, in which disputes between Muslims are settled by Islamic legal institutions considered to carry a religious legitimacy which the secular law does not have.[60] The unofficial system of "Muslim legal pluralism" is based on a variety of *shari'a* courts and councils that deal especially with cases of marriage and divorce according to Islamic *shari'a*.[61] (See page 189 for some examples.) Muslims in the UK have not abandoned their Islamic (and customary) family rules but have managed to reconstruct them, setting up an alternative voluntary framework to settle disputes according to Islamic law.[62] The Sharia Council of the Darul Uloom London even appears to assume the possibility of child marriages, as there are instructions on its website for how to deal with the divorce of a girl who has not yet reached puberty.[63]

English law accepts that people may voluntarily use arbitration tribunals administered by a third party to settle disputes. The judgement of the arbitrator is binding under domestic law, unless manifestly unreasonable. Many *shari'a* courts have turned themselves into recognised courts of arbitration.[64]

It would seem that there is virtually unlimited scope within the Muslim community for the establishment of such courts and councils, each with its specific sectarian, ethnic and cultural background. There is no doubt that at this time a whole alternative parallel unofficial legal system operates in the UK on a voluntary basis in the Muslim community.[65] On a BBC Radio 4 programme, "Law in Action", broadcast on 28 November 2006, Faizul Aqtab Siddiqi, a barrister and principal of Hijaz College Islamic University in Nuneaton, Warwickshire, predicted that a formal network of Muslim courts would function in Britain within a decade and imagined such courts dealing with crime.[66]

Evolution of an Islamic identity and the conflict of loyalties

Until the 1970s ethnicity rather than religion dominated the way Muslims perceived themselves.[67] In recent years there has been a determined push for Muslims to downplay racial, sectarian and linguistic differences, and present a united front towards the outside, non-Muslim world and the British authorities. This is linked to a push for the development of an overarching Muslim identity, i.e. for the upgrading of religion as the main ingredient in community identity. This has resulted in the visible presence of the Muslim community becoming a familiar part of British society, with a consequent shift in policies, resources, representation, etc. at local and government level as well as in many institutions. The process of re-defining themselves as a religious category also means that the concept of citizenship is marginalised for Muslims. When politicians, journalists and others use the phrase "the Muslim community" they are reinforcing this process.

Anti-racism has been supplanted by anti-Islamophobia activity, thus creating a split in the anti-racist alliance and alienating other minorities that were formerly allies in the anti-racism front such as Hindus, Sikhs and Jews. The recent push to Muslim identity politics seeks to downplay ethnic and cultural differences between Muslims; it also seeks to blame Islamophobia for negative indicators such as unemployment and low literacy, ignoring ethnic, cultural and local causes. This confuses the issues and makes the finding of effective solutions more difficult.

However there has, at the same time, been a growing rapprochement between the hard Left, anti-globalisation, anti-capitalist, anti-American, anti-Israel movement and radical Islamic organisations, particularly on matters relating to the Iraq War of 2003 onwards. Radical Islamic groups are increasingly being seen as representing justifiable liberation movements against the rich North.

Many Muslims in the West retain a primary loyalty to the *umma*, strengthened by the Islamist resurgence, while developing a secondary loyalty to their respective nation states. The first generation of Muslim immigrants, impoverished and lacking Muslim cultural facilities, tried to assimilate to some extent in their desire to improve their economic status. The better-off second and third generations are, however, rediscovering their Islamic identity, helped by a well established Western Muslim infrastructure constantly reinvigorated by contact with Muslim states from which come funds, imams, and radical ideologies. While many Muslims participate in the social, economic and political mainstream of their adoptive countries, often they simultaneously nurture a distinctive Muslim culture. They seek for Western states to adapt to the Muslim presence by adopting a pluralist communal type of political structure, in which each religious community is a recognised autonomous group under its religious leadership and law[68] in the way that the House of Islam has historically treated its own minorities.

Beyond the problem of how to balance two identities, the prioritising of the Muslim identity in recent years shows that the Islamist vision of supreme loyalty to the *umma* and its diverse worldwide causes is motivating many of the current leaders of the Muslim community in the UK. An extreme expression of disloyalty to Britain was the burning of the Union Jack outside the London Central Mosque in Regent's Park by members of the radical Islamist al-Muhajirun.[69]

Youth bulge – many alienated and unemployed

A marked characteristic of the British Muslim community is its youthfulness. The average age of the Muslim community is 28, compared with 41 for other groups. A third of the Muslim community are under the age of 16, compared with a fifth of the general population. This indicates a large population bulge of young Muslims compared with an ageing indigenous population.[70] As a result, in spite of education and training facilities, there is a growing segment of frustrated young Muslims who have not been able to complete their education or receive adequate professional training. Many of these are unemployed and are easily attracted to either crime or radicalism. Many are alienated from their parents who do not understand them and from society at large. In some inner city areas there are street gangs of young Muslims fighting for turf against white, Caribbean and non-Muslim Asian gangs.[71] However it should be recognised that there is a growing number of young Muslim professionals who are either embracing Western secularism and so adjusting to British society or embracing conservative Islamic positions.

Samuel Huntington has demonstrated how major disturbances across the world peak where the "youth bulge" (defined as 15- to 24-year-olds) in those areas exceeds 20% of the total population of the group.[72] Darryl Brock tested this theory on the Bradford riots of 2001 and found a conclusive link between areas of Bradford with the highest youth bulge percentages and the propensity of those areas to riot. For each of the 21 districts of Bradford that Brock analysed, the single common factor linking the areas that contributed most to the riots was a high Muslim population which was fuelling the youth bulge peaks.[73]

Effects of secularism: increasing criminality, divorce, drug addiction

Coming from Muslim-majority countries in which traditional views on religion, family, honour and shame, and Islamic law prevail, many Muslim immigrants are shocked by the secular, permissive and liberal society they find in Britain. They intuitively feel that excessive individual freedom endangers communal rights and considerations of the common welfare.

However, while Muslim spokesmen deplore rampant crime in British society as a sign of Christian decadence, the number of Muslim prisoners in 2005 constituted some 10% of the total prison population, about twice the proportion of Muslims in the population.[74] Two-thirds of these prisoners are young men between 18 and 30. The crimes committed include drug pushing, violent muggings and petty theft.[75]

Greater tendency to corruption among Muslim police officers

Complaints of misconduct and corruption against Asian (Muslim) police officers are ten times higher than against white officers. The Metropolitan Police prepared a secret report to investigate the reasons for this fact. The report concluded that the main causes were the cultural and family backgrounds of the Asian officers. Pakistani Muslim officers, in particular, are under greater pressure from their family and community to engage in activities that might lead to corruption than other officers. This is because in the Muslim community assisting one's family is considered a priority which outweighs other ethical considerations. The report supports its conclusions by citing cases in which Pakistani Muslim officers were accused of corruption and misconduct. The report was fiercely attacked by the Association of Muslim Police and by the Muslim Council of Britain. It was alleged it was racist and that it would alienate Muslim officers in a sensitive time when their loyalty was most needed.[76]

Homosexuality

Homosexual behaviour is considered a sin in Islam, is condemend by *shari'a* and carries the death penalty. In most Muslim states it is forbidden by law. Islam, however, is mainly concerned with public behaviour and morals, so while homosexuality was historically condemned, there was no strong reaction to the practice if not displayed in public. In Islamic history there was a paradoxical ambivalence toward homosexuality. Medieval European visitors to Islamic societies were shocked by the wide practice of "love between men and boys".[77] Many Muslim societies were lenient in their attitudes towards homosexuality, and it seems to have been widely practised, especially among the ruling classes. Before the twentieth century, Islamic societies discreetly incorporated a diverse set of homosexual practices which included the love of boys celebrated in poetry, the sexual use of male entertainers and military cadets, and the alternative gender status of the caste-like male *khanit* in Oman and the female *mustergil* in southern Iraq.[78] The male sexual urge was generally viewed as irresistible, requiring release,[79] and homosexual activities were seen as less dangerous than heterosexual illicit activities that threatened marriage, family responsibilities, inheritance, and brought great shame on the perpetrators and their extended families that could lead to lengthy blood feuds. Attitudes have recently hardened due to the Islamist resurgence and the growing strength of the puritanical Wahhabi and Salafi movements funded by Saudi Arabia.

In the contemporary West, some Muslim homosexuals have recently "come out" publicly despite vehement condemnation by Muslim leaders and communities. In Britain, a Muslim organisation for gay, lesbian, bisexual, and transgender Muslims was founded in 1999 as Al-Fatiha and is now known as Imaan. This organisation now has some 300 members, most of whom are still afraid to tell their families about their sexual orientation. However, they still see themselves as Muslims by religion and often pray together or celebrate Muslim feasts together.[80] Similar organisations are now active in the US and other Western countries.

In Canada Irshad Manji, a Muslim author calling for radical reform in Islam, has publicly stated that she is a lesbian. She has received many death threats but is still openly campaigning for her views.[81]

PROBLEMS FACED BY MUSLIM WOMEN IN BRITAIN

Marriage and divorce

Women are undoubtedly the main victims of the *shari'a* system which inherently favours the husband in marriage and divorce issues. British law recognises Muslim marriages that were performed abroad before the partners entered the UK. However British residents in the UK must contract marriage according to civil law in order for the marriage to be legally recognised. It is very common, even for well educated Muslims living in the UK, to think it unnecessary to register their marriages in the civil system. Some wrongly believe that the Islamic wedding ceremony is recognised by British law. In cases of divorce the women are then left with the much lesser legal rights of a "cohabitee". Some Muslim men knowingly exploit the ignorance of their wives so as not to have to pay maintenance and dowry should they divorce them. Widows may find they lack pension rights and rights to their husband's property.

Another problem is that many Muslim women in the UK may get divorced under *shari'a* only, without getting their divorce ratified by a civil court (decree absolute). Some believe they are free to remarry, but under British law, they are then committing bigamy (an offence punishable by seven years imprisonment).

Child marriages

In several Muslim countries child marriages are legal. For many traditional Muslims, child marriages are acceptable because Muhammad married his favourite wife 'Aisha when she was six years old and consummated the marriage when she was nine. This is why, following the Iranian Revolution, Iran's new rulers lowered the minimum age of marriage for girls to nine. Recently in India, the All India Muslim Personal Law Board attempted to gain an exemption for Muslims from the legal minimum marriage age of 18 set by Indian law. According to the board, child marriages are part of *shari'a* which is "absolute, final and non-negotiable". When such couples immigrate to Britain severe problems arise.

Polygamy

Under *shari'a* a man is allowed up to four wives. Polygamy is legal in many Muslim countries but prohibited in Britain. This raises problems of Muslim residents in the UK who married another wife either before their immigration or while visiting their home countries. Furthermore there are growing numbers of cases where a British Muslim marries one wife under British civil law and then others also in the UK but in *shari'a* ceremonies only; as a result he can have up to four wives under Islamic law but only one of them is recognised as his wife under British law.

The Muslim Parliament of Great Britain complained that many families are being forced to live outside the law because their polygamous marriages are not recognised in the UK.[82] It is difficult to ascertain the number of polygamous marriages, even those where all the wives are resident in the UK, although the number is certainly growing. This has led to Muslims petitioning the European Human Rights Commission to allow polygamous marriages on the basis that this is necessary for their religious liberty.[83]

Female genital mutilation

Female genital mutilation is a criminal offence in the UK under the 1985 Prohibition of Female Circumcision Act. However it is widespread among some Muslim communities, especially in Africa. Some Muslim leaders condemn it as un-Islamic but many see it as *shari'a*-ordained and essential for preserving women's chastity and family honour. In 1994 the former Sheikh of Al-Azhar, Jad Al-Haqq 'Ali Jad Al-Haqq, ruled that circumcision is an Islamic duty for women as well as for men.[84] An estimated 7,000 girls in Britain are at risk from this procedure at any given time.

The law is being evaded by families taking the girls abroad for a holiday and having the procedure carried out there. Further legislation passed in 2003 attempts to tackle this problem, making it unlawful to take girls abroad for genital mutilation, whether or not the procedure is lawful elsewhere. The same law increased the maximum penalty for both performing and procuring female genital mutilation from five to 14 years' imprisonment.[85]

Veiling

The discussion started in 2006 by then Home Secretary Jack Straw stating that he asked Muslim women to remove their veils when visiting his surgery has polarised views among the Muslim community on veiling. Some see it as a valid interpretation of the Muslim source texts, others as an instrument of male control. Some see it as a "liberating" choice made by enlightened Muslim women, others as a reactionary and discriminatory symbol of the oppression of Muslim women by men.

Both Qur'an and *hadith* urge modesty in women's dress and command them to cover themselves in public. The problem is a matter of interpretation of the original Qur'anic Arabic words used. One such word, *jilbab,* is obviously an outer garment, but what did it look like? Was it just a mantle-like garment that covered the under clothes, or did it cover head and face and ankles as well? Does another word, *juyub,* mean bosom only, or did it mean head, face, neck and bosom? Most contemporary Muslim women do not accept the stricter interpretations and just wear a headscarf and modest clothes. A small minority, especially in Afghanistan, Iran and the Arabian Peninsula adopt the strictest interpretation which totally covers the woman including her face.

Some modern Muslim women in the West are adopting this strictest version as a demonstration of their anti-secular worldview and assertive Muslim identity. Muslim organisations are manipulating the issue to further the Islamisation of their host societies. Wearing the veil is in many cases more a political statement than an act of piety. It challenges non-Muslim society, forcing non-Muslims to recognise the presence of Islam because of its visibility, and also to adapt to it in practices and procedures in contexts such as schools and courtrooms.

For example, in November 2006, Judge George Glossop at the immigration court in Stoke-on Trent adjourned a case, complaining that he had difficulties hearing a legal advisor, Shabnam Mughal, who twice refused to remove her full face covering (*niqab*). Following this dispute, the Judicial Studies Board Equal Treatment Advisory Committee issued new guidelines stating that Muslim women should be allowed to wear a veil in court; that decisions should be made on the merits of each case and veils should not interfere with the administration of justice; that any request to remove the veil should be considered carefully and be thoughtful and sensitive; and that should the woman be asked to remove the veil, the courtroom should be cleared of those not involved in the case. The principle appears to be that judges should assume that female Muslim lawyers are entitled to wear the veil.[86]

Women's clothing

This table gives the most common usage of the terms, but some are given different meanings in different parts of the world.

abaya – Arab outer garment, a loose robe covering the whole body apart from the face, feet and hands. Called a *chador* in Iran

burqa – Afghan outer garment, a loose robe with covers the whole body and face, with a mesh grille over the eyes

chador – Iranian outer garment, a long loose robe covering the whole body apart from the face, feet and hands

hijab – headscarf which covers the hair and neck. Literally "curtain" or "partition", *hijab* has come to mean the separation of the sexes.

jilbab – loose, ankle-length coat or robe covering the entire body except hands, feet and head

kumar (khimar) – headdress consisting of a circle of fabric with a whole cut for the face, usually reaches to the waist

niqab – opaque veil covering at least the lower half of the face. If it covers the whole face there is usually a slit for the eyes.

shalwar kameez – loose trousers and tunic as worn in Pakistan

---

Honour killings

Honour killings (i.e. the murder of women and girls for the sake of the family's reputation) are usually linked to cultural traditions in which patriarchal notions of family honour and shame are paramount. As family honour centres mainly on the modest and proper behaviour of the female members of the family, any perceived breach of the modesty code demands swift and severe punishment, often the death of the offending female at the hands of the male members of her family. In many Muslim states, such killings are not as severely punished as other murders, because the honour motive is recognised. As honour killings are integrated into traditional culture they are often assumed to be Islamic.

Honour killings take place within the British Muslim community. Statistics reveal that 13 people die every year in honour killings, but police and support groups believe the real figure is much higher.[87] While most Muslim leaders in Britain condemn honour killings as un-Islamic, some lay the blame on British secular society rather than on the Muslim individuals concerned. In September 2003 the Metropolitan Police set up a strategic taskforce to look into the frequency of honour killings and into how they could be stopped. Around a hundred files spanning the previous decade were reopened to search for common links and the possibility of honour killings.[88] Commander Andy Baker, head of homicide at the Metropolitan Police, spoke of the problems caused by the acquiescence of some family members and members of the community in honour killings. Other women in the family may even be accomplices in these murders.[89]

In most cases the presumed female offender against family honour is killed. In January 2003 in Birmingham, a 21-year-old Muslim woman, Sahjda Bibi, was stabbed to death in a frenzied attack by her cousin minutes before her planned marriage to another cousin. The proposed marriage was controversial in the extended family.[90] In another case, a Muslim father, Abdalla Yones, was convicted in September 2003 for killing his 16-year-old daughter Heshu because she had formed a relationship with a Christian boyfriend.[91] In April 2005, a young woman, Samaira Nazir, was stabbed to death by her father, brother and cousin because she rejected a number of suitors proposed by her family and preferred an Afghan asylum seeker whom she loved.[92] In May 2005, Sana Ali, a 17-year-old woman of Pakistani origin was stabbed to death by her husband in Bury in a suspected honour killing.[93]

Opinion polls and the trends they reveal

Opinion polls among British Muslims are confusing. An ICM poll conducted for the BBC in December 2002 indicated that "more than two-thirds of British Muslims consider the war on terrorism to be a war on Islam". The same poll also revealed that 56% of British Muslims believe al-Qaeda was not to blame for the 11 September 2001 attack on the World Trade Centre. Forty-four percent believed attacks by radical Islamist groups like al-Qaeda were justified because the US and its allies were killing Muslims. At the same time, two-thirds of British Muslims said they felt fairly or very patriotic to Britain.[94] A Guardian/ICM poll in June 2002 held that 41% of British Muslims believed their community must do more to integrate, while only 17% thought there had been too much integration. However 69% said the rest of society did not see them as an integral part of British life. The poll also revealed that British Muslims have a strong sense of solidarity with Muslims in other countries, especially in places of conflict like Kashmir, the Middle East and Afghanistan.[95]

An NOP poll in August 2006 found that 45% of British Muslims believed the 11 September 2001 attacks were an American-Israeli conspiracy. Almost 25% of British Muslims believe that the July 2005 London bombing was justified because of British involvement in the "war on terror". Thirty percent would prefer to live under *shari'a* rather than under British law; 28% hoped that Britain would one day become a fundamentalist Islamic state; 68% supported the arrest and prosecution of British citizens who insult Islam. The survey also reported that 9% of British Muslims are hardcore Islamists, while a further 29% are staunch defenders of Islam, willing to aggressively defend their religion.[96]

Such opinion polls reveal the diversity of attitudes within the British Muslim community, but also an underlying innate conservatism, an anti-British stance, and a loyalty to the Muslim *umma* and Islamic institutions.

RADICALISATION OF THE MUSLIM COMMUNITY IN BRITAIN

Islamists are very active in promoting the cause of Islam in the UK. They are making inroads into Muslim institutions and have managed to gain many key leadership positions in such institutions as well as positions of influence in the media, politics and academia.

In recent years the UK has been a haven for radical Islamists, who have been able to operate freely to plan international terrorism. British-born Muslim youths trained and fought in Afghanistan, and have carried out suicide bombings in Israel and the UK itself (7 July 2005). Mainstream Muslim leaders, while distancing themselves from Islamist terrorists, blame the West for creating the causes of terrorism and appear to have taken little action to try to marginalise or expel radicals from their communities. They also hamper the activities of the security forces by complaining that Muslims are disproportionately affected by anti-terrorist operations and precautions.

The identity crisis suffered by many young British-born Muslims is thought to be one of the reasons why so many are persuaded to follow radical Islamist groups. These promote a dedicated and austere lifestyle for those who are in training for leadership roles in the Islamic revolution. According to this viewpoint all forms of pleasure, from music and dance to watching films and television, should be foresworn in favour of more pious activities. Many aspects of the Islamic heritage are uncompromisingly and uncritically rejected. Some Muslims only remain true to this form of Islam during their student days, others move on to more radical ideologies and groups like al-Qaeda which favour immediate global *jihad* against all infidels.

Anti-Christian and anti-Jewish rhetoric and violence

Although rarely reported in the media, there have been a number of attacks on church buildings, church leaders and converts from Islam to Christianity.[97] These mostly happen in strongly Muslim areas, and the impression is given that the aim is to eradicate the Christian presence from such areas. Reports from south London suggest that gangs of young Muslims are trying to convert non-Muslims to Islam by force, and that one Christian boy who refused to convert was killed.[98]

There has been a growth in anti-Semitic attacks in the UK in recent years, apparently heightened by Palestinian-Israeli tensions in the Middle East. Some of this is due to Muslims, including a fatal stabbing on a London bus in 2000. Strongly anti-Semitic material is circulated in some sections of the Muslim community, some of it calling on Muslims to kill Jews.[99]

Planning for Islamic dominance

Powerful forces within the Islamic resurgence of recent decades have long been planning for the Islamic takeover of power wherever possible. Those involved are part of a broad alliance of the Wahhabi-Salafi movement with the Muslim Brotherhood, the Deobandis, the Jama'at-i Islami and similar groups. Saudi funding is an important part in the success of this alliance, but its main core is the convergence of the various ideologies. These movements are linked to a plethora of international organisations endorsed by Muslim states as well as networks of non-governmental organisations and institutions including violent *jihadi* groups.

Strategy for the Islamisation of the UK

Concerned to establish the power, honour and dominion of Islam, Islamists and their supporters have developed a programme for Islamising the UK in stages as set out by Sayyid Qutb and other Islamist thinkers (see page 40). This programme sees Muhammad's *hijra* as a paradigmatic model to be followed in all times. Its implementation is part of the political quest for the establishment of the Islamic state modelled on Muhammad's practice. Many Muslims in the West see themselves as equivalent to the "migrants" (*muhajirun*) of Muhammad's time, who helped him win Medina, set up the Islamic state and then expand its dominion. They dedicate themselves to this staged process of expanding Islamic hegemony in their host countries in the fields of politics, law, economics, education, and culture – initially by peaceful methods (the stages of weakness and of organisation) and in the final stage (the stage of strength) by the violent takeover of government and the establishment of an Islamic state under *shari'a*.

The plan of many Islamic activists is to gain power in the state and then use its coercive power to enforce *shari'a*. For them peace is only possible under Islamic rule. To attain their goals they work for:

1. Creation of Islamic consciousness in the Muslim community
2. Creation of Islamic institutions they can control
3. Creation of autonomous Muslim enclaves under *shari'a*
4. Infiltration of political, social, economic and educational structures in the state (Islamisation)
5. Finally, when strong enough, use of violence (*jihad*) as necessary to assume total power and set up an Islamic state.[100]

A group called Young Muslims UK sees four stages to be followed in emulating Muhammad's model:[101]

1. Private invitation to convert to Islam (call, mission, *da'wa*) and development: in this stage a vanguard of committed Muslims is recruited and trained.
2. Open invitation: this stage includes *da'wa* work among the Muslim and non-Muslim masses.
3. Establishment of the ideology: the mass turning to Islam and attendant reform of society will lead to the establishment of Islam and *shari'a* in government and law.
4. Once established in one state, the movement will co-operate with the global Muslim community (*umma*) to impose Islam on the whole world. This follows Muhammad's example, who after establishing the Islamic state in Medina first invited the surrounding tribes to Islam and then fought those who refused to submit to Islam until, within ten years the whole Arabian Peninsula was under Muslim control to a greater or lesser extent.

As early as 1977 Zakaria Bashier, a Sudanese born Islamist author and scholar, outlined the classical step-by-step strategy of Islamism in a talk at the annual conference of the Federation of Student Islamic Societies (FOSIS) in Britain. His reasoning was that the Qur'an promises Muslims political domination over non-Muslims:

> The Qur'an has promised victory and political domination to the true sincere Muslim workers. That is to say, if Islamisation is to be successful, then true, sincere workers of Islam must gain ascendancy and political sovereignty.[102]

This is to be achieved in stages, following Muhammad's *hijra* model:

> If the stages to it are fulfilled, then the political authority will inevitably be gained.[103]

The final stage entails using force to implement the Islamic system in the state:

> Only after the Islamic case is put forward clearly and convincingly and all legitimate grounds of genuine doubt removed, would the Muslim proceed to involve the necessary power to invoke it.[104]

In the UK the Muslim Brotherhood is not usually seen as an organisation which warrants concern. However, the Brotherhood's strategy for North America[105] has recently been uncovered and the threat it poses Western society as a whole has now been recognised. This concern is one which should now be reflected in the UK.

Paucity of intelligence from British Muslim community sources

Following the successful conclusion of the "Crevice trial" in May 2007, in which British Muslim terrorists were convicted of terrorist-related crimes, the head of the Metropolitan Police Anti-Terrorist Squad, Peter Clarke, hinted that most of the intelligence used had come from overseas, hardly any from the British Muslim community itself.

Community intelligence – titbits from friends and neighbours about aberrational behaviour – is crucial in spotting the early signs of radicalisation and in preventing acts of terrorism. The Muslim community constantly denies the real extent of such radicalism in its midst and seems reluctant to co-operate with the security forces in providing crucial intelligence; they prioritise loyalty to Muslims, no matter how criminal, over loyalty to the British state and its security.[106]

Radical Islamists highly active in Britain

A 2007 secret intelligence document asserts that radical Islamists intent on terrorism remain highly active in Britain, despite all security measures taken, especially after the July 2005 London bombings. Radicals continue to radicalise other Muslims, give them military training, and raise funds to support radicals elsewhere. British intelligence continues to detect high levels of operational activity of British extremist networks. This raises the likelihood of further terrorist attacks within Britain in the near future.[107]

Effects of British foreign policy on the Muslim community

Islamists have encouraged the Muslim attitude of a primary loyalty to the global Muslim *umma*. They have also propagated the view of Muslims as victims of mighty conspiratorial forces all over the world. As a result, British Muslims tend to judge the government not so much on its achievements in improving conditions for UK Muslims as on its foreign policy which they demand must be supportive of all Muslim causes around the world, regardless of British national interest or any other factors.

There is no doubt that British involvement in the invasions of Afghanistan in 2001 and of Iraq in 2003 has caused much anger within the British Muslim community. This has been further enhanced by the view pushed by radicals that the "war on terror" is actually a global war on Islam. Government policies are seen as part of the "clash of civilisations" between the West and Islam. Whether a change in these policies will moderate Muslim opinion is difficult to foresee, as some Muslims will only be satisfied by a new world order in which all outstanding conflicts involving Muslims anywhere in the world, including Israel/Palestine, Chechnya, Kashmir, the southern Philippines, southern Thailand, and many more, are resolved in favour of the radical Muslim positions.

Islamist impact on the media and the internet

Islamist organisations have been very skilful in using the media and the World Wide Web to further their goals. While more moderate spokesmen continue to assure the West that Islam is a religion of peace and tolerance, radical groups, through the *jihadi* violence broadcast on their websites and in videos and DVDs, are successfully recruiting many young Muslims to their cause. International Muslim media and TV stations like Al-Jazeera, funded by oil-rich Gulf states and businessmen, fulfil an important function in presenting news but also vilify the West as attacking Islam worldwide, glorify the *jihadi* "resistance" groups and spread the notion of Muslims everywhere as victims. Terrorism expert Professor Audrey Cronin of Oxford University states: "Blogs are today's revolutionary pamphlets, websites are the new dailies and list-servers are today's broadsides."[108]

The UK has become a centre of radical Islamist propaganda conducted in several languages, including English, Arabic and Urdu. These are published in a variety of media: print, internet, CDs, DVDs and videos. From Britain their message of hatred and violence is spread to the wider Muslim world as well as to the British Muslim community. It would seem that the relative freedom still allowed for the production and dissemination of radical Islamist propaganda makes Britain an attractive place for such activities. Other factors include the presence of networks of sympathisers and supporters within the British Muslim community and the availability of the technical know-how to produce high quality products and distribute them around the world.

As an example, the Palestinian Hamas operates a publishing house (Filastin al-Muslimah Publications) and a media centre in Britain for publication and distribution of Hamas materials. These include the Arabic monthly *Filastin al-Muslimah* which appears in both printed and internet versions. This paper incites hatred against the West and Israel, and glorifies terrorism and suicide bombings. Suicide bombers are depicted as role models for Muslims to emulate. The centre also publishes a bi-weekly children's newspaper *Al-Fateh* that serves to teach children the ideology of radical Islam as well as prepare them to participate in violence and terrorism. Books published by the Hamas publishing house include biographies of senior operatives in its terrorist wing, which glorify martyrdom and suicide bombings.

Research carried out in 2006–7 at important Islamic religious institutions and leading mosques in the UK discovered that radical literature was available either openly or "under the counter" at approximately 25% of them. This 25% included some of the "best funded and most dynamic institutions in Muslim Britain – some of which are held up as mainstream bodies". The radical literature, which was in the form of books and pamphlets in English, Arabic and Urdu, focused on loyalty to fellow believers and enmity to non-Muslims. It encouraged Muslims to feel disgust for non-Muslims and to separate themselves from people and things considered un-Islamic. In some instances there were exhortations to violence and *jihad* against the enemies of Islam.[109]

Small but growing liberal and secular Islam

Progressive Muslim reformers as well as liberal and secular Muslims are offering some really new interpretations of their faith, but in most Muslim societies they are a small minority and face determined and often violent opposition by the dominant traditionalist and Islamist forces.[110] Progressives represent a wide variety of approaches to the challenges of modernity, and are characterised by a peaceful approach to Western and other non-Muslim cultures. Many see themselves as good Muslims who oppose secularism as an atheistic ideology but embrace the separation of religion from state and politics. They accept what they consider to be a core of basic Islamic values, distilled from the Islamic source texts, as spiritual and moral norms that override coercive political and social interpretations. However they either ignore or reject traditional Islamic concepts and interpretations which contradict modern values of freedom and equality. They see a need to make some key changes to traditional orthodox Islam in such a way as to integrate liberal humanistic values at its very core.[111] A number of them have totally rejected Islam as a religion while seeing themselves as Muslims in the cultural sense.

Progressives are so few and their ideas are so opposed to the mainstream of traditional Islam, let alone to Islamism, that they put themselves at considerable risk when they publish. As UK-based reformer Ehsan Masood admits, Muslims advocating such reform are at present mainly living in the West – they could not articulate such ideas in Muslim states.[112] They are often accused by Islamists of the serious crimes of apostasy (*irtidad*), blasphemy and unbelief (*kufr*), and heresy (*ilhad*) – all of which are crimes under *shari'a* that incur the death penalty. Radicals also issue death threats against progressives and attack them physically.

Such progressives show immense courage in grappling with the thorny issue of the place of violence within the Islamic texts and within Islamic societies. The place of reason and its relation to violence in religion has been raised by some, but it has often brought them threats, intimidation and in some cases death.

Four British progressive reformers are described in the following chapter (pages 123–126).

5 MUSLIM THINKERS SHAPING BRITISH ISLAM

This chapter looks at 37 Muslim thinkers of the twentieth and twenty-first centuries who are impacting the nature of British Islam today. A number of them we have already met briefly in earlier chapters. Some are UK-born or UK-based. Others are not, and may never have even visited Britain, but with the ease of global communications today their thinking is nevertheless hugely influential.

ISLAMISTS

Main ideologues

The ideas and influence of the three main figures who shaped the modern Islamist movement – Hasan al-Banna, Sayyid Qutb and Abul A'la Mawdudi – continue to have a profound impact on Islamists around the world, including in the UK.

Hasan al-Banna (1906–1949)

In 1928 Hasan al-Banna, an Egyptian schoolteacher, founded the Muslim Brotherhood, the first grass-roots Islamic militant movement in modern times. Banna was influenced by the Salafi call of Afghani, Abduh and Rida to return to the original Islamic sources. He saw Islam as an integrated, self-sufficient, and comprehensive social and political system which must be implemented in the context of an Islamic state – there could be no separation between state and religion. It was the implementation of *shari'a* which made a government truly Islamic, and such implementation was a primary goal of the movement he founded.

The main objective of the Muslim Brotherhood is the establishment of an Islamic state under *shari'a* in Egypt, in all Muslim states and in all states in the world, leading ultimately to the re-establishment of a world-wide Islamic caliphate which will dominate the whole globe.

Banna stated that the goal of Islam is to rule all of humanity all over the world.

> The Noble Qur'an appoints the Muslims as guardians over humanity in its minority, and grants them the right of suzerainty and dominion over the world in order to carry out this sublime commission . . . it is our duty to establish sovereignty over the world and to guide all of humanity to the sound precepts of Islam and to its teachings, without which mankind cannot attain happiness.[113]

He glorified active *jihad*:

> The supreme martyrdom is only conferred on those who slay or are slain in the way of God. As death is inevitable and can happen only once, partaking in *jihad* is profitable in this world and the next.[114]

The Muslim Brotherhood movement soon developed branches in Syria, Palestine and Sudan. It then spread to most Arab and Muslim countries and established itself also in the West. Suppressed and persecuted by President Nasser in Egypt, many members fled to Saudi Arabia where they formed an alliance with the Wahhabi state against secular Arab regimes. The Syrian branch rebelled against the Ba'ath regime of President Hafiz al-Assad and was brutally suppressed in 1982.

It was Hasan al-Banna who founded the Muslim Brotherhood's secret armed wing, al Tanzim al Khas, which resorted to terrorism in the 1940s and early 1950s despite Brotherhood claims to be committed to non-violence and the use of legitimate means to achieve its objective. The movement still supports violent defensive *jihad* whenever Muslims are attacked. It has also given rise to numerous violent terrorist organisations.

The Muslim Brotherhood maintains a worldwide network of affiliated organisations, many of them viewed as mainstream by Western governments.

Sayyid Qutb (1906–1966)

Sayyid Qutb was the ideologue of the Egyptian Muslim Brotherhood in the 1950s and 1960s. He was tortured and executed by President Nasser for his book *Milestones (Ma'alim fil Tariq)* which reinterpreted traditional Islamic concepts to justify a violent takeover of the state. This reinterpretation was the catalyst for the rise of radical Islamic groups. Qutb posits a real battle taking place between the forces of good (true Islam) and evil (those who oppose true Islam). This world is the battlefield and, although in this world there are only partial victories, the final victory of true Islam is assured.

For Qutb, Islam is a perfect system which integrates freedom, equality and social justice and is in accord with the cosmic order and the laws of nature. Islam is a comprehensive ideology that must regulate all of life by implementing *shari'a* as the legal system of the state. Reason and public welfare are useful principles of interpretation, but only when kept in the framework of *shari'a*.

Qutb wrote a Qur'anic commentary called *In the Shade of the Qur'an (Fi Zilal al-Qur'an)* which is extremely popular in the contemporary Muslim world. He embeds his radical interpretation of Islam in the Qur'anic text, using Qur'anic stories and concepts as paradigms applicable to the modern world. Pharaoh is the prototype of the evil dictators and tyrants of today who want to destroy Islam and must be fought. Moses is the prototype of the true Muslim leader who fights to liberate his people by bringing them under the yoke of *shari'a* – true worship of God. Qutb sees the Qur'an as a unity which mirrors and demands the unity of the Muslim *umma*.[115]

Qutb taught that the main cause of moral decadence affecting modern societies is the return of humanity to paganism (*jahiliyya*) and the dethroning of God from His rightful sovereignty and rule (*hakimiyya*). He saw the paganism, ignorance and immorality of pre-Islamic Arabia being replicated in the neo-paganism of the modern secular world, both Western and Muslim.[116] In his view, *jahiliyya* is not a pre-Islamic historical era of paganism but rather an ever-present condition of denying God's rule, usurping his authority, and living by man-made laws that enslave men to their rulers thus creating oppression. Qutb identifies the enemy as all *jahili* societies, thus giving a specific focus for revolutionary action. *Jahiliyya* is always evil in whatever form it manifests itself, always seeking to crush true Islam. *Jihad* by force (*bil saif*) must be used to annihilate *jahili* regimes and replace them by true Muslim ones.[117] Islam is God's truth; all that opposes it is inevitably false, a deviation from submission to the one God and his law. There is only one true system, Islam – all other systems are *jahiliyya*. The concepts of the two systems are totally incompatible, so there is no possibility of compromise or coexistence between them.

Qutb embraced the Khariji doctrine of *takfir,* the process of judging Muslims (individuals, regimes, societies and states) to be apostates or infidels if they do not wholly conform to *shari'a*. Those thus defined must be fought by *jihad*, deposed and killed. Qutb believed that the first step towards Islamic renewal is to judge all societies, institutions, and regimes by the criteria of true *hakimiyya*. All those that do not fulfil these criteria are proclaimed *jahili*. Qutb held that no truly Islamic state existed and therefore denounced every contemporary society, whether Western or Muslim, as *jahili*.

This use of *takfir*, as promoted by Qutb, created for other radicals the possibility of condemning rival groups and individuals as *kuffar*. This paved the way for indiscriminate terror as practised by al-Jama'at al-Islamiyya and al-Jihad in Egypt, by the Armed Islamic Group (GIA) in Algeria and by al-Qaeda.[118]

In Qutb's view *jihad* was not merely specific wars against unbelievers, but the permanent conflict between the Islamic system and all other systems which will continue until the end of the world. He put an emphasis on the *qital* (fighting) aspect of *jihad*,[119] and strongly rejected the argument that *jihad* is for defence only.[120] He saw *jihad* as a method for actively seeking to free all peoples on earth from non-Islamic authority.[121]

As we have already seen (page 40), Qutb conferred a new depth of meaning on the term *hijra* (emigration) and saw in Muhammad's migration from Mecca to Medina a model of separation from *jahili* society which he said all true Muslims should follow. He held that such separation is a necessary condition for any modern renewal, enabling Muslims, once separated from *jahiliyya*, to transform themselves by immersion in the Qur'an, and prepare themselves for the next stage of *jihad* and the radical change of society.

Qutb believed in a worldwide conspiracy of the Christian West, Marxist communism and world Jewry against true Islam. These three forces he considered to be *jahiliyya* at its worst, enemies of God always plotting the destruction of Islam. Modern imperialism is a secret crusade by the Christian West, aided by the Jews, to attain world domination. Atheistic Marxists, who had replaced God with their own ideology, joined this attack on Islam.[122] Qutb saw hostility to Islam as inherent to the West since Crusader days, and detected this attitude in Orientalism, the Spanish *Reconquista*, the fall of Constantinople, and the Reformation. He held that, in spite of Western rationalism, an irrational prejudice against Islam survived and believed that Western imperialism saw Islam as the main obstacle to achieving world domination.[123]

Qutb had a key role in the spread of a virulent modern form of anti-Semitism amongst Muslims. He used racist stereotypes and Western anti-Semitic forgeries such as the Protocols of the Elders of Zion (translated into Arabic and widely distributed in the Muslim world).[124] It is largely as a result of Qutb's work that contemporary Islamism sees itself in an eternal struggle against "the Jews".[125] For Qutb, modern-day Jews are identical to the Jews of Arabia at the time of Muhammad, who opposed the Prophet and plotted against the early Muslim community.[126] Since then, all Jews have always been enemies of Islam, and all enemies of Islam are Jewish agents.[127] Jews are inherently evil because all through the ages they have rebelled against God. They are characterised by ingratitude, selfishness, fanaticism, isolationism, and hatred for all others, encouraging dissension in their host societies, and exploiting disasters to profit from the misery of others. They utilise usury to accumulate wealth, infiltrate societies, and dominate the whole world.[128] Qutb states that Jews have been behind every misfortune that befell the Muslims through the ages, Zionism being but the latest in the long line of Jewish plots against Islam. Jews have subverted Muslim states by bribing political leaders to betray their own people: "Therefore the struggle between Islam and the Jews continues in force and will continue, because the Jews will be satisfied only with the destruction of this religion (Islam)."[129]

Abu'l A'la Mawdudi (1903–1979)

Abu'l A'la Mawdudi was an immensely influential Pakistani Muslim scholar and activist. He was influenced by Hasan al-Banna and founded the Jama'at-i Islami in 1941 in British India as an elitist organisation aimed at establishing an Islamic state order. His goal was the complete transformation of individual, society and politics in line with Islamic ideology, a transformation that should be attained gradually through the efforts of a highly motivated vanguard of enlightened Muslims acting as catalysts of the revolution. An Islamic state ruled by *shari'a* was seen as the solution to all the problems Muslims faced worldwide.[130]

Mawdudi's writings – many of which are misogynistic and strongly anti-Western – are still immensely popular and widely available in Islamic bookshops. His simple confidence in the virtues of Islam and its ultimate victory has great appeal to pious Muslims.

Mawdudi wrote his commentary on the Qur'an, *Tafhim al-Qur'an,* with the objective of presenting a unitary "Islamic message" for *da'wa* purposes. He analysed the text of the Qur'an according to his Islamist ideology which saw it as a revolutionary manifesto and a manual for Islamist activists. While using the form of the traditional Qur'anic commentary, it is a very political book.

Mawdudi pictures true Islam and its past and present leaders as a modern-style revolutionary party engaged in a revolutionary struggle (*jihad*) to reshape the world:

> Islam is a revolutionary ideology which seeks to alter the social order of the entire world and rebuild it in conformity with its own tenets and ideals. 'Muslims' is the title of that 'International Revolutionary Party' organized by Islam to carry out its revolutionary program. *'Jihad'* refers to that revolutionary struggle and utmost exertion

which the Islamic Nation/Party brings into play in order to achieve this objective....There is no doubt that all the Prophets of Allah, without exception, were Revolutionary Leaders, and the illustrious Prophet Muhammad was the greatest Revolutionary Leader of all.[131]

Mawdudi divides the world into Muslim and non-Muslim rather than good and evil. It is an Islamic variant of Marxism and Fascism, a totalitarian ideology which is detrimental to individual freedoms. Mawdudi argues that as Islam means submission to God, so *kufr* means disobedience to God. Muslims recognise and obey their Lord, while *kuffar* (infidels) neither recognise him nor obey him. God loves Muslims but dislikes *kuffar*.[132]

While embracing the classic military understanding of *jihad*, Mawdudi considered that *jihad* also included non-violent methods such as campaigning by speech and writing. He defined *jihad* as the struggle "to bring about a revolution and establish a new order in conformity with the ideology of Islam." This new order would be just, would eliminate evil and would enforce *shari'a*. In this struggle Muslims are duty-bound to expend their possessions and lives in the fight to "wipe out oppression, wrongdoing, strife, immorality, arrogance and unlawful exploitation from the world by force of arms . . . and to reinstate good in the place of evil." Under an evil government evil systems flourish, so authority must be wrested from them and transferred to true Muslims.[133]

According to Mawdudi, Islam must be dominant in the whole world:

Islam wishes to do away with all states and governments anywhere which are opposed to this ideology and programme of Islam . . . Islam requires the earth – not just a portion, but the entire planet – not because the sovereignty over the earth should be wrested from one nation or group of nations and vested in any one particular nation, but because the whole of mankind should benefit from Islam, and its ideology and welfare programme.[134]

At the core of Islam is a constant striving for political power and supremacy in all states and societies in order to set up an Islamic system of government enforcing *shari'a*.

These aims cannot be realized so long as power and leadership in society are in the hands of disbelieving rulers and so long as the followers of Islam confine themselves to worship rites . . . Only when power in society is in the hands of the Believers and the righteous, can the objectives of Islam be realized. It is therefore the primary duty of all those who aspire to please God to launch an organized struggle, sparing neither life nor property, for this purpose. The importance of securing power for the righteous is so fundamental that, neglecting this struggle, one has no means left to please God.[135]

Islam must eventually eliminate **all** non-Islamic governments and regimes and rule in their place:

The aim of Islam is to bring about a world revolution . . . the Muslim Party should not be content just with establishing the Islamic system of government in one territory, but should extend its sway as far as possible all around . . . if the Muslim Party commands enough resources, it will eliminate unislamic governments and establish the power of Islamic government in their place.[136]

Mawdudi took a severe stand against non-Muslims, apostates, and anyone who differed from his view. He argued that Islam is not simply a religion like Christianity, but a complete order of life embracing all spheres and serving as the basis of society, state and civilisation. As such, it is cannot allow itself to be made "the toy of individual free wills". Fundamental differences cannot be accepted in such a system and an apostate who has demonstrated that he is not willing to assimilate into his society's order must be expelled from it, for he has rejected its very foundation. Mawdudi stated that it is preferable for an apostate to emigrate from a Muslim state, but if the apostate chooses to stay he must be subject to the death penalty so that he cannot endanger society by spreading his views.[137] With regard to non-Muslims (not apostates), Mawdudi favoured implementing classical Islamic discriminatory rules including imposing the *jizya* tax on them, excluding them from military service or involvement in affairs of state, and relegating them to an inferior status.[138]

Abdel-Aziz Ibn Baz (1911–1999)

The Grand Mufti of Saudi Arabia from 1993 to 1999, Abdel-Aziz Ibn Baz was seen by many Wahhabis and Salafis as the leading scholar of his generation. He wrote over 60 books, most of them dealing with everyday aspects of Islamic faith and practice such as Qur'anic interpretation, *hadith*, *tawhid*, *fiqh*, prayer, *zakat* and pilgrimage. He actively supported *da'wa* around the world.

Ibn Baz was very conservative and true to the original Wahhabi teachings of purifying Islam by a literal return to the original sources of Qur'an and *hadith*. He condemned those who called for *ijtihad* and other "innovations" in Islam. His views were condemned by both militants and liberals. Ibn Baz banned Muslims from employing non-Muslim maids in their homes and banned women from driving cars.[139] He objected to radical Islamist calls to overthrow Muslim rulers and effect regime change by force, and he asserted that only a legitimate Muslim ruler can proclaim *jihad*. He considered it his duty to legitimise the rule of the Saudi royal family and approved the muffling of more radical Salafi scholars, those who criticised the government and approved the use of force. Most prominent judges and religious scholars in Saudi Arabia today are former students of Ibn Baz.

Muhammad ibn Saalih al-Uthaymeen (1925–2001)

Uthaymeen was one of the four main Salafi clerics (the other three of his stature being Abdel-Aziz Ibn Baz, Muhammad Nasir ud-Din al-Albani and Muqbil ibn Haadee al-Waadi'ee). His works are widely quoted amongst Salafis. For many years he was a lecturer at the Grand Mosque of Mecca. He also taught religious fundamentals at the Shari'a Faculty of the Imam Muhammad ibn Saud Islamic University. He was also a member of the Senior Scholars Committee of Saudi Arabia. He wrote over 50 books, mainly on *fiqh*.

Uthaymeen warned that loving non-Muslims was wrong and un-Islamic. He held that living in non-Muslim countries is one of the greatest dangers Muslims face and leads to great harm because it involves mixing with unbelievers and paying allegiance to a non-Muslim state. It is dangerous for Muslim manners and morals as many become sinners and some apostatise. Living in a non-Muslim country is only legitimate if Islam can be freely practised, otherwise Muslims should migrate to a Muslim land. Nevertheless, he taught that there are various legitimate reasons for a sojourn among non-Muslims. These reasons include Islamic *da'wa* (which he saw as a type of *jihad*); study of non-Muslim customs so as to warn Muslims and prepare them to deal with *kafir* wiles; representing Muslim states in official capacity; and a temporary stay for education, trade or medical treatment.[140]

Disciples of the main ideologues

Khurshid Ahmad (1948–)

Khurshid Ahmad is a disciple of Mawdudi. He is an economist and a vice-president of the Jama'at-i Islami in Pakistan and editor of its monthly journal, *Tarjumanul Quran*. He was the Pakistani Minister of Planning under President Zia ul-Haq (1978–79) and a member of Pakistan's Senate for two terms (1985–1997).

Khurshid Ahmad founded the Islamic Foundation, Leicester, in 1973 and was its first director and chairman. He is also rector of the Markfield Institute of Higher Education near Leicester, where a new campus was opened by the Prince of Wales in 2003.

Hailed in the West as a moderate, he has in Pakistan consistently espoused extreme anti-Western rhetoric while calling for an Islamic state under *shari'a*. At a Jama'at-i Islami world conference near Peshawar in 2005, he stated that the United States and its allies had crippled the economies of Muslim countries by taking over their resources. He argued that the only way to recover from this subjugation was by waging *jihad*. God had directed Muslims to increase their power, which included economic strength.[141]

He is committed to a totalitarian Islamist ideology which sees no division between the religious and the secular, and to the aim of changing all human societies into ideal Islamist ones:

> It [Islam] welds the religious with the secular and treats life as one integrated and harmonious whole . . . Islam stands for total change

as against all contemporary ideologies and some religious systems which are content with partial change. It purifies the individual and reconstructs society . . . Islam's strategy for the establishment of such a world order consists in inviting all human beings to take this path . . . It wants the new order to be established for all human beings in all parts of the world . . . Islam also launches a social movement, an international movement requiring all those who accept these ideals and values to establish the new order. Islam is eager to establish the new model in any part of the world . . . Its prospects depend very much upon the Islamic movement that is trying to spearhead this social effort for the establishment of a new world order.[142]

Khurshid Ahmad admired many aspects of the Taliban regime in Afghanistan.[143] In an article in July 2003 on his party's website, he wrote: "All of that area which was controlled by the Taleban had become the cradle of justice and peace."[144]

Ahmad sees the implementation of *shari'a* as the main goal of his movement and as the solution to all of Pakistan's internal and external problems. He supports the efforts to implement *shari'a* in the North West Frontier Province and accuses President Musharraf of fighting against Islam because of his opposition to this.

Targeting the passage of Shariah Bill in NWFP he [Musharraf] opened the second front, apparently against MMA, but in fact against Islam and its system of law, culture and civilization . . . So there is the General on one side, who is nothing more than unelected and self-styled president. On the other hand is the elected provincial assembly and a leadership, which attempts . . . to realise the objective . . . employ democratic and educational means to enforce Shariah.[145]

Ahmad likewise criticises the small Christian minority in Pakistan for opposing the implementation of *shari'a*, accusing them of not respecting the will of the majority and of being agents of the West. In his eyes, Pakistani Christians are an insignificant minority who should support the imposition of *shari'a* (despite *shari'a* being biased against non-Muslims):

The Islamic movement in this context had invited the nation and its leadership to realize that a real and lasting solution of these problems lies in the enforcement of Shari'ah . . . Christian leadership has also plunged into the fray vowing it would not allow Muslims to introduce Shari'ah in their own country! Despite their tall claims of upholding democracy and respecting the will of the majority, the Western media and policy makers are rearming this tiny minority in Pakistan . . . All should strive to strengthen the movement for the enforcement of Shari'ah and to settle this issue constitutionally and legally once and for all . . . Islamic law is not only a religious, ideological and spiritual code, but, at the same time, it is also the law for the state and judiciary . . . Being a religious law, it is a matter of belief for every Muslim, which requires him to act thereupon . . . Besides the call of the conscience, the state and administrative and judicial systems, all act in unison in the process of enforcement of Shari'ah . . .[146]

Ahmad is strongly opposed to Israel's right to exist and to any efforts by the Pakistani government to recognise it:

To us, the State of Israel has no legitimacy . . . recognizing Israel would be an error of Himalayan proportions on our part, and that it would incite nation's hatred and protest besides inviting Allah's wrath . . . The Zionist state of Israel possesses no legitimacy – historical, Biblical or juridical – in the place where it has been established. Nor does it posses any moral legitimacy.[147]

He believes that Islam will sweep away the hated Western system and Muslim regimes allied to it, and set up a new Islamic world order.

Numerical strength plus the Muslim states' geographical location have given Muslims a strategic position in today's world . . . the strength and centrality which the Muslim ummah enjoy today has no match in its history . . . The current Islamic revival comprises . . . rejection of Western culture . . . creation of a number of similar other institutions which are symbols of unity of Muslim ummah and indicators of their ideological awareness . . . it is quite obvious that Islam is the only constructive force for the future. Indeed much has yet to be done. It has to strengthen its moral values, gain intellectual creditability in order to motivate the masses. It is also utmost desirable to get rid of those rulers of the Muslims countries who are under the influence of the West. Once the masses and the leadership work for the same ideology and destination and instead of confrontation the energies are used for new and positive objectives, change is sure to come. In order to achieve this objective firm belief, determination and continuous efforts are essentially required. God willing, the ummah is going to have new and bright future in the 21st Century.[148]

As an economist, Ahmad wove the theme of an Islamic economy into the discourse of the Islamist struggle to weaken the West in preparation for the ultimate phase of establishing Muslim political hegemony in the world.[149] He has helped establish Islamic economics as an academic discipline. Ahmad was elected first president of the International Association for Islamic Economics founded in 1986.

Khurram Murad (1932–1996)

Khurram Murad was a former Director of the Islamic Foundation, Leicester, (1978–1986) and vice-president of the Jama'at-i Islami in Pakistan (1987–1996). He translated many of Mawdudi's works into English. Murad argued that it is not possible fully to live Islam as a minority in a non-Muslim environment.

> Islam means living in total surrender to Allah, in private and in public, inwardly and outwardly. This has two clear, important implications. One, as most of human lives comprises of relationships with other people, living in surrender to Allah cannot be actualized fully unless other people join us in our endeavour, unless the whole society lives in surrender.[150]

Da'wa is the means by which all of society is brought to submit to Allah i.e. to become Muslim. Murad recommends contextualising da'wa methods to the culture of Western society while retaining the core message of Islam. As an example, he suggests avoiding terms like "Islamic state" that might frighten off Westerners:

For example, the language of 'Islamic state' may not be a suitable language for a Western society; instead, a Just World Order based on surrender to the One God and obedience to His Messengers, is likely to evoke a more favourable response.[151]

This type of language means hiding the real goal (an Islamic state under *shari'a*) from the target audience and using deceptive terms to mislead the hearers so they will turn to Islam before recognising the missionaries' real aim. This is a good example of the use of *taqiyya*, conscious dissimulation, to further the cause of Islam, in this case of Islamising Britain.

Dilwar Hussain Sayeedi

Dilwar Hussain Sayeedi is a prominent leader of the Bangladeshi Jama'at-i Islami and a member of its Consultative Council.

He has supported attacks by his followers on members of the Ahmadiyya movement in Bangladesh.

Sayeedi often visits the UK to speak to Bangladeshis in Britain. His main venue in London is the East London Mosque, a hub of Jama'at-i Islami organisations in Britain. Sayeedi supporters in the UK have beaten up community elders opposed to his visits.[152]

Sayeedi was a member of the al-Badr militia in East Pakistan (Bangladesh) in 1971 which opposed its secession from Pakistan. Al-Badr is alleged to have been involved in massacres, rapes and other crimes against humanity during the struggle that led to the emergence of the independent state of Bangladesh.[153]

Sayeedi has compared Hindus to excrement:

> Why should we feel sad when the Hindu brothers chose to leave our country? Do we mourn when we have indigestion and materials leave our bodies?[154]

Kalim Siddiqui (1931–1996)

Kalim Siddiqui moved from Pakistan to Britain in 1954 and was for a time a journalist working for *The Guardian*. He was influenced by the Khilafa movement in the subcontinent and by

Islamism, and he founded the Muslim Institute for Research and Planning in London in 1972. Radicalised by the 1979 Islamic Revolution in Iran, he went on to found the Muslim Parliament of Great Britain in 1992. His thought was influential in the polarisation between Muslims and British society and the radicalisation of many British Muslims.

During the 1988–1989 "Rushdie Affair", Siddiqui voiced the traditional Islamic outrage to any perceived insult to Islam. He stated that protecting Islam from insult could involve violence and perhaps the creation of Muslim areas in which non-Muslims were not allowed:

> Muslims will insist, and continue to insist for as long as it may be necessary, that the British State provide them, their religion and culture protection from gratuitous insult, obscenity and abuse . . . Muslims make it clear to the State, and all sections of British society, that they do not expect to be and will not tolerate being insulted and abused on grounds of their religion, culture and traditions . . . At some stage we may have to engage in a campaign of civil disobedience in Britain . . . We are a law abiding community seeking a peaceful settlement of a dangerous conflict. Such conflicts, unless peacefully settled, often lead to violence . . . The operation of existing laws against blasphemy shows that their extension to protect Islam as well is unlikely . . . The Muslim community may have to define 'no go' areas where the exercise of 'freedom of speech' against Islam will not be tolerated.[155]

According to Siddiqui, Islam must always dominate other civilisations:

> What was established in Madinah by the Prophet was a civilization. But the civilization of Islam could not be a subservient civilization, a fringe civilization . . As the *Seerah* of the Prophet shows, Islam became the dominant civilization. Islam became the dominant civilization of the Arabian Peninsula in the lifetime of the Prophet. Soon afterwards Islam emerged to defeat the then world powers, the Persian Empire and the Byzantine Empire, and to establish the most far-flung civilization of history. This Islamic civilization remained the dominant civilization of the world for more than a

thousand years . . . The Islamic civilization, once established, remained dominant, dynamic, growing for more than a thousand years.[156]

Siddiqui advocated the primacy of the *umma* over all secondary loyalties. The method of struggle for achieving the ultimate goal of setting up a universal Islamic state is to emulate Muhammad's transition from Mecca to Medina. As we have already seen, every Muslim enclave is potentially a base for the expansion of Muslim rule:

> New Islamic States will be established in the newly liberated parts of the *Ummah* until, one day, the entire *Ummah* will consist of Islamic States that are united in a hierarchy of institutions under a single *imam/khalifah* . . . The goal of the total transformation of the *Ummah* requires a total struggle. An important part of the method of Prophet Muhammad, upon whom be peace, was to acquire control over the environment around him . . . The Islamic movement recognises no frontiers in the *Ummah*. The struggle for the liberation of any one part of the *Ummah* can be carried out from any other part of the *Ummah*. Every part of the *Ummah* is a potential asset for all other parts. This means that every obstacle in the path of the Islamic movement in one part of the *Ummah* is also an obstacle for the entire Islamic movement. Every Muslim engaged in the struggle in any part of the world, however remote or isolated, is engaged in a global struggle. Every group that is engaged in the struggle, however small or remote, is also part of the global struggle between Islam and *kufr*. We have to eradicate all traces of nationalism from the Islamic movement before we can challenge and defeat the power of nationalism established in territorial nation-States and a worldwide international system dominated by the mobilized power and resources of the enemies of Islam.[157]

The conflict of loyalties experienced by many Muslims in Britain is exemplified by Kalim Siddiqui's call to Muslims to give only conditional obedience to the laws of the state, i.e. to obey them as long as they do not conflict with the principles of Islam and loyalty to the *umma*:

Muslims living under the protection of a non-Muslim State must obey the laws of the State, so long as such obedience does not conflict with their commitment to Islam and the Ummah ... There are laws on the British statute Book that are in direct conflict with the laws of Allah; these relate to such matters as usury, abortion, homosexuality, gambling, sale and consumption of alcohol, and the abolition of capital punishment; Muslims can neither agree with nor condone any part of a legal and social agenda which so flagrantly violates the laws of nature as well of God ... We are Muslims first and last.[158]

Siddiqui calls for the development of a separate Muslim identity, ignoring internal differences[159]and presenting a unified front to the outside world. They must gradually establish Muslim autonomous spheres, meanwhile Islamising the majority community.

According to Siddiqui, Muslims in Britain must be involved in *jihad,* either participating personally in the armed struggle or giving it material or moral support:

Jihad is a basic requirement of Islam and living in Britain or having British nationality by birth or naturalization does not absolve the Muslim from his or her duty to participate in jihad; this participation can be active service in armed struggle abroad and/or the provision of material and moral support to those engaged in such struggle anywhere in the world.[160]

Azzam Tamimi[161] (1955–)

Azzam Tamimi is a Palestinian Islamist activist. He was born in Hebron in 1955 and migrated with his family to Kuwait in 1965. He completed a PhD in Political Theory at Westminster University, London, in 1998. From 1990 to 1991 Tamimi was the official spokesman for the Islamic Action Front in Jordan, and Director of the Islamic Movement Parliamentary Office in Amman 1990–1991, both fronts for the Jordanian Muslim Brotherhood.

Tamimi presents himself as a moderate Muslim, a specialist in Islam and democracy, and a disciple of the Tunisian Islamist leader

Rashid al-Ghannoushi. He now heads the Institute of Islamic Political Thought in London, and is also a senior lecturer at the Markfield Institute of Higher Education (linked to the Islamic Foundation) near Leicester. Tamimi is a favourite lecturer in Muslim communities across the world as well as to academic and political audiences in the West. He pleads for Western audiences to understand the democratic and tolerant nature of Islam.

Tamimi, however, is a member of the Muslim Brotherhood and of its Palestinian offshoot Hamas, which has been involved in intensive suicide bombings against Israeli civilians for many years.[162] He opposes the PLO and the Palestinian Authority ("no more than contractors hired by the Israeli establishment"),[163] as well as the peace process with Israel. He supports the hardline stance of Hamas which rejects the legitimacy of the state of Israel and calls for its destruction, and hints at support for Palestinian suicide bombers as real Islamic martyrs. He opposes all moderate regimes in Muslim states as tools of the West and supports radical Islamist movements wanting to overthrow them.

Like other Islamists in the West, Tamimi strives to present a sanitised view of Islam. This generates sympathy for Islamic causes and ensures militants the freedom to organise their networks in the West. Tamimi joins many Muslim and Western apologists in presenting Islam as a religion of peace. He offers supporting proof for this from Muhammad's example while living in Mecca.

> Islam is a religion of peace and tolerance. There is an abundance of Quranic and historical evidence to show that it does not approve of coercion [sic.]. Throughout the thirteen years of his mission in Makka, the Prophet disallowed the use of force by his followers even though they were persecuted by non-believers.[164]

He fails to mention that the Meccan period was essentially abrogated by the later Medinan stage of Muhammad's life, in which *jihad* against all non-Muslims was instituted. The peaceful episode in Muhammad's life is therefore not considered to be normative by most Muslims.

Azzam Tamimi translates traditional *jihad* terminology into "politically correct" euphemisms, more palatable to Westerners.

Jihad thus becomes the imperative to fight all political or economic oppression or tyranny, a sort of permanent revolution against any and every evil. This actually permits Muslims anywhere and at any time to rebel and fight the legitimate regimes of their states. Tamimi repeats the traditional teaching on heavenly rewards for martyrdom in *jihad*.

> One of the basic features of the Islamic faith is that it generates within the believer a passion for freedom . . . it liberates man from servitude and renders him un-slaveable . . . This is where the concept of jihad lies. Jihad is the constant endeavour to struggle against all forms of political or economic tyranny; for life has no value in the shade of despotism. Islam wages war against despotism using the weapon of al-amr bilma'ruf wan-nahyu 'anil-munkar (enjoining good and forbidding evil) through a series of actions the minimum of which is by the heart, that is by boycotting evil and disliking it. This may then progress, depending on ability and resources, to condemning evil through the use of various means of non-violent expression, such as speaking up, writing or demonstrating, or eventually to the use of force. What matters here is that oppression should never be given a chance to establish itself in society . . . Not only does the Islamic faith permit a Muslim to resist despotism and rebel against it, but it makes it incumbent upon him to do so with whatever means available to him. It is understandable that a Muslim may lose his life struggling against oppression, and for this he or she is promised a great reward in the life after death. In other words the effort made is not wasted and the sacrifice is not in vain.[165]

Tariq Ramadan (1962–)

Tariq Ramadan is a popular and controversial figure in European Islam who is now a visiting lecturer at St Antony's College, Oxford University, and has been an advisor to former Prime Minister Tony Blair on Muslim affairs. His father was secretary to Hasan al-Banna and a pioneer in establishing the Muslim Brotherhood in the West, and his mother was Banna's daughter.

Tariq Ramadan presents a moderate and sophisticated face of Islamism to Western audiences. On the one hand he calls on

Muslims in the West to stop blaming others for their problems and start criticising themselves so as to find the right solutions. On the other hand, he is fairly orthodox in his views on *shari'a*. Ramadan is against assimilation of Muslims as individuals into Western society and supports the concept of European Islam as a separate but integrated community which will challenge secularism.[166]

In March 2005 Ramadan issued a call for a moratorium (rather than an annulment) on the *hudud* punishments. These are the brutal physical punishments which *shari'a* says are compulsory for certain crimes, for example, flogging for drinking alcohol, amputation for theft, stoning for adultery, and crucifixion for highway robbery.[167] His call was widely applauded as a call for a reformation of *shari'a*, though some Muslim scholars accused him of coming close to heresy. Actually, what he meant was that because these punishments are so repulsive to Westerners it would be better to postpone their implementation until Western societies have been islamised to the point where they are ready to accept them.

Tariq Ramadan has invented the term *Dar al-Shahada* (House of Witness) for the West, implying it is no longer a House of War, but a space where Muslims can live without feeling any guilt as long as they are free to witness to their faith. He uses the *shari'a* principle of "all that is not strictly forbidden is allowed" to permit Muslims in the West to embrace whatever good they encounter in Western culture and law. As long as the state allows the free practice of Islam, Muslims are bound to be both faithful to their religion and to the laws of the land. Ramadan criticised the negative consequences of minority *fiqh* and the *darura* principle which encourage a ghettoisation of Muslims. According to Ramadan, Western Muslims are starting to re-interpret Islamic texts and *shari'a* in the light of their social context, attempting to reconcile Islamic values with Western democratic and human rights norms.[168]

Ramadan is a puzzling and contradictory figure. Some observers feel that, although he seems to encourage Muslims to integrate into Western society, his real agenda is Muslim domination of the West. Using sophisticated Western philosophical discourse and terms, Ramadan tries to place Islam in the forefront of the anti-globalisation movement. He is against the local nation-state expressions of Islam which he deems have failed. Muslims need to recapture a universal vision which will place Islam in a universal leadership position once again as it leads the anti-globalisation movements around the world.

Gilles Kepel, a leading French analyst of contemporary Islam, has this to say on Tariq Ramadan:

> As was the case with Western communism, it is hard to know whether changes in Islamist vocabulary accurately track structural transformations in ideology or are merely rhetorical artifices to mask a hidden agenda. This is an important point of contention, not just for the Muslim Brothers' descendants in Europe and the US today, but for those betting for and against them . . . An interesting new development here is the way Islamists are hijacking the political agenda of the anti-globalisation left, which lacks any political compass of its own. Tariq Ramadan has attended the last two European Social Forums in Paris and London, and has formed an alliance with the far left, in hope of becoming the public voice not only of French Muslim communities but of a "universalist" political agenda. For him, Islam is the destination not the starting point, and the vehicle is created by a fusion of radical "pro-*hijab*" elements within the European Social Forum with the more deluded anti-globalisation activists . . . The more relevant point is about the kinds of alliance he seeks to form with the extreme left, calculating that it is unlikely to long resist the Islamists' much more potent and organised ideology.[169]

According to Kepel, even Muslims find Ramadan disconcerting because of his double talk. Kepel quotes a Muslim complaining on an internet chat room that:

> For a long time now Tariq Ramadan has been saying two different things. He tells us Muslims one thing, and he tells *kouffars* [unbelievers] what they want to hear.[170]

Ramadan attacks liberal reformers whom he considers are too subservient to the West:

Far from creating a bridge between two worlds, they implicitly deny the legitimacy of one of the partners to speak about its universal principles. Acknowledged and envied in Western intellectual circles, they have often lost all legitimacy amongst Muslims but what is more serious is that certain amongst them have become objective allies of the most obtuse Islamaphobes. Yet another paradox of this period of crisis which forces us to identify the nature of criticism: who is talking and from where? In the name of what? And, fundamentally, why?[171]

Ramadan envisages a long struggle in which Islam, allied to anti-globalisation forces in the developing world and in the West, emerges victorious and sets up a dominant Islam, reformed in the way he seeks, that liberates Mecca from Wahhabi ideology as well as Jerusalem from Israeli rule.

> Those who are engaged in the struggle know full well that the road will be a long one, that labels and suspicions remain the norm. But it is up to them to face up to their responsibilities at this time when new partnerships are being forged. It is up to them, allied to the forces of the South, to develop a global vision of reform; it is up to them to take up the universality of Muslims values and to set the terms for an equitable dialogue with the West; it is up to them to finally engage in a demanding and fruitful internal debate where constructive self-criticism is permitted. Their responsibilities are immense and we are only at the beginning of the journey: for the Muslim conscience it means that the political liberation of Jerusalem, occupied by another, cannot make us forget the need for an ideological, economic, and political liberation of Mecca by our own wanderings alienated and betrayed.[172]

Yusuf al-Qaradawi (1926–)

Yusuf al-Qaradawi is a very prominent and popular Qatar-based scholar and cleric (originally from Egypt) who is acknowledged as the main spiritual leader of the Muslim Brotherhood and of their networks in Europe. He has helped set up numerous global Islamic institutions and was behind the founding of Al Jazeera television channel. He appears on the popular Al Jazeera programme "*Shari'a* and Life" and is behind the website IslamOnline. He is also a significant *shari'a* advisor in the field of Islamic finance to many large institutions. He is the Head of the European Council for Fatwa and Research and on the boards of numerous Islamic organisations in the West.

Qaradawi has tried to create a new path for Islam between Salafism and the kind of reform advocated by Abduh, a path which he calls the Middle Way. While *shari'a* is absolute and unchangeable, the duty of scholars is to determine pragmatically the priorities of *fiqh* in each specific context and era. He has pushed for the development of a special Islamic jurisprudence for Muslim minorities, *Fiqh al-Aqalliyyat,* to enable Muslims in the West to function as autonomous communities, implementing *shari'a* as far as possible.[173]

In the West Qaradawi is often perceived as a moderate conservative, yet many Muslims regard him as dangerously radical and a supporter of violence. While he advocates a form of democracy as equivalent to the Islamic concept of *shura*, he also legitimises suicide bombings and violent *jihad*.

Yusuf al-Qaradawi rejects the call for separation of state and religion, considering this effectively apostasy from Islam:

> Since Islam is a comprehensive system of 'Ibadah (worship) and Shari'ah (legislation), the acceptance of secularism means abandonment of Shari'ah, a denial of the Divine guidance and a rejection of Allah's injunctions. (...) The call for secularism among Muslims is atheism and a rejection of Islam. Its acceptance as a basis for rule in place of Shari'ah is a downright apostasy.[174]

He sees *jihad* (if successful) as creating conditions in which conversion to Islam can easily take place supported by the state institutions and without opposition from powerful enemy forces.

> [*Jihad*] would be aimed at liberating Muslim lands, fighting the forces that oppose the Islamic *da'wah* and the Muslim Ummah . . .[175]

He argues that the initial Islamic conquests were:

> In reality a rescue of the oppressed and wronged people from the tyranny of wrongdoers and the injustice of oppressors, and a liberation of the people from the domination of Persian Monarchs and Roman Caesars.[176]

This justification for the first *jihad* implies that similar contemporary aggression would be perfectly acceptable by this interpretation of Islam, and could thus justify any Muslim aggression against any non-Muslim state in the world today, as they are all considered by Islamists to be illegitimate and oppressive.

Qaradawi holds that *jihad* can be an offensive means of expanding the Muslim state as well as being defensive:

> A *jihad* which you seek [an attack], and a *jihad* in which you repulse an attack. In the *jihad* which you are seeking, you look for the enemy and invade him. This type of *jihad* takes place only when the Islamic state is invading other [countries] in order to spread the word of Islam and to remove obstacles standing in its way. The repulsing *jihad* takes place when your land is being invaded and conquered... [In that case you must] repulse [the invader] to the best of your ability. If you kill him he will end up in hell, and if he kills you, you become a martyr [Shahid].[177]

We have already seen (page 49) that Qaradawi believes that territory which has once been in the possession of Muslims must never be yielded to non-Muslims.

Qaradawi calls for the support of all Muslim minority demands for independence or autonomy as well as for outright rebellions against central governments. This is practised in Kashmir and the Philippines.

> The Islamic Movement should consider itself at the 'beck and call' of every Islamic Cause and respond to every cry for help wherever that cry may come from. It should stand with Eritrea in its *jihad* against the unjust Marxist Christian regime . . .by Sudan against the treacherous Christian racist rebellion . . . It should support the Muslims of the Philippines against the biased Christian regime . . .

it should also help the Muslims of Kashmir . . . support the Muslims of Somalia . . . mobilise the Muslims of the world for the Palestine Cause . . .[178]

Qaradawi states that the contemporary *jihad* against the Jews is in principle only over the problem of sacred land. The Jews have taken Muslim land in Palestine to set up the state of Israel. (The fact that Muslims first seized these lands by force from non-Muslims is not considered relevant.)

> Our war with the Jews is over land, brothers. We must understand this. If they had not plundered our land, there wouldn't be a war between us . . . We are fighting them in the name of Islam, because Islam commands us to fight whoever plunders our land, and occupies our country. All the school of Islamic jurisprudence – the Sunni, the Shi'ite, the Ibadhiya – and all the ancient and modern schools of jurisprudence – agree that any invader who occupies even an inch of land of the Muslims must face resistance. The Muslims of that country must carry out the resistance, and the rest of the Muslims must help them. If the people of that country are incapable or reluctant, we must fight to defend the land of Islam, even if the local [Muslims] give it up . . . They must not allow anyone to take a single piece of land away from Islam. That is what we are fighting the Jews for.[179]

Qaradawi has issued multiple calls for *jihad* against the US-led invasion of Iraq in 2003. The Association of Muslim Scholars, led by Qaradawi, issued a statement at its Beirut conference in November 2004 that:[180]

> The *jihad*-waging Iraqi people's resistance to the foreign occupation, which is aimed at liberating the [Iraqi] land and restoring its national sovereignty, is a Shari'a duty incumbent upon anyone belonging to the Muslim nation, within and outside Iraq, who is capable of carrying it out. Allah has permitted this by saying: 'Permission (to fight) is given to those upon whom war is made because they are oppressed [Koran 22:39]," and He said to the Muslims: 'Fight for the sake of Allah against those who fight against you [Koran 2:190].'

In his capacity as head of the European Council for Fatwa and Research, Qaradawi gave a report to the Council at their meeting in Stockholm in July 2003, which approved Palestinian suicide attacks on the basis that it was a situation of extreme necessity and thus normal prohibitions (such as the prohibition on suicide) became irrelevant.

> What weapon can harm their enemy, can prevent him from sleeping, and can strip him of a sense of security and stability, except for these human bombs – a young man or woman who blows himself or herself up amongst their enemy? This is a weapon the likes of which the enemy cannot obtain, even if the U.S. provides it with billions [of dollars] and the most powerful weapons, because it is a unique weapon that Allah has placed only in the hands of the men of belief. It is a type of divine justice on the face of the earth ... it is the weapon of the wretched weak in the face of the powerful tyrant...[181]

He also argued that suicide attacks were not suicide as such but martyrdom, because of the different motives – advance and attack by self-sacrifice for a higher goal, or escape and retreat by fleeing life because of failure and weakness.[182]

Qaradawi supports the death penalty for apostasy. He advocates certain forms of female genital mutilation, while stating it is not obligatory.

Muhammad Taqi Usmani (1943–)

Mufti Taqi Usmani is a leading Deobandi scholar in Pakistan. He specialised in Islamic jurisprudence under the supervision of his father Mufti Muhammad Shafi, Grand Mufti of Pakistan, at the Deoband Dar-ul-Ulum in Karachi (established in 1951). This is the largest institution of Islamic learning in Pakistan and the Pakistani centre of the Deoband movement. After graduating he became a lecturer at the Dar-ul-Ulum teaching *hadith* and *shari'a,* later becoming its vice president. While the college appears a model for other seminaries to emulate, it plays a role in promoting violent *jihad*. Both Taqi Usmani and his brother Maulana Mohammed

Rafi Usmani (president of the Dar-ul-Ulum and chief Deobandi mufti of Pakistan), have given practical help to *jihadi* organisations, which are allowed to preach and collect donations from the Dar-ul-Ulum's mosques and its twelve branches in Karachi. Students are not permitted to participate in *jihad* during their studies but many go on to do so afterwards.

Taqi Usmani has been the Deputy Chairman of the Islamic Fiqh Academy of the Organisation of the Islamic Conference in Jeddah. He has published over 60 books, including more than a dozen available in English. He has served as judge of the Supreme Court Shariat Appellate Bench, and is advisor to a large number of Islamic financial institutions. He is Chairman of the Islamic Economy Centre in Pakistan. He sits on the Shari'a Supervisory Board of the Dow Jones Islamic Markets Indexes. He serves on the HSBC Amanah Finance independent "Shariah Supervisory Committee", which regularly reviews the bank's products and transactions to make sure they comply with *shari'a*. He also serves on the International Advisory Council of the Markfield Institute of Higher Education.

In his book *Islam and Modernism*, Taqi Usmani asserts that an aggressive expansionist military *jihad* should be waged by Muslims against non-Muslim lands to establish the supremacy of Islam worldwide. He argues that Muslims should live peacefully in countries such as Britain, where they have the freedom to practise Islam, but only until they gain enough power to engage in battle. The book is a polemic against Islamic modernists who are accused of seeking to convert the Qur'an into a book of poetry and metaphor. He accuses them of having been bewitched by Western culture and ideology.

His book refutes those who believe that only defensive *jihad* (fighting to defend a Muslim land that is under attack or occupation) is permissible in Islam. He also denies the suggestion that *jihad* is unlawful against a non-Muslim state that freely permits the preaching of Islam. Aggressive *jihad* has always been commendable, he says, for establishing the glory of Islam, and there is no need to change this doctrine.

Taqi Usman urged all Muslims to support the Taliban *jihad*.

Taqi Usman was the religious mentor of the Imam of the Red Mosque in Islamabad, who with his students had to be overcome by the Pakistani security forces in 2007 when they tried to forcefully implement *shari'a* and attacked other citizens.

Sheikh Salman al-Awdah

Awdah is a Saudi Wahhabi-Salafi scholar who became a leading opponent of the Saudi regime in the early 1990s following the stationing of US troops in Saudi Arabia during the First Gulf War. His stand was praised by al-Qaeda's leader, Osama bin Laden. He later supported the *jihadi* fighters in Iraq against the Western invaders. Awdah taught that the conflict between true Islam and its enemies is part of the apocalyptic battle between the forces of good and evil. In this battle Muslims may use any weapon available against their enemies.

Awdah was one of the clerics behind the Salafi awakening in the 1990s which wrested the initiative from the liberals and modernists who seemed to have gained the upper hand at the beginning of the 1980s. Following the Gulf war of 1990–1991, he shifted to politics, and criticised the authorities for their relations with the US. He was supportive of Osama bin Laden. He was arrested in 1994 and spent five years in prison. He then moderated his sermons and spoke out against self-proclaimed *jihadis*.[183] In 2007 he called on bin Laden to end terrorist acts in Iraq and elsewhere which caused the killing of innocent Muslims and others.[184]

Abu Ameenah Bilal Philips (1947–)

Philips is a Jamaican who grew up in Canada and was converted to Wahhabi-Salafi Islam in 1972. He preaches in the UK, Saudi Arabia and the Gulf. He studied Arabic and Islamic theology in Saudi Arabia and lectures at the American University in Dubai.

Some Western sources have alleged that he was associated with the blind Egyptian Sheikh Omar Abdul Rahman, who was jailed in the US for his involvement in the 1993 bombing of the World Trade Centre, but these allegations have not been substantiated.

However he was deported from the US and has been refused entry to Australia.

Philips sees Western culture, led by the US, as the main enemy of Islam. He has written several books, some against Christian beliefs and against Sufism. He divides *jihad* into defensive and offensive. While defensive *jihad* is an individual obligation, offensive *jihad* can only be carried out under the command of the legitimate Islamic ruler of the state and under his banner.[185]

Ahmad Thomson

A white Briton who converted to Islam in 1973, Ahmad Thomson is a well known British Islamist barrister and author, who is the deputy chairman of the Association of Muslim Lawyers. He acted as advisor to the Blair government on Islamic issues until the media revealed his radical views. Thomson sees a worldwide conspiracy of Jews and Freemasons working to achieve world dominion. He has expounded his views in the books *The Next World Order* (1994) and *Dajjal: The Anti-Christ* (1997). His writings include anti-Semitic statements and holocaust denial.[186]

At the fifth Annual Conference of the Association of Muslim Social Scientists (AMSS) held in London in February 2004, Ahmad Thomson argued that the British government is under a legal duty to safeguard Muslim human rights by incorporating Islamic personal law into UK domestic law. This, he said, should include the legal recognition of Muslim marriages, divorces and inheritance. This incorporation would mean the setting up of *shari'a* courts whose verdicts would be recognised and enforced by the UK civil courts.[187]

Organisational activists

Sir Iqbal Sacranie (1952–)

Iqbal Abdul Karim Mussa Sacranie was secretary general of the Muslim Council of Britain (2002–2006). During his time as secretary general of the MCB, the British government treated Sacranie as their preferred spokesperson for what they considered responsible and moderate Islam. (See pages 134–36 for other opinions on the stance of the MCB.) Sacranie received a knighthood in 2005 in recognition of his "services to the Muslim community, to charities and to community relations".

Sacranie came to Britain from Malawi where he was born. Educated in London, he trained as an accountant and went on to become managing director of the family business.

He first came to prominence in 1989 in connection with the UK Action Committee on Islamic Affairs (UKACIA), which was founded in 1989 by several Muslim organisations to respond to the publication of Salman Rushdie's *The Satanic Verses*. Iqbal Sacranie was a Joint Convenor of UKACIA and a founding member of its steering committee. He commented on Rushdie:

> Death, perhaps, is a bit too easy for him? His mind must be tormented for the rest of his life unless he asks for forgiveness to Almighty Allah.[188]

The UKACIA argued that Muslim interests were best served by working within the British system rather than against it. This approach was continued by the new umbrella group which developed from it, the Muslim Council of Britain (MCB).[189]

In 1999 *The Observer Magazine* produced a Power List of 300 most powerful people in the UK and Sacranie was numbered at 246. *The Guardian* named him in 2002 as "the most influential Muslim in the UK". In 2005 *GQ* magazine produced a list of 100 Most Powerful Men in Britain and he was ranked at number 10 as the voice of Muslims in Britain, who plays a vital role as mediator in multi-cultural Britain. Sacranie has grown in that role and in stature and has become the first port of call to be consulted by the British media on all issues related to the Muslim community.

As Britain was preparing for the invasion of Iraq in 2003, Iqbal Sacranie warned Tony Blair in a letter that a war with Iraq would "breed bitterness and conflict for generations to come" within the UK. Sacranie described he plans for war as a colonial policy, and said Muslims were deeply cynical of the government's motives.[190] Sacranie also said that Muslims were likely to perceive British foreign policy as "an indiscriminate war on Islam".[191]

During discussions on the subject of legislation to ban incitement to religious hatred, Sacranie said in a debate on BBC Radio 4's *The Moral Maze* that he wished to see Muhammad protected from insult or disrespect, and that any "defamation in the character of the Prophet Muhammad (PBUH)" would be "a direct insult and abuse on the Muslim community".[192] Sacranie's hope was that the new law once passed would be used to protect Muhammad from any negative criticism. Sacranie made it clear that he would see a law against incitement to religious hatred as being in effect a blasphemy law whereby Muslims could protect their prophet from any criticism or disrespect. During a *Newsnight* television debate in July 2004 Sacranie announced that people should be allowed not to believe in Islam, but should not be permitted to criticise or defame it.[193] He expected that the new law would prohibit references to Islamic terrorism:

> There is no such thing as an Islamic terrorist. This is deeply offensive. Saying Muslims are terrorists would be covered [i.e. banned] by this provision.[194]

In December 2004 Sacranie stated that Muslims were seeking "safeguards against vilification of dearly cherished beliefs".[195]

In the light of such demands from the head of the MCB, it is more than a little ironic that the MCB also requested an amendment to the bill to grant exemption for the Qur'an and *hadith*, in other words to ensure that neither text could ever be held to be a cause of incitement to religious hatred. Such a request suggests a Muslim recognition that their source texts could be particularly vulnerable to the accusation of inciting religious hatred. The requested exemption was not granted.[196]

Sacranie was greatly disappointed with the form in which the religious hatred bill was eventually passed on 31 January 2006, and complained of injustice and impediments to the promotion of a cohesive and harmonious society in Britain.

Muhammad Abdul Bari (1954–)

Muhammad Abdul Bari MBE is secretary general of Muslim Council of Britain (MCB), having taken over from Sir Iqbal Sacranie in June 2006. He had previously been the deputy secretary general of the MCB for four years. He is the first person of Bangladeshi origin to become MCB leader. He has a winsome personality, and communicates very effectively in interviews and face-to-face meetings.

Bari is an educationalist with a PhD and Post Graduate Certificate in Education from King's College, London, as well as a management degree from the Open University. He has worked as an Air Force officer in Bangladesh, a researcher in physics and a science teacher. Bari is an author of several books on parenting and issues of youth and identity. These include: *Building Muslim Families*, *A Guide to Parenting* and *Race, Religion and Muslim Identity in Britain*.

Bari is a longstanding member of the Jama'at-i Islami and former founding president of Islamic Forum Europe created in 1988 that represents the Bangladeshi wing of Jama'at-i Islami.[197] He is also chair of the East London Mosque Trust in Whitechapel, London, a stronghold of the Bangladeshi Jama'at-i Islami movement in Britain.[198]

Bari is a member of the Inner Cities Religious Council and sits on the Greater London Authority's Faith Advisory Group. He is also on the organising committee for the 2012 Olympic Games in London.

In July 2006 Bari welcomed Dilwar Hussain Sayeedi to the East London Mosque. As we have seen (page 94) Sayeedi is a leader of the Bangladeshi Jama'at-i Islami and is alleged to have committed grave war crimes during the Bangladesh War of Independence.

As chair of the East London Mosque, Dr Bari was considered instrumental in helping controversial MP George Galloway secure his parliamentary seat in the 2005 general election by telling Muslims they had a duty to vote.

Dr Bari was one of the signatories of an open letter dated 11 August 2006 to then Prime Minister Tony Blair which attacked British foreign policy as "ammunition to extremists".

On the eve of the fifth anniversary of the "September 11" terrorist attack Bari threatened that unless Muslim demands were met, Britain would have to deal with two million terrorists:

> Some police officers and sections of the media are demonising Muslims, treating them as if they're all terrorists—and that encourages other people to do the same. If that demonisation continues, then Britain will have to deal with 2 million Muslim terrorists—700,000 of them in London.[199]

Radical Islamists espousing violence

Abdullah 'Azzam (1941–1989)

Abdullah 'Azzam, a Palestinian graduate of al-Azhar University, Cairo, was a member of the Muslim Brotherhood and a prominent *jihad* fighter in Afghanistan in the 1980s. He established the Afghan Service Bureau (Maktab al-Khidmat) to coordinate the efforts of the foreign fighters who came to Afghanistan. 'Azzam was considered by many to be Osama bin Laden's mentor.

'Azzam created a synthesis of classical *jihad* and Qutbist doctrine. He saw military *jihad* as the greatest religious obligation after faith (*iman*), an act of communal worship. He considered that *jihad* was God's ordained method for establishing Islam in the world, a "battle ... for the reformation of mankind, that the truth may be made dominant and good propagated."[200] 'Azzam held that *jihad* is the final stage of a process that includes *hijra*, preparation, and *ribat* (frontline defence) Only the ill, the disabled, children, women who cannot emigrate, and the elderly are excused from this duty, which is an act of communal worship of God conducted under a recognised leader.[201]

'Azzam claimed that the obligation of *jihad* had been forgotten, and its neglect is the cause of contemporary Muslim humiliation. When not under direct attack by unbelievers, *jihad* is a communal obligation (*fard kifaya*) for which it is sufficient that the armed forces protect the borders and the caliph sends out an army at least once a year "to terrorise the enemies of Allah".[202] However, when unbelievers occupy Muslim land, *jihad* becomes a compulsory individual obligation on every Muslim (*fard 'ayn*) and remains so until the liberation of the last occupied piece of Muslim land. 'Azzam offered quotes from the four Sunni schools of law to support this view.[203] He stressed the doctrine of sacred space which obliges all Muslims to fight an enemy who has entered an Islamic land or a land that was once part of the Islamic lands.[204] He argued that, in the modern world, infidels occupy Muslim lands in Palestine, Afghanistan (in the 1980s), Kashmir, and other places, so that at present *jihad* is a personal duty for every Muslim as an individual.[205]

'Azzam also calls for Muslims to give up narrow nationalism and let their vision extend beyond national borders "that have been drawn up for us by the Kuffar". He rejects all arguments against the immediate implementation of *jihad*, such as the lack of a qualified leader, internal squabbles among Muslims, or insufficient manpower. On the contrary, he asserts that conducting *jihad* is part of the process of uniting Muslims and establishing the real caliphate.[206]

Omar Bakri Muhammad (1958–)

Omar Bakri Muhammad is a Syrian cleric who lived for a time in Saudi Arabia and then sought asylum in Britain. Originally a member of the Muslim Brotherhood, he later joined Hizb ut-Tahrir and was the founder of their UK branch, which he left in 1996 to found al-Muhajirun. Omar Bakri Muhammad has written numerous booklets and articles, and has organised many conferences and demonstrations supporting Islamist causes around the world. In 1998 he was co-signatory of Osama bin Laden's infamous call for *jihad* against the West and the Jews. Bakri expressed delight at the 11 September 2001 atrocities, and he praised the terrorists involved as "the magnificent nineteen". Al-Muhajirun has been quite successful in recruiting young Muslims at mosques and universities to join terrorist groups abroad.[207] Though it had only several thousand adherents, its radical message increasingly influenced young British Muslims.[208]

Omar Bakri Muhammad drove a wedge between Muslims and British law. He preached non-cooperation with *kafir* legislation and hostility to the police force. He also established himself as the self-appointed judge of his own Sharia Court for the UK, issuing numerous *fatwas* on various subjects. One was a death sentence for blasphemy against Terrence McNally, a playwright who wrote a play depicting Christ as a homosexual.[209] Another decreed a *jihad* against Israel, calling on Muslims worldwide to attack Israeli interests anywhere.[210] At the beginning of 2003, in anticipation of the allied invasion of Iraq, he issued another *fatwa* forbidding Muslims to help the British and American military in any way. According to this *fatwa*, any Muslim aligning himself to the allied troops in Iraq would be considered an apostate and a legitimate target for the *mujahidin:*

> He is at war with Islam and Muslims, and his life and wealth will have no sanctity. He like the disbelievers is a clear enemy of Islam and Muslims and consequently becomes a legitimate target for the Mujahideen, and if they die they will die outside of the fold of Islam, and they will never be dignified in their death nor buried with the Muslims.[211]

In January 2005 Omar Bakri Muhammad issued a declaration stating:

> I believe the whole of Britain has become Dar ul-Harb (land of war) . . . The kuffar (non-believer) has no sanctity for their own life or property.[212]

Omar Bakri blamed the British government and the British public for provoking the July 2005 London bombings. He said that by re-electing Tony Blair the British people had invited the bombings.[213] He is suspected of interaction with the bombers.

Omar Bakri Muhammad left for Lebanon in August 2005, one day after the government announced its intention to ban al-Muhajirun and Hizb ut-Tahrir. The home secretary forbade his return to the UK.

Abu Qatada (1960–)

Abu Qatada is a Palestinian Islamist militant who fought in the Afghan *jihad* against the Soviets and then moved to London in 1993, where he was granted asylum in spite of having been twice convicted in Jordan on terrorist charges and a Jordanian request for his extradition. He served as a key recruiter for Islamist terrorist groups including al-Qaeda and the GIA, and was described as an inspiration for the September 11 terrorists. His lectures appear on numerous *jihadi* websites and his *fatwas* have justified and promoted terrorist attacks against infidels.[214]

European security services connected him to suspected terrorists in various parts of the continent, and he was on the American government's most wanted list of terrorists. Videos of his speeches were found in the Hamburg flat of Muhammad Atta, the ringleader of the September 11 hijackers. In October 2002 Reda Hassaine, a security agent who had infiltrated the Finsbury Park Mosque in London, supplied information linking Abu Qatada and Abu Hamza to recruiting and fundraising for Islamist terrorist organisations. This information led to Abu Qatada's arrest the following year.[215] Four European countries have named him as "al-Qaeda's spiritual ambassador in Europe", and he allegedly had ties to the European network of the brutal head al-Qaeda In Iraq, Al-Zarqawi, (killed in Iraq in 2006). The Spanish police want to question him about the Madrid bombing of trains in March 2004.[216] Abu Qatada videos were also found by anti-terrorist police in Cremona, Italy, in which he called for an attack on Rome:

> "Rome is a cross. The West is a cross and Romans are the owners of the cross. Muslims' target is the West . . . We will split Rome open. The destruction must be carried by the sword. Those who will destroy Rome are already preparing their swords. Rome will not be conquered with the word but with the force of arms.[217]

Abu Qatada was arrested in 2003 and is awaiting extradition to Jordan.

Abu Hamza al-Masri (1958–)

Abu Hamza is a charismatic preacher who first came to London in 1979 to study engineering. He became radicalised in the 1980s, and travelled to Afghanistan in1990 where he trained in *jihadi* camps, losing an eye and both hands in a land mine explosion. He returned to London in 1996 where he became an imam in the Finsbury Park Mosque, turning it into a centre for terrorist activities where many *jihadis* were recruited.

Abu-Hamza organised a group called Supporters of Shariah, dedicated to implementing *shari'a* and raising support for radical groups by recruiting and fundraising. He and his Supporters of Shariah group were allied to the GIA of Algeria and to al-Qaeda. Richard Reid, the "shoe bomber", and Zacharias Moussaoui, a member of the 11 September 2001 conspiracy, were both recruited in the Finsbury Park mosque. According to Abu Hamza,

> Islam needs the sword . . . Whoever has the sword – he will have the earth.[218]

Abu Hamza was charged with terrorist activities by the government of Yemen, who has asked for his extradition. He was also linked to the bombing of the *USS Cole* in Aden. Italian security services have linked him to extremist Islamist cells in the Milan area. In 1999 he was questioned by Scotland Yard detectives on suspicion of terrorism offences, but was released after a few days without charge.

The Charity Commission, while examining allegations that he used the mosque for political means, sent him a Provisional Removal Order telling him to leave the mosque in January 2003. In the spring of the same year, the Home Office moved to have Abu Hamza's British citizenship annulled in preparation for his expulsion.[219]

Abu Hamza was finally arrested on 27 May 2004, following an extradition warrant from the US who claims to have evidence linking him to a terrorist hostage-taking Islamist group in Yemen, the Islamic Army of Abyan, who kidnapped 16 Western tourists in 1998, resulting in the death of three Britons. The kidnappers had links with ten young British Muslims from the Supporters of

Shariah on a study visit to Yemen, including his 16-year old son and 18-year old stepson. The US also alleges that he was linked to efforts to set up a terrorist training camp and weapons depot in the US.[220]

Abu Hamza's trial began in January 2006 at London's Central Criminal Court. He faced 15 charges including soliciting to murder and incitement to racial hatred. In February 2006 he was found guilty on 11 of the charges and sentenced to seven years in jail.[221]

Abdullah al-Faisal

Abdullah al-Faisal is black Jamaican convert to Islam. He toured Britain for four years, preaching hatred to all non-Muslims, before being arrested. In 2003 he was convicted on three charges of incitement to murder and jailed for seven years. In 2007 he was released and deported to Jamaica.

Faisal, who had studied in Saudi Arabia, urged his audiences to kill Jews, Hindus and Westerners by any means available. He stated that young Muslims should follow Osama bin Laden's teachings, learn how to use weapons, and fulfil their mission of killing unbelievers. His lectures were recorded and sold in Islamic bookshops under titles such as *Jihad, No Peace with the Jews, Treachery from within,* and *Declaration of War.* Examples of his exhortations include:

> So you go to India and if you see a Hindu walking down the road you are allowed to kill him and take his money . . . His wealth isn't sacred and nor is his life.
>
> Jews are rotten to the core and sexually perverted, creating intrigue and confusion to keep their enemies weak. They should be killed very soon, as by Hitler.
>
> You can use chemical weapons to exterminate the unbelievers. Is that clear? If you have cockroaches in your house, you spray them with chemicals.[222]

Faisal's book *Natural Instincts* is imbued with a deep hatred towards all non-Muslims, described as *kafirs* (infidels). These he considers to be followers of Satan and purveyors of pornography, people whom Muslims must hate without exception. The Muslim world would experience greater success if Muslims expressed more hatred to non-Muslims. There is no substitute for a violent *jihad* against the non-Muslims.[223]

Anjem Choudary (1967–)

A British-born lawyer, Choudary joined Omar Bakri Muhammad's al-Muhajirun and was its spokesman. After Bakri's departure to Lebanon in 2005, he became leader of the group, now known as al-Ghurabaa. He is active in organising radical demonstrations in London and preaches hatred against the West and Western values. He called for the execution of the Pope Benedict XVI following the Pope's remarks on Muhammad and violence in September 2006.[224]

Abu 'Izzadeen (1976–)

A convert to Islam of Jamaican origin, he is now leader of the Saviour Sect, a spin-off of al-Muhajirun. He briefly made the headlines when he verbally attacked then home secretary John Reid at a public meeting in East London in September 2006.

ABDUH-TYPE REFORMERS

Zaki Badawi (1922–2006)

Zaki Badawi was an Egyptian scholar who was educated at al-Azhar University in Cairo where he received the King Faruq First Prize for the best post-graduate student in 1947. He then studied psychology at University College, London, obtaining his bachelor degree in 1954 and moving on to a doctorate from London University in Modern Muslim Thought. He returned to teach at al-Azhar for a while, and then went on to teach Muslim communities in Malaysia, Nigeria and Singapore, before he came to Britain and was appointed the first chief imam at London's Regent's Park Mosque and Cultural Centre in 1978.

Badawi was a member of the Muslim Brotherhood in his early years in Egypt. However he became a supporter of Abduh-type reformism rather following the Salafi influence of Rida and al-Banna.

During his time at the Regent's Park Mosque, Badawi was instrumental in establishing the Shariah Council as a facility to reconcile conflicts between Islamic law and the British civil code. The Shariah Council now operates under the auspices of the Imams and Mosques Council. Badawi was elected chairman of the Imams and Mosques Council by the National Conference of Imams and Mosque Officials of the UK in 1984.

Badawi was also active in Islamic finance. He joined the board of the Islamic Banking System in Luxembourg and participated in the delegation that negotiated with the Bank of England to establish the first Islamic financial institution licensed in the UK, the Islamic Finance House which was founded in 1983. Badawi published many articles on banking, finance and business ethics in regards to Muslim law. He also gave annual lectures in business ethics to MBA (Masters of Business Administration) students at Cranfield University Business School, UK.

Badawi established the Muslim College in London in 1986 as a postgraduate seminary for the training of imams and Muslim leaders in the West. The curriculum includes the study of Islam as well as Western society and religions and emphasises interfaith dialogue. He challenged the traditional inward-looking, rule-based education of most British imams with a broad, multi-faith training grounded in Western philosophical study.[225]

He was a co-founder of the Three Faiths Forum, vice chairman of the World Congress of Faiths and director/trustee of the Forum Against Islamophobia and Racism. In addition Badawi was chairman of The Arabic Forum, the Islamic Religious Council and the National Council for the Welfare of Muslim Prisoners (established in 2001).

Badawi co-edited *Encounter Magazine* which publishes news on interfaith matters. He also edited *Islamic Quarterly* for four years and contributed an article to *al-Arab* daily newspaper every Friday for many years.

Zaki Badawi was the unofficial leader of Britain's Muslims for many years. He pleaded for a moderate Islam and opposed Islamism. He held that the Qur'an is the word of God and has absolute authority, but that interpretations of the Qur'an are not sacred and can change from time to time.[226] He was committed to improving relations between Muslims and Christians and was involved in interfaith dialogue at many levels.

Nevertheless Badawi affirmed the classical Islamic requirement for political power and Islam's inability to function as a minority:

As we know the history of Islam as a faith is also the history of a state and a community of believers living by Divine law. The Muslims, jurists and theologians, have always expounded Islam as both a Government and a faith. This reflects the historical fact that Muslims, from the start, lived under their own law. Muslim theologians naturally produced a theology with this in view – it is a theology of the majority. Being a minority was not seriously considered or even contemplated. The theologians were divided in their attitude to minority status. Some declared that it should not take place; that is to say that a Muslim is forbidden to live for any lengthy period under non-Muslim rule. Others suggested that a Muslim living under non-Muslim rule is under no obligation to follow the law of Islam in matters of public law. Neither of these two extremes is satisfactory. Throughout the history of Islam some pockets of Muslims lived under the sway of non-Muslim rulers, often without an alternative. They nonetheless felt sufficiently committed to their faith to attempt to regulate their lives in accordance with its rules and regulations in so far as their circumstances permitted. In other words, the practice of the community rather than the theories of the theologians provided a solution. Nevertheless Muslim theology offers, up to the present, no systematic formulation of the status of being a minority. The question is being examined. It is hoped that the matter will be brought into focus and that Muslim theologians from all over the world will delve into this thorny subject to allay the conscience of the many Muslims living in the West and also to chart a course for Islamic survival, even revival, in a secular society.[227]

However, following in Abduh's path, he tried to form a moderate and modern British Islam that can accept its minority role and support the British state and its values.

> There is no theological problem in Islam taking on a great deal of western culture and values and incorporating them.[228]

Badawi seems to have struggled to reconcile his belief in classical Islam with the need he could see to adapt it for a modern minority context.

He opposed forced marriages and female genital mutilation, which he saw as having cultural rather than Islamic bases. He coined the term "British Islam" and predicted that:

> Within a couple of generations Muslims will lose their cultural baggage. Indian and Pakistani ways will disappear. They will adopt western cultural values and the whole community will be brought together as British Muslims.[229]

He opposed the culture of proliferating *fatwas*, and, while unhappy with Salman Rushdie's book *The Satanic Verses*, declared on television that if Rushdie was being chased and knocked at his door, he would give him refuge.[230]

Badawi saw *jihad* as purely defensive and stated that most wars in Islamic history were not real *jihads* but manipulated as such to gain support; he considered this an abuse of the term *jihad*. Many of the initial Islamic wars of expansion were simply for booty and gain. He opposed the teachings on *jihad* of Mawdudi and Qutb and of the radicals who followed their interpretations. He defined Britain as a House of Islam (*Dar al-Islam*) because Muslims can live there in peace and security and worship freely.[231]

Within 24 hours of the September 11 attacks, Badawi had issued a statement condemning the terrorism as contrary to Islam. As chairman of the Shariah Council UK, he also drafted a *fatwa* decreeing that Muslims in the American and British forces have a duty to obey orders and fight against the Taliban in Afghanistan.

PROGRESSIVE REFORMERS

Ziauddin Sardar[232] (1951–)

Ziauddin Sardar is a British Muslim scholar, born in Pakistan. He is a cultural critic, journalist and writer calling for a serious rethinking of Islam to make it compatible with modernity.

According to Sardar, Islam has acquired a "pathological strain" because of relying on old interpretations that do not fit contemporary contexts. Muslims tend to blame all their problems on outside forces rather than examining and reforming Islam. Islam's source texts have been "frozen" in contexts of long ago, so they can have no meaning for today.[233] Sardar argues that this freezing of Islam has had devastating effects, causing "three metaphysical catastrophes: the elevation of the Shariah to the level of the Divine, with the consequent removal of agency from the believers, and the equation of Islam with the state".[234]

Sardar believes that only the Qur'an can be considered as divine in Islam. He holds that there is nothing divine about the *shari'a*, which is simply a human construction. Wherever *shari'a* is imposed, Muslim societies acquire a medieval feel.[235] Sardar argues that *shari'a* is a set of guiding principles for Muslim societies that should be constantly and dynamically changing to produce solutions to new problems Muslims face. The Qur'an itself has to be constantly reinterpreted in changing contexts, only its text remains unchanged.

Sardar accuses Islamism of reducing Islam to a "totalitarian" ideology that leads to a totalitarian state order as exemplified by the Taliban, Iran, Sudan, and Saudi Arabia.

> The transformation of Islam into a state-based political ideology not only deprives it of all moral and ethical content, it also debunks most Muslim history as un-Islamic. Invariably when Islamists rediscover a 'golden past', they do so only in order to disdain the present and mock the future. All we are left with is messianic chaos, as we saw so vividly in the Taliban regime, where all politics as the domain of action is paralyzed and meaningless pieties become the foundational truth of the state.[236]

In Islamic history, clerics and religious scholars gradually prevented the people from having any say, and authoritarianism, theocracy and despotism became supreme. Traditional Muslims and Islamists today dispense with moral reasoning and ethics as they defend despots like Saddam Hussein simply because they are Muslims and reduce *jihad* to a violent holy war against anyone identified as an enemy. For Sardar, *jihad* must be understood only as a multifaceted spiritual, intellectual and social concept. It includes personal struggle, intellectual endeavour, and social construction as well as the non-violent struggle for peace and justice for all people everywhere.[237]

Sardar acknowledges the difficulty in motivating Muslims to examine themselves and their religion.[238]

> The most significant answers to the contemporary plight of the Muslim people are buried deep within the history, social practice and intellectual and political inertia of Muslims themselves. Muslims, on the whole, are very reluctant to look at themselves or to examine the process through which they have transformed Islam into a suffocating and oppressive ideology.[239]

He also accepts that in recent decades the debates within Islam have produced a narrow, intolerant, obscurantist, illiberal, brutal and confrontational interpretation of Islam.[240] He hopes that new trends within Islam will result in a reinterpretation of *shari'a*, which will be viewed not as divine and immutable but open to be modified or reformulated in its entirety. He also hopes to see the separation of religion from state to ensure an Islam that is authentic, moderate, liberal, tolerant, open and democratic.

Ehsan Masood

Ehsan Masood, Project Director for the Gateway Trust in Woking, argues for a revision and reinterpretation of Muslim sources.[241] He wants to see a revision of aspects of *shari'a* to keep up with modern times, especially in the areas of human rights and the rights of children and minorities. He also calls for a reinterpretation of the meaning of Qur'an and *hadith*. The Qur'an especially must be read in its historical context, meaning that not all passages are relevant for contemporary Muslims. Masood would also like to see a reform in the role of authority in Islam.

Masood recognises the extreme opposition which progressive reformers face, but he hopes that recent atrocities by Muslim terrorists, the emergence of Islamic reformers in the West and the availability of modern communications will carry the message or progressive reform across the Muslim world and finally initiate the desired reform.

Fareena Alam (1978–)

Fareena Alam, managing editor of the London-based Muslim magazine *Q-News,* calls for a reformation of Islam that would distance it from the Wahhabi-influenced narrow *jihadi* outlook.[242] Her suggestions include:

1. Promote discourse over violence. The classical Muslim values that stress civility, moderation, diversity and discussion must be renewed.
2. Promote spirituality and morality. Mercy, humility, service and the individual's spiritual experience with God need to be stressed.
3. Reject the wrong kind of support. The US supported its Wahhabi allies even as they destroyed the classical Islamic heritage and replaced it with their narrow literalist and aggressive form of Islam.
4. Divorce state from religion. Remove the *ulama* (Islamic scholars) from state control. State and scholars need to be independent of each other so they can keep one another in check.
5. Promote pride in Muslim culture. Revive Muslim art and culture in such areas as literature and music which Islamists label as not permissible.

Maruf Khwaja

Maruf Khwaja is a Muslim journalist, raised in Pakistan and now working in Britain. He considers that it is virtually impossible to reform Islam because for centuries reactionary Islamic scholars and clerics have used threats, intimidation and outright murder to resist it. "Islamic graveyards are full of unsuccessful reformers."[243] However, although reform is an almost impossible task, Khwaja sees a ray of hope arising among the Muslim communities in the West as a new generation of thinkers emerges that is free from the almost instinctive fear of Muslim thinkers in Muslim states. The long-term answer to Islamic terrorism is the reform of Islam. He believes that Islamic reformers must re-examine pre-modern practices and concepts; reject Islamic radicals who want to apply *shari'a* laws to Muslims in the democratic West; abandon sectarian dogmas that perpetuate intra-communal conflict; consign the theological disputes of early Islam to the past; and update or discard rigid rules that have no relevance today.[244]

DEVELOPING TRENDS IN MUSLIM LEADERSHIP

Leadership within the Muslim community in the UK is becoming more diffuse and diverse. In addition to the traditional leaders of official institutions and organisations (like the Muslim Council of Britain), there is a whole array of activists: radical preachers, veterans of combat in *jihad*, self-styled *amirs* of small groups, and others moving around the country and communicating their radical message to ever expanding circles. These operate in small groups, mosques, prisons and streets. They are also adept at using modern electronic communications media. Radicalised by *jihadi* ideology from a variety of sources, they are connected in a loose non-hierarchical network or web. They often serve as first contact points for young Muslims entering the world of radical Islam.

Some of the younger generation radical Islamist terrorist leaders and activists

Muhammad Sidique Khan (1974–2005)

Khan was a British Muslim of Pakistani background who became the leader of the 7 July 2005 London bomb attacks. In a videotape broadcast by al-Qaeda, Khan explained his beliefs and reasons for the attack against civilians:

> Your democratically elected governments continually perpetrate atrocities against my people all over the world. Your support makes you directly responsible. We are at war and I am a soldier. Now you too will taste the reality of this situation.

Omar Khayam (1983–)

A British Muslim of Pakistani origin, he became the leader of the terrorist cell arrested during "Operation Crevice" and convicted of plotting attacks against the Bluewater shopping centre in Kent, nightclubs and other targets in Britain.

Babar Ahmad (1975–)

A computer expert from Tooting, south London, Ahmad was arrested for allegedly operating websites supporting terror and of urging Muslims to fight *jihad* against the West. The websites called for support for terrorist causes in Afghanistan and Chechnya, and asked for the transfer of money and useful equipment via the sites. It is also alleged that Ahmad tried to set up a terrorist training camp in Arizona. He was arrested and is facing extradition to the USA.

Former radicals who have rejected extremism

Several Muslims who were involved in radical Islamist groups have recently rejected the radical ideologies and come out of the radical Islamist groups they were involved in.

Ed Husain[245] (1975–)

Ed Husain comes from a Bangladeshi background, and grew up in London's East End. His family was traditionalist Barelvi Sufi, followers of the Fultoli *pir*, worshipping at the Brick Lane mosque. Husain's early recollections are of Islam as a spiritual mystical religion, with no mention made of politics.

At the age of 15, he was introduced by a classmate to the ideas of Islamism i.e. to Islam as a political ideology. He was also introduced to young members of the Jama'at-i Islami linked groups the Young Muslims Organisation UK (YMOUK) and Islamic Forum Europe. They explained that Islam prescribed a specific political system and that all Muslims should strive to establish an Islamic state implementing *shari'a*. Islam was the solution to all of the world's problems. He was introduced to the writings of Mawdudi and Qutb that were mandatory reading in these groups, and became a radical Islamist activist in the Islamic Society of his college. The strategy was to provoke confrontation, radicalise the Muslims, antagonise the non-Muslims, and gain publicity. One aim was to use the Islamic Society as a recruiting ground for YMOUK.

While in college Husain became involved with the more radical Islamist group Hizb ut-Tahrir (HT). In the HT he was introduced to the concepts of a global methodology for changing the world and the quest for a universal Islamic state, the *khilafa* (caliphate). Whereas the YMOUK sought to Islamise democracy, HT viewed democracy as un-Islamic.

After a college student was stabbed to death by HT sympathisers, Husain gradually tried to distance himself from HT and *jihadi* ideology. He spent some time in Saudi Arabia, where he saw a society that, in spite of its Islamic credentials, was inherently unequal, racist, sexually frustrated and strictly controlled by state Wahhabi ideology and religious police. In Syria he found a society more free from the stifling control of puritan Islam, yet even there he missed the freedoms and opportunities offered by British society. After the July 2005 London bombings he determined to warn the public of the dangers of Islamist groups and their ideology.[246]

Hassan Butt (1980–)

Hassan Butt, from a Pakistani Kashmiri background, was a 17-year-old college student when he was radicalised and recruited by what he terms the British Jihadi Network (BJN). He was first approached by Hizb ut-Tahrir[247] and later became a member of al-Muhajirun. He claims to have personally recruited some 50–75 young British Muslims to receive *jihadi* training in Pakistan. According to Butt there is a dedicated camp in Pakistan specifically for training British Muslims in *jihad*. Regular groups attend the camp for up to three months before returning to Britain or heading for the Middle East.

At the age of 20 Butt went to Pakistan to help young British Muslims fight in Afghanistan.[248] He rejected Omar Bakri Muhammad's concept of a covenant of security with Britain, considering it to be un-Islamic. A Muslim's only allegiance was to Allah and the *umma*.[249] In 2002 in an interview with BBC radio he warned that British Muslims would return home from Afghanistan to take terrorist action in the heart of Britain against government and military institutions and individuals.[250]

When he heard that the Pakistani authorities were about to arrest him, he flew back to Britain where he was arrested, questioned for five days and then released without charge. He continued to recruit and raise funds for *jihad*. Butt claims that his biggest contributors were middle class businessmen, doctors and professionals, but also criminals like drug dealers who were promised their donations would cleanse their activities and profits.[251]

In 2004, in an interview with the journalist Aatish Taseer, he still described himself as a radical and yearned to have the honour of becoming a terrorist. He also argued that the British government and security services could not destroy Islamic radicalism because they had lost the ability to analyse and understand how Islamists think. He rejected the argument that economic deprivation led to radicalisation. Muslims, said Butt, were being attacked all over the world, and he called on every Muslim to work for the implementation of *shari'a* as a political system by getting involved in revolutionary action.[252]

Following the July 2005 London bombings, Butt began to have doubts and asked theological questions of his handlers. He wanted to know whether the bombings could be justified in Islam. He received no answers, only fresh orders to go to Iraq for re-programmimg. He then came to the conclusion that killing in the name of Islam was prohibited, and that the Islamist-*jihadi* ideology is a "cancer" in the Muslim world that needs to be dealt with. He left the network in February 2006 and in July 2006, at a debate at Cambridge University, he publicly announced that he had left the network and that he would confront radicalism. He attacked the position that Islam has nothing to do with terrorism, arguing that denial blocks the possibility of reform. Muslims must acknowledge that there is a violent streak in Islam. As a result of his change of mind, his family labelled him a traitor and former friends threatened his life.[253]

Butt disagrees with the widely held view that the main cause of Islamist terrorism is Western foreign policy, especially in Iraq. He relates that he and his fellow radicals would laugh and celebrate when hearing such views on TV. The radicals felt that the media and personalities such as Ken Livingstone were doing their propaganda work for them by these assertions, blaming the government and drawing attention away from any examination of the real driving force behind Islamist violence which is Islamic theology. Butt argues that what motivated him and others like him to plot acts of terror in Britain and abroad was the goal of fighting for the creation of a revolutionary Islamic state that would enforce justice in the world. Starting with the classical Islamic teaching on *Dar al-Islam* and *Dar al-Harb*, modern radicals went further by reasoning that there was no real Islamic state in existence in our time, so the whole world was *Dar al-Harb*, or as they often called it *Dar al-Kufr* (House of Unbelief). As Islam has declared war on unbelief, radicals feel justified in declaring war on the whole world. They thus legitimate the destruction of the five rights granted by Islam: life, wealth, land, honour and belief. In war against infidels the end justifies the means, including the killing of civilians. Butt argues that the unwillingness of mainstream Islam in Britain to discuss these issues of violence within Islam allows radical preachers to recruit many young Muslims to their cause. Mainstream Muslims repeatedly asserting that "Islam is peace", deny the violent aspects of Islamic theology, and hope the problems will disappear, but this simply leaves the field open for radicals and their ideologies.[254]

Butt offers a line of reasoning to help radicals towards a new mindset. In his view Muslims in the West no longer live in the bi-polar world of the Middle Ages. Muslims in Britain are not migrants in the Land of Unbelief, but equal citizens who can freely practise their religion. They must cease ignoring the passages in Qur'an and *hadith* which speak of killing unbelievers and challenge the centuries-old theology of *jihad*. They must recognise that *jihadi* scholars like Abu Qatada are extremely learned and that their opinions have validity within the broad canon of Islam. Muslim scholars must therefore refashion Islamic theology, creating a reformed Islam for Muslims living in what he calls the Land of Co-existence. They must develop a new set of rules of rights and responsibilities which will enable Muslims to liberate themselves from ancient theological models that legitimised killing in the name of Islam.[255]

Shiraz Maher[256] (1981–)

Shiraz Maher served as a regional officer in north-east England for Hizb ut-Tahrir. In 2005 he left the organisation in the aftermath of the London bombings and as he discovered the rich heritage of moderate Islam during his PhD studies. He has rejected the ideology of political Islam. He states that Islamist terrorism does not exist in a vacuum but in a wider infrastructure of mainline Islamism that provides the ideology. Focusing on the violent groups will therefore not solve the problem. The mainline Islamist ideology, which has the same ultimate aims as the terrorist groups, must be confronted and dealt with. The Muslim community must come out of its attitude of denial and discover the riches of moderate peaceful Islam.

COUNTER-MCB LEADERSHIP

In order to counter the negative impact of the Muslim Council of Britain, the British government has encouraged and supported the founding of new moderate organisations linked to Sufism, among them the Sufi Muslim Council and the British Muslim Forum, dedicated to a peaceful, non-political Islam.

Haras Rafiq (1965–)

Haras Rafiq is co-founder of the Sufi Muslim Council. He states that Sufis are the silent majority among Britain's Muslims whose voice has not yet been heard. He has committed himself to building alliances with others to combat the evil of political ideology. He believes that the Islamists, who falsely claim to represent the whole Muslim community, have to be isolated.[257]

6   MUSLIM ORGANISATIONS IN THE UK

This chapter and the following five chapters describe some of the main organisations linked to important movements within British Islam. Because of limitations of space it has not been possible to distinguish every nuance of doctrine and ideology, and some generalisation has been necessary.

Furthermore, when seeking to establish the beliefs of any particular organisation it is important to bear in mind the Islamic doctrine of *taqiyya* which permits Muslims to dissimulate in times of danger. Many Muslims understand this doctrine as allowing them to deceive non-Muslims in order to advance the cause of Islam. As a result some Muslim organisations vary their discourse to suit different audiences; their real intentions are made known in what they say to fellow-Muslims. As Dr Taj Hargey, Chairman of the Muslim Education Centre, Oxford (MECO) explained in an interview with BBC Panorama researcher John Ware,

> We have one vocabulary in private and we have another vocabulary for the public domain and that's why you don't hear it because you're the public domain.[258]

This can be especially relevant when seeking to understand the stance of Islamist organisations. While some Islamists openly express their hostility to the West, other Islamists prefer a gradual, staged approach as the best tactic for achieving their goal of the Islamisation of their host society. They may present themselves as liberals and moderates to the general public and to the authorities while concealing their real goals.

UMBRELLA ORGANISATIONS

The Muslim Council of Britain (MCB)

The MCB was launched in 1997 at the instigation of the British government who wanted a Muslim organisation that could give "moderate" mainline Muslims a national voice, and could act as the main representative of the whole Muslim community in the UK to government and to the British public. The MCB draws its support from a network of mosques and community groups and has almost 400 affiliated Muslim bodies. Its leadership grew out of the 1988–1989 anti-Rushdie campaign that had first brought many Muslims together in a united front. Sher Azam of the Bradford Council of Mosques and Iqbal Sacranie of the UK Action Committee for Islamic Affairs (UKACIA) were instrumental in its founding.[259] (For more on Iqbal Sacranie, head of the MCB from 2002 to 2006, see pages 109–111.)

However the MCB has faced sharp criticism from within the Muslim community, not least by those who claim that it does not effectively represent the great variety of ethnic and religious groups in British Islam.[260] Some criticise it for not condemning the British and American wars on Afghanistan and Iraq more strongly.[261] The Muslim journal *Q-News* argued that the MCB is "unrepresentative and irrelevant . . . In its obsession to establish itself as the sole representative body of British Muslims the MCB has ended up being nothing more than an isolated, aloof and exclusive organisation . . ." It is accused of being totalitarian, exclusive and secretive in its operations, striving hard to exclude competing Muslim bodies, leaders and views as far as possible, using bullying tactics and defamation.[262] Yvonne Ridley, a white British journalist who converted to Islam, claimed in her Islam Channel programme "The Agenda" on 9 June 2005 that the MCB wants to control all mosques in the UK and the contents of their Friday sermons.[263]

According to *Q-News*, the real force behind the MCB are Jama'at-i Islami activists including people from the UK Islamic Mission mosque network and others from the Federation of Student Islamic Societies. As a result, in spite of its activism, it is alien to the vast majority of British Muslims, and especially to the "young, women, refugees, poor and non-subcontinentals".[264] Media investigations have repeated the allegations that the MCB has its roots in radical Pakistani groups, especially the Jama'at-i Islami and the Ahl-i Hadith.[265] The current secretary general of the MCB, Muhammad Abdul Bari (see pages 112–113), has been involved in the Jama'at-i Islami linked Islamic Forum Europe. If Jama'at-i Islami activists and ideology are really at the heart of the MCB, then it is far from being the moderate, mainstream organisation as which it is often presented.

Critics claim that the MCB's approach to the media is "control and complain". As an example they present the MCB's reaction to a *Panorama* television programme (broadcast 19 August 2005) about British Muslim leadership. Before it was shown, the MCB tried to exercise some control over the film's content. When that failed, it mobilised supporters to bombard the BBC with complaints of bias and unfair treatment. Once the programme had been aired, it pressured the BBC to offer some kind of "redress".[266]

MCB and the incitement to religious hatred law

In an effort to appease British Muslims upset by new anti-terrorism legislation, the government introduced a law banning incitement to religious hatred, which was passed on 31 January 2006. The reason given was that, while Sikhs and Jews were protected by race laws, Muslims who are not a race but a multiethnic religious group, were not. The original draft was framed in such a way that it appeared to prohibit any kind of negative comment about another faith, no matter how mildly phrased or accurate and no matter whether or not there was any intention to incite hatred of the followers of that faith. Many non-Muslims were alarmed about the implications for freedom of speech, but many Muslim leaders, including Iqbal Sacranie from the MCB, welcomed the proposed law. (See page 111.) At the same time the MCB also requested a special exemption to prevent the Qur'an and *hadith* from being held to incite religious hatred, but this was not granted.

Pakistan's non-Muslim minorities are subject to a so-called "blasphemy law" whose most feared aspect is a mandatory death sentence for anyone who "defiles the name" of Muhammad. This reflects the Muhammad veneration which is such a characteristic of South Asian Islam – and likewise of Islam in the UK. Sacranie made it clear that he would see a law against incitement to religious hatred as being in effect a blasphemy law whereby Muslims could protect their prophet from any criticism or disrespect. Considering the passionate devotion which so many British Muslims give to their prophet, it is not hard to imagine a spate of cases resulting, which would probably soon create a most unwelcome degree of self-censorship amongst non-Muslims.

Shift in the government's attitude to the MCB

Following the July 2005 London bombings, government attitudes to Muslim organisations changed. A primary cause was the MCB's perceived failure to confront extremism. The government realised that several of the Muslim groups it had supported (including financially) believing them to be moderate and mainstream, were actually Islamist in ideology. In October 2006 Ruth Kelly, Secretary of State for Communities and Local Government, publicly warned the MCB that "funding and engagement must shift significantly" towards organisations "tackling extremism and defending our shared values". There was also unease at the MCB's refusal to observe the annual Holocaust Memorial Day in 2005 on the sixtieth anniversary of the liberation of Auschwitz. The rift deepened when the MCB joined 38 Muslim associations in sending an open letter dated 11 August 2006 to Prime Minister Tony Blair expressing concerns about British foreign policy.[267]

Muslim Parliament of Great Britain[268]

The Muslim Parliament was founded by Kalim Siddiqui in 1992 in the aftermath of the "Rushdie Affair" with the goal of giving British Muslims a united separatist political voice. Siddiqui was influenced by the ideology of the Muslim Brotherhood and the Jama'at-i Islami, but he mistrusted these groups because of their close ties to Saudi Arabia. He looked to the Iranian Islamic Revolution as an ideal Islamic model.

Siddiqui rejected integration leading to assimilation, and established the Muslim Parliament as a separate communal minority political system which he hoped would represent all Muslims in the UK and would evolve into a unified autonomous Muslim system. The Manifesto of the Muslim Parliament, published under his name in 1990, declares: "The option of integration and assimilation that is on offer as official policy in Britain must be firmly resisted and rejected". We have already seen that Siddiqui also predicted the possible creation of "no go" areas where Muslims would be safe from what he called "the exercise of 'freedom of speech' against Islam".[269]

The Muslim Parliament demanded that proposed new legislation should first pass its jurisdiction before being applied to British Muslims. Its agenda includes imposing *shari'a* family law and extending the blasphemy law to include material offensive to Islam. It controls the Halal Food Authority.

Following the founder's death in 1996, there have been leadership struggles within the Parliament and several members have left to found their own new Institute of Contemporary Islamic Thought and others the Islamic Human Rights Commission. It now has few followers left in the British Muslim community and has become a marginal institution.

Institute of Contemporary Islamic Thought (ICIT)[270]

Following the death of Kalim Siddiqui in 1996, there were leadership struggles within the Muslim Parliament of Great Britain. Several members left to start their own Institute of Contemporary Islamic Thought in 1998 to carry on the founder's original hardline vision.

The Director is Zafar Bangash, based in Toronto, Canada. Iqbal Siddiqui, projects co-ordinator, is based in London. The organisation publishes a magazine, *Crescent International*.

The Halal Food Authority (HFA)[271]

The Halal Food Authority (HFA) was set up in 1994 as a voluntary, non-profit making organisation. It is controlled by the Muslim

Parliament of Great Britain. The HFA's remit is to monitor and regulate red meat and poultry in the UK intended for consumption by Muslims. It separates *halal* meat from non-*halal* meat by marking or tagging the *halal* carcasses in the slaughterhouses soon after slaughter.

The HFA also licenses slaughterhouses, distribution centres, retailers and providers of meat and poultry. These licences are granted on an annual and contractual basis. The HFA inspectors audit and monitor compliance to Islamic laws and British and European slaughter regulations.

The HFA also tries to regulate, endorse and authenticate other food stuffs, pharmaceuticals, confectionery, toiletries, flavourings, emulsifiers, and colourings for Muslim usage. This is done on an annual contractual basis by licensing the provider, after auditing ingredients, method of manufacture and process together with packaging and labelling.

The HFA works closely with the Food Standards Agency on a consultation basis on issues such as animal feed, beef labelling, sheep and poultry strategy, and health and hygiene in food manufacture that need to comply with Islamic dietary laws.

UK Action Committee on Islamic Affairs (UKACIA)

The UKACIA was founded in 1989 by several Muslim organisations to respond to the Salman Rushdie crisis: co-ordinate protests against Rushdie, combat the circulation of Rushdie's *The Satanic Verses*, and guide the Muslim community in their efforts to express their anger and hurt. Iqbal Sacranie, later leader of the Muslim Council of Britain (MCB), was a founding member of the UKACIA steering committee. It aimed to support Muslim interests by working within the British system, rather than against the system. The MCB developed from the UKACIA.[272]

FOSIS in the UK & Ireland[273]

FOSIS, the Federation of Student Islamic Societies, is the premier Muslim student representative body. It was established in 1962 after a meeting held in Birmingham by students from Birmingham, Leeds, Liverpool, London, Wolverhampton and Dublin who realised the need to co-ordinate the work of Islamic Societies across the UK and Ireland. Its headquarters are in north-west London.

According to its website, its aims and objectives are:

- Unite all existing student Islamic Societies in the UK and Ireland on Islamic principles
- Encourage the formation of new Islamic Societies on campuses and support the activities of existing ones
- Protect and promote the interests of Muslim students
- Develop the understanding, character and skills of Muslim students
- Invite students from other faiths to Islam, as a complete, balanced and comprehensive way of life
- Initiate mechanisms for regular communication and co-ordination among Islamic societies

FOSIS is Islamist in tenor and campaigns on behalf of Palestine, Kashmir, Chechnya and other places where it perceives Muslims to be oppressed.

British Muslim Forum (BMF)

The BMF is a federation of some 300 Barelwi mosques and community institutions, set up as an alternative to the MCB, because the latter is perceived to be Deobandi-controlled. The BMF defines its aims as:[274]

To communicate the balanced opinions and impartial ways of Islam and promote its peace-loving morals and etiquettes

To promote values that are common to all humanity through teachings of fearing God and serving humanity as per the education of the Sufiya (spiritual leaders)

To instil such values in the next generation of Muslims that will lead to improved cohesion in a multi-religious, multi-cultural and multi-racial and intellectually open thinking society

To support, strengthen and supervise the existing efforts and projects of Muslim females that are acceptable to Islamic regulation

To strengthen the existing multi-faith links that promote understanding and tolerance amongst faith communities

To establish a network of official, political, social and educational organisations of Muslims addressing their problems and concerns and taking appropriate steps to resolve them

To work to protect the rights of the affiliate organisations, institutes and mosques and to try to stabilise and improve their educational and financial welfare

To establish a link with all areas of the media, forwarding to them the concerns and reservations of the Muslims, and to offer through general consensus the endorsed opinions of the Muslims on issues that are of concern to them

To take appropriate actions in attempt to reduce or eliminate terrorism, extremism and religious and racial discrimination

Mosques and Imams' National Advisory Board (MINAB)[275]

After the London bombings on 7 July 2005 the government consulted the Muslim community extensively in the framework of Preventing Extremism Together (PET). One of the recommendations was the establishment of the Mosques and Imams' National Advisory Board (MINAB) to consider the need for reform of teaching in some mosques. Its goal is to promote best practice in British mosques.

The MCB is only one among four organisations in MINAB, thus increasing the representation of other Muslim streams. The other organisations are the Barelwi Sufi-orientated British Muslim Forum, the Muslim Brotherhood-affiliated Muslim Association of Britain, and the Twelver Shi'a al-Khoei Foundation.

The Sufi Muslim Council (SMC)[276]

The Sufi Muslim Council, with 102 affiliates mainly from the north-west of England, was launched in July 2006 at the House of Commons with Ruth Kelly giving the keynote speech. It was founded to represent the "silent majority" Muslims in the UK who are mainly Sufi and Barelwi, and as a counterweight to the many Islamist organisations linked to Deoband, Jama'at-i-Islami and the Muslim Brotherhood. It is linked to the Naqshbandi Sufi order headed by Hisham Qabbani. Its launch was backed by the British government and other faith groups worried that existing Muslim organisations had not done enough to tackle radical extremism within the Muslim community. (See page 132 for more on Haras Rafiq, one of the SMC's co-founders.)

SUNNI ORGANISATIONS

Barelwis and Barelwi organisations

Barelwis form the majority of South Asian Muslims in Britain, accounting for some 70% of Britain's Pakistani-origin Muslim population and are also found amongst those with roots in Bangladesh. They practise a traditional form of Islam in which Sufism and folk Islam play an important part. The movement takes its name from the home town of its founder, Ahmad Raza Khan of Bareilly, Uttar Pradesh (1856–1921), who was a member of the Qadiri Sufi order.

It is estimated that about 50–60% of British mosques are Barelwi-controlled. The Barelwi movement has integrated Sufism with strict adherence to the Hanafi school of *shari'a*, and a number of Sufi orders are linked to them. Shrines and *pirs* are an important part of their faith, and their most distinctive characteristic is veneration for the person of Muhammad.

Barelwis have tended to settle in concentrated geographical clusters, both reflecting their villages in Pakistan and the general wish to live in a Muslim environment. The older generation are very attached to their home countries, Pakistan and Bangladesh, and live much as if they were still "back home", interacting little with those outside their community. Using their own customs and languages, with shops, schools and other local facilities that are effectively Muslim, and Muslim newspapers, radio and TV, often in their own language as well, they are effectively sealed off from the rest of British society. Although there are some Muslims who would like to integrate with mainstream society, their leaders often discourage them from doing so and they appear to be a minority of their community.

Barelwi imams usually came from the same South Asian village or area as do their respective congregations and often do not speak much English. It is still the norm for English not to be used in Barelwi mosques and *madrassas*. These imams tend to be unfamiliar with mainstream British culture, and to reject Western values of democracy, human rights, freedom of speech etc.

There is a wide gulf between older Barelwis and the younger British-born generations of Barelwis. It is debatable how many second and third generation Muslims from Barelwi backgrounds living in the UK consciously define themselves as "Barelwi". Many young people from Barelwi backgrounds have little interest in theological arguments and are therefore less likely than their parents to identify themselves as Barelwi. Also, the use of Urdu in mosques alienates the younger English-speaking generations, as does Barelwi literature produced in Pakistan in a style unfamiliar to British-bred youngsters. The imams, who have little understanding of mainstream British culture, are unable to give much help to British-born Muslims wrestling with the question of how to be a Muslim in the UK. These second and third generation Muslims often face a real crisis of identity, torn between the expectations of their elders with regard to marriage and lifestyle, and what they see around them in society. Their response is often to move from the traditional, non-extreme religious observance of their parents and grand-parents towards one or other of two extremes: either a Western secular lifestyle or radical Islam.

The young radicals, who look chiefly to the Qur'an and *hadith* for guidance, tend to find their identity as trans-national members of the global *umma*, rather than as either British or, say, Bangladeshi. This is leading to tensions over the "Arabisation" of

South Asian Islam as in the case of 16-year-old Luton school-girl Shabina Begum who won the legal right in March 2005 to wear the ankle-length robe, the *jilbab*, rather than the *shalwar kameez* (loose trousers and tunic) which was allowed by her school's uniform policy. The judicial committee of the House of Lords later ruled in favour of the school in June 2006.[277] The point here is that the *jilbab* is an Arab cultural response to the Islamic dress code, whereas the *shalwar kameez* is the South Asian response. Shabina Begum was of South Asian heritage, yet she was fighting for the right to wear the Arab-style clothing. She was opposed by the school, which had a Muslim head-mistress and 79% Muslim pupils.

It can be said that, in effect, the conservatism and traditionalism of the Barelwi and their attachment to South Asia has hindered the integration of younger generations into mainstream British culture, and has left the young people open to radical Islamist movements which they perceive as better meeting their needs. Older Barelwis are increasingly worried that they are "losing" the younger generation. As a result Barelwis have established *darul ulums* (seminaries) to train a new generation of British Barelwi scholars.[278]

The challenge of Islamist groups like the Deobandi, Wahhabi and Ahl-e Hadith has pushed the Barelwis to attain more cohesion and define themselves in distinction to these groups. They call themselves as *ahl-i-sunnat wa-jamaat* (people of the *sunna* and community), to indicate that they consider themselves the true Sunni Muslims.[279]

Despite their normal passivity, the Salman Rushdie affair which began in 1988–1989 motivated the Barelwis to organised political action. When touched on the sensitive area of Muhammad's honour, their high veneration for him caused them to react more strongly than other Muslims to the perceived insults against him in Rushdie's *The Satanic Verses*. They took the lead in the demonstrations and linked with other groups to defend his honour and lobby the government and the media.

It is important to note that in Pakistan the Barelwi have organised into powerful political parties, notably Jamiat Ulema-e-Pakistan which is one of the key members of the Islamic coalition

Muttahida Majlis-e Amal (MMA). Many observers were surprised that Barelwis and Deobandis would join the same coalition. However, the power this coalition has gained in Pakistan means that they are unlikely to leave it now. The MMA is notable for anti-Western (particularly anti-American) rhetoric and calls for the introduction of *shari'a* in Pakistan.[280]

Furthermore, some Barelwis in Pakistan have shown they are willing to engage in violence to defend their conservative version of Islam. Barelwi groups such as the Sunni Tehrek have launched sectarian attacks against Deobandis and members of groups linked to the Ahl-e Hadith. They have also attacked religious minorities in Pakistan including Christians.[281] The Sunni Tehrek have called for the enforcement of *shari'a* and have become more insistent on this than the Deobandis.[282]

Barelwis are represented in most Muslim umbrella organisations such as the Muslim Council of Britain (MCB). Specifically Barelwi organisations include:

The Fultoli Movement[283]

The Fultoli Movement is led by Abdul Latif Chowdhury who was born in the village of Fultoli, Sylhet in Bangladesh. Chowdhury is said to be a descendant of Shah Kamal, a disciple of Shah Jalal who spread Islam in Sylhet in the fourteenth century. He is based in Bangladesh. The Fultoli Movement has many followers in the Birmingham Bangladeshi community, mainly among the older generation. Some mosques in Aston, Lozells and Handsworth follow the Fultoli Movement in terms of religious practices and beliefs. Abdul Latif Chowdhury visits Britain regularly to preach at *wa'z mahfil* (religious conferences). The movement's political wing, Anjumane Al-Islah, is not very influential in Britain.

Jamaat-i Tabligh al-Islam

Founded in 1963 by Pir Maroof Hussain Shah, the Jamaat-i Tabligh al-Islam was the first Barelwi organisation in Britain. Its aim is to spread Islam amongst Muslims and non-Muslims. It is also committed to follow Sufi teachings of the Qadiri, Chishti, Naqshbandi and Suhrawardi orders. The organisation is based in the Bradford Southfield Square Mosque controlled by Pir Maroof. The majority of the Barelwi mosques in Bradford and also some mosques in Sheffield and Oldham are members. It distributes Islamic teaching materials and *da'wa* materials to the mosques and provides them with personnel. Pir Maroof also set up the Islamic Missionary College in Bradford in 1974 to train Barelwi imams.[284]

World Islamic Mission[285]

The World Islamic Mission was founded in 1973 in Bradford by Pir Maroof Hussain Shah. It was intended to be an alternative to the Muslim World League backed by Deobandis and Ahl-e Hadith. The World Islamic Mission aspires to be an international umbrella group and the UK centre has set up branches in Canada, Western Europe, the Middle East and Africa. It aims to support a traditional form of Islam throughout the world, and also to engage in Muslim *da'wa* and publishing.

International Muslim Organisation

The International Muslim Organisation is a breakaway from the World Islamic Mission which was founded by Pir Abdul Wahhab Siddiqi from Coventry who died in 1994. The organisation was aligned with the Muslim Parliament which is unusual given the opposition to Sufism by Kalim Siddiqi, founder of the Muslim Parliament. It is now based in London and has at various times issued statements describing Islam as a religion of peace, calling for Muslims to wage *jihad* within the law, and voicing concerns about the wars in Iraq and Afghanistan.

Hanafia Association

The Hanafia Association is a rival organisation to Pir Maroof's Jamaat-i Tabligh al-Islam, based in Bradford's Hanafia mosque. Its founders are devotees of a Kashmiri *pir*, Alauddin Siddiqui.[286]

145

Sultan Bahu Trust[287]

The Sultan Bahu Trust is another rival organisation to Pir Maroof's Jamaat-i Tabligh al-Islam. (See Naqshbandi Sultan Bahu, page 177.)

Suffatul Islam (UK) Association

The Suffatul Islam (UK) Association is also a rival organisation to Pir Maroof's Jamaat-i Tabligh al-Islam. It is based in Bradford.[288]

Minhajul Qur'an (Path to the Qur'an)

The Minhajul Qur'an (MQ) movement emerged from Barelwi Islam in Pakistan in the 1980s, where it has a chain of schools and colleges as well as a university in Lahore. It has become an international movement and claims to have offices in over 80 countries. Its founder Tahirul Qadri criticises the traditional Islamic scholars for their backwardness and for their sectarian bias against the Shi'a and other Muslim groups. He blames the traditional *madrassa* system for creating decadence in the *umma*.

The British headquarters of the MQ is in east London. Qadri makes regular visits and uses literature, audio-visual material and the internet to spread his message amongst British Asians and to raise funds for educational and welfare activities in Pakistan. The movement has sometimes provided imams for the traditional Barelwi mosques. But conflict has arisen when the MQ has tried to absorb the mosques into its organisational structures.

British Muslims who are attracted to the MQ tend to be well educated and economically successful people, who are looking for an alternative to the traditional interpretation of Islam. MQ members also include many "sons-in-law" i.e. Asian-born men who have come to the UK to marry British Muslim women. Although well educated they often lack the social and language skills which would help them to feel at home in British society and are therefore very dependent on their wife's family. (In traditional South Asian marraiges the wife becomes dependent on her husband's family.) MQ offers such men a broader social network in a culturally familiar environment.[289]

Jamaat-i al Sunnat[290]

The Jammat-i al Sunnat arranges conferences in Britain for Barelwi scholars from the Indian subcontinent in order to discuss political and religious issues.

Configuration of Sunni Mosques Midlands

This grouping was created to link together all Barelwi mosques in the Midlands. Muhammad Saleem Akhtar is chairman of its executive committee. It has achieved agreement on times of prayer and dates of beginning and end of Ramadan.[291]

Faizan-e Islam[292]

Faizan-e Islam is an educational and missionary organisation based in Manchester which aims to establish fully functioning secondary schools in Britain run by Barelwis.

Deobandis and Deobandi organisations

The strict and puritanical Deobandi Islamist movement, followed by a large minority of South Asian British Muslims, makes no concessions to modernity or Western cultural norms and also rejects the folk Islam of their rivals the Barelwis. Deobandis seek to follow the Qur'an literally. As such they have much in common with many Islamist movements and with the Wahhabis of Saudi Arabia. (The notoriously strict Taliban of Afghanistan came originally from the Deoband movement.) They have therefore received far more Saudi funding and support than the Barelwis have. They see the *shari'a* as a protection against non-Islamic Western influences which are deemed inherently sinful. It is alleged that Deobandis control more than 600 of Britain's mosques and 17 of the 26 seminaries in the UK.[293]

Many Deobandis in Britain come from India, especially from Gujarat. Deobandis are more likely to be originally from an urban background in their home country than the Barelwis.

Jami'at-i Ulama Britannia (JUB)

The umbrella organisation for Deobandi scholars in the UK, founded in 1967, Jami'at-i Ulama Britannia is based in Birmingham. About half the mosques in Bradford are affiliated to this organisation. The JUB mosque committee includes Sher Azam (a successful local businessman, president of the Bradford Council for Mosques during the *Satanic Verses* affair). It provides education and advice on Islam and its observance. An important JUB goal is for Parliament to accept *shari'a* family law. Another goal is to contest the legitimacy of the Ahmadiyya in the UK. JUB organises conferences and seminars, produces posters and calendars and has developed a network of trained *muftis* to deliver *fatwas* in response to questions on the application of Islamic law.[294]

Deobandi Darul Ulum (Seminary), Bury[295]

This seminary was founded in 1975 to train British Deobandi imams. It offers a six-year programme of studies. The principal Yusuf Motala studied in India at the Mazahir-i Ulum seminary near Deoband, and was commissioned by a leader in Tablighi Jama'at to found a Deobandi seminary in England. Bury has developed links to al-Azhar University in Egypt and to Medina University in Saudi Arabia.

Deobandi Darul Ulum (Seminary), Dewsbury[296]

Founded in 1982, this seminary serves as the European centre of Tablighi Jama'at, a Deobandi offshoot. It hosts a weekly Thursday evening teach-in and an annual Europe-wide conference at Christmas at the Dewsbury Darul Ulum. It has some 300 students, and is more radical than the Bury seminary.

Tablighi Jama'at (The Group that Propagates the Faith)[297]

Tablighi Jama'at is a grassroots *da'wa* movement that is dedicated to bringing Muslims back to their faith. It follows Deobandi precepts and is opposed to the Barelwi tradition. In general it tries to avoid being drawn into local or national politics. Tablighi missionaries use door-to-door visitation, group activities and travelling missionaries to try to bring about a Muslim revival.

Tablighi Jama'at (TJ) was founded in India in 1927 by a student of the university in Deoband, Muhammad Ilyas. When working with Muslims who are not from South Asia, the Tabligh is not particularly closely linked to Deobandi Islam; however when the Tabligh works with South Asian Muslims it is always strongly associated with the Deoband movement and does not work amongst Barelwis. Tablighi Jama'at describes itself as non-political, but is very conservative, advising Muslims to emphasise their Islamic identity, to keep women separate from men, to avoid voting and to disengage from Western society because of its corruption.

The movement began a rapid penetration into non-Muslim countries in the 1970s as it established cordial relationships with the Saudi Wahhabis. While Wahhabis are dismissive of most other Islamic movements, they supported TJ in spite of their opposition to some of its Sufi-inspired practices. The late Saudi Sheikh Abdel-Aziz Ibn Baz, the most influential Wahhabi cleric in the late twentieth century, approved of the Tablighis and encouraged Wahhabis to join their mission work so as to guide and advise them. This co-operation involved large-scale Saudi financing of Tablighi Jama'at. Saudi money subsidises transportation costs for thousands of poor Tablighi missionaries. Some of the vast sums spent by Saudi organisations such as the World Muslim League on proselytism benefit Tablighi Jama'at. In 1978 the World Muslim League subsidised the building of the Tablighi mosque in Dewsbury, which has become the headquarters of Tablighi Jama'at in Europe. Wahhabi sources pay Tablighi missionaries in Africa good salaries to spread the faith. In Western countries, Tablighis operate interchangeably out of Deobandi and Wahhabi controlled mosques and Islamic centres.[298]

The British headquarters of TJ are in Dewsbury. In London one of its main mosques is the Markazi Masjid on Christian Street in Tower Hamlets where it seems to attract young Bangladeshis through its *da'wa* work. The TJ controls a large number of mosques in the Muslim areas of Birmingham, among Bangladeshi, Pakistani and Gujarati communities. As in Tower Hamlets, it has been successful in attracting second and third generation Muslims. It effectively uses its long established local network of mosques and *madrassas* and its *da'wa* activities to spread its influence.

The Tablighi Jama'at has come under the spotlight in the UK as the main sponsor of a plan to build the largest mosque in the UK, able to hold 40,000 worshippers (or according to local sources 70,000 in the original plans), close to the Olympic complex in London. The proposed "London Centre" has a futuristic design and would have the largest capacity of any religious building in Britain.[299] Questions have been raised about the security implications and the possibly divisive nature of the project.

The mainstream TJ says that it follows a policy of non-intervention in politics. On this basis the Pakistani government allowed public servants and military officers to join it, and the TJ was frequently invited to preach in military barracks. It is however alleged that TJ was infiltrated by the Pakistani Inter-Services Intelligence (ISI) and the Jama'at-i-Islami to recruit fighters for the *jihad* in Afghanistan and Kashmir.

The trend towards the radicalisation of the TJ was accelerated in the 1990s when its Pakistani branch was headed by Lt. Gen. (retd) Javed Nasir. Nasir was the director-general of the ISI, but in 1993 he was removed from his post by then prime minister Nawaz Sharif responding to American pressure. Russia and other countries have since banned the TJ.

It is alleged that a breakaway faction of the TJ, led by Sufi Iqbal and with its headquarters at Taxila, Pakistan, had been advocating active involvement in politics and military *jihad*.

In September-October 1995 the Pakistani army arrested a group of 36 army officers and 20 civilians led by Maj. Gen. Zaheerul Islam Abbasi on a charge of plotting, in association with the TJ and the Harakat-ul-Mujahidin, to kill then Prime Minister Benazir Bhutto and senior army officers and then proclaim the formation of an Islamic state. It was reported that Lt. Gen. Ghulam Mohammad Malik, Commander of the 10 Corps, who was an active member of the TJ, was prematurely retired by Mrs Bhutto because of strong suspicion that he was the main inspiration behind the plotters. Mohammad Rafiq Tara, a former president of Pakistan, is also active in TJ.

Western security agencies are increasingly concerned that the movement once viewed as apolitical may have become a fertile recruiting ground for terrorists. It is believed that, after joining Tablighi Jama'at groups at a local mosque and partaking in several local *da'wa* missions, Tablighi officials invite the most promising recruits to the Tablighi center in Raiwind, Pakistan, for four months of additional training. There, representatives of terrorist organisations approach the students and invite them to undertake military training. [300]

The security services in the Netherlands have expressed the fear that Tablighi Jama'at furthers the social isolation and radicalisation of segments of the Dutch Muslim community. They consider that it spreads an ultra-orthodox version of Islam which may be vulnerable to abuse by radical Islamists. [301]

Some British suicide bombers have been linked to TJ. Mohammed Sidique Khan, leader of the July 2005 London suicide bombers, lived in Dewsbury and attended the Tabligh mosque there. Shehzad Tanweer, another July 2005 bomber, attended a Tablighi mosque in Leeds. Assad Sarwar and Waheed Zaman, two of the alleged terrorists who plotted to blow up transatlantic airliners and were arrested in August 2006, are also linked to Tablighi Jama'at. Assad Sarwar who was arrested in High Wycombe is said to have become a Tabligh follower after dropping out of university. Waheed Zaman who was arrested in Walthamstow, East London, was also involved in Tablighi gatherings. [302]

Tablighi Jama'at is also very active in North Africa. It was involved in the founding of the Islamic Salvation Front in Algeria. In Morocco, the authorities have prosecuted 60 members of the Moroccan Tablighi offshoot Da'wa wa Tabligh in connection with the May 2003 terrorist attack on a Casablanca synagogue. [303]

Ahl-e Hadith organisations

Ahl-e Hadith is a radical movement of Pakistani origins which condemns Sufi practices such as visiting shrines and seeking the intercession of saints. It emphasises the unity of God. It rejects democracy as un-Islamic and advocates government by a "pious ruler" under guidance of their own version of *shari'a*. In Pakistan it has a military wing called Lashkar-e-Taiba which is engaged in violent *jihad* against India for possession of Kashmir. The Ahl-e Hadith reject the authority of the standard schools of *shari'a* and seek to implement a more radical kind of Islamic law. They have called on Muslims to separate themselves from non-Muslim society and also engage in Muslim mission. They are more radical than the Deobandis, who adhere to the Hanafi school of *shari'a*. The Ahl-e Hadith are closer to the Wahhabis and Salafis. Most members of Ahl-e Hadith in the UK come originally from the Punjab. A Channel 4 *Dispatches* programme revealed preachers in Ahl-e Hadith mosques in Birmingham disseminating a radical message of hatred to non-Muslims, glorification of *jihad* and a call to not recognise the democratic system. This is part of the effort to make Islam superior in Britain and establish *shari'a* as the law of the land.[304]

Markazi Jamiat Ahl-e Hadith

This is the main Ahl-e Hadith organisation in the UK, founded in 1975. Its headquarters is the Markazi Jamiat Ahl-e-Hadith (mosque) in Small Heath, Birmingham. It is an umbrella organisation for over 60 other organisations around the UK and controls 44 mosques across Britain: 12 in the south; 12 in the Midlands; 18 in the north; and two in Scotland.

The centre operates a well-maintained website (formerly www. ahlehadith.co.uk now http://www.mjah.org) which used to call on Muslims to avoid wearing Western clothes or integrating into Western society.[305] They urge Muslims to focus on *da'wa*, to establish centres across the UK and form links to European *da'wa* organisations. Markazi Jamiat Ahl-e Hadith issues two publications: *Straight Path* (in English) and *Sirat-e-Mustaqeem* (in Urdu).[306]

Jama'at-ud-Da'wa (JUD)

Jama'at–ud-Da'wa is another name for the Pakistan-based terrorist group Lashkar-e-Taiba. It also engages in charitable work, providing free medical care and education services. It was active in helping the victims of the 2005 Kashmir earthquake. Following the discovery of the airliners plot in 2006, the *New York Times* alleged that Jama'at-ud-Da'wa offices in the UK were responsible for channelling funds for the plot, which were raised under the guise of earthquake aid.[307]

Jama'at-i Islami (JI) and linked organisations

The Jama'at-i Islami movement, founded in Pakistan in 1941 by Abu'l A'la Mawdudi, exists to establish an Islamic world order by Islamising individuals, society and politics, with no separation of secular from sacred.[308] Mawdudi's ideology is made clear in his writings (see also pages 86–88).

> . . . Our Constituent Assembly should unequivocally declare:
>
> (i) That the sovereignty in Pakistan belongs to God Almighty alone and that the government of Pakistan shall administer the country as His agent.
>
> (ii) That the basic law of the land is the Islamic *Shari'ah* which has come to us thorough our Prophet Muhammad (peace be upon him).
>
> (iii) That all those existing laws which may be in conflict with the *Shari'ah* shall in due course be repealed or brought into conformity with the basic law and no law which may in any way be repugnant to *Shari'ah* shall be enacted inn the future.
>
> (iv) That the State, in exercising its powers, shall not be competent to transgress the limits laid down by Islam.[309]

The political mobilisation of all Muslims in the *umma* is an important objective, but at the same time, the Jama'at-i Islami sees itself as the training ground for an elite vanguard preparing the way for the Islamic state. It stresses Islamic education and activist political involvement.

The Jama'at-i Islami maintains a network of linked institutions and organisations in the UK. These are often dependent on personnel from the subcontinent or from subcontinent background.[310] These organisations work closely together with other Islamist networks having similar aims, especially the Muslim Brotherhood.

UK Islamic Mission (UKIM)[311]

The UKIM was founded in 1963 by a group of professionals and students as the main bearer of the Jama'at-i Islami message in Britain. It claims over 30 centres and 45 branches in Britain.[312] From its headquarters in Birmingham it concentrates on *da'wa* to non-Muslims, aiming at converting the majority of the British population to Islam so as to set up a society and state based on *shari'a*. It conducts much of its *da'wa* through youth work and education, runs a series of mosques and does community work. It seeks to create an elite of well-trained and committed activists, and some of its leaders have gone on to found other organisations. UKIM was involved in the establishment of the monthly journal *Impact International*.

Islamic Foundation (IF)[313]

The Islamic Foundation is the Jama'at-i Islami's central think tank, research, training and publishing institution for outreach in the UK and Europe. It is based at a conference centre in Markfield, near Leicester, and is registered as an educational institution. The Islamic Foundation was founded in 1973 by Professor Khurshid Ahmad, an economist and a vice-president of the Jama'at-i Islami in Pakistan. Ahmad was the first director of the IF until he returned to Pakistan to become minister of planning under President Zia ul-Haq. He was succeeded by Khurram Murad, another leading member of the Pakistani Jama'at-i Islami. The current director is Dr Manazir Ahsan with a background in the Bangladeshi Jama'at-i Islami. The IF has established itself as a major representative of Islamist interests to the opinion formers of the UK.

The IF often presents a moderate public face, but its aim is to propagate the Jama'at-i Islami's brand of Islam at all levels in Western European society – academic, interfaith, and popular – with the ultimate goal of Islamising the West.

In its early years the Foundation was involved in establishing some twenty mosques and community centres in the UK. It was the first British Islamic organisation to establish ties with higher education institutions such as Leicester University and the Centre for the Study of Islam and Christian-Muslim Relations at Selly Oak Colleges, Birmingham.

In the 1980s the IF increasingly concentrated on publishing. Its publications include hundreds of books and several journals, magazines and newsletters in English and other European languages. The IF has published the main works of the radical Islamists Abu'l A'la Mawdudi and Sayyid Qutb in English translation. Many mosques have built up lending libraries of English-language books for children and the young, mainly supplied by the Foundation.

IF has also established the Markfield Institute of Higher Education.

Muslim Educational Trust (MET)[314]

Founded in 1966, the Muslim Educational Trust is the longest-running organisation for promoting Islamic education in the UK. The MET produces Islamic literature in English, and furthers the teaching of Islam in state schools by providing curricula and training teachers. It also provides visiting teachers to take classes in Islam outside of normal teaching hours. A main aim is to establish fully Islamic schools across the country, with all their staff and pupils Muslims.

For many years the director of the MET was Ghulam Sarwar. He wrote a textbook *Islam: Beliefs and Teaching* that has sold almost 200,000 copies and is often assumed to represent mainstream British Islam. It is, however, written from an Islamist perspective. The book is used to teach Islam both in Muslim schools and as part of Religious Education in mainstream state schools. Its Islamist ideology is clear from passages such as the following which deals with Islam and politics.

> Religion and *politics* are one and the same in Islam. They are intertwined . . . Just as Islam teaches us how to say *Salah*, observe *Sawm*, pay *Zakah* and undertake Hajj, so it teaches us how to run a state, form a government, elect councillors and members of parliament, make treaties and conduct business and commerce . . . There are many more laws in the Qur'an concerning our life and those laws must be put into practice by an Islamic state for the greater good of human beings.

> The Islamic state is duty bound to implement the laws of the *Qur'an* and the *Sunnah* . . . There is not a perfect Islamic state in the world today. There are many Muslim countries. An Islamic state is based on the model of Prophet Muhammad's (*pbuh*) state in Madinah while a Muslim state is one which has a majority Muslim population and some Islamic features . . . However, organised efforts are being made in many parts of the world to bring about total change in society by setting up an Islamic system of government to implement the laws of *Qur'an* and *Sunnah*. Notable among the organisations which have been working to Islamise society are: *Al-Ikhwanul Muslimun* in the Middle East, *Jama'at-e-Islami* in Pakistan, Bangladesh and Kashmir, *Milli Salamat Party* (renamed *Rifah Party* and now banned) in Turkey, *Dewan Dakwah Islamiah (DDII)* in Indonesia, *Islamic Salvation Front (FIS)* in Algeria, *National Islamic Front in Sudan* (now defunct), *Angkatan Belia Islam Malaysia (ABIM)*, and *Hizb An-Nahdah* in Tunisia.[315]

Islamic Society of Britain (ISB)[316]

The Islamic Society of Britain (ISB) was established in 1990 by members of the UK Islamic Mission and former members of Young Muslims UK to promote Islam and Islamic values as relevant to modern Britain. Its youth wing is the Young Muslims UK (YMUK). It seeks to present Islam as rooted in Britain rather than being a South Asian import, and thus to revive the faith of the Muslim community and mobilise Muslims so as to impact the wider society.

Its membership reflects the diversity of the British Muslim landscape. ISB engages in what it terms sincere and constructive *da'wa* and dialogue. It also describes itself as working at establishing cordial relations with non-Muslims in order to promote better understanding of Islam in multi-cultural British society.

Young Muslims UK (YMUK)[317]

Young Muslims UK was founded in 1984 by young followers of Jama'at-i Islami influenced by the UK Islamic Mission (UKIM). Khurram Murad, then Director of the Islamic Foundation, provided them with training programmes and a meeting-place in the premises of the Foundation. Young Muslims UK affiliated itself with the Young Muslims Organisation, the equivalent organisation inspired by Jama'at-i Islami in Bangladesh.

YMUK members tend to be radical in their views. They were vociferous in their support of the Islamist regime in Sudan and of the Chechnya Islamist rebels, while attacking the Saudi regime as oppressive and treacherous. YMUK has supported *jihad* across the world and the restoration of the *khilafa*.[318]

Within the constitution, which was drafted with assistance from UKIM, is a clause giving UKIM the power to disband the leadership of Young Muslims UK should UKIM consider that they are straying from the right Islamic path. This has enabled the UK Islamic Mission to maintain control over the speed and type of changes which the members of the youth movement may want to introduce. In April 1994 Young Muslims UK became the youth wing of the Islamic Society of Britain. Young Muslims UK has forged alliances with other youth organisations in Britain sharing the same ideology, a process accelerated by their connection with the ISB.

The members of Young Muslims UK were nearly all born in Britain. They are predominantly of Pakistani background, but also include Bengalis (the leadership is one-third Bengali), Somalis, Yemenis and others. There is a small but significant number of English converts to Islam. The majority of members are university undergraduates and graduates.

The organisation stresses *da'wa* activity and training, and has been instrumental in bringing lapsed Muslims back to Islam. They like to use English as a means of reaching out to young Muslims in the UK, and they try to adapt to Western culture rather than to feel threatened by it. They are able to appeal to Muslim youth in Britain seeking an Islamic identity in a non-Islamic environment. It is their belief that the purest form of Islam will develop in the West because it is the most contaminated environment.

Da'watul Islam

Da'watul Islam was created in 1978 in Tower Hamlets by Bangladeshi members of the UK Islamic Mission, who were also involved in the Jama'at-i Islami and its student organisation, Islami Chatra Shibir, in Bangladesh before coming to Britain. The decision to form a separate organisation for Bengalis was based on tensions resulting from the Bangladeshi War of Independence against Pakistan, but its ideology is indistinguishable from that of UKIM.[319] The Jamiatul Ummah (mosque and *madrassa*), Bigland Street, Tower Hamlets, London is its base.

Islamic Forum Europe (IFE)[320]

Islamic Forum Europe (IFE) was founded in London in 1988 by mainly Bangladeshi Islamists as an umbrella group for several organisations linked to Jama'at-i-Islami. These include: Young Muslim Organisation UK, Junior Muslim Circle, and a young women's organisation Muslimaat UK. IFE has branches across Britain including in Oldham and Birmingham as well as in Austria, France, Belgium, Cyprus, Finland, Germany, Greece, Italy, Portugal, Sweden and Switzerland. It publishes *Insight* magazine. It is linked to the East London Mosque and its affiliate the London Muslim Centre. Based in Tower Hamlets, IFE is committed to bringing about change in accordance with Islamic *shari'a*.

According to its website, IFE has the following goals:

1. *Da'wa* (mission): bringing revival to Muslims and inviting non-Muslims to Islam

158

2. *Jama'a* (organisation): to organise committed Muslims so they can be effective in attaining their goals

3. *Tarbiyyah* (training): includes developing Islamic education, Islamic character and Islamic purification, in order to produce trained Muslims who can resist temptations and difficulties

4. *Iqamat-ud-Deen* (establishing Islam as a way of life): to help in the struggle of establishing Islam, to rid humanity from servitude to man and bring it to the servitude of Allah. To support justice, human rights, the oppressed and weak of the Muslim *umma*. To strengthen Muslim community infrastructure through institutions, projects and community service.

An elected consultative body (*shura* council) oversees the organisational activities. Programmes are mainly in English, although other languages are also used. IFE activities include: study circles, training camps, seminars and conferences, exhibitions, Islam awareness weeks, Arabic language courses, Qur'an and *shari'a* courses, publications, production of audio-visual material, local radio stations, evening and weekend Islamic schools, building/supporting mosques and Islamic centres, raising funds for the poor, establishing and supporting social welfare organisations, art and cultural activities.

Islamic Council (formerly the Islamic Council of Europe)[321]

The Islamic Council of Europe was founded in 1973 with its headquarters in London. This was in accordance with decisions made at the Third Islamic Conference of Foreign Ministers held in Jeddah, Saudi Arabia in 1972 and the Fourth held in Bengazi, Libya, in 1973.

Its declared objectives are the protection, preservation and promotion of the religious and cultural life of Muslims in Europe, and the development of a better understanding of Islam in the West.

The Council works in close co-operation with international Islamic organisations and the governments of Muslim-majority states. Its first secretary general was an Egyptian called Salem Azzam who had close links to both Saudi Arabian Wahhabism and to the Muslim Brotherhood in Egypt. It aims to coordinate the efforts of more than 24 Muslim organisations in the UK, Germany, France, Scandinavia, Italy, Switzerland, Austria and other countries of northern Europe.

It has published a variety of Islamist books. It produced the Universal Islamic Declaration in 1980 and the Islamic Declaration of Human Rights in 1981. In 1980 it published a book called *Muslim Communities in Non-Muslim States* which set out an agenda for the Islamisation of Europe. In 1983 it also published *A Model for an Islamic Constitution*. The Council has also organised several large international Islamic conferences.

During the Gulf War of 1990–91 the Council condemned Saudi reliance on American military assistance and the presence of foreign troops on Saudi soil.

The Muslim Brotherhood (MB) network[322]

The Muslim Brotherhood has several networks of organisations in Europe, led by Egyptian-born Yusuf al-Qaradawi. Most MB members in Europe are first generation immigrants from the Arab world, especially Egypt, Iraq, Syria, Libya and Tunisia. Some were already affiliated with the MB in their countries of origin while others became members after settling in Europe. A minority are second generation immigrants, many of whom joined the MB in the 1980s. Some see their affiliation not as formal membership but as their intellectual or religious heritage.

Although MB numbers in Europe are small, their influence on European Muslims is disproportionately great because they are well educated activists. The Muslim Brotherhood is very active amongst students, welfare organisations, study groups and social and sporting events. It spreads its message by preaching, conferences, literature, audio-visual materials and the internet. Muslim Brotherhood members have started or joined many Muslim associations, not all of which are openly associated with the MB.

Members focus on maintaining a Muslim lifestyle and separate identity in non-Muslim contexts, promoting a positive image of Islam amongst non-Muslims, combating imperialism, colonialism and perceived injustice, and supporting the Palestinian cause. The establishment of the European Council for Fatwa and Research, whose president is Yusuf al-Qaradawi, was part of the process of developing guidance on how to live as Muslims in the West. Some of the key intellectuals associated with the MB include Rachid Ghannouchi, Tareq Oubrou and Tariq Ramadan, who are attempting to define a new European Muslim identity.

The various organisations have a hierarchical structure with local associations affiliated to national and European level groupings. Links to the Muslim Brotherhood in the Arab world tend to be informal. Because of state repression, the MB developed a culture of secrecy in the Arab world. This is being abandoned to some extent in the freedom Europe offers. A large number of MB members in the West are well-educated professionals, including imams, scholars, scientists and engineers.

Funding comes from both public and private sources, including from Saudi Arabia.

In the UK the Muslim Brotherhood maintains close links with the Jama'at-i Islami network.

Muslim Association of Britain (MAB)[323]

The MAB is the main representative of the Muslim Brotherhood in the UK. It was founded in 1997 by Kamal al-Helbawy, the London-based spokesman in Europe for the Muslim Brotherhood, and some other Arabs linked to the Muslim Brotherhood. The MAB aims to draw attention to perceived injustices against Muslims throughout the world, particularly Palestine, often expressed through extreme anti-Israeli and anti-Jewish propaganda. It seeks to mobilise both Muslims and non-Muslims to campaign on these and similar issues. The MAB was one of the main groups involved in organising the "Stop the War Coalition" at the time of the 2003 invasion of Iraq.

The MAB aims to encourage a "comprehensive Islam that encompasses all aspects of life" i.e. its long-term goal is the creation of an Islamic state under *shari'a* in the UK. Its short-term goals are for British law to be shaped by Islamic principles, for Islam to have a positive image amongst non-Muslim Britons, and to facilitate the conversion of non-Muslims to Islam. An example of its efforts to influence domestic policy in Britain is its campaign against the banning of the *hijab* in British schools.

The MAB president is Muhammad Sawalha, a Palestinian who came to the UK in 1990. He was member of the military structure of Hamas where he organised and facilitated terrorist activities. It has been alleged that he is still engaged in continued support to terrorist activities by sending activists to the West Bank with money and instructions for organising terrorist activities.[324] His current Hamas status is unknown. Anas al-Tikriti, a past president of the MAB, is the son of Osama al-Tikriti, the leader of the Muslim Brotherhood in Iraq. He stood as a candidate for George Galloway's Respect Party in the elections to the European Parliament, thus encouraging the alliance of radical Islam with the radical Left.

Azzam Tamimi is a senior MAB activist who has represented MAB at many Muslim and anti-war meetings. Tamimi acts as advisor to the Hamas leadership in the Middle East and describes himself as a "sympathiser and supporter" of Hamas. He is a personal friend of Khalid Meshal, chief political officer of Hamas.

Like a number of other extremist organisations in the UK, MAB takes considerable care to present a moderate exterior to the non-Muslim public and to conceal its core ideology. It is thus seen as mainstream by many in the British media. It is one of the most successful Muslim organisations in Britain. It encourages Muslims to enter the democratic process and use their numbers to affect election results in a way benefiting Muslim causes and to help elect pro-Muslim candidates. One of their goals is for Muslims to be involved in legislation, the shaping of political and social decision-making procedures, and the installation of governments in Britain.[325]

The Federation of Islamic Organisations in Europe (FIOE)[326]

Based in Markfield, near Leicester, this umbrella grouping links together the various member organisations and institutions of the Muslim Brotherhood in Europe. It has 52 organisations amongst its membership in 28 countries.

Linked organisations in Europe include the Muslim Association of Britain (MAB); Union des Organisations Islamiques de France, (UOIF, France); Ligue des Musulmans de Suisse (Switzerland); and Islamische Gemeinschaft in Deutschland e.V. (Germany). These all serve as umbrella organisations for MB institutions in their respective countries. For instance, the French UOIF claims 200 member organisations.

The leader of FIOE is Dr Ahmad Al-Rawi, originally from Iraq, who came to Britain in 1975. He asserted in October 2004 that attacks against British soldiers in Iraq were justified.[327]

The European Council for Fatwa and Research (ECFR), sometimes called the Islamic Cultural Centre in Ireland[328]

Although the ECFR is now based in Dublin, it qualifies for inclusion in this list because it was founded in London. The creation of ECFR in 1997 was an initiative of the Federation of Islamic Organisations in Europe. It is a largely self-selected body of Islamist clerics and scholars linked to the Muslim Brotherhood, who believe that *shari'a* is superior to civil law and democracy. The president is Yusuf al-Qaradawi.

The aim of the ECFR is to provide a unified voice teaching Muslims in Europe how to live as a minority within non-Muslim contexts. The Council issues collective *fatwas* to provide guidance on how to apply *shari'a* to various issues which arise in a European context. The ECFR is one of the main channels for the publications of *fatwas* by al-Qaradawi and other communications by him in English.

During its 2003 annual conference the Council issued a *fatwa* supporting suicide bombing operations against coalition forces in Iraq as well as against Israelis.[329] In April 2004 IslamOnline published a *fatwa* in which the Council's deputy, Faisal Mawlawi, stated that it is permissible to mutilate the dead in a case of retaliation, as Muslims are allowed to take vengeance for their mutilated dead fighters.[330]

The ECFR wants to promote, and control, the local education of imams for the Muslim minorities in European countries. It also strives to gain recognition by non-Muslim authorities as an approved religious authority in all countries where Muslims are a minority.

The European Institute of Human Sciences (EIHS)[331]

Located in a manor house in Llanbydder, Wales, the European Institute of Human Sciences is an Islamist college which was founded in 1999 and registered as a charity in 2001. It is academically validated by the University of Wales. Many of its 80 students come from Muslim countries to the UK to study at EIHS, and teaching is conducted only in Arabic. Its proclaimed aim is to educate a new generation of imams who understand British society.

International Association of Muslim Scholars (IAMS)[332]

Yusuf al-Qaradawi is founder and president of the association, which was officially launched on 11 July 2004, in London, and is based in Dublin. It defines itself as a pan-Muslim body and comprises approximately 200 Muslim scholars from many different countries, including Sunnis, Shi'as, Sufis and Ibadis. The founding communiqué defined IAMS as "an independent body working on safeguarding the Muslim identity and bridging the gap between the peoples and their rulers in the Islamic countries". Al-Qaradawi has stated that he wants the association to warn Muslims of the perils which globalisation and modernity pose to their faith and identity.

The IAMS aims to unite the majority of the *umma* on common ground, presenting a united Islamic front to non-Muslims, and issuing authoritative decisions and opinions. It presents itself as an alternative to the global network of radical Islamists, but appears to be quite radical itself. For example, it has defined the *jihad* in

Palestine and Iraq as a *fard 'ayn* (individual obligation) i.e. causes which every member of the *umma* should be joining and assisting.

Although it is independent of governments, the group's leaders include Ayatollah Muhammad Ali Taskhiri, an advisor to Iran's supreme leader, and Ahmad bin Hamad al-Khalili, Grand Mufti of Oman.

Hamas

The terrorist organisation Hamas is apparently represented in the UK by Mashreq Media Services, based in Cricklewood, London, which publishes the Hamas newspaper *Filistin al-Muslima*.[333] As early as 1996, the CIA was aware that Hamas fronts such as Human Appeal International and Human Relief International were operating offices in London.[334]

A variety of Islamist groups in the UK serve as organs for Hamas as they include Palestinian Islamists in their leadership. These include the MAB, Interpal, Friends of al-Aqsa, the Palestine Return Centre, the pro-Hamas English publication *Palestine Times*, and others.

Dr Azzam Tamimi is a Hamas sympathiser in the UK. He is a spokesman for the MAB, lectures at the Markfield Institute and has set up his own organisation, the Institute of Islamic Political Thought.[335]

Hizb ut-Tahrir (HT) and its offshoots[336]

Hizb ut-Tahrir is active in the UK where it is also known by the English version of its name, the Islamic Liberation Party. It calls for a Muslim communal identity in the UK, linked to the worldwide *umma* but separate and isolated from the general British identity. It rejects British identity, British values and all forms of integration into British society on the grounds that they are secular and un-Islamic. Muslims in Britain are not "British Muslims" but simply "Muslims".

While HT's activities in most parts of the world must be clandestine, in the UK it has the freedom to operate openly, and is attracting an increasing number of followers, mainly among young people and in particular students. HT opposes any form of political participation in the British system, including elections or lobbying Parliament, and considers democracy to be un-Islamic. It opposes all activities that bring Muslims in contact with non-Muslims.

Hizb ut-Tahrir sees itself as an Islamist political party which is active internationally. Its ideology is centred on the revival of the Islamic *umma* as a restored caliphate (*khilafa*) under a recognised caliph (*khalifa*), by creating a single Islamic state on the ruins of existing regimes in Muslim lands. This state would export true Islam throughout the world – first by invitation and call, then by force. By politicising Muslims it aims at creating a "fifth column" to prepare for the Islamic state which will be established in due time. It regards the rightful caliph as the only person authorised to wage *jihad*; thus HT can assert that it opposes all forms of violence. It denies links to violent groups and on 31 July 2005 disavowed its association with Al-Muhajirun, a movement that had earlier acted as a front for the party in Britain. However it also asserts that defensive *jihad* is a duty at all times upon Muslims and does not need the caliph's permission.

This advocacy of inaction, coupled with the party's extreme rhetoric, appears to be what makes HT so attractive to disaffected young British Muslims disturbed by what they see as the weakness of the *umma*. HT offers a recipe that allows adherents to consider themselves radicals, express their anger, and denounce Western governments, Western society and other Muslims, yet without committing themselves to any concrete action. All meaningful action must await the dream of the re-established caliphate. In the meantime, members can lead a comfortable life taking advantage of all that the UK offers, advance themselves professionally, and bring up their children. However some HT members are so fired by the radical rhetoric that they move into groups dedicated to immediate violence.

HT was banned by the National Union of Students in 1994, and the Committee of Vice-Chancellors issued a warning about them in 1998. To allow it continuing access to university campuses and other recruiting venues, HT has used a variety of aliases and false names including: the Islamic Society, the Islamic Front, the International Islamic Front, the Islamic Forum Against Communism, Al Khilafah Publications, the Young Liberating Party, East London Youth Forum, the Debate Society, the Muslim Women's Cultural Forum, the One Nation Society, the Millennium Society, and the 1924 Committee. Other localised fronts include the Asian Youth (Waltham Forest), the Muslim Media Forum (University College London), Muslim Current Affairs Society (Leeds University), and the New World Society (Nottingham and Sheffield universities).

The leaders of HT in the UK are mainly young professionals of South Asian origin who have given HT a more diplomatic and polished look. They also succeeded in gaining for the UK branch a central role in the HT international movement. Many administrative and publishing functions have been transferred to London, enabling HT to better compete for influence and recruits with other groups such as the Muslim Brotherhood. HT publishes an attractive online magazine *New Civilization*, through which it seeks to project a moderate image.[337]

A number of British residents linked to HT have been involved with terrorism. In 1995 Faisal Moustafa, Shafihur Rehman and Iftikar Sattar were arrested and charged with conspiring to assassinate the Israeli ambassador. It was alleged that they were in possession of HT literature and had helped organise HT meetings in Manchester. The 2003 Tel Aviv suicide bombers, Omar Khan Sharif and Asif Hanif, had been in touch with HT before moving on to more radical organisations. Mohammad Babar, linked to seven men tried in London on charges of planning terrorist attacks between January 2003 and April 2004, stated that he was a member of HT while in college. It is thus clear that HT serves as a catalyst for recruits who then move on to violent groups.[338]

Internationally the UK is believed to be the hub of operations for HT in Europe; this has been alleged by both Danish and German police who are were investigating its activities in their respective countries.[339] HT's London base may also be leading activities in other parts of the world, particularly in Central Asia where HT has gained much influence.

Al-Muhajirun, the Saviour Sect, al-Ghurabaa, Ahlus Sunnah wal Jammah

Al-Muhajirun was founded in 1996 by Omar Bakri Muhammad, then leader of Hizb ut-Tahrir (HT) in the UK, when he split to form his own group. It was committed to the same basic ideology as HT but called for greater activism in the UK and allied itself openly with Osama bin Laden and al-Qaeda. It is believed to have been involved in recruiting British Muslims for *jihad* in Afghanistan, Palestine, Iraq and elsewhere.

Omar Bakri Muhammad disbanded Al-Muhajirun in October 2004 because of pressure from the British authorities, but started other groups such as the Saviour Sect and al-Ghurabaa in order to continue the work of Al-Muhajirun. The Saviour Sect and al-Ghurabaa merged in November 2005 forming Ahlus Sunnah wal Jammah, led by Anjem Choudary.

Wahhabi and Salafi organisations

Some Wahhabi and Salafi organisations are supported by Saudi Arabia while others are more radical and oppose the Saudi regime as insufficiently Islamic. The Saudis have funded many British mosques, placing Wahhabi or Wahhabi-friendly imams in many of them.

World Assembly of Muslim Youth (WAMY)[340]

The World Assembly of Muslim Youth is an umbrella organisation of Muslim youth movements funded by Saudi Arabia and linked to the Organisation of the Islamic Conference (OIC). It was founded by the International Islamic Federation of Students Organisations (IIFSO) in Riyadh, Saudi Arabia, in 1972. WAMY is strongly engaged in propagating the Wahhabi form of Islam to young people across the world. It maintains an office in London that organises camps, training, *da'wa* exhibitions, venture scouts activities and matchmaking. It also distributes *Discover Islam* leaflets, posters and other *da'wa* material.

Muslim World League or World Muslim League (Rabitat Al-'Alam Al-Islami)

The Muslim World League is the largest Islamic relief and development agency in the world, and its aim is to promote Wahhabism. It works particularly in the developing world to spread Wahhabi Islam through its charitable activities and has established 100 branches in 30 countries. It is linked to the International Islamic Relief Organisation (IIRO). It sends out missionaries, distributing the works of main Wahhabi ideologists (especially Ibn Taymiyya and Ibn al-Wahhab) and raises funds for building mosques and subsidising Islamic associations all over the world. The League identifies worthy beneficiaries, invites them to Saudi Arabia, and gives them recommendations (*tazkiya*) that later provide them with generous assistance from wealthy private donors, members of the Saudi royal family, or a rich businessman.

The Muslim World League opened an office in London in 1984 in the Saudi Embassy, which engages in *da'wa,* social and cultural activities. It also has offices in other locations in London.

Committee for the Defence of Legitimate Rights (CDLR)[341] (now called the Party for Islamic Renewal)

This group, led by Muhammad al-Mas'ari, is effectively the opposition party to the current Saudi regime. Presenting itself as a human rights organisation, it actually seeks to install a more strongly Islamic rule in Saudi Arabia and indeed the whole world. It has campaigned for the deposition of the Saudi royal family and the establishment of a Saudi Islamic Republic.

Mas'ari represents a very radical form of Wahhabi Islam and is close to Hizb ut-Tahrir, al-Muhajirun and Osama Bin Laden. He has recently changed the name of his organisation to Party for Islamic Renewal.

A breakaway group, the Movement of Islamic Reform in Arabia (MIRA), is also based in London. Its leadership under Sa'ad al-Fagih separated from the CDLR in 1996. They seem to share many of the goals of the CDLR, but are critical of it for not focusing exclusively on Saudi Arabia.[342]

Al-Qaeda

Security forces believe al-Qaeda has a network in the UK, including "sleeper cells" of operatives who may have been living here for years without engaging in terrorist activity, simply waiting for orders to act. In August 2004 a senior al-Qaeda operative in Britain, codenamed Bilal and also known as Abu Musa al-Hindi, was arrested under anti-terror legislation. It is alleged that he was in the final stages of planning an attack on Heathrow Airport. Pakistani intelligence, who had arrested and interrogated several al-Qaeda members, claimed that Bilal was receiving direct orders from Osama bin Laden. Outline plans for the attack on Heathrow were sent to Bilal whose task was to carry out the operation.[343]

However Bilal's arrest did not prevent the four suicide bombs in London on 7 July 2005, which were undertaken by hitherto unknown sleeper cells.

Dhiran Barot (also known as Isa al-Britani), a Hindu convert to Islam, is a senior British al-Qaeda plotter arrested in 2004. He was engaged in feasibility studies of various types of large-scale attacks on targets in Britain and the US, including the employment of radioactive materials. He used a forged pass to carry out some research into radioactive materials at Brunel University London. In November 2006 he was sentenced to life imprisonment after pleading guilty to planning terrorist attacks to inflict "indiscriminate carnage, bloodshed and butchery" in Britain and America.[344]

Following the foiled airliner bomb plot in 2006, allegations have been made linking several of the plotters to al-Qaeda.[345]

The Director-General of MI5 stated in November 2006 that al-Qaeda in Pakistan had links with the al-Qaeda network in the UK, providing guidance for tens of plots preparing mass–casualty terrorist attacks in the UK. She claimed that al-Qaeda guidance and training for its UK foot soldiers was on an extensive and expanding scale.[346]

SHI'A ORGANISATIONS

There is no accurate assessment of how many Shi'a Muslims are living in Britain, but estimates suggest some 100,000 to 200,000, amounting to less than 10% of the total British Muslim population. Many are originally of South Asian origin, mainly from the Punjab or Gujarat; some of these came to the UK via East Africa after being expelled from Uganda in 1972. The other main influx has been from the Middle East, particularly refugees from Iran and Iraq. There are also Shi'as from Lebanon and Turkey.

Shi'a mosques are sometimes multi-ethnic (in contrast to what is normal for Sunni mosques). For example, the Shi'a Ithna-Ashari Community of Middlesex claims to have been formed by a group from both South Asian and Middle Eastern backgrounds.[347] However, this unity around a common identity is not always present and they can also be divided along sectarian, ethnic and linguistic lines. The Shi'a community are not nearly as well provided with mosques as the Sunni community, and Shi'a living in provincial parts of Britain either have to travel a long way to attend a mosque or do not attend a mosque at all because there is none within reach.

The majority of Shi'a in Britain are Twelvers (Imamis). These are divided between followers of various Grand Ayatollahs. Some follow the more radical Khamenei of Iran while others follow less radical Ayatollahs such as Sistani or Al Khoei. Some mosques have a reputation for being more extreme than others. One accused of extremism by other Shi'a is the Idara-e-Ma'rif-e-Islam mosque in Birmingham.

Whilst the Shi'as are represented in the Muslim Council of Britain, the strong Shi'a element in Pakistani Islam(25% of Pakistani Muslims are Shi'a) is rarely recognised. Not only are there far fewer Shi'a in British Pakistani Islam but also most British Pakistani Muslims are strongly anti-Shi'a in disposition.

Twelver organisations

World Ahlul-Bayt Islamic League (WABIL)[348]

WABIL is a non-profit organisation dedicated to the service of the worldwide Twelver Shi'a community. It is an international socio-religious charitable organisation with offices in more than 80 countries spanning five continents, including one in London. Its activities include educational, medical and other charitable works, Shi'a religious centres, human rights activities and *da'wa*.

Al-Khoei Foundation[349]

Founded in the 1980s by the late Grand Ayatollah Abolqassem Al-Khoei (1899–1992) with headquarters in London, Al-Khoei Foundation is now led by Sayyed Yousef Al-Khoei, the founder's son. It is involved in worldwide religious, social and cultural activities, as well as in *da'wa*, education, youth work and social and welfare relief. It has a general consultative status at the United Nations. It operates the main Shi'a mosque in London as well as an Islamic Centre. It owns many buildings and controls many charities. In London it runs an Arabic and English-language magazine called *Noor* or *Light*. It publishes and distributes material from New York to India.

Abolqassem Al-Khoei was a famous Iraqi *mujtahid* (senior legal scholar) who practised a quietist version of Shi'a Islam. He remained largely outside Middle East politics. However, together with Iranian Ayatollah Ruhollah Khomeini, he openly criticised the Shah in the 1960s. Al-Khoei's friendship with Khomeini did not last, as they disagreed over the question of the involvement of Islamic clerics in politics. Al-Khoei argued that they should do no more than offer religious guidance to politicians.

World Federation of Khoja Shi'a Ithna-Asheri Muslim Communities[350]

Founded in 1980 and based in Stanmore, Middlesex, this organisation seeks to promote the Shi'a Ithna-Asheri faith (i.e.

Twelver Shi'a Islam) throughout the world, relieve poverty amongst its communities, and run various initiatives focusing on education. The general secretary of the organisation is Dr Ahmed Hassam who was elected in 2003. Its member organisations appear to be mostly in Britain, Canada and Australia.

Islamic Centre of England (ICE)[351]

The ICE was founded in 1995 by Sheikh Mohsen Araki and is based in London. It is closely associated with the Iranian government. Araki has also founded the Islamic Thought Association in the UK and was the editor of the journal *Al-Fikr*. The Islamic Centre of England engages in the propagation of Shi'a Islam, organises conferences on the history of Islam, and is involved in various cultural and sporting activities. It has a Religious Enquiries Section which answers enquiries according to the *fatwas* of the Iranian Ayatollah and Supreme Guide Ali Khamanei.

Bahrain Liberation Movement (also known as the Bahrain Freedom Movement)[352]

The Bahrain Liberation Movement is the dominant Shi'a opposition movement in Bahrain and has its central office in London. It enjoys widespread support as the only serious force defending Shi'a rights in Bahrain. Its leadership are well-educated and they maintain contact with Shi'a Islamist groups in Lebanon and around the world, some Sunni Islamist groups, as well as with leftist Bahraini opposition movements. The BLM has a secret internal leadership connected to Sheikh 'Abd al-Amir al-Jamri who has been in and out of prison a number of times, as well as an external leadership abroad, mainly in the UK.

Hizbullah[353]

Hizbullah is a Shi'a terrorist organisation based in south Lebanon but founded and supported by the Islamist regime in Iran.

Hizbullah is known to operate a vast support network around the world, especially in countries with a significant Lebanese Shi'a diaspora. While Hizbullah has no official organisation in the UK representing it, it is alleged to have a support network of fundraisers, operators and propagandists as well as "sleeping" terror cells.[354]

Several incidents have been reported involving British residents linked to Hizbullah. A Hizbullah operative was killed in a London hotel while handling explosives in 1989. In 1996 another Hizbullah agent, Hussein Makdad, travelled to Israel on a forged British passport. He was severely injured in a Jerusalem hotel while preparing explosives.[355] In 2001 Jihad Shuman, a Lebanese with British nationality, was arrested in Israel on charges of planning to collect intelligence for a major terrorist attack. It was alleged that he had met in Britain with a Hizbullah operative who had briefed him on his mission. He then received equipment supplied by a UK-based Hizbullah logistical cell.[356]

Sevener (Isma'ili) organisations

British Isma'ilis are mainly from the Indian subcontinent and East Africa. They are divided into the Nizari faction (Khojas) led by the Agha Khan and the Musta'li (Bohra) faction.

Institute of Isma'ili Studies (IIS)[357]

The Institue of Isma'ili Studies is a Nizari London-based academic research centre which was founded by the Aga Khan in 1977 with the object of promoting scholarship and research, especially into Isma'ili intellectual and literary history. It has links to several main universities and an extensive publications programme.

Agha Khan Foundation (AKF)[358]

The Agha Khan Foundation, another Nizari organisation, is the British branch of the worldwide Agha Khan network. On its website it describes itself as a development agency committed to supporting disadvantaged Isma'ili communities around the world. It aims at promoting solutions to social development problems primarily in Asia and East Africa. AKF provides opportunities for disadvantaged people aimed at improving their income, health, children's education, and the sustainability of their environment. It is linked to the Agha Khan Development Network (AKDN).

Bohra organisations

British Bohras number some 15,000. Most are Dawoodi Bohras who hail from Gujarat. Their international leader is Dr Syedna Mohammed Burhanuddin Saheb, a descendant of the Fatimid caliphs, who resides in Mumbai (Bombay), India. Their main British centre is the Masjid complex in Northolt, Middlesex (London), which includes the Al-Masjid al-Husayni mosque and the offices of the Anjuman-e-Burhani Trust that runs the affairs of the community. The Dawoodi Bohras are building a new mosque in Bradford.

SUFI ORGANISATIONS

Sufis tend to be quietist and secretive in comparison with Islamists who actively publicise their ideology and programmes. Sufis concentrate mainly on their devotional practices and are less political than other Muslim groups, so there is less written material emanating from Sufi sources. However, in Muslim history, Sufi orders were at times engaged in *jihad* activities, so their passive stance could potentially shift to militancy given the necessary conditions.

In the UK Sufism is usually most closely linked with Barelwi Islam, but other Islamic traditions are also involved in Sufism. The two Sufi *tariqa* most commonly found amongst British Barelwis are the Chishtiya and the Naqshbandis. Most Sufis however are devoted more to their own favourite *pir* rather than to the *tariqa* as a whole. A characteristic of Sufism is the belief that the saintliness of a *pir* sanctifies the ground on which he places his residence, and it thus becomes Islamic sacred space forever; this has important implications in non-Muslim contexts. Furthermore there are now a number of saintly shrines (*mazars*) in Britain, where Sufi saints are buried. The first generation of immigrants has thus actively reconstructed their familiar religious world despite the radically different environment in the UK.

In 1973 there were only two subcontinent *pirs* in Britain: Pir Maroof of Bradford and Sufi Abdulla Khan in Birmingham (both Naqshbandis). By 2005 there were numerous Naqshbandi *pirs* spread across various Muslim locations in the UK and several important British centres of Naqshbandi Sufism. Many *pirs* have preferred to keep a low profile, operating from the privacy of their own homes rather than from mosques and large centres. It is difficult to estimate how many *pirs* are currently operating in Britain in this low profile manner, but it is likely to be a substantial number.

The Chishtiya order does not appear to have any *pirs* resident in the UK or any central organisation in the UK; its focus remains in South Asia and its followers in the UK are dispersed throughout the Barewli communities.

The Sufi Muslim Council was formed in 2006 (see page 141).

Qadiri organisations

Qadiri Naushahi

Pir Maroof is the spiritual guide of the Qadiri Naushahi order. Like other Sufi Barelwi *pirs,* he has established himself in a mosque and set up a mosque-based organisation for his order, which is located in Bradford.

Naqshbandi organisations

Naqshbandi Zindapir

Sufi Abdullah Khan was sent by his sheikh, Sufi Zindapir, from Pakistan to Britain to guide lapsed Barelwi immigrants back to Islam. He established the Darul Ulum Islamiyya in Birmingham as his centre. His followers form a distinct cult within the Naqshbandi order, known as the Naqshbandi Zindapir.

Naqshbandi Sultan Bahu (The Sultan Bahu Trust)

This organisation was founded in the 1980s in Birmingham by Sultan Fiazul Hasan Bahu, a descendant of a Sufi saint in Pakistan. It also has mosques in Leicester, Bradford and London and followers in Leeds, Newcastle and Glasgow. It maintains links with other Barelwi centres.

Naqshbandi-Haqqani[359]

The Naqshbandi-Haqqani order has its roots in Turkey, Cyprus, Lebanon and Syria. It has emerged since the mid-1970s as one of the fastest-growing Sufi orders in western Europe and North America. In the 1970s it established a centre in London.

This conservative, *shari'a*-minded mystical movement has been successful in attracting non-Muslim Europeans and Americans to both Islam and Sufism. The order's teachings promote appealing mystical themes that include spiritual growth, love, respect for the natural environment and religious toleration. The message is effectively distributed to a wide following on the internet, in books and pamphlets, and through a well-organised network of national Sufi centres and local circles that gather for weekly *zikr* (Sufi devotional acts).

The two main leaders of the order, Sheikh Nazim Haqqani and his deputy Sheikh Hisham Kabbani, reinforce these teachings and cement powerful personal ties with their followers through constant touring and travel.

Other Sufi orders

Shadhili-Alawiyya

The Shadhili-Alawyiyya order was founded in Britain by the Yemeni Sheikh Abdullah Ali al-Hakimi and his disciple Sheikh Abdul Qadir (died 1999) originally in Cardiff. The main centre is the *zawiya* in Cardiff called al-Markaz al-Islamiyya wal-Zawiya al-Alawiyya, and there are also centres in Birmingham, London, Hull and Glasgow. Under Abdul Qadir the order managed to be effective in organising the Yemeni community in Britain.

Nimatullahi

The Nimatullahi order was brought to Britain by Sheikh Javed Nurbakhsh, a physician and psychiatrist from Tehran, in 1983. It is active in reaching out to non-Muslims and stresses universal spirituality and the Unity of Being.

Radical Sufi orders

Although most Sufis in the UK are traditional and quietist, there are several radical Sufi groups which have espoused Islamist ideology.

Murabitun Worldwide Movement[360]

The Murabitun Worldwide Movement is a Sufi order which includes many Muslims of European descent. It is radical in its commitment to establishing a renewed caliphate.

The founder was a Scot, Ian Dallas (born 1930), who converted to Islam in 1963 while visiting Morocco. He joined the Shadhili-Darqawi *tariqa*, and headed a Sufi *zawiya* in London for a while. He later changed his name to Sheikh Abdul Qadir al-Sufi. Claiming authorisation from two Morrocan Sufi sheikhs of the order, he proclaimed himself leader of the Shadhili-Darqawi *tariqa*. He insisted his followers become Arabic-speaking. He was also a firm supporter of the Maliki school of *shari'a*. He claimed to represent pure Islam, that had been lost, and opposed what he called the "Jew-tolerant" Islam of the contemporary West. Abdul Qadir al-Sufi condemned all other schools of thought as deviant innovations.

He established a new headquarters in Norwich which he developed as a "pure Muslim village" centred around the Ihsan Mosque. From there he published his manifesto *Jihad: A Ground Plan*, which is a programme to establish Islamic rule over the whole world. He also established the Norwich Academy for Languages and Continuing Education. Later he renamed his order as the Murabitun Sufi order and changed his name again to Abdul Qadir al-Sufi al-Maliki al-Murabit.

Dr Umar Ibrahim Vadillo, the present UK leader of Murabitun, lives in Inverness. He promotes the concept of the "Islamic dinar", calling for all currencies in the Muslim world to be replaced by a gold dinar minted to resemble an ancient Islamic coin. More than 250,000 people have bought the dinars from the Islamic Dinar project's headquarters in Malaysia. The idea is to implement the Qur'anic instruction that Muslim wealth should not be entrusted to non-Muslims.[361]

ISLAMIC OFF-SHOOTS CONSIDERED HERETICAL BY MAINSTREAM ISLAM

Ahmadiyya

The Ahmadiyya is an offshoot of Sunni Islam with adherents (called Ahmadis) all over the Muslim world and in the West. It is very active in proselytising.

It was founded in the Punjab, India, by Mirza Ghulam Ahmad in 1889, and has many followers in modern Pakistan. Mirza Ghulam Ahmad proclaimed himself *mahdi* and a "non-legalising" prophet (i.e. not introducing a new law to replace *shari'a*) renewing Islam. It is because of this belief in an ongoing prophethood after the death of Muhammad that Ahmadis are considered heretical by most other Muslims. Ahmadis also believe Jesus revived after his crucifixion and went on to preach in India where he died. Ahmadis were declared non-Muslims in Pakistan in 1971 and are forbidden to call themselves Muslims; they face much repression and persecution there. The movement has divided into two factions, the Qadiani and the Lahori.

Ahmadiyya roots in the UK go back to 1913 when its first mission was established in Woking. It took over a mosque which had been built in 1889 by Dr G.W. Leitner for Muslim students at an institute he had hoped to establish for the study of oriental languages, culture and history. The first purpose built Ahmadiyya mosque was the Fazal Mosque in Southfields, south-west London, which was built in 1924. The Woking mosque was returned to mainstream Sunni control in 1967 or 1968.[362]

Because of persecution in Pakistan, the Ahmadiyya leader, Hadhrat Mirza Tahir Ahmed, left Pakistan in 1984 and established a new headquarters for the movement in London. The Ahmadis claim to have 80 community centres and branches across the UK. Some 30,000 Ahmadis gather for their annual conferences in the UK, usually in their centre at Tilford near Farnham, Surrey. In 2003 a new Ahmadiyya mosque was opened in Morden, south London, which can accommodate 10,000 worshippers.

The Muslim Council of Britain declared in 2003 that Ahmadis are non-Muslims and their centres are not mosques. Anti-Ahmadiyya propaganda is prevalent in many Muslim areas of Britain, especially those where Pakistani-background Muslims predominate.

Bahai

The Bahai faith was founded by Bahaullah (1817–1892) who proclaimed himself *mahdi* in 1863. It developed out of the Twelver Shi'a Babist movement in Iran. The political and religious authorities combined in efforts to suppress the movement, and the hostility of the Shi'a clergy to Bahaism has remained intense. Bahaism is now a separate universalistic religion with its own scripture, *Kitab Akdas,* which stresses the brotherhood of all peoples, equality of the sexes, and pacifism. Its international headquarters are in Haifa, Israel, where Bahaullah's tomb is located. Bahais in Iran have been severely persecuted since the 1979 Islamic Revolution.

A Bahai community has been present in the UK since the end of the nineteenth century. The UK National Spiritual Assembly of the Bahais was established in 1923, and Bahai communities now exist in many towns and regions of the UK. In 2001 there were some 6,000 Bahais in the UK, of whom some 40% were of Iranian origin. Many came seeking asylum from persecution in Iran. The *UK Baha'i Journal* is the organ of the British Bahai community.

The grave of Shoghi Effendi (1987–1957), last Guardian of the Bahai Faith, is situated in the New Southgate Cemetery in London. Shoghi Effendi had been appointed in 1921 by his grandfather Abdul Baha (son and successor of the founder Bahaullah), as Guardian and sole interpreter of the faith.

7 ISLAMIC EDUCATIONAL INSTITUTIONS

Many Muslim parents in the UK are unhappy with sending their children to secular schools. As a result there are an estimated 120 to 150 independent Muslim schools and eight state-funded Muslim schools in the UK.[363] Because of the way in which Muslims tend to live close to each other, there are also many secular state schools whose catchment area is almost 100% Muslim. The government is keen to expand the faith school network in Britain, including Muslim schools. In 2005 the Department for Education and Skills gave the Association of Muslim Schools £100,000 to make the transition to state-funded status smoother for independent Islamic schools.[364]

There are however fears that such schools will increase the segregation of Muslim young people from mainstream society as well as potentially be a source of radicalism. Unlike Christian faith schools, which are almost all church schools where organisational responsibility is accepted by the Roman Catholic Church or the Church of England, in Muslim schools there is no overarching organisation to accept responsibility for them and hence it is more difficult to ensure that Muslim schools are not taken over by radical ideologies or movements.

The issues which concern parents of Muslim children at non-Muslim schools usually centre on religious education, assemblies, *halal* food, prayer rooms, modest clothing for PE lessons, girls to be allowed to wear the *hijab,* and an unwillingness for their children to have sex education or study music, drama or art. Many would like languages such as Urdu and Arabic to be offered. Organisations like the Muslim Educational Trust are active in trying to influence what is taught about Islam. There also appears to be some activity to try to control the content of history lessons (see pages 183–185).

Madrassas

Madrassa – the Arabic word for "school" – is used in Islam to mean "a school for the teaching of Islam" and the term can describe a variety of institutions. Most British mosques offer after-school classes, often two hours each evening, for children from the age of five to 15 where they are taught Qur'an, Arabic and other subjects relating to Islam. These classes are called *madrassas*.

Islamic secondary schools or colleges, usually with boarding facilities, are also termed *madrassas* (or *darul ulum*). These take young people from 13 to 21 and offer Islamic subjects in the morning and GCSE or A-Level studies in the afternoon. The initial elements of the Islamic teaching take six years to complete. Islamic studies include Arabic, Qur'an, Islamic law, Islamic morality and manners, and Islamic history and thought. Students who go through the full six years are encouraged to go into higher education. Some become teachers and a few attend higher Muslim seminaries to become imams.

Madrassas can be institutions where anti-Western, anti-Christian and anti-Jewish attitudes are fostered from an early age, as many texts in the Qur'an and *hadith* can be interpreted this way. Much depends on the ideological and financial affiliation of the *madrassas*. Those following Islamist interpretations foster a more hard-line approach towards non-Muslims.

Some *madrassas* in other countries, such as Pakistan and Indonesia, are known to be breeding grounds for extremism and militants.[365] Concern has been expressed that the same may be happening in some British *madrassas*, depending on the ideological affiliation and funding base of each one.[366]

Tertiary education

A growing number of Islamic centres and similar departments at British universities have received endowments from Muslim donors, especially from Saudi Arabia and the Gulf. These funds usually have some strings attached, such as certain requirements about who can be appointed to staff positions in that specific department. An increasing number of lecturers originate from Muslim states. This has certain advantages but also risks, as some might be restricted in their academic freedom by political or other pressures from the home country which can influence their research and teaching. Another consequence of such funding is an increasing number of Islamists in positions of authority in British universities.

Another cause for concern is the increased recruitment of young Muslim students to radical ideologies and organisations. There have been several cases of Islamic terrorists who were radicalised during their studies at British universities and colleges. Omar Sheikh studied at the London School of Economics before joining a terrorist group in Pakistan and murdering the American journalist Daniel Pearl in 2002. Zacarias Moussaoui, linked to the September 11 2001 plot, had studied at South Bank University in London. Two of the July 2005 London bombers had studied at Leeds University.[367]

Re-writing history

There appears to be an extensive campaign to re-write history to give it a more pro-Muslim slant. Events such as the Crusades are presented with the Muslims as innocent victims instead of as the original aggressors. Medieval Islamic empire-building and conquest are played down, while Islam's contribution to European civilisation and scholarship is played up. Many historical characters are "revealed" to be Muslims or have Muslim leanings, such as Napoleon Bonaparte, William Shakespeare and the eighth-century Saxon King Offa II.[368] It is not clear at present how much of this is being incorporated into school text-books.

Much emphasis is being placed on what Britain has learned from Islam in history with the implication that British history and culture should therefore be inclusive. A typical example from a British Muslim is:

> The west, including Britain, has been enriched with a previously unacknowledged Muslim heritage that most of us are not aware of. This heritage has become part of British mainstream culture over the centuries and is, for example, manifest in quintessentially English national architectural icons such as the domes of St Paul's Cathedral and the Royal Pavilion in Brighton. Even the way we speak demonstrates a ubiquitous linguistic influence; many English words, such as blighty, candy, magazine, tabby, Trafalgar, summit and zero, have their roots in the Arabic language and reflect a vast cultural interconnectivity that has enriched western civilisation over many centuries.[369]

Many non-Muslims are taking up the same theme. Trevor Phillips, head of the Human Rights and Equality Commission, has called for British history to be rewritten to make it more inclusive of Muslims and other minority groups. Citing as an example the baseless assertion[370] that Turks saved England in 1588 by holding up the Spanish Armada at the request of Elizabeth I, he said:

> Sometimes we have to go back into the tapestry and insert some threads that were lost.... When we talk about the Armada, it's only now that we realise that part of it is about Muslims.[371]

What is not often recognised is that, while in a global world most cultures and religons have interacted with each other and so have shaped their common histories, it is a gross distortion to believe that Islam has had the impact on Western culture which so many now claim. Unfortunately British academia, media and politicians have often, for the sake of pragmatism, political correctness or out of fear, sought to embrace ideas which may have no intellectual basis. For some in the Muslim community, presenting arguments about how Muslims have shaped British history and culture is part of their *da'wa*, part of their efforts to create suitable conditions for the thoroughly Islamic society they hope to see instituted one day. For if it could be shown that British and European history and civilisation rest on Islamic foundations, then why not embrace the religion itself?

Some examples of Islamic educational institutions

Islamia Primary School[372]

Islamia Primary School is a co-educational, multi-ethnic and multi-lingual primary school. It is probably the best known Muslim school in Britain, due to its founder and chairman of governors being Yusuf Islam (formerly Cat Stevens) who purchased a property on Brondesbury Road, Kilburn for the purpose. The school started with a nursery class in October 1983. It now has classes of 30 children from reception (age 4) until year six (age 11).

Yusuf Islam made the first application for state funding in April 1986 but was refused for several years. In 1998 it became the first Muslim school to get state funding.

The Islamia School says that it is "committed to developing and providing a high quality education in a secure Islamic environment through the application of the Quran and Sunnah".

Al-Muntada Islamic School[373]

Al-Muntada Islamic school is an independent day school for boys and girls aged 3–11 established in 1989. Situated in the Parsons Green area of the London Borough of Hammersmith and Fulham, it draws its pupils from a wide area of Greater London and beyond. It is housed in an educational and social centre owned by the Al-Muntada Al-Islami Trust, which is a Muslim welfare and educational organisation which maintains schools in several different countries. It has 198 pupils of more than ten different nationalities. The school has no public funding and is dependent on fees and voluntary contributions.

The school prospectus states its aims as:

- to provide its pupils with an Islamic environment where they can receive a high standard of elementary education with Islamic input and knowledge about their religion and way of life

185

- within a strong Islamic ethos to aim sensitively at developing children with good moral values and character so that they may actively become responsible young people within the community and outside

Feversham College[374]

Feversham College is a girls' secondary school in Bradford. In 2001 it became the first Muslim state secondary school in England. It has 530 pupils, and has become the top school in the country for helping its students to make the best academic progress between the ages of 11 and 16.

Leicester Islamic Academy[375]

Leicester Islamic Academy is an independent Islamic school which includes a co-educational primary and a girls' secondary school. It was founded in 1981 in a mosque with just seven pupils. In 1991 existing school premises were bought to enable enlargement. It aims "to promote a wholly Islamic approach to learning within the bounds of *shari'a*". In addition to the general National Curriculum subjects, it offers classes in Islamic subjects such as Qur'an and *fiqh* as well as Arabic and Urdu.

Islamic College for Advanced Studies[376]

The College is situated in Willesden, London, and offers A-level studies and a BA in Islamic studies. The BA (Hons) Islamic Studies is validated by Middlesex University. It "provides an opportunity to study the foundation and development of Islamic knowledge, from a broad and multidisciplinary perspective. The course includes core modules on Islamic studies, while offering the flexibility to choose from a broad selection of related courses on Islam and Muslim society."

The College also operates a Shi'a Hawza Ilmiyya of London. The *hawza* is the traditional Shi'a religious college for training Islamic scholars and jurists. The London Hawza Ilmiyya states that "it is enhancing and extending the fruitful history of *hawza* by responding to the needs of the society by launching a new intertwined system; this new system answers the call of academe for the need of Islamic Scholars in various fields: politics, economics, media studies, law and Islamic banking and simultaneously provides the traditional approach for religious education."[377]

The Markfield Institute of Higher Education (MIHE)[378]

The Markfield Institute of Higher Education was founded in September 2000 by the Islamic Foundation. Based in Markfield, Leicestershire, it offers Muslim students the opportunity to study Islam in an Islamic institution. It currently offers PG (post graduate) Certificate, PG Diploma, MA and PhD programmes, most of which are validated and awarded by Loughborough University.

At MA level it offers courses in Islamic Studies; Muslim Community Studies; and Islamic Banking, Finance and Management.

Like the Islamic Foundation, it represents an Islamist view of the world based especially on Jama'at-i Islami ideology.

Students and staff benefit from the Islamic Foundation library, which contains over 30,000 books and periodicals and 250 journals.

The Institute has recently introduced three additional new diploma courses on Islamic Medical Ethics; Islamic Finance (Banking, *takaful* and stock exchange); and Islamic Jurisprudence (Islamic family law and Islamic law of inheritance).

8   ISLAMIC LEGAL INSTITUTIONS

The primary characteristic of an authentic Islamic state is that it should be governed by Islamic law, *shari'a*. The subject of *shari'a* in the UK is one which divides the Muslim community. Some argue that Muslims living in the UK are in a state of *darura* (necessity). According to *shari'a*, extreme necessity transforms the unlawful into the lawful and therefore, by this argument, Muslim minorities in the West can "live their religions maybe with difficulty but peacefully".[379] They adapt to Western norms and Western legal systems while voluntarily keeping to *shari'a* norms as much as possible.

The alternative argument is that Muslims must live by *shari'a* wherever they are, especially in family matters such as marriage, divorce and inheritance. A Guardian/ICM poll which surveyed 500 British Muslims in 2004 found that 61% wanted Islamic courts operating on *shari'a* principles to be introduced to handle civil cases relating to the Muslim community "so long as the penalties did not contravene British law".[380]

Muslims who reject the British legal system as un-Islamic have developed an extensive alternative unofficial system of arbitration and dispute settlement of family matters by *shari'a* courts and councils which apply Islamic law to the cases brought to them. Thus a *de facto* parallel legal system has come into being in the UK. (See also pages 61–62.) Not the least of the issues here is the conflict between *shari'a* and Western norms of human rights. (See box on pages 190–191.)

As Sunni Islam does not recognise one overarching authority, a variety of *shari'a* courts and councils have been established by different bodies. The main one is the Islamic Shariah Council of UK and Ireland (see below).

The Muslim Law (Shariah) Council was established in 1978 at the Islamic Cultural Centre, Regent's Park, London, during the tenure of Dr Zaki Badawi. Its aims are to resolve disputes between Muslims in the UK, to give *fatwas* in answer to questions posed by Muslims, and to resolve conflicts between civil and *shari'a* law especially in the field of family law.[381]

The Islamic Cultural Centre also instituted a Fatwa Committee for Muslims wanting clarification or advice on legal matters pertaining to *shari'a*.[382]

Omar Bakri Muhammad, formerly leader of Al-Muhajirun, established his own *shari'a* court in London.[383]

In Birmingham the Markazi Jamat Ahl-e Hadith UK has established "The Islamic Judiciary Board – United Kingdom".[384]

Darul Uloom London, a boys' secondary school, has set up a Sharia Council, mainly to help solve marital problems.[385]

There are also a range of institutions which offer advice to Muslims on aspects of *shari'a,* such as the Islamic Shariah Institute established in 1995 in Birmingham provides confidential advice and counselling services regarding aspects of Islamic law.[386] In 1997 the European Council for Fatwa and Research was established in the UK with the famous Islamist scholar Yusuf al-Qaradawi as chairman.[387]

The Islamic Shariah Council of UK and Ireland[388]

This is the main *shari'a* council in Britain and was established in Birmingham in 1982. It claims to issue *fatwas* and verdicts based on all four Sunni schools of law. By April 2002 the Council had dealt with almost 4,000 cases, mainly concerning divorce, as many Muslim husbands would not accept divorces which their wives obtained in the British courts. The founders of the council feel that its establishment and increasing use by Muslims are preparing the way for the final goal of legal acceptance by the British authorities.

Aspects of *shari'a* which conflict with the Western understanding of human rights

Hudud punishments

The *shari'a* prescribes severe punishments for some offences seen as being against God himself. These are called *hudud* (singular *hadd*) punishments and include the death penalty for adultery, amputation for theft, and flogging for drinking alcohol.

Status of women

In addition to discriminating on the basis of religion (see below), *shari'a* also discriminates on the basis of gender. Men are regarded as superior. *Shari'a* rules enforce modesty in dress and behaviour and place women under the legal guardianship of their male relatives. A man is allowed up to four wives, but women can have only one husband. A man can divorce his wife easily; a woman faces great obstacles should she wish a divorce from her husband. A daughter inherits half as much as a son, and the witness of a woman in court is worth only half that of a man. In cases of murder or injury, the compensation for a woman is less than that given for a man.

Dhimmi status of Jews and Christians

Discrimination on grounds of religion is fundamental to *shari'a*, which determines the personal identity and social status of people according to religious criteria. Muslims are treated as superior to any other religious group who are marginalised and excluded from the power structures of society.

Jews and Christians are defined as protected people (*dhimmi*). This protection means that they are allowed to live and practise their faith, but does not imply equality of rights with Muslims. The Muslim state will protect them from other enemies. This protection is conditional on the *dhimmi* submitting to a raft of humiliating discriminatory laws. They are not allowed to bear arms, have to pay a special poll tax (*jizya*) and demonstrate in their clothes, their buildings, their form of transport and many other ways their subservience to Muslims. They are not allowed to have authority over

Muslims. They must practise their faith in a self-effacing way, so as not to disturb the Muslims. *Dhimmi* cannot testify in a *shari'a* court against a Muslim and get less compensation than a Muslim for any given injury. (According to the Maliki and Shafi'i schools of law, *dhimmi* are not allowed even to testify against each other.)

The general attitude of contempt for non-Muslims produced by centuries of application of such rules means that, even in modern secular Muslim states that have constitutionally guaranteed equal rights to all citizens, non-Muslims are discriminated against in numerous ways.

Apostasy from Islam

According to *shari'a*, it is forbidden for Muslims to convert to another faith. The punishment specified is death (see page 24). This obviously runs completely contrary to the modern human rights concept of freedom of religion, as affirmed for example in the United Nations Universal Declaration of Human Rights.

The Muslim view is that apostasy from the faith is equivalent to treason against the *umma* and hence the death penalty is justified. This derived from the political and military context of early Islam. However, for most contemporary Muslims across the spectrum of beliefs and ideologies, apostasy is even today considered unthinkable, bringing the most appalling shame on the family of the apostate because of the connotations of betrayal of one's community and rejection of one's heritage. Some Muslim individuals feel they would be right in the eyes of God to personally murder an apostate. It is ironic, to put it mildly, that Islam itself is a missionary religion active in encouraging non-Muslims to convert to Islam.

The Association of Muslim Lawyers (AML)[389]

The Association of Muslim Lawyers was founded in 1995 and is based in High Wycombe, Buckinghamshire. The AML offers advice, referrals to lawyer members and access to expert witnesses on matters of Islamic law. It describes itself as working on issues of importance to Muslims in the UK as well as highlighting international issues that affect Muslims. Its main aim is to provide a platform for debating the issues and for setting up procedures to help resolve them. It promotes research into *shari'a* and English law in matters relevant to British Muslims. The AML organises seminars and conferences and publishes a magazine *The Muslim Lawyer*.

Aina Khan Partnership[390]

Aina Khan is the Senior Partner and founder of Aina Khan Partnership. She qualified as a solicitor in 1991 and specialises in family law. The law firm, based in east London, specialises in Islamic law and providing expert opinions to other solicitors and to local authorities. The team of specialist solicitors provide solutions under English law which are compatible with Islamic law. Areas dealt with include divorce, *haq mehr* (financial settlements in marriage) and forced marriages.

9   ISLAMIC FINANCIAL INSTITUTIONS

A 2004 survey of 34 UK-based key players and investors in the field of international Islamic finance indicated that the UK was considered to have the most *shari'a*-friendly environment (in terms of human capital and expertise, institutional and legal framework and political environment) of all European countries.[391]

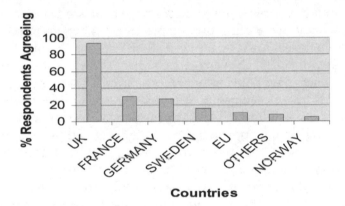

Countries with a Shari'a-Friendly Environment

Western institutions and governments have begun to introduce *shari'a*-compliant products into the Western system. The American Dow Jones company now has more than 70 Islamic Market Indexes (DJIM).

According to experts, the global market for Islamic financial products in 2005 was worth over $500 billion and is expected to grow at 12–15% a year over the next ten years. It is likely to account for some 50–60% of the total savings of the world's 1.2 billion Muslims within the next decade.[392]

Various British financial institutions have begun to offer financial products which are promoted as *shari'a*-compliant. This means not only avoiding investing in industries linked to un-Islamic activities such as alcohol, gambling or pornography, but also avoiding the payment of interest. As already discussed (page 54), the view that **all** interest is forbidden in Islam is not at all a mainstream view but rather is promoted by radical Islamists. So there are many Muslim countries where finance works in the normal Western way with interest payments, whereas the UK has aligned itself with the more extreme interpretation. The non-Muslim British media have in recent years helped to further the cause of the Islamists by promoting their view that *shari'a* unambiguously prohibits the taking of any interest, as if it were the mainstream view.

A number of articles in the media have expressed sympathy for Muslims who were allegedly unable to get mortgages, take out student loans or invest in Western stock markets because of their religious principles. (Nevertheless, some 70% of British Muslim home-owners have conventional mortgages.) The solution, at least as regards home ownership, was a *shari'a*-compliant mortgage, which works as follows. The bank buys the house and rents it out to the buyer until he or she has paid off an agreed price, at which time the house is registered in the buyer's name. Formerly this meant paying stamp duty twice, first when the bank bought the property and later when it was transferred into the buyer's name.

The Bank of England set up a working group to research the problem of how to make Islamic mortgages more accessible, and in 2003 the government changed the rules governing stamp duty for *shari'a*-structured mortgages in order to avoid the double taxation. Under the new rules, stamp duty will be paid only once, making these Islamic alternatives cheaper and more competitive. In October 2004 Islamic (*murabaha*) mortgages became regulated by the Financial Services Authority (FSA).

Some observers have expressed concern that the move to Islamise finance is a part of the overall Islamist strategy to facilitate worldwide Islamic dominion in every society.

The British Treasury Board welcomed the idea of starting an Islamic bank in the UK, arguing that having an Islamic financial market in London gives Britain an economic advantage. (There are 5,000 Muslim millionaires in the UK.) Treasury officials have also indicated that there are no objections in principle to the introduction of *shari'a*-compliant financial products into the UK market. Further discussions are being held as to whether other regulations are needed (like the new stamp duty regulations) for *shari'a*-structured property investment vehicles.

Various mainstream banks and building societies, such as HSBC, Barclays, West Bromwich Building Society and Yorkshire Building Society, are now offering Islamic products. Most have set up internal *shari'a* supervisory committees (or councils or boards) with Muslim scholars to ensure their products comply with a strict interpretation of *shari'a*.

A survey of Islamic companies showed that the UK is the most favoured European location for *shari'a* investors.[393]

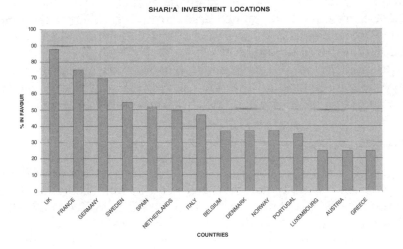

SHARI'A INVESTMENT LOCATIONS

Institute of Islamic Banking and Insurance[394]

Based in Grosvenor Crescent, London, this institute states that its aim is to provide education and training in Islamic banking and insurance as well as developing Islamic financial instruments. It operates a postgraduate diploma course and uses publications, lectures, seminars, workshops and research to achieve its goals. The institute also provides *shari'a* advisory services, personalised overseas training programmes and operates a website. It publishes a monthly journal *New Horizon*. It also publishes books (including an encyclopaedia and directories on Islamic finance), and produces an Islamic banking databank on CD-ROM.

Islamic Bank of Britain (IBB)[395]

The Islamic Bank of Britain was the first Islamic retail bank to open in any Western country. It started its operations in the UK on 9 August 2004 and is regulated by the FSA. Its headquarters are in Edgware Road, London. By 2007 it had eight branches across the UK in London, Birmingham, Manchester and Leicester. Customers outside of branch areas are offered Direct Banking Services. At end of 2006, it had 30,814 customers, an increase of 120% compared to 2005.

Its products include mortgages, current accounts, savings accounts and personal finance. The bank is also planning to introdcue an internet banking service and launch its own credit card.

HSBC Amanah Finance, UK[396]

The HSBC banking group was the first high street bank in Britain to offer *shari'a*-compliant mortgages and current accounts. These products are offered through its Amanah Finance division. HSBC Amanah is the global Islamic financial services division of the HSBC Group, and was established in 1998 with the aim of making HSBC the leading provider of value added Islamic financial services worldwide. Its headquarters are in the United Arab Emirates and it has regional representatives in the UK, US, Saudi Arabia, Malaysia, Bangladesh, Indonesia, Singapore and Brunei.

10 ISLAMIC CHARITIES

Many Islamic charities function in the UK, and almost all have international links. There have been allegations that some of the charities use funds to promote terrorism directly or indirectly. This is justifiable in the eyes of Muslims because of an interpretation of Qur'an 9:60, a verse which lists what charitable giving can be used for. One of these possible uses is "for Allah's Cause" which in the *Noble Qur'an* (Hilali and Khan's version) is explained by an interpolation in the text as meaning "for Mujahidin – those fighting in holy battle".

Muslim Aid[397]

Muslim Aid was founded in 1985 in London by 23 leading British Muslim organisations, in response to continuing conflicts and disasters around the world. It provides emergency relief, mainly to Muslim countries affected by natural disasters, wars, and famine, for example, Muslims affected by floods in Bangladesh, and conflict in Darfur, Sudan and Iraq.

It also engages in long-term development programmes to tackle the root causes of poverty in Muslim societies such as provision of clean water, shelter, education, income-generation projects and healthcare. It has field offices in Sudan, Bangladesh and Somalia where over 60 local staff are employed.

Muslim Aid saw contributions to its funds in 2003 rise about 10 percent over the previous year to £5 million.[398] In 2005 its income was £2,100,335 and its expenditure was £1,226,025.[399]

Muslim Aid is thought to be linked to Jama'at-i Islami.[400]

Islamic Relief Worldwide, (formerly Islamic Relief)[401]

Islamic Relief Worldwide is an international relief and development charity aiming to alleviate the suffering of the world's poorest people. It was founded in the UK in 1984 by Egyptian Dr Hany El Banna who is also its current president and was awarded an OBE in the New Year's Honours List 2004. The international head office is in Birmingham. IR has consultative status with the UN Economic and Social Council. It works in several sectors including emergency relief, health and nutrition, development, water and sanitation, income-generation and orphan sponsorship.

Islamic Relief Worldwide has fundraising offices in Belgium, France, Italy, Germany, Mauritius, Netherlands, South Africa, Sweden, Switzerland, UK and US. t has field offices in Afghanistan, Albania, Bangladesh, Bosnia, Chechnya, China, Egypt, Kosovo, Indonesia, Mali, Pakistan, Palestine, and Sudan, and carries out further projects in Ethiopia Jordan, Kenya, India, Iraq Somalia, and Yemen.

Its 2006 income was £35,233,471 and its expenditure amounted to £41,152,655.[402]

Following the South Asia earthquake in October 2005, the charity was designated the lead agency for all the Islamic NGOs in Pakistan. It led the need assessment of all the affected areas, and several leading charities and governments approached Islamic Relief to co-ordinate the work in the region. The government of South Africa pledged to channel its aid through Islamic Relief.[403]

The UK government's Department for International Development (DFID) has channelled funds for humanitarian relief and development through IR, amounting to £3.6 million by March 2005.[404]

Interpal (The Palestinian Relief and Development Fund)[405]

Founded in 1994 and based in north-west London, Interpal is the most important Palestinian fund operating in the UK. It describes itself as a non-political, non-profit-making British charity that focuses solely on the provision of relief and development aid to needy Palestinians around the world. The Chairman of the Board of Trustees is Ibrahim Hewitt.

Interpal transfers large sums of money collected in the UK and elsewhere to charitable societies and committees operating in the Palestinian Authority administered territories.

Israel has alleged that most of those charitable societies and committees are actually Hamas-operated and contribute significantly to maintaining the Hamas civilian and terrorist-operational infrastructure. Interpal was outlawed by Israel in 1997 and declared a terrorist organisation in 1998.[406] In August 2003 President George W. Bush ordered the US Treasury to block and freeze all Interpal's assets, declaring the charity to be a specially designated global terrorist organisation. The US authorities alleged that Interpal was the fund-raising co-ordinator of Hamas and a principal charity utilised to hide the flow of funds to Hamas.

However, in the UK, the Charity Commission announced after they had conducted an investigation that the US authorities were unable to substantiate claims that Interpal channelled money to Hamas for terrorist and political activities. Investigators lifted a month-long freeze on Interpal's bank accounts and allowed it to continue operating normally.[407]

Al-Muntada al-Islami

A report prepared by Bangladeshi intelligence agencies confirmed links between Islamic NGOs and radical Islamist violence. Ten NGOs with links to extremist activity were named, among them al-Muntada al-Islami.[408] This is a Saudi-funded, UK-based charity with branches in many other countries.

In March 2004 its branch in Kano, Nigeria, was accused of being involved in violence. A Muslim cleric, Alhaj Sharu, involved in the January 2004 "Taliban" raid in Yobe state, confessed to the police that he was a middleman between Nigerian radicals and the al-Muntada al-Islami Trust. He said that charity funds had been used to propagate a Wahhabi version of Islam in Nigeria and to fund religious violence. Authorities also arrested Muhideen

Abdullahi, a Sudanese businessman who was the local director of the trust, on charges of financing attacks on Christians.[409]

In Kenya, Mhawiye Hussain Abu-Waid, the Sudanese executive director of the Nairobi branch of al-Muntada al-Islami, was deported by the authorities on 10 January 2004 over alleged terror links.[410]

11 ISLAMIC MONITORING AND LOBBYING ORGANISATIONS

British society is very conscious of the possibility of anti-Muslim rhetoric, discrimination or violence, particularly in the aftermath of terrorism incidents attributed to Muslims, such as the World Trade Centre attack in New York on 11 September 2001, or the London Transport suicide bombings of 7 July 2005. Political and church leaders are quick to affirm the Muslim community and rightly condemn any hostility or attacks on them. Sadly, such attacks do occur, but contrary to the impression often given by Muslim spokesmen they are relatively few. The Crown Prosecution Service's Racist and Religious Monitoring report for 2005–2006 identified only 18 prosecutions specifically involving hatred of Muslims. The statistics covered cases involving violence, public order offences and criminal damage which are the most common of all offences and covered the period after the July 2005 London bombings when both police and prosecution were specifically on the look out for "Islamophobic" revenge attacks.

The concept of "Islamophobia" has been used in recent years as a way of shielding Islam and Muslims from criticism. All negative comments are automatically condemned as Islamophobic without considering whether the comments have any validity. The majority society in the UK appears to be very vulnerable to such arguments – perhaps because of post-colonial guilt – and has developed a tendency to self-censorship, even in the arts. This was particularly marked in the media for some time, as a spate of pro-Muslim programmes and articles appeared. (However, it is possible that the pendulum is now swinging back the other way, and various exposés of radical Islam in the UK have been publicised.

The remarkable difference in treatment of Muslims compared with other British minorities has also begun to excite comment.)

British Muslims have established a number of organisations to lobby mainstream society on their behalf. The aim appears to be to place Islam and Muslims beyond criticism, which would be tantamount to achieving a privileged status in comparison with all other British communities. The Muslim community has come a long way since the anti-Salman Rushdie public demonstrations in 1989. It is now sophisticated and well organised, expert at relating effectively to both media and government. It offers cultural sensitivity training to government offices and public organisations, and networks with the power elites.[411]

The monitoring and lobbying agencies include the Muslim Council of Britain (see page 135) and its Media Committee.[412] Other important organisations performing this function include:

Islamic Human Rights Commission (IHRC)[413]

Although the name might be thought to indicate a modernist and secular organisation, the IHRC is Islamist and radical. It was established in 1997 to monitor discrimination against Muslims and Islamophobia, and is based in Wembley, London.[414] Its founder and chairman is Massoud Shadjareh, an Islamist activist and formerly a close colleague of Dr Kalim Siddiqui in the Muslim Parliament of Great Britain. His wife, Arzu Merali, is the IHRC's Director of Research.

The IHRC has tried to move away from the confrontational tactics of the Muslim Parliament and to collaborate with other faith groups. It tends to attract many Shi'a in addition to its Sunni constituency.[415]

The IHRC defines its work as including submission of reports to governments and international organisations, writing articles, monitoring the media, cataloguing war crimes, producing research papers, organising vigils, and taking on discrimination cases.

Its aims include the promotion of "a new social and international order, based on truth, justice, righteousness and generosity, rather than selfish interest". The IHRC also states that its aims include "to gather information about, and to publicise, atrocities, oppression, discrimination, and other abuses of divinely-granted rights; to campaign for redress, and to support the victims, of such crimes; to campaign to bring the perpetrators and their accomplices to justice."

Among its advisers it lists Muhammad al-Mas'ari in London and Ibrahim al-Zakzaky, leader of the Muslim Brothers in Kaduna, Nigeria – both radical Islamists with terrorist links.[416] In the media it is reported as a moderate group whose advice is sought by the Home Office.[417] Its report *Anti-Muslim Discrimination and Hostility in the United Kingdom, 2000* was launched by Lord Ahmed at an event in the House of Lords addressed by then Home Office minister Mike O'Brien.[418] It is also involved in radical Islamist pro-Palestinian activities and organises the annual Quds Day demonstration in London, on the last Friday of Ramadan, initiated by the late Ayatollah Khomeini to protest against Israel's rule in Jerusalem.

The IHRC uses the label "Islamophobe" to stigmatise a wide variety of British public figures, and runs an annual "Islamophobe of the Year" event. In 2004 it granted this appellation to US President George W. Bush, French President Jacques Chirac and Israeli Prime Minister Ariel Sharon. In the same event *The Guardian* journalist Polly Toynbee won the appellation "Most Islamophobic Media Personality" award for her investigative work into how Islam treats women.[419]

Following the July 2005 London bombings, Massoud Shadjareh stated that the British government must take responsibility for the political environment in which the attacks took place. It must address the underlying factors that created it before there was further loss of life.[420]

Tel Aviv University's Stephen Roth Institute claims that the IHRC supports *jihad* groups around the world, campaigns for the release of convicted terrorists and promotes the notion of a Western conspiracy against Islam.[421]

Forum Against Islamophobia and Racism (FAIR)[422]

The Forum Against Islamophobia and Racism was established in 1986 to raise awareness of Islamophobia and related prejudices and practices and to combat them. It has a "Media and Popular Culture Watch" to monitor and identify incidences of Islamophobia in print, internet, novels, cinema, theatre, museums, art galleries, fashion, music and broadcast media.[423]

FAIR emphasises partnership and multi-agency working and co-operates with various organisations across numerous disciplines. It aims to identify specific incidences of harassment and violence towards Muslims and deal with them by case-specific means. It also aims to work towards the elimination of religious discrimination at all levels; to promote a more balanced and positive image of Islam and Muslims through the promotion of Islamic arts and culture, to promote interfaith co-operation and dialogue; to campaign and lobby to highlight and critique unjust laws affecting the Muslim community in Britain; and to monitor the way anti-discrimination legislation is working and recommend improvements.

FAIR's first chairman was the late Dr Zaki Badawi. Among its patrons are Baroness Pola Uddin, Lord Amir Bhattia, and Lord Patel of Blackburn. Its Board of Trustees includes Adeela Rashid, Ahmed Al-Rawi, Batool Al-Toma, Dr. Anas Al-Shaikh-Ali, Khalida Khan, Omar Megerisi, Rizk Toema, Yousif Al-Khoei and Yusuf Islam.

FAIR seems to be more mainstream than the IHRC. This is evidenced by its willingness to publish its structure and the names of those involved in its board and committee. (Most Islamist organisations try to keep such information secret.)

Muslim Public Affairs Committee UK (MPAC-UK)[424]

A radical Islamist organisation, the aim of the MPAC-UK is to defend Muslim interests and Islam in Britain through a system of media monitoring, political lobbying and grass-roots community and institutional activism.[425] It is quick to label public figures pro-Zionist and Islamophobic.

Asghar Bukhari is Chief Executive of the MPAC-UK. He is a design consultant and a freelance journalist and has written extensively about issues affecting the Muslim community in Britain. He has used his professional credentials and expertise to launch the MPAC-UK. Muddassar Ahmed is projects manager for MPAC-UK.[426]

It is claimed that Bukhari and the MPAC-UK have radicalised British Muslim involvement in the UK's political and electoral systems, galvanising Muslim political activity especially during the 2005 general election. Before the election it "established teams on the ground to confront pro-war and pro-Israeli MPs such as Jack Straw, Lorna Fitzsimmons, Mike Gapes, and Andrew Dismore, interventions which received much media coverage". MPAC-UK believed that their campaigning had a significant influence on the election results, especially because of the Iraq war issue.

> Muslims were simply the vanguard of a crest of national disillusion with both Tories and Labour over the war. This must be remembered by Muslims for the future; they can influence results when the wider public are in sympathy with them. This underlines the necessity of engaging with non-Muslims at grass roots level, rather than simply courting the power elite.[427]

The MPAC-UK has labelled political lobbying as a political *jihad*, and seeks to use the Muslim vote to further Muslim causes. It asserts that the Conservatives "hate Muslims", it encouraged Muslims in Jack Straw's constituency to vote against him, it constantly criticises the "unjust British foreign policy" in Iraq, and excuses terrorism as an inevitable reaction of angry young Muslims who have no other outlet for their rage.[428] It also states that suicide bombings of civilians are the only weapon available to "the weaker and more resource hungry party" in conflicts where, it claims, both sides target civilians. It also argues that in any case there are no innocent civilians and non-combatants – in times of war the whole nation is a legitimate target.[429]

MPAC-UK leaders argue that the traditional leaders of the Muslim community in Britain are unsophisticated elderly men from abroad who do not have the necessary expertise to help young British-born Muslims to understand the British political system.[430] The British-born generation are considered "more Islamic, concerned for the global Ummah, and though only a minority are from Palestine or Iraq, it is these issues – even more than Kashmir – which galvanise them".[431]

12   MUSLIM PERIODICALS IN ENGLISH

Most of the earliest Muslim print publications in English had strong links to Pakistan and especially to the Islamist ideology of Mawdudi and his Jama'at-i-Islami. They concentrated more on affairs in the Muslim world than with problems Muslims faced in Britain. This has changed since the 1990s with the emergence of new publications dealing more with the concerns of the UK Muslim community. Even so, most (with the exception of *Q-News*) tend to avoid criticism of Muslims or of Islam.[432] The following is but a sample of the growing number of Muslim periodicals in English published in Britain.

The Muslim News[433]

The Muslim News, founded in 1990, claims to be the only independent monthly Muslim newspaper in the UK. According to its own publicity, it is not backed by any state, organisation or party, and is the most consulted paper in the UK on Muslim domestic and international issues by various media, institutions and researchers – both Muslim and non-Muslim. It describes its readership as ethnically diverse and mainly second and third generation Muslims.

The Muslim News highlights human rights abuses against British Muslims, and reports many issues which the non-Muslim media do not report. It claims to have exposed the institutionalised Islamophobia of the British media and establishment on various issues – political (both domestic and international), education, employment and religion. It is highly critical of Western society and of the British government. *The Muslim News* mainly tackles domestic issues, but also Islamic theology and political theory. Its editor is Ahmad Versi, a Tanzanian Asian.

The Muslim Weekly[434]

The Muslim Weekly is published by Muslim Media Ltd. in east London. It was founded in October 2003 by Ahmed Abdul Malik (editor in chief) and Mohammed Shahed Alam (managing editor). It is published every Friday and provides its Muslim readership with domestic and international news, religious, social and sports reports, alongside commentary, editorials and a letters page for readers. It has an average circulation of 40,000.

The Muslim Weekly appears to be more Islamist than *The Muslim News*. It has published some radical Islamist articles such as "Islam, faith and power" by Abid Ullah Jan, a leader in the radical Islamist Pakistani movement, Hizb-i Islami.[435] In this article, published the day after the 7 July 2005 London bombings, Abid Ullah Jan argues that Muslims should strive to gain political and military power over non-Muslims, that warfare is obligatory for all Muslims, and that the Islamic state, Islam and *shari'a* should be established throughout the world. At the same time he criticises secular and modernist tendencies in contemporary Islam.

The editor is Sabera Salam and the marketing manager is Shahid Butt. In response to the July 2005 London bombings Butt is reported to have blamed British foreign policy for the attacks and said that he believed the threat to Britain would be reduced if it pulled its troops out of Iraq.

> At the end of the day, these things [violent incidents] are going to happen if current British foreign policy continues. There's a lot of rage, there's a lot of anger in the Muslim community. We have got to get out of Iraq, it is the crux of the matter. I believe if Tony Blair and George Bush left Iraq and stopped propping up dictatorial regimes in the Muslim world, the threat rate to Britain would come down to nearly zero.[436]

Impact International

Impact International is a journal linked to the Jama'at-i Islami and the Islamic Foundation.[437] It was set up in 1971 by professionals linked to Mawdudi[438] and deals mainly with political contexts outside the UK. The monthly journal invariably supports Islamist movements and Islamist leaders against the moderate secular governments in Muslim states. For instance, in Sudan it was in favour of the 1989 Islamist-military *coup d'état,* mounted by General Omar al-Bashir and supported by Hasan al-Turabi that overthrew the democratically elected government of Sadiq al-Mahdi, replacing it with an Islamist government:

> This was the National Salvation Revolution. Sudan had been salvaged and virtually reborn.[439]

Other articles have praised Hamas as the Palestinian liberation movement and opposed all PLO moves to an agreement with Israel. The 1991 Gulf War against Iraq was presented as a conspiracy led by the US and Britain "to save the Zionist project from total collapse".[440]

The West is seen as the main enemy of Islam, and the cause of all problems Muslims face around the world:

> The main issue is the aggression, physical occupation and exploitation of resources by the West – a process that has been going on for almost three centuries . . . So the clash lies in the unwillingness of the West to respect Islamic beliefs and values.[441]

President Musharraf of Pakistan is seen as a US lackey who betrayed Afghanistan to the Americans, and will do the same to Kashmir and to Pakistan itself. He is accused of enforcing a secular Islam while suppressing the authentic Islam of the Pakistani people.[442]

The invasions of Afghanistan and Iraq, led by the US and Britain, are likened to the Nazi occupation of Europe, and the violent resistance in these countries is lauded.[443] These invasions are part of a recolonisation process in which the West imposes its rule by appointed proxies, "through Hamid Karzais, people who look like Muslims but behave like their masters" and who are readily available as "there is no dearth of quislings in Muslim countries".[444]

Secular and liberal Muslims who argue for a modern interpretation of Islam adapted to the needs of Muslims in the twenty-first century are accused of seeking to destroy Islam from within, especially by their attempt to deconstruct the Qur'an.

> For them, the only way to progress goes through a deconstructed Islam in which everything is relativized to the nth degree . . . The most dangerous are those who have found a niche in the academic institutions . . . They sit, eat and drink and converse with those who are bent on destroying the last remains of Islamic civilisation. This is how they earn their morsels. Indeed, they have bartered their soul for a very small price.[445]

Q-News[446]

Q-News is a monthly magazine started in March 1992 by Fuad Nahdi. It describes itself as the first Muslim publication in the UK not linked to a specific "denomination" or financed by a specific state or regime. It argues that it is Britain's leading Muslim magazine, providing independent analysis, critique and review of politics, culture and ideas. It has a print run of 20,000 and claims to be read by almost 60,000 people, including second and third generation British Muslims, parliamentarians, policy makers and educators. A third of the readership is not Muslim. It aims to be an alternative, both to the mainstream media and to the existing Muslim media, developing a unique and relevant Western Muslim discourse.

The editor is Fareena Alam. Most of the staff, publishers and supporters of *Q-News* are committed Sufis, as is Hamza Yusuf, the American Muslim imam (a convert from the Greek Orthodox Church) used by the magazine as a doctrinal point of reference.[447]

For some examples of Arabic publications see pages 78–79.

CONCLUSION

Islam in Britain is highly complex and multi-faceted. It poses peculiar challenges to British society not seen perhaps since the sixteenth century. Because it has political, legal, economic and social as well as spiritual dimensions, the question of how a secular context can best accommodate Islam the religion needs considerable thought. The issue of how Muslims as individuals can live within the UK is also complex. For, if Islam in its conservative garb guides the Muslim community towards the opinion that integration is essentially an integration of communities as opposed to an integration of individuals, then there will be some Muslims who see their presence in Britain in an increasingly isolated if not parallel way.

Careful thought needs to be given to the future of society in the United Kingdom. Is it to follow the communalism model of British India in which each separate religion is empowered and enshrined? Or is it to follow the route where all religions are given space but there is an integration of individuals and a vision of one society and one overarching community?

Many British politicians, including the leader of the Conservative Party, David Cameron,[448] offer the view of British Islam as an ideal society of peace, tolerance and moral values. The Prince of Wales has expressed similar views. The reality, however, includes a rather different aspect. High crime rates, street gangs, oppression of women and radicalisation leading to terrorist violence seem equally to characterise the community and reveal the deep problems and rifts within it. Ignoring such problems will only exacerbate them rather than help eradicate them.

SOME IMPLICATIONS FOR BRITAIN

1. *Shari'a*

We have seen that the British Muslim community is developing an alternative legal system. The move to implement *shari'a* in the UK, both within the Muslim community and within the British legal system, must be seen as part of Islam's inherent compulsion to dominate every society within which it finds itself. Part of the Islamic legal tradition is that it treats individuals not as persons in their own rights, but only as members of a religious community. The community has inherent rights, but far less so the individual. While some expressions of this drive might seem harmless, and may be justified in providing for Muslims wishing to abide voluntarily by *shari'a*, there are real dangers in the use of strong communal pressure on individual Muslims to accept *shari'a* litigation (not least for Muslim women who are disadvantaged under *shari'a*). Integrating *shari'a* precepts into British law would gradually impose elements of Islamic religious law on non-Muslims in the UK. Both trends contradict the human rights and freedoms of individuals which are enshrined in modern Western states. British law is based on territorial jurisdiction – all citizens within the state territory have equal rights before the law. Muslims pushing for *shari'a* integration into British law are actually asking for a new system that treats citizens in different ways according to their religious community.

What would be the implications of dual legal systems? Some Muslim countries, for example Pakistan and Malaysia, have this situation, and it can cause severe difficulties (especially when Muslims change their faith). It has been argued by some Muslim commentators that such a development would merely follow the practice of the British Empire and that within the UK there are already differences in law between England and Wales, Scotland and Northern Ireland. This seems a persuasive argument but ignores the fact that the differences between the laws of England and Scotland are territorial not personal or communal. Scots in England have always been governed by English law just as an English person in Scotland has to abide by Scottish law. The recognition of *shari'a* law within parts of the Empire was simply a pragmatic acceptance of an existing situation and not a decision in principle. Similarly when Britain conquered Quebec it preserved Quebec's French legal system, but nobody has ever suggested that because of this decision French people in England should be governed by French law.

Throughout English history no group has ever before suggested that it should be governed by its own separate law. The English legal tradition has always been that there is one law that applies to all citizens equally. *Shari'a* law by contrast would transcend national boundaries and depend on an individual's professed religion. Another issue concerns the principle that laws should apply equally to everyone within the society. What would happen if laws were passed which discriminated in favour of one group? For example, if a Muslim man were allowed to have four wives, why should a non-Muslim man not have this freedom as well? If polygamy is to be permitted according to *shari'a*, then surely polyandry should be legalised as well, otherwise women would be discriminated against? Also since we now have same-sex civil partnerships do we also introduce same-sex polygamous partnerships? It may well be argued that these are ridiculous suggestions but they indicate the fundamentally discriminatory nature of having laws which apply to only one, self-selecting, group within society. How far should a religion impose its own demands on society, and how much should it accept that in order to live within a secular society it must be accommodating and willing to compromise to a degree? If Muslims wish to have time off for prayers on Friday, extra leave to make the pilgrimage to Mecca, and to have exam times adjusted to avoid the Ramadan fast, should these demands be met or should Muslims accept that as a religious minority, living within a secular framework, they must conform to the ways of the majority society?

2. Women's and children's rights

The case brought by Shabina Begum on 2 March 2005 (see page 143) in an attempt to force her school to change its uniform policy was part of a general tendency to emphasise Arab traditional clothes such as the all-enveloping *jilbab* and the *niqab* (face veil) as the only true forms of "Islamic" dress in place of non-Arab clothing such as the Pakistani *shalwar kameez*. Increasingly Muslim men require their women to be fully covered and, as Yasmin Alibhai-Brown has powerfully noted,[449] the clothes can literally cover the evidence of male brutality on a wife's or daughter's body. How far can mainstream society facilitate the covering of women and girls, knowing that it can be abused in this way?

It is said by many female supporters of the *hijab* that their wearing of it is a personal decision of faith. For many that is undoubtedly the case, but what of those women who do not want to wear the *hijab* or *jilbab*? Once it is permitted in school it is easy for fathers or elder brothers to insist that it be worn. Even under the strictest interpretation of *shari'a* there is no need for pre-pubescent girls to veil but there are already young Muslim girls in Britain sent to infant school wearing the *hijab*. Used in this way the *hijab* ceases to fulfil a religious function and becomes instead a mark of identity and a political statement. In that situation an older Muslim girl who chooses not to wear the *hijab* is seen as separating herself from the Muslim community and could even be regarded as an apostate. How does this affect the issue of school uniforms? Is the *hijab* now a political symbol as well as a religious symbol, and what might be the consequences for Muslim girls and women who do not want to wear the *hijab*. What rights do they have?

It is now recognised that "honour killing" is an evil which cannot be tolerated, and so is the forced marriage of Muslim girls. However, the discriminatory treatment of women must be addressed by the wider community and not just left to the concerns of the religious minority involved. Only a minority of British mosques are currently registered for civil marriage ceremonies, and many Muslim women do not realise the need to insist on a civil ceremony as well as a religious ceremony. The result is that many Muslim marriages are not legally recognised. This puts the wife at a serious disadvantage, for. according to *shari'a*, she can be divorced at whim by her husband and is then left bereft, with none of the rights she would have had if her marriage had been recognised by the state.

3. Prioritising the Muslim umma identity

The concept of supreme loyalty to the Muslim worldwide *umma*, and only a secondary loyalty to the UK, has unfortunate results. This is evident in the common trend among Muslim leaders and media in Britain to judge the British government and society not on objective grounds of developments in Britain, but almost exclusively on their view of British foreign policy, especially as regarding Muslim states. Any kind of attack on any Muslim state, however unjust or brutal its regime may be, is inevitably seen as an attack on Islam, and thus by inference, also on Muslims in Britain. This presents the government with a no-win situation in its relations with Muslims in the UK. No matter how well accepted and treated Muslims are in Britain, many are inherently dissatisfied with the British system because of their focus on foreign policy. This creates a breeding ground for radical Islamists and Islamist terrorism.

4. Roots of radicalism

The basis of Muslim radicalism in Britain is the self-understanding of most Muslims as members of a religious community theologically destined for world dominion. Many Muslims still see Islam as a religious and political ideology inherently committed to expansion into unoccupied infidel territory, which must be sacralised for Islam. The rise of Islamism within the British Muslim community, with Islamist activists gaining control of most representative institutions has only strengthened this trend. Radicalism and violence are inherent in much of traditional Muslim theology, ideology, sectarianism and history. Only a new Islam that rejects this theological basis will be able to resist the allure of radicalism.

In its search for a solution, the government must face up to these basic facts. Appeasement of Muslim demands for privileged

215

treatment (i.e. above that given to other citizens and groups) will only worsen the situation by feeding a growing appetite for concessions. It will lead to a fragmentation of British society, the creation of Muslim-controlled enclaves, and increase the potential for riots and civil strife. The British government, politicians and public bodies ought to initiate an effective campaign to counteract the influence of radical teachings, but at the same time not consolidate separatism or inadvertently initiate a process that leads to the subversion of society.

One important way to fight radical Islamism is by supporting progressive forms of Islam, those which seek to bring about an enlightenment, and giving them an institutional shape.[450] It is crucial that Muslim leaders encourage a new British Islam that isolates the radicals and the ideologies that motivate them, and reinterprets Islamic doctrine in a liberal manner that allows for a Muslim minority to live peacefully in a non-Muslim majority society without having recourse to legalistic ruses that do not resolve the underlying tensions and paradoxes. For non-Muslims to assist this process is not straightforward, as their visible support could be counter-productive.

5. Muslim concept of mission (da'wa)

The Muslim concept of mission includes the conversion of individuals, but prioritises the Islamisation of the non-Muslim majority society in order to create an environment conducive to Islam. Islam being inherently political, all moves to change British society and impose Muslim concepts and practices must be seen as steps in that direction. They are not necessarily harmless discrete calls for meeting the needs of individual Muslims, but could fit into a wider pattern of the Islamisation of Britain. It must be recognised that there is a link between *da'wa*, radicalisation and a jihadist ideology.

6. Muslims and education

Much Muslim activity in the educational sphere aims at wresting the education of Muslim children from state schools, and placing them instead within strictly Muslim and Islamist systems, isolated from majority society. This is all part of the general strategy of controlling their community, denying individual members freedom of choice.

To justify the trend, Islam is presented to the public in a sanitised form that does not conform to reality. Christianity and other non-Muslim religions are to be taught in a biased manner, if at all. Although non-Muslim children must be taught Islam, Muslim children must be insulated from any expressions of Christianity and from an objective teaching of it. These trends could damage Muslim-Christian relations and radicalise future generations.

Much emphasis is being put upon introducing children at the primary level to other religions and cultures on the basis that it will facilitate better understanding and remove prejudices. But is it right for small children to be taken by their teachers to a mosque, or for that matter to a church? Should this not be left for secondary school, by which time the youngsters will have a better understanding of their own faith, as a basis for going on to look at other faiths?

Equally, the development of faith schools needs to be addressed from the basis of the development of a parallel society. For if the ethos of the child is shaped by education, then by educating children of different faiths separately, we are facilitating the evolution of separate societies. This applies in particular to Muslim schools, because of the very different value system which the children there absorb in comparison with other faith schools. Such children, prevented from encountering any other value systems, can hardly be blamed if they grow up without any understanding of mainstream British society.

7. Muslim electoral power

The growing efforts to utilise the electoral power of Muslims in Britain have inherent dangers. While the political involvement of individual Muslims is to be welcomed, trends in all Muslim societies around the world reveal an inherent drift to radicalism and violence as Muslim politicians compete with each other in Islamic terms. In Muslim states, such trends are often limited by the regime in power. In democratic Western states, such limits are not present. Radicals take over leadership positions, legitimising their demands by reference to Islam. There is a real danger that the Muslim political leadership in the UK will become ever more radical, pushing the Muslim community into greater estrangement and alienation from majority society.

8. Whom to empower?

The UK government has sought through the Muslim Council of Britain to empower the Muslim conservatives instead of seeking out the modernists and liberals within Muslim society. Effectively they have worked to consolidate the power of the imams and mullahs, something which very few governments in Muslim-majority countries do. Abd Al-Rahman Al-Rashed, Director General of Al-Arabiyya TV, has criticised the British government for choosing Muslim advisers from only one section of the Muslim community. The message of these advisers, said Rashed, was that the July 2005 bombings were justified by the British involvement in the Iraq war and by the poor socio-economic condition of Muslims in the UK. The government was not hearing from the many Muslims who support British intervention in Iraq or who do not hold that poverty and unemployment justify terrorism.[451] Rather than empower radicals, the government ought to support progressive and secular Muslim groups. It should help them build up well funded organisations powerful enough to take control of Muslim institutions and counteract radicalisation within the community.

Alternatively, there are those who feel the government should refrain from trying to empower any particular section of the Muslim community, and leave them to evolve without government interference, as other religions do.

9. Islamisation of British media

The influence of Islam in the British media has given Islam a privileged position not granted to other religions. As a result the British public is often presented with a sanitised view of Islam that does not correspond to reality. Although the media may examine the violent facets of Islam and problems within the Muslim community, there is virtually no critical attention given to the fundamentals of Islam e.g. the position of Muhammad and the status of the Qur'an. This contrasts with the frequent programmes questioning or ridiculing Christianity and Christian history.

10. Islamic economics

The development of Islamic financial institutions, which has been welcomed by many, has not been fully assessed in relation to overall British society. How far will the creation of separate Islamic financial institutions help to deepen the separation of Muslims from non-Muslim society? The British authorities have accepted Islamist interpretations of *shari'a* economic principles as representative of all of Islam. This has empowered Islamists, while weakening moderates and progressives. It has also placed individual Muslims under increasing communal pressure to use so-called *shari'a*-compliant financial products.

11. Overseas funding

There is an immense amount of funding coming into the UK from Muslim countries, principally Saudi Arabia, to fund mosques and other Muslim infrastructure and activities. Given the radical ideology which is favoured by many of these funding sources, it may be advisable to consider introducing cash limits on the amount of foreign support for building places of worship and other religious activities. This would be comparable to the limit on foreign founding of British political parties.

12. Muslim hate propaganda

While Muslims are very vocal in their complaints about Islamophobia, there are many expressions of Muslim antipathy to Christians, Jews, Hindus and other groups. Anti-Semitism among Muslims has become very widespread. The vast Islamist propaganda apparatus and its outpourings of hate messages against the West, the Jews and other non-Muslims who are blamed for all misfortunes of Muslims around the world cannot but reap a harvest of violence and conflict, which is already seen in growing violence towards non-Muslim minorities in many Muslim-majority societies. Such attitudes can also bear the seeds of communal strife and violence within the UK.

13. Policing

Much headway has been made in policing "with the consent of the community". Police forces have sought to respond to the charge of institutional racism by reviewing their force structure and operations at every level. However there may be a danger that moving too far in that direction could unwittingly empower certain sections of a religious minority, causing fear to the rest of the population.

Whilst Sikh police officers have been allowed to wear turbans, there are real issues as to whether this small precedent should be extended to other religious forms of dress. When a Muslim wears a turban it is a symbol of religious authority and not merely religious belief. So if Muslims police officers are permitted to wear turbans this may not be welcomed by some within their community. To create a religious police force on the basis that it is policing by consent would mean creating a police force that does not meet the needs of the whole of the local community. How are other minorities, such as Hindus, Sikhs, Afro-Caribbeans and Jews expected to view an overtly Muslim police officer? We have already noted that this possiblity was rejected by a judge in Philadelphia (see page 32) who commented that "prohibiting religious symbols and attire [in police uniform] helps to prevent any divisiveness on the basis of religion both within the force itself and when it encounters the diverse population of Philadelphia." Therefore the judge rejected the Islamisation of police uniform because of the need for police neutrality in a multi-cultural, multi-faith society. What of the secularised young Muslim woman who wants to wear jeans or short skirts and is threatened becase of offending her family's honour? How would she feel about reporting these threats to a police woman wearing a *hijab* with her uniform? If the police are meant to be neutral, surely this should be displayed in their dress code and personal appearance?

THE WAY FORWARD

For almost 1400 years Islam has had a largely negative effect on non-Muslims, constraining their liberties, minimising their rights, and always seeking to increase its own power, influence and territory. In the context of Muslim minorities within non-Muslim countries, Muslim demands are insatiable and often smack of brinkmanship. The more concessions that are made to Islamic demands, the less integration and the more separation there will be, until Islam eventually becomes dominant.

The rise of Islamic radical groups committed to terrorist violence is a symptom of a deeper crisis within Islam itself. The strong opposition to reform and reinterpretation of Islam and its sources leaves the rigid and narrow interpretations dominant. Muslim leaders and societies must engage in a process of genuine self-examination leading to a genuine reformation of Islam. They must grapple with the complicated question of why violence seems endemic in contemporary Islam, why the problem has not been squarely faced up to but denied and suppressed, and how this situation can be changed.

Only an enlightenment-type reform of mainstream Islam, including a complete reinterpretation of its violent and intolerant theological strands, supported by the majority of its religious and political leadership, can stop the drift to an ever more radical and aggressive Islam. Otherwise, Islam will continue to produce new movements and organisations bent on regaining Islamic dominance in the world by subversion, violence, terrorism and war.

Only a clear rejection of militant and intolerant doctrines by the majority of Muslims, and especially by the dominant forces within Islamic states and societies worldwide, would be able to mitigate the effects of the contemporary resurgence of aggressive Islam. An acceptance of secularism and the separation of religion from state is crucial. *Shari'a* must be adhered to only voluntarily and never be imposed by the state.

When peaceful Muslims remain silent, radicals are seen to speak for all Muslims. It is time that peaceful and progressive Muslims rescued Islam by taking a strong stand against its violent aspects and supporting its reformation and reinterpretation in a way that denies the validity of the violent and intolerant strands of their faith. All violent and aggressive passages in the sources must be interpreted as one-time events limited to their immediate historical context. All confrontational passages must be reinterpreted as only spiritually valid against the evil within the individual. Liberal Muslims must fight against all forms of prejudice, hatred, and intolerance within Muslim ranks and must forcefully advocate the peaceful resolutions of conflicts relating to Muslims around the world.

In the preface of this work, we noted the dramatic changes taking place within the UK. Many who came to the country as immigrants, like the author, have gladly embraced British culture, its history and its institutions, despite their non-British origins. Britain has become a far more tolerant society than anyone could have imagined. The author himself, as an Asian Caribbean settling in the UK in 1959, has seen changes for the better which could never have been envisaged half a century ago. There are race relations laws that are just and sound, there is a remarkable degree of social cohesion, and economic prosperity for most. Small wonder that people still stream to the UK, for it continues to offer peace, stability, material security, freedom and a desirable way of life.

The move towards multiculturalism, however, has had serious consequences, which were not foreseen by the well-intentioned individuals who have promoted this doctrine so successfully. It has now become clear that the key issue is not that of race but rather of culture and religion. It is this that will pose the great challenges to the United Kingdom in the future. If many citizens and residents of the UK do not integrate as individuals but only in terms of their community (as defined by religion and culture), thus creating a parallel society, then as Trevor Phillips has noted, we are "sleepwalking our way to segregation".[452]

This development of a parallel society is no accident. As long ago as 1978, the Islamic Council of Europe was arguing for the integration not of individuals but of communities.

> Once a community is well organized, its leaders should strive to seek the recognition of Muslims as a religious community having its own characteristics by the authorities. Once recognized the community should continue to request the same rights as other religious communities enjoy in the country. Eventually, the community may seek to gain political rights as a constituent community of the nation. Once these rights are obtained then the community should seek to generalize its characteristics to the entire nation.[453]

Such a pattern of integration is not just sociological, but has its roots in the belief system which is at the heart of Muslim identity. Dr Lois Lamya' al-Faruqi, writing in the context of gender relations, has stated:

> Islam and Islamic traditions therefore are seen today by many Muslims as the main source of cohesiveness for nurturing identity and stability to confront intruding alien influences and the cooperation needed to solve their numerous contemporary problems... It is only through establishing that identity and stability that self-respect can be achieved.[454]

The idea here is that Muslims require self-respect. But in Islamic culture, self-respect is based on respect received from others – that is, honour – and hence, in the Muslim understanding, ultimately on power. Muslims still feel humiliated by the colonial period and by earlier military defeats they suffered from time to time at the hands of Western countries, as well as by what they see as the current occupation of Muslim lands by non-Muslims. They also resent the global dominance of Western culture. To sum up the problem, "Muslims are convinced of the superiority of their religion and culture and also obsessed by the inferiority of their power."[455]

The need for self-respect based on honour and power is so important for Muslims that without it violence can (and in Muslim contexts often does) ensue. But if the rest of British society yields to Muslim demands on this count and grants them the power they want, it would be the first step towards separatism based on religious identity, which would ultimately threaten social cohesion.

The attitudes and concerns of Muslims in Britain or indeed the West as a whole should not be considered in isolation from what is happening in the rest of the Muslim world, both in the past and in the present. A new consciousness of Islamic identity and expectation of renewed power was sweeping across the *umma* as much as three decades ago, and this had its effects on Muslims in Britain. The year 1979 was pivotal in the renewal movement of Islam in the modern period. The date 20 November 1979 was the start of a new century in the Islamic calendar, 1 Muharram 1400. In Islamic thought the turn of any century is expected to be a time of reformation and religious revival when Islam returns to its original sources. Much was expected of the fifteenth Islamic century in particular, perhaps even the final triumph of Islam worldwide. One reason for this expectation was that Imam al-Suyuti, the greatest scholar of medieval Egypt, had predicted in his book *al-Kashf an mujawazat hadhihi al-umma al-alf (Proof that this umma will survive the millenium)* that Jesus and the Antichrist (*al-masih ad-dajjal*) were most likely to appear in the fifteenth Islamic century. It was certainly no coincidence that the Iranian Revolution took place in 1979 and that the mosque in Mecca was attacked on 20 November 1979 itself.

Ayatollah Khomeini had stated at a press conference in Paris in February 1979, shortly before his return to Iran to lead the Islamic Revolution there:

There is not a single true Islamic state in existence today where social justice is practised. Our task will be to endeavour in modern history to approach this ideal as closely as is practically possible. This will take many years but I have been called, together with my religious leaders, to make a start in that direction. We are striving for the ideal society as the Prophet himself saw it...[456]

It is interesting to note that Altaf Gauhar sounded a warning in the same month in *The Guardian*:

> There is genuine fear that Muslims may be creating a great deal of trouble for themselves and the rest of the world by unleashing forces which they may not be able to control or direct.[457]

Less than two months later an editorial in *The Guardian Weekly* commented:

> As a creed with which Europe and America has to do business, Islam has begun to make Marxism look decidedly familiar and manageable ... It presents itself as a powerful third force in international affairs.[458]

Despite such comments, the gradual penetration of the UK together with other Western societies (and indeed Muslim countries) by radical Islam has gone largely unnoticed until the subversion of systems is now well entrenched. The process of penetration has been the result of a deliberate Islamic strategy to transform Britain and Western Europe into an Islamic entity. Commenting on Islam in Germany, Albrecht Hauser points out that:

> Part of the da'wa strategy ... is not primarily to get as many converts as possible but rather to instrumentalize structures and institutions of a given society, in order to create more favourable conditions for an Islamic way of life. Therefore it is part of the da'wa strategy to keep a society, including its media, the press and the legal institutions, busy with an Islamic agenda. The Muslim opinion-shapers are quite clever in turning even possible negative headlines into positive PR mileage. The legal proceedings for allowing school teachers as civil servants to wear the headscarf (hijab) has to be seen as part of this da'wa strategy. The aim and stages of the Islamization of society are the creation of an Islamic consciousness, then the establishing and consolidation of Islamic institutions; out of this flows a strategic engagement in political and social structures.[459]

What Hauser describes for Germany is also true for the UK.

The ultimate transformation of Britain and Europe has been predicted by the Libyan president, Colonel Qadhafi, who saw that demographics alone might eventually produce a Muslim continent.

> We have fifty million Muslims in Europe. There are signs that Allah will grant Islam victory in Europe – without swords, without guns, without conquests. The fifty million Muslims of Europe will turn it into a Muslim continent within a few decades.[460]

Qadhafi warned that the only way in which the West could prevent itself being islamised would be by warfare.

> Europe is in a predicament, and so is America. They should agree to become Islamic in the course of time, or else declare war on the Muslims.[461]

Yusuf al-Qaradawi likewise expects a peaceful "conquest" of Europe by Islam.

> Some friends have quoted a *hadith* that says Islam would conquer Rome. Does this mean that we will vanquish the Europeans once again? ... The conquest of Rome – the conquest of Italy, and Europe – means that Islam will return to Europe once again. Must this conquest necessarily be through war? No. There is such a thing as peaceful conquest. ... The peaceful conquest has foundations in this religion, and therefore, I expect that Islam will conquer Europe without resorting to the sword or fighting. It will do so by means of *da'wa* and ideology.[462]

It will be recalled that the Muslim Brotherhood (of which Qaradawi is the main spiritual leader in Europe) have a detailed strategy for islamising North America (reproduced in Appendix 2).

The reader may want to protest that statements from a selection of Muslim leaders are not necessarily a fair representation of the aspirations of the whole *umma*, that one cannot ascribe extremists' opinions to moderates who may well form the majority of Muslims in the UK. However, the real difficulty lies in interpreting this theologically. It is certainly true that there is a great diversity of opinion amongst Muslims, as this book has sought to show. But can one separate rain from water? Can one separate moderates (i.e. traditionalists) from extremists when their theological basis is one and the same?

The assumption, which has been assiduously propagated by many in the UK (both Muslims and non-Muslims) that Islamic extremists are a tiny minority and that Islam is moderate and peace-loving will need to be re-examined. It is true that most Muslims are peace-loving and desire principally the economic and social benefits of Western society, but when it comes to addressing Islam as a power it is not so easy to make distinctions such as moderate and extremist. For the extremists – Islamists – are able to define and support their actions and concepts from the source texts of Islam, just as the moderates do. If both moderate/ traditionalist and extremist Muslims (though not liberal Muslims) are agreed that these texts are eternal, cannot be changed and are binding for today, then the consequences will indeed be grave. If both want to be a territorial power as well as a faith, how will they exist in a society based on liberalism and a secular space? It is not inconceivable that a new balkanisation will take place, with all its attendant difficulties.

We cannot separate Islam in Britain from events taking place across the world. Wars in Iraq and Afghanistan, coupled with the "war on terror", have created great anguish and great anger in the Muslim community, as they watch what they see as the subjugation of Muslim lands and the killing of Muslims based on American and British foreign policy decisions. Furthermore, the increasing move towards conservatism across the Muslim world has had a direct impact on Islam in Britain. It is impossible to separate out the two; each impacts on the other.

Much discussion has taken place concerning the proposed inclusion of Turkey in the European Union, with the British government strongly advocating such a move. Going even further, the foreign secretary, David Miliband, has argued that a process should be started to enable the countries of North Africa and the Middle East to join the European Union in due course.[463] If Turkey (let alone the Arab countries) is given membership of the European Union, if population growth continues according to forecasts (i.e.

with a far higher birth rate amongst Muslims than amongst non-Muslims), and if immigration patterns continue as they are, then the European Union would gradually find itself becoming a Muslim-majority entity. The implications for Europe, including Britain, would be profound.

Many politicians, like Miliband, do not seem to view the loss of Europe's Judaeo-Christian heritage as important. For them, the vital thing is to embrace Turkey, which they see as embracing moderate Islam and thereby, they hope, not only neutralising radical Islam but also creating a bridge to the Middle East. As secular individuals themselves, they fail to recognise that Islam is not just a faith but also a power with a territorial basis.

The future of the UK is now inextricably linked to Europe for better or for worse. If Islam in Britain is established as a power as well as a faith then there will be potential for, first of all, serious social conflict and even violence, and then enforced peace as non-Muslims are subjugated by a dominant Islam. David Miliband spoke of "a bleak scenario for 2030: a world more divided by religion both between and within countries. Greater threats – both at home and abroad – from terrorists and rogue states. Growing hostility towards the West." He argues for an "alternative to the narrative which says the West and the Islamic world are destined to clash."[464] His proposed enlargement of the European Union is part of the solution he recommends. But does he realise that avoiding violence by this method is in effect to make non-Muslim Europeans into voluntary *dhimmis*? It is interesting to note that Islamic scholars have given much thought to categorising Islamic territory in various ways according to how the Muslims originally obtained power in any particular piece of territory. Miliband's Europe of the future would either be in the category of land gained from infidels through treaty or the category of land acquired from infidels "accidentally, effortlessly, owing to their evacuating it in fear."[465] Additionally, opening the doors of Europe to mass immigration from Turkey and the Arab world will greatly facilitate Muslims engaged in the *hijra* method of islamisation.

The real question which politicians, social scientists and others need to address is: what kind of society do we want in the UK? Is it a society with a secular space allowing all religions to exist? Do we want a fragmented and fractured society based on a voluntary apartheid where groups of people opt out of the wider societal framework on the basis of their religious identity? Or is it going to be a cohesive society where individuals are protected but religions are not protected? Some would argue that a precedent has been set by the "protection" of the Church of England, but this so-called protected status does not exempt the Anglican Church or Anglican people from criticism, marginalisation or powerlessness.

In the preface it was noted that Britain has lost its Judaeo-Christian moorings and that the Church in general not only is steadily losing its influence but also is in a state of rapid numerical decline. This is true overall despite the fact that certain sections of the Church in the UK are thriving, including those where congregations are drawn largely from new immigrant communities, be they African or eastern European. However, Britain is facing a challenge unlike anything faced for many centuries. It is the challenge of a new religion, which is both a faith and a territorial power, a religion which could easily become numerically and structurally the dominant religion in coming years.

Answers are not easy to see. There is no precedent of a non-Muslim society successfully halting the advance of Islam by peaceful means, and one certainly cannot advocate any means which are not peaceful. Perhaps the solution lies in learning to prize and value once more the good things of British culture, which we have inherited from our forebears and which, so often, were won by them at great cost. These liberties and equalities, which many think must be universal human values so deeply are they embedded in the Western psyche, would be at risk if the Islamic faith, with its discriminatory *shari'a*, were to gain the power it craves. But this need not happen if we treasure them and safeguard them. As Christ himself would say, "Hold fast what you have." (Revelation 2:25)

APPENDIX 1

The Development of Sunni Islam

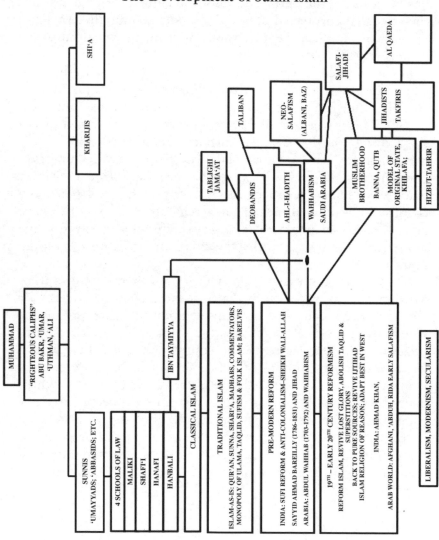

APPENDIX 2

Muslim Brotherhood Strategy for North America

An Explanatory Memorandum on the General Strategic Goal for the Group in North America[466]

22 May 1991

بسم الله الرحمن الرحيم
الحمد لله رب العالمين و الصلاة و السلام على سيد المرسلين

مذكرة تفسيرية

للهدف الإستراتيجي العام للجماعة في أمريكا الشمالية

١٩٩١/٥/٢٢

المحتويات :

١- مقدمة في التفسير .
٢- مفهوم التوطين .
٣- عملية التوطين .
٤- مؤسسات التوطين الفاعلة .

بسم الله الرحمن الرحيم
الحمد لله رب العالمين و العاقبة للمتقين

التاريخ : ٢٢/ ٥ /١٩٩١

الأخ الحبيب / فضيلة المسؤول العام حفظه الله .
الأخ الحبيب / أمين مجلس الشورى حفظه الله .
الأخوة الأحبة / أعضاء مجلس الشورى حفظهم الله .
السلام عليكم و رحمة الله و بركاته ... و بعد

أتمنى على الله تعالى أن تكونوا و أهليكم و من تحبون ممن حولكم على أحسن حال ترضيه عز و جل .
أتوجه اليكم بخطابي هذا راجيا أن يحظى اهتمامكم و ينال حسن رعايتكم فأنتم أهل المسؤولية و أصحاب
الأمانة . بين أيديكم « مذكرة تفسيرية » اجتهدت في تدريتها على لا تبلى حبهما الصدر و العقل . و لكي
أشاركم جزءا من المسؤولية الملقاة على عواتقنا في قيادة الجماعة في هذه البلاد .
و لعل الذي شجعني على أن أتقدم بالمذكرة في هذا الوقت بالذات هو احساسي « بمبارقة أمل » و اشرافة خير
تبشر بأننا بدأنا ندخل مرحلة جديدة من مراحل العمل الاسلامي في هذه القارة .
و الأوراق التي بين أيديكم ليست ترفا زائدا أو خيالات و هواجس مرّت في مخيلة لمد إخوانكم . و إنما هي
آمال و طموحات و تمنيات أرجو أن تشاركوني فيها أو معظمها . و لا أتمنى لها العصمة و الصواب المطلق .
و إنما هي اجتهاد يحتاج منكم الى دراسة و نظر و تفصيل و تأصيل .
و طلبي من إخواني... أن يقرأوا المذكرة و يكتبوا ما شاءوا من تعليقات و تصويبات . مع العلم أن الذي بين
أيديكم ليس غريبا أو طرحا جديدا مبتدأ لا أصل له . و انما هو محاولة لتقصير و شرح بعض ما جاء في
الخطة بعيدة المدى . و التي اعتمدناها وأقررناها في مجلسنا و مؤتمرنا عام (١٩٨٧) .
فلا تبخل أخي الكريم بإلقاء هذه الاوراق بمهدأ لكثرة انشغالك و مسوغك .. كل الذي أطلبه منك أن تقرأها و
تعلق عليها . علّنا نستكمل مع بعضنا مشروع خطتنا و عملنا الاسلامي في هذه البقعة من العالم . و لئن
فعلت لأكونّ لك من الشاكرين المثنين .
و كما و أرجو من أخي الكريم أمين المجلس حفظه الله أن يدرج موضوع المذكرة على جدول أعمال المجلس في
إجتماعه القادم .

و جزاكم الله خيرا و حفظكم ذخرا لدعوته

أخوكم / محمد أكرم

232

(١)

بسم الله الرحمن الرحيم
الحمد لله رب العالمين و العاقبة للمتقين

الموضوع : مشروع لمذكرة تفسيرية للهدف الاستراتيجي العام للجماعة في أمريكا الشمالية
الوارد في الخطة بعيدة المدى .

أولا : تستند هذه المذكرة الى :

١- الهدف الاستراتيجي العام للجماعة في أمريكا و المعتمد من قبل مجلس الشورى و المؤتمر التنظيمي
لعام [١٩٨٧] و هو « تمكين الاسلام في أمريكا الشمالية أي : ايجاد حركة اسلامية فعالة و مستقرة بقيادة
الاخوان المسلمين ، تتبنى قضايا المسلمين محليا و عالميا، و تعمل على توسيع القاعدة الاسلامية الملتزمة،
و تهدف الى توحيد و توجيه جهود المسلمين، و تطرح الاسلام كبديل حضاري ، و تدعم دولة الاسلام العالمية
أينما كانت » .

٢- الأولوية المعتمدة من قبل مجلس الشورى لعمل الجماعة في دورته الحالية و السابقة و هي: «التوطين» .

٣- تطور العلاقة ايجابيا مع الاخوة في الحلقة الاسلامية في محاولة الوصول الى الوحدة الاندماجية .

٤- الحاجة الدائمة للتفكير و التخطيط المستقبلي و محاولة استشرافه و العمل على « تطويع » العاصر
ليستوعبهم و يتلائم مع احتياجات و تحديات المستقبل .

٥- ورقة الأخ فضيلة المسؤول العام حفظه الله التي أرسلها مؤخراً الى أعضاء المجلس .

ثانياً : مقدمة في مذكرة التفسير :

- لكي نبدأ بالتفسير لابد من « استفسار » السؤال الآتي و - وضعه نصب أعيننا لأن علاقته مهمة و لازمة
بالهدف الاستراتيجي و بمشروع التفسير الذي نحن بصدده- . . السؤال هو : « كيف نحب أن ترى حركة
الاسلام في أمريكا الشمالية بعد عشرة أعوام ؟ » أو « استصحاب» الجملة التالية -عند التخطيط و العمل-
و هي : « العمل الاسلامي في أمريكا الشمالية عام (٢٠٠٠) : رؤية استراتيجية » .

- و لابد -أيضا- من استفسار و إستصحاب « عناصر » الهدف الاستراتيجي العام للجماعة في أمريكا
الشمالية و مؤكرزها « مرتبة » متمماً و هي :
[١- ايجاد حركة اسلامية فعالة و مستقرة بقيادة الاخوان المسلمين .

٢- تبني قضايا المسلمين محليا و عالميا .

٣- توسيع القاعدة الاسلامية الملتزمة .

٤- توحيد و توجيه جهود المسلمين .

(٢)

٥- طرح الإسلام كبديل حضاري .
٦- دعم إقامة دولة الإسلام العالمية أينما كانت [.

- و لابد من التأكيد على أنه أصبح من الواضح و من « المعلوم عن الواقع بالضرورة » أنّ الجميع متفقون
على أننا نريد أن « نوطّن » أو « نمكّن » الإسلام و حركته في هذه البقعة من الأرض .

- فلابد ـ إذن ـ من تبني فهماً مشتركاً لمدلول التوطين أو التمكين . نفسّر في سياقه و على أساسه الهدف
الاستراتيجي العام ـ بعناصره الستة ـ للجماعة في أمريكا الشمالية .

ثالثاً : مفهوم التوطين :

وردت هذه الكلمة في « معجم » و وثائق الجماعة بمصطلحات متعددة . بالرغم من أن الجميع قصد بها أمراً
واحداً . و نعتقد أن الفهم في المضمون مشترك . و سنحاول هنا تفسير الكلمة و « مرادفاتها » تفسيراً
عملياً ذو دلالة حركية واقعية و ليس تفسيراً لغوياً تأسيساً . مع التأكيد أن تفسيرنا لايكتمل الا بعد استيعاب
تفسيرنا لعملية « التوطين » ذاتها و التي ترد في الفقرة اللاحقة . فنقول بإختصار ما يلي :

التوطين - « أن يكون الإسلام و حركته جزءاً من الوطن الذي يحيا فيه » .
التأسيس - « أن يتحول الإسلام الى مؤسسات ثابتة الأركان تقوم عليها قواعد الحضارة و البناء و الشهود » .
الاستقرار - « أن يكون الإسلام مستقرا في الأرض التي يتحرك عليها أهله » .
التمكين - « أن يكون الإسلام متمكناً من نفوس و عقول و حياة أهل البلد الذي يتحرك فيه » .
التأصيل - « أن يكون الإسلام أصيلا و ليس طارئا أي متأصلا «متجذرا» في تربة البقعة التي يتحرك عليها و
ليس نبتا غريبا عنها » .

رابعاً : عملية التوطين :

- و لكي يكون الإسلام و حركته « جزءا من الوطن » الذي يحيا فيه و « مستقراً » في ارضه و « متأصلاً » في
نفوس و عقول أهله و « متمكناً » من حماة مجتمعه و له « مؤسسات » ثابتة الأركان يقوم عليها البناء
الاسلامي و يتحقق بها الشهود الحضاري . فلا بد أن تخطط الحركة و تجاهد من أجل امتلاك « مفاتيح » و
أدوات هذه العملية لإنجاز المهمة العظيمة كمسؤولية « جهادية حضارية » تقع على عاتق المسلمين و على
رأسهم الاخوان المسلمين في هذه البلاد . و من هذه المفاتيح و الأدوات ما يلي :

١- تبني مفهوم التوطين و أدراك دلالاته العملية :

ركّزت المذكرة التفسيرية على البعد الحركي و الواقعي لمفهوم عملية التوطين و على دلالاتها العملية دون
الالتفات الى الاختلاف في الفهم بين من هو المقيم و غير المقيم ؟ أو من هو المستوطن أو غير المستوطن؟

234

(٢)

و نعتقد أن الذي جاء في النقطة بعيدة المدى بهذا الصدد فيه الكفاية .

٢) إحداث نقلة نوعية في منهجية تفكيرنا و عقليتنا لتتناسب مع تحديات مهمة التوطين :
المقصود بإحداث النقلة - و هو تعبير ايجابي - هو الاستجابة للتحديات الكبيرة لمهمة التوطين ، و نعتقد
أن أية استجابة تغييرية تبدأ بمنبع التفكير و مركزه العقل أولاً . و لكي يتضح ما نقصد بالنقلة التي ننادي
بها كمفتاح يؤهلنا لخوض ميدان التوطين . نقول باختصار شديد ....أن يتحقق :

- الانتقال من عقلية التفكير الجزئي الى عقلية التفكير الشمولي .
- الانتقال من عقلية التخطيط الجزئي «المبتور» الى عقلية التخطيط الشمولي «المتواصل» .
- الانتقال من عقلية الحذر و التحفظ الى عقلية المجازفة و التحرر المنضبط .
- الانتقال من عقلية تنظيم النخبة الى عقلية التنظيم الشعبي .
- الانتقال من عقلية الوعظ و الإرشاد الى عقلية البناء و الإنشاء .
- الانتقال من عقلية أحادية الرأي الى عقلية تعددية الرأي .
- الانتقال من عقلية التصادم الى عقلية الاستيعاب .
- الانتقال من عقلية الفرد الى عقلية الفريق .
- الانتقال من عقلية الترقب الى عقلية المبادرة .
- الانتقال من عقلية التردد الى عقلية الحسم .
- الانتقال من عقلية المبادئ الى عقلية البرامج .
- الانتقال من عقلية الأفكار المجردة الى عقلية المؤسسات العتيقة [و هنا بيت القصيد و لب المذكرة].

٢- فهم المراحل التاريخية التي مرّ بها العمل الاسلامي الاخواني في هذه البلاد :
يعتقد كاتب المذكرة أن فهم و استيعاب المراحل التاريخية للعمل الاسلامي الذي قاده و يقوده الاخوان
المسلمون في هذه القارة مفتاح مهم جداً في العمل من أجل التوطين . نلمح من خلاله الجماعة مسيرها و
اتجاه حركتها و مسلسلها و منعطفات دربها . و سنكتفي هنا بذكر عنوان [العنوان هنا يعبر من السنة
التالية للمرحلة] كل مرحلة من هذه المراحل [و لعل التفصيل يكون في دراسة مستقبلية أخرى [، و أغلب
الظن أن المراحل هي :
أ- مرحلة البحث عن الذات و تحديد الهوية .
ب- مرحلة البناء الداخلي و إحكام التنظيم .
ج- مرحلة المساجد و المراكز الاسلامية .
د- مرحلة انشاء المؤسسات الاسلامية -الطور الاول - .
ه- مرحلة انشاء المدارس الاسلامية -الطور الاول- .

235

(٤)

و- مرحلة التفكير في الحركة الاسلامية العلنية -الطور الأول- .

ز- مرحلة الانفتاح على الحركات الاسلامية الاخرى و محاولة الوصول الى صيغة للتعامل معها -الطور الأول-

ح- مرحلة اعداد و استكمال انشاء المؤسسات الاسلامية -الطور الثاني- :

نعتقد أن المساحة على أبواب هذه المرحلة في طورها الثاني عليها أن تغلق الباب و تفتحه كما فعلته أول مرة .

٤- تقيم طبيعة دور الاخ المسلم في أمريكا الشمالية :

إنّ عملية التوطين - عملية جهادية حضارية - بما تحمل الكلمة . و لابد أن يستوعب الاخوان أن عملهم في أمريكا هو نوع من أنواع الجهاد العظيم في إزالة و عدم المدنية أو الحضارة الغريبة من داخلها و "تغريب" بيئتها الحقيّة بأيديهم و أيدي المؤمنين لكي يتم جلاؤهم و يظهر دين الله على الدين كله . و دون هذا المستوى من الاستيعاب ، فاننا دون التحدي و لمّا نمّد أنفسنا للجهاد بعد . نقدر المسلم ان يجاهد و يعمل حيثما كان و حيثما حلّ حتى قيام الساعة و لا مفرّ من هذا القدر الا لمن اغتال القعود .. و لكن هل يستوي القاعدين و المجاهدين .

⊙ ادراك أننا لاتستطيع أن نقوم بمهمة التوطين بمفردنا أو بمعزل من الناس :

إنّ مهمة بهذه الجسامة و الضخامة كمهمة التوطين ، تحتاج الى جهود عظيمة و مضنية . و ان يستطيع الاخوان - بامكاناتهم و مواردهم البشرية و المالية و العلمية - أن يقوموا بهذه المهمة بمفردهم أو بمعزل من الناس ، و الذي يعتقد هذا فهو مخطئ . و الله أعلم . أما دور الاخوان فهو المبادرة و الريادة و القيادة و رفع الراية و دفع الناس بهذا الاتجاه . ثم يعملون على توظيف و توجيه و توحيد جهود و قوى المسلمين لهذه العملية . و من أجل ذلك لابد أن يتعمق عندنا فقه » التحالفات » و فن » الاستيعاب » و أدب » التعاون » .

٦- ضرورة تحقيق المزاوجة و الاندماجية المتدرجة المتوازنة بين العمل الخاص و العمل العام :

نظن أن ما كتب حول هذا الموضوع كثير و فيه الكفاية و لكن يحتاج منا الى تأطير زمني و عملي بحيث ينطلق المطلوب بشكل متدرج و متوازن و متواكب مع متطلبات عملية التوطين .

٧- القناعة بأن نجاح توطين الاسلام و حركته في هذه البلاد هو نجاح للحركة الاسلامية العالمية و اسناد حقيقي للدولة المنشودة بإذن الله تعالى :

هناك فهم - تخالفه هذه المذكرة - و هو أن تركيز عملنا في محاولة توطين الاسلام في هذه البلاد سيؤدي الى تقصيرنا و إغفالنا بدورنا في أداء واجبنا تجاه الحركة الاسلامية العالمية في دعم مشروعها في قيام الدولة . نعتقد أن الاجابة من شقين : الأول _ ان نجاح الحركة في أمريكا باقامة قاعدة اسلامية ملتزمة ذات قوة و فعالية و تأثير سيمكن خير عون و دعم و اسناد لمشروع الحركة العالمية .

236

(ه)

و الثاني ـ هو أن الحركة العالمية لم تنجح بعد في « توزيع الأدوار » على فروعها للعدد لهم المطلوب منهم كأحمد المشاركين أو المساهمين في مشروع قيام الدولة الاسلامية العالمية . و يوم أن يتم هذا فسيكون لابناء الفرع الاخواني الامريكي أياد و مواقف بيضاء يفخر بها الآباء .

٨- استيعاب المسلمين و كسبهم بكل فئاتهم و ألوانهم في أمريكا و كندا لصالح مشروع التوطين و جعله قضيتهم و مستقبلهم و أساس حياتهم الاسلامية في هذه البقعة من العالم:

هذه المسألة تحتاج منا الى « فقه للتعامل مع الاخرين » . فالناس معادن و الناس كإبل مائة . نحن نحتاج الي اعتماد المبدأ الذي يقول « خذ من كل الناس ..أفضل ما عندهم » . أفضل ما عندهم من تخصصات و خبرات و فنون و طاقات و كفاءات . و التسود بالناس هنا من داخل الصف أو خارجه من الافراد و المؤسسات . و سياسة « الأخذ » تكون بما يحقق خدمة الهدف الاستراتيجي و عملية التوطين . و لكن التحدي الكبير الذي أمامنا هو : كيف نربطهم جميعا في « فلك » خطتنا و « دائرة» حركتنا لتحقيق «نقاط » مصلحتنا ! و ليس لنا خيار ـ في ظني ـ الا التحالف و التناهم مع من يرغب في ملتنا . و يرضي بمطمعنا في العمل . و الساحة الاسلامية الامريكية مليئة بهؤلاء ينتظرون ....الرواد .

المهم أن نوصل الناس الى مستوى ادراك التحدي الذي أمامنا كمسلمين في هذا البلد و الاقتناع بمشروعنا في التوطين . و ادراك مصلحة اللقاء و التعاون و التحالف . حينها لو طلبنا المال سيأتي ثلاثاً . و لو طلبنا الرجال لجاءوا صفوفا . المهم أن تكون خطتنا هي« المعيار و الميزان » في علاقاتنا مع الاخرين .

و هنا ينبغي تسجيل نقطتين ، الاولى : نحن بحاجة الى ادراك و فهم موازين القوى الاسلامية على الساحة الامريكية [و لعل هذا يكون مشروع دراسة مستقبلية] . و النقطة الثانية : أن الذي توصلنا اليه مع الاخوة في « اكنا » يعتبر خطوة في الاتجاه الصحيح و بداية الخير و أول الغيث . يحتاج منا إنماءً و ترشيحاً .

٩- إعادة النظر في هياكلنا التنظيمية و الادارية و تنمية القيادات و أساليب اختيارها بما يتلائم مع تحديات مهمة التوطين :

ستمنعك الفكرة من التفصيل في هذا البند لحين أخر مع أنه أمر بعضي و فيه قول كثير .

١٠- تنمية و تطوير مصادرنا و مواردنا و امكانياتنا المالية و البشرية بما يتناسب مع ضخامة المهمة الكبيرة :

لو استعرضنا الموارد البشرية و المالية التي يملكها الاخوان لوجدنا في هذا البلد لشعرنا و شعر غيرنا بالفخر و الاعتزاز . و لو ضممنا اليها موارد أصدقائنا و حلفائنا و من هم في فلكنا يصبحون و لرايتنا ينتظرون . لأدركنا اننا يمكن أن نقوض بحر التوطين و نستعرضه لإعلاء كلمة الله سبحانه .

237

(٦)

١١- اعتماد المنهج العلمي في التخطيط و التفكير و اعداد الدراسات التي تحتاجها عملية التوطين :

نحن نحتاج الى هذا المنهج ، و نحتاج الى العديد من الدراسات التي تعين في عملية الجهادية الحضارية . و لعله تكتفي هنا بذكر بعضها بإيجاز :

- تاريخ الوجود الاسلامي في أمريكا .
- تاريخ العمل الاسلامي الاخواني في أمريكا .
- الحركات و المنظمات و المؤسسات الاسلامية : تحليل و نقد .
- ظاهرة المراكز و المدارس الاسلامية : تحديات و إحتياجات و احصاءات .
- الاقليات الاسلامية ،
- الجاليات الاسلامية و العربية .
- المجتمع الامريكي ، تركيبة و سياسة .
- نظرة المجتمع الامريكي الى الاسلام و المسلمين ... و غيرها كثير من الدراسات التي يمكن ان توجه اليها موارنا و حلفاؤنا لاعدادها اما من خلال دراساتهم الاكاديمية أو من خلال مراكزهم العلمية أو من خلال تكليفاتهم الحركية . المهم ان نبدأ .

١٢- الاتفاق على « آلية » مرنة و متوازنة و واضحة لتنفيذ عملية التوطين ضمن « اطار زمني » محدد و متدرج و متوازن و متواكب مع متطلبات و تحديات عملية التوطين .

١٣- فهم المجتمع الامريكي من جوانبه المختلفة فهماً يُؤهلنا « من الهام » بمهمة توطين دعوتنا في وطنه و و « إستئبانها » على أرضه .

١٤- تبني « فقه » مدوّن يتضمن قواعد و مبادئ و سياسات و تفسيرات شرعية و حركية لتلائم مع حاجات و تحديات عملية التوطين .

١٥- الاتفاق على « معايير » و موازين تكون بمثابة « حاسة الاستشعار » أو « برج المراقبة » للتأكد من أن أولوياتنا و خططنا و برامجنا و هياكلنا و قياداتنا و اموالنا و نشاطنا كلها تسير باتجاه عملية التوطين.

١٦- تبني سيفة عملية مرنة يتكامل فيها عملنا المركزي مع عملنا المحلي .
[البنود من ١٢ الى ١٦ سهرد فيها التفصيل لاحقاً] .

١٧- ادراك دور و طبيعة عمل « المركز الاسلامي » في كل مدينة بما يحقق عملية التوطين :

إن المركز الذي نسمي له هو الذي : يُمثّل « محور » حركتنا و « محيط » دائرة عملنا و « نقطة » ارتكازنا و « قاعدة » انطلاقنا و « دار أرتحنا » لتربيتنا و امدادنا و إنفاذ سرايانا بالاضافة الى انه «مصرابه» حماياتنا .

(٧)

حتى يتحول المركز الاسلامي -بالفعل- لا بالقول الى نواةٍ « لمجتمع اسلامي» صغير يكون انعكاساً و مرآةً لمؤسساتنا المركزية . ينبغي أن يتحول المركز الى « خلية نحل » يُخرج شهداً على المذاق . فيتحول بذلك المركز الاسلامي الى مكان الدرس و الاسرة و الكتيبة و الدورة و الندوة و الزيارة و الرياضة و المدرسة و النادي الاجتماعي و ملتقى المرأة و محضن الناشئة و الناشئات و مكتب صنع القرار السياسي العملي و مركز توزيع صحفنا و مجلاتنا و كتيبنا و أشرطتنا السمعية و المرئية .

باختصار نقول : أننا نريد أن يصبح المركز الاسلامي « دار الدعوة » و « المركز العام » بالمضمون أولاً قبل الاسم ، و على قدر امتلاكنا و توجيهنا لهذه المراكز على مستوى القارة .. على قدر ما يمكننا القول أننا نسير بنجاح نحو توطين الدعوة في هذه البلاد .

أي أن يكون دور « المركز » كدور « المسجد » على عهد رسول الله صلى الله عليه و سلم عندما انطلق يباشر « توطين » الدعوة في عهدها الاول في المدينة المنورة . و من المسجد إستأنف الحياة الاسلامية و قدم للعالم أروع و أبهى حضارة عرفتها الإنسانية .

و هذا يحتّم أن تتحول -بعد حين- المنطقة و الشعبة و الأسرة الى « غرف عمليات » للتخطيط و التوجيه و المراقبة و القيادة للمركز الاسلامي ليكون مثلاً و نموذجاً يُحتذى .

١٨- اعتماد نظام يؤكد على ان « فرز » العاملين و « توزيع الأدوار و « تقليد » المناصب و المسئوليات يكون على أساس التخصص و الرغبة و العامة و بما يحقق عملية التوطين و يُسهم في إنجاحها .

١٩- تحويل مبدأ التفرغ لمسئولي المواقع الرئيسية في الجماعة الى قاعدة و أساس و سياسة في العمل . و بدونه قد تتعطل عملية التوطين [و الكلام حول هذا الموضوع يحتاج الى تفصيل و تأصيل [.

٢٠- ادراك أهمية النقلة « المؤسساتية » في عملنا الحركي . و الجهاد من أجل تحقيقها على أرض الواقع بما يخدم عملية التوطين و يعجّل نتائجه بأذن الله عزّ و جلّ :

إنّ سبب تأخير هذا البند على أهميته القصوى هو أنه يمثل سر و لب هذه المذكرة . و يمثل أيضا المظهر العملي و المعيار الحقيقي لنجاحنا أو إخفاقنا في سيرنا نحو هدف التوطين . و الحديث عن المؤسسات و العقلية أو الظاهرة « المؤسساتية » لا يحتاج منا الى تفصيل كثير . و يكفينا أن نقول أن أول رائد لهذه الظاهرة كان نبينا محمد صلى الله عليه و سلم اذ أنه وضع الأساس لأول مؤسسة حضارية و هي المسجد فكانت بحق « المؤسسة الشاملة » .. ثم هكذا كان فعل رائد الدعوة الاسلامية المعاصرة الامام الشهيد حسن البنا رحمه الله عندما أحسّ هو و إخوان بضرورة اعادة « تأسيس » الاسلام و حركته من جديد . فأقام المؤسسات بكل أنواعها : الاقتصادية و الاجتماعية و الاعلامية و الكشفية و المهنية و حتى العسكرية . و يجدر القول أننا في بلد لا يفهم الا لغة المؤسسات و لا يحترم و يحسب وزناً لأي مجموعة بدون مؤسسات فاعلة و مؤثرة و قوية .

239

(٨)

و من حسن الطالع أن بهتنا من إخواننا من صفوفنا بالقول و العمل من عنده هذه «النزعة» أو الطلبة أو الميل لإنشاء المؤسسات . مما يدفعنا الي القول بشجاعة و صراحة ـ كما قالها مرة ذات مرة السادات في مصر «نحن نريد أن نقيم دولة المؤسسات» ـ كلمة حق أراد بها الباطل . و أنا أقول لإخواني دعونا لرفع شعار الحق لإقامة الحق « نحن نريد أن نقيم جماعة المؤسسات » ، اذ ان بدونها لن نضع أقدامنا علي الطريق الصحيح .

ـ و من أجل أن تتم عملية التوطين لابد أن نخطط و نعمل من الآن علي تهيئة و اعداد أنفسنا و إخواننا و أجهزتنا و أقسامنا و لجاننا لكي تتحول الي مؤسسات شاملة بشكل متفرع و متوازن و متواكب مع الحاجة و الواقع . و الذي يشجعنا علي ذلك ـ بالاضافة الي الذي ذكر سابقاً ـ هو أننا نملك « أندية » لكل مؤسسة من المؤسسات التي تنادي بوجودها . [انظر الي الملحق رقم (١)] .

ـ«كل الذي نصاعبه هو أن تحكم ربطهم و كتشّل عملهم و نمتّع عناصرهم و نوحّد جهودهم مع غيرهم ثم نصلهم بالخطة الشاملة التي تسمى لها .

تعلى سبيل المثال :

عندما نواة لمؤسسة « اعلامية و فتية شاملة » : نملك مطبعة + جهاز صف حروف متطور + مركز سمعيات و بصريات + مكتب اخراج فني + مجلات و صحف بالعربية و الانكليزية [الآفاق و الأمل و السماسي و الي فلسطين و الملتقطات الصحفية و الزيتونة و الراصد الفلسطيني و مجلة العلوم الاجتماعية [...] + فرقة فنية + مصورين + مخرجين + مقدمي برامج + مصورين + بالاضافة الي خبرات اعلامية و فنية أخرى » .

مثال آخر :

عندما نواة لمؤسسة « دعوية تربوية شاملة » : عندنا قسم الدعوة الاسلامية في الاسنا + مؤسسة الدكتور جمال بدوي + المركز الذي يديره الأخ حامد الغزالي + مركز الدعوة الذي تسمى له لجنة الدعوة الآن و الاخ شاكر السيد + بالاضافة الي جهود دعوية هنا و هناك ... » .

و هكذا يمكن أن نقيس علي جميع المؤسسات التي تنادي بايجادها .

ـالتحدي الكبير الذي أمامنا هو أننا كيف تحمل من هذه الأندية أو العناصر « المبعثرة » مؤسسات شاملة مستقرة « متوطنة » مرتبطة بحركتنا و تدور في ذلك خطتنا و تأتمر بتوجيهنا . و لا يمنع ـ بل يفضي ـ أن يكون لكل مؤسسة مركزية لفروعها المحلية و لكن ارتباطها بالمركز الاسلامي في المدينة شرط .

ـالمطلوب : أن تسمى لتهيئة الأجواء و السبل لتحقيق « الاندماج » بحيث تكون الاقسام و اللجان و المناطق و الشعب و الاسر هي لب و جوهر المؤسسات ـ بعد حين ـ .

أي أن تحصل النقلة و التحول كما يلي :

(٩)

١- قسم التنظيم + قسم الامانة	- المؤسسة التنظيمية و الادارية - المركز العام
٢- قسم التربية + لجنة الدعوة	- المؤسسة الدعوية و التربوية
٣- قسم الاخوات	- المؤسسة النسوية
٤- قسم المال + لجنة الاستثمار + الوقف	- المؤسسة الاقتصادية
٥- قسم الناشئة + قسم المنظمات الشبابية	- المؤسسة الشبابية
٦- اللجنة الاجتماعية + لجنة الزواج + م. الرحمة	- المؤسسة الاجتماعية
٧- اللجنة الامنية	- المؤسسة الامنية
٨- القسم السياسي + لجنة فلسطين	- المؤسسة السياسية
٩- محكمة الجماعة + اللجنة القانونية	- المؤسسة القضائية
١٠- قسم العمل المحلي	- تتوزع أعماله على بقية المؤسسات
١١- مجلاتنا + المطبعة + فرقنا الفنية	- المؤسسة الاعلامية و الفنية
١٢- مؤسسة الدراسات + دار النشر + دار الكتاب	- المؤسسة الفكرية و الثقافية
١٣- الجمعيات العلمية و الطبية	- المؤسسة العلمية و التعليمية و المهنية
١٤- المؤتمر التنظيمي	- المؤتمر التأسيسي الاسلامي الامريكي
١٥- مجلس الشورى + لجنة التخطيط	- مجلس شورى الحركة الاسلامية الامريكية .
١٦- المكتب التنفيذي	- المكتب التنفيذي للحركة الاسلامية الامريكية
١٧- المسئول العام	- رئيس الحركة الاسلامية و الناطق الرسمي لها -
١٨- المناطق + الشعب + الاسر	- القيادات الميدانية للمؤسسات و المراكز الاسلامية،

خامساً : مؤسسات التوطين الشاملة :

- ثم نسعى و نجاهد من أجل أن تصبح كل مؤسسة من هذه المؤسسات المذكورة أعلاه « مؤسسة شاملة » على مدى الايام و السنين و ما قدّر لنا أن نكون في هذه الديار ..المهم يكفينا اعتزازاً أننا وضعنا اللبنات و يأتي من بعدنا أقوام و أجيال تكمل المسيرة و الطريق و لكن بهدي سابق واضح المعالم ،

و لكي يتضح القول بمقصدنا من المؤسسة الشاملة المتخصصة . نذكر هنا ملامح و مظاهر كل مؤسسة من المؤسسات « الواحدة » :

١- دعوياً و تربوياً [المؤسسة الدعوية و التربوية] : بحيث تشمل على :
- مؤسسة نشر الدعوة (مركزية و فروع محلية) .
- معهد لتخريج الدعاة و المربين .
- علماء و دعاة و مربين و مهجرين و ملدمي برامج .
- فنون و تقنية الاتصال و التبليغ و الدعوة .

(١٠)

-محطة تلفزيونية .
-مجلة دعوية متخصصة .
-محطة اذاعية .
-المجلس الاسلامي الاعلى للدعاة و المربين .
-المجلس الاعلى للمساجد و المراكز الاسلامية .
-جمعيات الصداقة مع الاديان الاخرى ... و ماشابه ذلك .

٢- سياسيا [المؤسسة السياسية] : بحيث تشمل على :
-حزب سياسي مركزي .
-مكاتب سياسية محلية .
-رموز سياسية .
-ملفات و تحالفات .
-المنظمة الامريكية للعمل السياسي الاسلامي .
-مراكز معلومات متطورة ... و ماشابه ذلك .

٢- اعلاميا [المؤسسة الاعلامية و الفنية] : بحيث تشمل على :
-جريدة يومية .
-مجلات اسبوعية شهرية و فصلية .
-اذاعات .
-برامج تلفزيونية .
-مركز سمعيات و بصريات .
-مجلة للطفل المسلم .
-مجلة للمرأة المسلمة .
-مطبعة و أجهزة صف حروف .
-مكتب اخراج .
-استديو تصوير و تسجيل .
-فرق فنية للتمثيل و الانشاد و المسرح .
-مكتب تسويق و انتاج فني ... و ماشابه ذلك .

(١١)

٤- اقتصاديا [المؤسسة الاقتصادية] : بحيث تشمل على :
- بنك اسلامي مركزي .
- اوقاف اسلامية .
- مشاريع استثمارية .
- مؤسسة للقروض الحسنة ... و ماشابه ذلك .

٥- علميا و مهنيا [المؤسسة العلمية و التعليمية و المهنية] : بحيث تشمل على :
- مراكز بحث علمي .
- معاهد تقنية و تدريب مهني .
- جامعة اسلامية .
- مدارس اسلامية .
- مهني للتعليم و البحث العلمي .
- مراكز لتدريب المعلمين .
- جمعيات علمية في المدارس .
- مكتب للتوجيه الاكاديمي .
- جهاز للتأليف و المناهج الاسلامية ... و ماشابه ذلك .

٦- ثقافيا و فكريا [المؤسسة الثقافية و الفكرية] : بحيث تشمل على :
- مراكز للدراسات و البحوث .
- منظمات ثقافية و فكرية مثال : [جمعية العلماء الاجتماعيين - جمعية العلماء و المهندسون ...] .
- معهد للفكر و الثقافة الاسلامية .
- دار نشر و ترجمة و توزيع للكتاب الاسلامي .
- مكتب للتدوين و التأريخ و التوثيق .
- مشروع ترجمة القرآن الكريم و الحديث الشريف ... و ماشابه ذلك .

٧- اجتماعيا [المؤسسة الاجتماعية الخيرية] : بحيث تشمل على :
- نوادي اجتماعية للشباب و ابناء و بنات الجاليات .
- جمعيات محلية للرعاية الاجتماعية و الخدمات مرتبطة بالمراكز الاسلامية .
- المنظمة الاسلامية لمكافحة الامراض الاجتماعية للمجتمع الامريكي .
- مشاريع المساكن الاسلامية .
- مكاتب الزواج و القضايا العائلية ... و ما شابه ذلك .

(١٢)

٨- شبابيا [المؤسسة الشبابية] : بحيث تشمل على :

-منظمات شبابية مركزية و محلية .

-فرق و نوادي رياضية .

-فرق كشفية ... و ماشابه ذلك .

٩- نسويا [المؤسسة النسوية] : بحيث تشمل على :

-جمعيات نسوية مركزية و محلية .

-معاهد التدريب و التشغيل الفني و التدبير المنزلي .

-معهد لتدريب الداعيات .

-دور الحضانة الاسلامية ... و ماشابه ذلك .

١٠- تنظيميا و اداريا [المؤسسة الادارية و التنظيمية] : بحيث تشمل على :

-معهد للتدريب و التنمية و التطوير و التخطيط .

-خبراء بارزين في هذا المجال .

-أنظمة عمل و لوائح و دساتير تصلح لادارة اغلب الاجهزة و المؤسسات .

-مجلة دورية في التنمية و الادارة الاسلامية .

-امتلاك مخيمات و قاعات للانشطة المختلفة .

-بنك للمعلومات و الحصر و الاحصاء البشري .

-شبكة اتصالات متطورة .

-أرشيف متطور لتراثنا و انتاجنا ... و ما شابه ذلك .

١١- أمنيا : [المؤسسة الامنية] : بحيث تشمل على :

-نوادي للتدريب و تعلم وسائل الدفاع عن النفس .

-مركز يعتني بالشؤون الامنية [فنها و فكريا و تقنيا و بشريا] ... و ماشابه ذلك .

١٢- قانونيا : [المؤسسة القانونية] : بحيث تشمل على :

-مجلس فقهي مركزي .

-محكمة اسلامية مركزية .

-جمعية المحامين المسلمين .

-المنظمة الاسلامية للدفاع عن حقوق المسلمين ... و ما شابه ذلك .

و الله ولي التوفيق

الملحق رقم (٢) :

قائمة بمؤسساتنا و مؤسسات أصدقائنا

[تخيل لو أنها كلها تسير وفق خطة واحدة !!!]

1- ISNA = ISLAMIC SOCIETY OF NORTH AMERICA
2- MSA = MUSLIM STUDENTS' ASSOCIATION
3- MCA = THE MUSLIM COMMUNITIES ASSOCIATION
4- AMSS = THE ASSOCIATION OF MUSLIM SOCIAL SCIENTISTS
5- AMSE = THE ASSOCIATION OF MUSLIM SCIENTISTS AND ENGINEERS
6- IMA = ISLAMIC MEDICAL ASSOCIATION

7- ITC = ISLAMIC TEACHING CENTER
8- NAIT = NORTH AMERICAN ISLAMIC TRUST
9- FID = FOUNDATION FOR INTERNATIONAL DEVELOMENT
10-IHC = ISLAMIC HOUSING COOPERATIVE
11-ICD = ISLAMIC CENTERS DIVISION
12-ATP = AMERICAN TRUST PUBLICATIONS
13-AVC = AUDIO-VISUAL CENTER
14-IBS = ISLAMIC BOOK SERVICE
15-MBA = MUSLIM BUSINESSMEN ASSOCIATION
16-MYNA = MUSLIM YOUTH OF NORTH AMERICA
17-IFC = ISNA FIQH COMMITTEE
18-IPAC = ISNA POLITICAL AWARENESS COMMITTEE
19-IED = ISLAMIC EDUCATION DEPARTMENT

20-MAYA = MUSLIM ARAB YOUTH ASSOCIATION
21-MISG = MALASIAN ISLAMIC STUDY GROUP
22-IAP = ISLAMIC ASSOCIATION FOR PALESTINE
23-UASR = UNITED ASSOCIATION FOR STUDIES AND RESEARCH
24-OLF = OCCUPIED LAND FUND
25-MIA = MERCEY INTERNATIONAL ASSOCIATION

26-ICNA = ISLAMIC CIRCLE OF NORTH AMERICA
27-BMI = BAITUL MAL INC
28-IIIT = INTERNATIONAL INSTITUTE FOR ISLAMIC THOUGHT
29-IIC = ISLAMIC INFORMATION CENTER

Bate #ISE-SW/ 1B10/ 0000413

In the name of God, the Beneficent, the Merciful
Thanks be to God, Lord of the Two Worlds,
Prayers and peace be upon the master of the Messengers

An Explanatory Memorandum
On the General Strategic Goal for the Group
In North America
5/22/1991

Contents:

1- An introduction in explanation
2- The Concept of Settlement
3- The Process of Settlement
4- Comprehensive Settlement Organizations

Page 2 of 18

Bate #ISE-SW/ 1B10/ 0000414

In the name of God, the Beneficent, the Merciful
Thanks be to God, Lord of the Two Worlds
And Blessed are the Pious

5/22/1991

The beloved brother/The General Masul, may God keep him
The beloved brother/Secretary of the Shura Council, may God keep him
The beloved brothers/Members of the Shura Council, may God keep them
God's peace, mercy and blessings be upon you.... To proceed,

I ask Almighty God that you, your families and those whom you love around you are in the best of conditions, pleasing to God, glorified His name be.
I send this letter of mine to you hoping that it would seize your attention and receive your good care as you are the people of responsibility and those to whom trust is given. Between your hands is an "Explanatory Memorandum" which I put effort in writing down so that it is not locked in the chest and the mind, and so that I can share with you a portion of the responsibility in leading the Group in this country.
What might have encouraged me to submit the memorandum in this time in particular is my feeling of a "glimpse of hope" and the beginning of good tidings which bring the good news that we have embarked on a new stage of Islamic activism stages in this continent.
The papers which are between your hands are not abundant extravagance, imaginations or hallucinations which passed in the mind of one of your brothers, but they are rather hopes, ambitions and challenges that I hope that you share some or most of which with me. I do not claim their infallibility or absolute correctness, but they are an attempt which requires study, outlook, detailing and rooting from you.
My request to my brothers is to read the memorandum and to write what they wanted of comments and corrections, keeping in mind that what is between your hands is not strange or a new submission without a root, but rather an attempt to interpret and explain some of what came in the long-term plan which we approved and adopted in our council and our conference in the year (1987).
So, my honorable brother, do not rush to throw these papers away due to your many occupations and worries. All what I'm asking of you is to read them and to comment on them hoping that we might continue together the project of our plan and our Islamic work in this part of the world. Should you do that, I would be thankful and grateful to you.
I also ask my honorable brother, the Secretary of the Council, to add the subject of the memorandum on the Council agenda in its coming meeting.

May God reward you good and keep you for His Daw'a.

Your brother/Mohamed Akram

Page 3 of 18

Bate #ISE-SW/ 1B18/ 0000415

(1)

In the name of God, the Beneficent, the Merciful
Thanks be to God, Lord of the Two Worlds
And Blessed are the Pious

Subject: A project for an explanatory memorandum for the General Strategic goal
for the Group in North America mentioned in the long-term plan

One: The Memorandum is derived from:

1- The general strategic goal of the Group in America which was approved by the Shura Council
and the Organizational Conference for the year [1987] is "Enablement of Islam in North
America, meaning: establishing an effective and a stable Islamic Movement led by the Muslim
Brotherhood which adopts Muslims' causes domestically and globally, and which works to
expand the observant Muslim base, aims at unifying and directing Muslims' efforts, presents
Islam as a civilization alternative, and supports the global Islamic State wherever it is".

2- The priority that is approved by the Shura Council for the work of the Group in its current and
former session which is "Settlement".

3- The positive development with the brothers in the Islamic Circle in an attempt to reach a unity
of merger.

4- The constant need for thinking and future planning, an attempt to read it and working to
"shape" the present to comply and suit the needs and challenges of the future.

5- The paper of his eminence, the General Masul, may God keep him, which he recently sent to
the members of the Council.

Two: An Introduction to the Explanatory Memorandum:

- In order to begin with the explanation, we must "summon" the following question and place it
in front of our eyes as its relationship is important and necessary with the strategic goal and the
explanation project we are embarking on. The question we are facing is: "How do you like to see
the Islam Movement in North America in ten years?", or "taking along" the following sentence
when planning and working, "Islamic Work in North America in the year (2000): A Strategic
Vision".

Also, we must summon and take along "elements" of the general strategic goal of the Group in
North America and I will intentionally repeat them in numbers. They are:

[1- Establishing an effective and stable Islamic Movement led by the Muslim Brotherhood.

2- Adopting Muslims' causes domestically and globally.

3- Expanding the observant Muslim base.

4- Unifying and directing Muslims' efforts.

Page 4 of 18

248

Bate #ISE-SW 1B10/ 0000416

(2)

5- Presenting Islam as a civilization alternative
6- Supporting the establishment of the global Islamic State wherever it is].

- It must be stressed that it has become clear and emphatically known that all is in agreement that we must "settle" or "enable" Islam and its Movement in this part of the world.
- Therefore, a joint understanding of the meaning of settlement or enablement must be adopted, through which and on whose basis we explain the general strategic goal with its six elements for the Group in North America.

Three: The Concept of Settlement:
This term was mentioned in the Group's "dictionary" and documents with various meanings in spite of the fact that everyone meant one thing with it. We believe that the understanding of the essence is the same and we will attempt here to give the word and its "meanings" a practical explanation with a practical Movement tone, and not a philosophical linguistic explanation, while stressing that this explanation of ours is not complete until our explanation of "the process" of settlement itself is understood which is mentioned in the following paragraph. We briefly say the following:

Settlement: "That Islam and its Movement become a part of the homeland it lives in".
Establishment: "That Islam turns into firmly-rooted organizations on whose bases civilization, structure and testimony are built".
Stability: "That Islam is stable in the land on which its people move".
Enablement: "That Islam is enabled within the souls, minds and the lives of the people of the country in which it moves".
Rooting: "That Islam is resident and not a passing thing, or rooted "entrenched" in the soil of the spot where it moves and not a strange plant to it".

Four: The Process of Settlement:
- In order for Islam and its Movement to become "a part of the homeland" in which it lives, "stable" in its land, "rooted" in the spirits and minds of its people, "enabled" in the live of its society and has firmly-established "organizations" on which the Islamic structure is built and with which the testimony of civilization is achieved, the Movement must plan and struggle to obtain "the keys" and the tools of this process in carry out this grand mission as a "Civilization Jihadist" responsibility which lies on the shoulders of Muslims and - on top of them - the Muslim Brotherhood in this country. Among these keys and tools are the following:

1- Adopting the concept of settlement and understanding its practical meanings:
The Explanatory Memorandum focused on the Movement and the realistic dimension of the process of settlement and its practical meanings without paying attention to the difference in understanding between the resident and the non-resident, or who is the settled and the non-settled

Page 5 of 18

249

Bate #ISE-SW 1B10/ 0000417

(3)

and we believe that what was mentioned in the long-term plan in that regards suffices.

2- Making a fundamental shift in our thinking and mentality in order to suit the challenges of the settlement mission.
What is meant with the shift - which is a positive expression - is responding to the grand challenges of the settlement issues. We believe that any transforming response begins with the method of thinking and its center, the brain, first. In order to clarify what is meant with the shift as a key to qualify us to enter the field of settlement, we say very briefly that the following must be accomplished:
- A shift from the partial thinking mentality to the comprehensive thinking mentality.
- A shift from the "amputated" partial thinking mentality to the "continuous" comprehensive mentality.
- A shift from the mentality of caution and reservation to the mentality of risk and controlled liberation.
- A shift from the mentality of the elite Movement to the mentality of the popular Movement.
- A shift from the mentality of preaching and guidance to the mentality of building and testimony
- A shift from the single opinion mentality to the multiple opinion mentality.
- A shift from the collision mentality to the absorption mentality.
- A shift from the individual mentality to the team mentality.
- A shift from the anticipation mentality to the initiative mentality.
- A shift from the hesitation mentality to the decisiveness mentality.
- A shift from the principles mentality to the programs mentality.
- A shift from the abstract ideas mentality the true organizations mentality [This is the core point and the essence of the memorandum].

3- Understanding the historical stages in which the Islamic Ikhwani activism went through in this country:
The writer of the memorandum believes that understanding and comprehending the historical stages of the Islamic activism which was led and being led by the Muslim Brotherhood in this continent is a very important key in working towards settlement, through which the Group observes its march, the direction of its movement and the curves and turns of its road. We will suffice here with mentioning the title for each of these stages [The title expresses the prevalent characteristic of the stage] [Details maybe mentioned in another future study]. Most likely, the stages are:
A- The stage of searching for self and determining the identity.
B- The stage of inner build-up and tightening the organization.
C- The stage of mosques and the Islamic centers.
D- The stage of building the Islamic organizations - the first phase.
E- The stage of building the Islamic schools - the first phase.

Page 6 of 18

Bate #ISE-SW 1B10/ 0000418

(4)

F- The stage of thinking about the overt Islamic Movement - the first phase.
G- The stage of openness to the other Islamic movements and attempting to reach a formula for dealing with them - the first phase.
H- The stage of reviving and establishing the Islamic organizations - the second phase.
We believe that the Group is embarking on this stage in its second phase as it has to open the door and enter as it did the first time.

4- Understanding the role of the Muslim Brother in North America:

The process of settlement is a "Civilization-Jihadist Process" with all the word means. The Ikhwan must understand that their work in America is a kind of grand Jihad in eliminating and destroying the Western civilization from within and "sabotaging" its miserable house by their hands and the hands of the believers so that it is eliminated and God's religion is made victorious over all other religions. Without this level of understanding, we are not up to this challenge and have not prepared ourselves for Jihad yet. It is a Muslim's destiny to perform Jihad and work wherever he is and wherever he lands until the final hour comes, and there is no escape from that destiny except for those who chose to slack. But, would the slackers and the Mujahedeen be equal.

5- Understanding that we cannot perform the settlement mission by ourselves or away from people:

A mission as significant and as huge as the settlement mission needs magnificent and exhausting efforts. With their capabilities, human, financial and scientific resources, the Ikhwan will not be able to carry out this mission alone or away from people and he who believes that is wrong, and God knows best. As for the role of the Ikhwan, it is the initiative, pioneering, leadership, raising the banner and pushing people in that direction. They are then to work to employ, direct and unify Muslims' efforts and powers for this process. In order to do that, we must possess a mastery of the art of "coalitions", the art of "absorption" and the principles of "cooperation".

6- The necessity of achieving a union and balanced gradual merger between private work and public work:

We believe that what was written about this subject is many and is enough. But, it needs a time and a practical frame so that what is needed is achieved in a gradual and a balanced way that is compatible with the process of settlement.

Page 7 of 18

Bate #ISE-SW 1B10/ 0000418 (Cont'd)

7- The conviction that the success of the settlement of Islam and its Movement in this country is a success to the global Islamic Movement and a true support for the sought-after state, God willing:
There is a conviction - with which this memorandum disagrees - that our focus in attempting to settle Islam in this country will lead to negligence in our duty towards the global Islamic Movement in supporting its project to establish the state. We believe that the reply is in two segments: One - The success of the Movement in America in establishing an observant Islamic base with power and effectiveness will be the best support and aid to the global Movement project.

Bate #ISE-SW 1B10/ 0000419

(5)

And the second - is the global Movement has not succeeded yet in "distributing roles" to its branches, stating what is the needed from them as one of the participants or contributors to the project to establish the global Islamic state. The day this happens, the children of the American Ikhwani branch will have far-reaching impact and positions that make the ancestors proud.

8- Absorbing Muslims and winning them with all of their factions and colors in America and Canada for the settlement project, and making it their cause, future and the basis of their Islamic life in this part of the world:
This issues requires from us to learn "the art of dealing with the others", as people are different and people in many colors. We need to adopt the principle which says, "Take from people... the best they have", their best specializations, experiences, arts, energies and abilities. By people here we mean those within or without the ranks of individuals and organizations. The policy of "taking" should be with what achieves the strategic goal and the settlement process. But the big challenge in front of us is: how to connect them all in "the orbit" of our plan and "the circle" of our Movement in order to achieve "the core" of our interest. To me, there is no choice for us other than alliance and mutual understanding of those who desire from our religion and those who agree from our belief in work. And the U.S. Islamic arena is full of those waiting...., the pioneers.
What matters is bringing people to the level of comprehension of the challenge that is facing us as Muslims in this country, conviction of our settlement project, and understanding the benefit of agreement, cooperation and alliance. At that time, if we ask for money, a lot of it would come, and if we ask for men, they would come in lines. What matters is that our plan is "the criterion and the balance" in our relationship with others.
Here, two points must be noted; the first one: we need to comprehend and understand the balance of the Islamic powers in the U.S. arena [and this might be the subject of a future study]. The second point: what we reached with the brothers in "ICNA" is considered a step in the right direction, the beginning of good and the first drop that requires growing and guidance.

Page 8 of 18

Bate #**ISE-SW 1B10/ 0000419** (Cont'd)

9- Re-examining our organizational and administrative bodies, the type of leadership and the method of selecting it with what suits the challenges of the settlement mission:
The memorandum will be silent about details regarding this item even though it is logical and there is a lot to be said about it.

10- Growing and developing our resources and capabilities, our financial and human resources with what suits the magnitude of the grand mission:
If we examined the human and the financial resources the Ikhwan alone own in this country, we and others would feel proud and glorious. And if we add to them the resources of our friends and allies, those who circle in our orbit and those waiting on our banner, we would realize that we are able to open the door to settlement and walk through it seeking to make Almighty God's word the highest.

Bate #ISE-SW 1B10/ 0000420

(6)

11- Utilizing the scientific method in planning, thinking and preparation of studies needed for the process of settlement:
Yes, we need this method, and we need many studies which aid in this civilization Jihadist operation. We will mention some of them briefly:
- The history of the Islamic presence in America.
- The history of the Islamic Ikhwani presence in America.
- Islamic movements, organizations and organizations: analysis and criticism.
- The phenomenon of the Islamic centers and schools: challenges, needs and statistics.
- Islamic minorities.
- Muslim and Arab communities.
- The U.S. society: make-up and politics.
- The U.S. society's view of Islam and Muslims... And many other studies which we can direct our brothers and allies to prepare, either through their academic studies or through their educational centers or organizational tasking. What is important is that we start.

12- Agreeing on a flexible, balanced and a clear "mechanism" to implement the process of settlement within a specific, gradual and balanced "time frame" that is in-line with the demands and challenges of the process of settlement.
13- Understanding the U.S. society from its different aspects an understanding that "qualifies" us to perform the mission of settling our Dawa' in its country "and growing it" on its land.
14- Adopting a written "jurisprudence" that includes legal and movement bases, principles, policies and interpretations which are suitable for the needs and challenges of the process of settlement.
15- Agreeing on "criteria" and balances to be a sort of "antennas" or "the watch tower" in order to make sure that all of our priorities, plans, programs, bodies, leadership, monies and activities march towards the process of the settlement.
16- Adopting a practical, flexible formula through which our central work complements our domestic work.
[Items 12 through 16 will be detailed later].

17- Understanding the role and the nature of work of "The Islamic Center" in every city with what achieves the goal of the process of settlement:
The center we seek is the one which constitutes the "axis" of our Movement, the "perimeter" of the circle of our work, our "balance center", the "base" for our rise and our "Dar al-Arqam" to educate us, prepare us and supply our battalions in addition to being the "niche" of our prayers.

Page 10 of 18

Bate #ISE-SW 1B10/ 0000421

(7)

This is in order for the Islamic center to turn - in action not in words - into a seed "for a small Islamic society" which is a reflection and a mirror to our central organizations. The center ought to turn into a "beehive" which produces sweet honey. Thus, the Islamic center would turn into a place for study, family, battalion, course, seminar, visit, sport, school, social club, women gathering, kindergarten for male and female youngsters, the office of the domestic political resolution, and the center for distributing our newspapers, magazines, books and our audio and visual tapes.

In brief we say: we would like for the Islamic center to become "The House of Dawa'" and "the general center" in deeds first before name. As much as we own and direct these centers at the continent level, we can say we are marching successfully towards the settlement of Dawa' in this country.

Meaning that the "center's" role should be the same as the "mosque's" role during the time of God's prophet, God's prayers and peace be upon him, when he marched to "settle" the Dawa' in its first generation in Madina. from the mosque, he drew the Islamic life and provided to the world the most magnificent and fabulous civilization humanity knew.

This mandates that, eventually, the region, the branch and the Usra turn into "operations rooms" for planning, direction, monitoring and leadership for the Islamic center in order to be a role model to be followed.

18- Adopting a system that is based on "selecting" workers, "role distribution" and "assigning" positions and responsibilities is based on specialization, desire and need with what achieves the process of settlement and contributes to its success.

19- Turning the principle of dedication for the Masuls of main positions within the Group into a rule, a basis and a policy in work. Without it, the process of settlement might be stalled [Talking about this point requires more details and discussion].

20- Understanding the importance of the "Organizational" shift in our Movement work, and doing Jihad in order to achieve it in the real world with what serves the process of settlement and expedites its results, God Almighty's willing:

The reason this paragraph was delayed is to stress its utmost importance as it constitutes the heart and the core of this memorandum. It also constitutes the practical aspect and the true measure of our success or failure in our march towards settlement. The talk about the organizations and the "organizational" mentality or phenomenon does not require much details. It suffices to say that the first pioneer of this phenomenon was our prophet Mohamed, God's peace, mercy and blessings be upon him, as he placed the foundation for the first civilized organization which is the mosque, which truly became "the comprehensive organization". And this was done by the pioneer of the contemporary Islamic Dawa', Imam martyr Hasan al-Banna, may God have mercy on him, when he and his brothers felt the need to "re-establish" Islam and its movement anew, leading him to establish organizations with all their kinds: economic, social, media, scouting,

Page 11 of 18

Bate #ISE-SW 1B10/ 0000421 (Cont'd)

professional and even the military ones. We must say that we are in a country which understands no language other than the language of the organizations, and one which does not respect or give weight to any group without effective, functional and strong organizations.

Bate #ISE-SW 1B10/ 0000422

(8)

It is good fortune that there are brothers among us who have this "trend", mentality or inclination to build the organizations who have beat us by action and words which leads us to dare say honestly what Sadat in Egypt once said, "We want to build a country of organizations" - a word of right he meant wrong with. I say to my brothers, let us raise the banner of truth to establish right "We want to establish the Group of organizations", as without it we will not able to put our feet on the true path.

- And in order for the process of settlement to be completed, we must plan and work from now to equip and prepare ourselves, our brothers, our apparatuses, our sections and our committees in order to turn into comprehensive organizations in a gradual and balanced way that is suitable with the need and the reality. What encourages us to do that - in addition to the aforementioned - is that we possess "seeds" for each organization from the organization we call for [See attachment number (1)].

- All we need is to tweak them, coordinate their work, collect their elements and merge their efforts with others and then connect them with the comprehensive plan we seek.
For instance,
We have a seed for a "comprehensive media and art" organization: we own a print + advanced typesetting machine + audio and visual center + art production office + magazines in Arabic and English [The Horizons, The Hope, The Politicians, Ila Falastine, Press Clips, al-Zaytouna, Palestine Monitor, Social Sciences Magazines...] + art band + photographers + producers + programs anchors + journalists + in addition to other media and art experiences".
Another example:
We have a seed for a "comprehensive Dawa' educational" organization: We have the Daw'a section in ISNA + Dr. Jamal Badawi Foundation + the center run by brother Hamed al-Ghazali + the Dawa' center the Dawa' Committee and brother Shaker al-Sayyed are seeking to establish now + in addition to other Daw'a efforts here and there...".
And this applies to all the organizations we call on establishing.

- The big challenge that is ahead of us is how to turn these seeds or "scattered" elements into comprehensive, stable, "settled" organizations that are connected with our Movement and which fly in our orbit and take orders from our guidance. This does not prevent - but calls for - each central organization to have its local branches but its connection with the Islamic center in the city is a must.

Page 12 of 18

Bate #ISE-SW 1B10/ 0000422 (Cont'd)

- What is needed is to seek to prepare the atmosphere and the means to achieve "the merger" so that the sections, the committees, the regions, the branches and the Usras are eventually the heart and the core of these organizations.

Or, for the shift and the change to occur as follows:

Page 13 of 18

257

Bate #ISE-SW 1B10/ 0000423

(9)

1- The Movement Department + The Secretariat Department	- The Organizational & Administrative Organization - The General Center
2- Education Department + Dawa'a Com.	- Dawa' and Educational Organization
3- Sisters Department	- The Women's Organization
4- The Financial Department + Investment Committee + The Endowment	- The Economic Organization
5- Youth Department + Youths Organizations Department	- Youth Organizations
6- The Social Committee + Matrimony Committee + Mercy Foundation	- The Social Organization
7- The Security Committee	- The Security Organization
8- The Political Depart. + Palestine Com.	- The Political Organization
9- The Group's Court + The Legal Com.	- The Judicial Organization
10- Domestic Work Department	- Its work is to be distributed to the rest of the organizations
11- Our magazines + the print + our art band	- The Media and Art Organization
12- The Studies Association + The Publication House + Dar al-Kitab	- The Intellectual & Cultural Organization
13- Scientific and Medial societies	- Scientific, Educational & Professional Organization
14- The Organizational Conference	- The Islamic-American Founding Conference
15- The Shura Council + Planning Com.	- The Shura Council for the Islamic-American Movement
16- The Executive Office	- The Executive Office of the Islamic-American Movement
17- The General Masul	- Chairman of the Islamic Movement and its official Spokesman
18- The regions, branches & Usras	- Field leaders of organizations & Islamic centers

Five: Comprehensive Settlement Organization:

- We would then seek and struggle in order to make each one of these above-mentioned organizations a "comprehensive organization" throughout the days and the years, and as long as we are destined to be in this country. What is important is that we put the foundation and we will be followed by peoples and generations that would finish the march and the road but with a clearly-defined guidance.

Page 14 of 18

Bate #**ISE-SW 1B10/ 0000423** (Cont'd)

And, in order for us to clarify what we mean with the comprehensive, specialized organization, we mention here the characteristics and traits of each organization of the "promising" organizations.

1- From the Dawa' and educational aspect [The Dawa' and Educational Organization]: to include:
- The Organization to spread the Dawa' (Central and local branches).
- An institute to graduate Callers and Educators.
- Scholars, Callers, Educators, Preachers and Program Anchors.
- Art and communication technology, Conveyance and Dawa'.

Bate #**ISE-SW 1B10/ 0000424**

(10)

- A television station.
- A specialized Dawa' magazine.
- A radio station.
- The Higher Islamic Council for Callers and Educators.
- The Higher Council for Mosques and Islamic Centers.
- Friendship Societies with the other religions... and things like that.

2- Politically [The Political Organization]: to include:
- A central political party.
- Local political offices.
- Political symbols.
- Relationships and alliances.
- The American Organization for Islamic Political Action
- Advanced Information Centers....and things like that.

3- Media [The Media and Art Organization]: to include:
- A daily newspaper.
- Weekly, monthly and seasonal magazines.
- Radio stations.
- Television programs.
- Audio and visual centers.
- A magazine for the Muslim child.
- A magazine for the Muslim woman.
- A print and typesetting machines.
- A production office.
- A photography and recording studio
- Art bands for acting, chanting and theater.
- A marketing and art production office... and things like that.

Page 15 of 18

Bate #ISE-SW 1B10/ 0000425

(11)

4- Economically [The Economic Organization]: to include:
- An Islamic Central bank.
- Islamic endowments.
- Investment projects.
- An organization for interest-free loans.... and things like that.

5- Scientifically and Professionally [The Scientific, Educational and Professional Organization]: to include:
- Scientific research centers.
- Technical organizations and vocational training.
- An Islamic university.
- Islamic schools.
- A council for education and scientific research.
- Centers to train teachers.
- Scientific societies in schools.
- An office for academic guidance.
- A body for authorship and Islamic curricula.... and things like that.

6- Culturally and Intellectually [The Cultural and Intellectual Organization]: to include:
- A center for studies and research.
- Cultural and intellectual foundations such as [The Social Scientists Society - Scientists and Engineers Society....].
- An organization for Islamic thought and culture.
- A publication, translation and distribution house for Islamic books.
- An office for archiving, history and authentication
- The project to translate the Noble Quran, the Noble Sayings....and things like that.

7- Socially [The Social-Charitable Organization]: to include:
- Social clubs for the youths and the community's sons and daughters
- Local societies for social welfare and the services are tied to the Islamic centers
- The Islamic Organization to Combat the Social Ills of the U.S. Society
- Islamic houses project
- Matrimony and family cases office....and things like that.

Page 16 of 18

Bate #ISE-SW 1B10/ 0000426

(12)

8- Youths [The Youth Organization]: to include:
- Central and local youths foundations.
- Sports teams and clubs
- Scouting teams....and things like that.

9- Women [The Women Organization]: to include:
- Central and local women societies.
- Organizations of training, vocational and housekeeping.
- An organization to train female preachers.
- Islamic kindergartens...and things like that.

10- Organizationally and Administratively [The Administrative and Organizational Organization]: to include:
- An institute for training, growth, development and planning
- Prominent experts in this field
- Work systems, bylaws and charters fit for running the most complicated bodies and organizations
- A periodic magazine in Islamic development and administration.
- Owning camps and halls for the various activities.
- A data, polling and census bank.
- An advanced communication network.
- An advanced archive for our heritage and production.... and things like that.

11- Security [The Security Organization]: to include:
- Clubs for training and learning self-defense techniques.
- A center which is concerned with the security issues [Technical, intellectual, technological and human].....and things like that.

12- Legally [The Legal Organization]: to include:
- A Central Jurisprudence Council.
- A Central Islamic Court.
- Muslim Attorneys Society.
- The Islamic Foundation for Defense of Muslims' Rights...and things like that.

And success is by God.

Page 17 of 18

Bate #ISE-SW 1B10/ 0000427

Attachment number (1)

A list of our organizations and the organizations of our friends
[Imagine if t they all march according to one plan!!!]

1- ISNA   = ISLAMIC SOCIETY OF NORTH AMERICA
2- MSA   = MUSLIM STUDENTS' ASSOCIATION
3- MCA   = THE MUSLIM COMMUNITIES ASSOCIATION
4- AMSS   = THE ASSOCIATION OF MUSLIM SOCIAL SCIENTISTS
5- AMSE   = THE ASSOCIATION OF MUSLIM SCIENTISTS AND ENGINEERS
6- IMA   = ISLAMIC MEDICAL ASSOCIATION

7- ITC =   ISLAMIC TEACHING CENTER
8- NAIT   = NORTH AMERICAN ISLAMIC TRUST
9- FID   = FOUNDATION FOR INTERNATIONAL DEVELOPMENT
10- IHC   = ISLAMIC HOUSING COOPERATIVE
11- ICD   = ISLAMIC CENTERS DIVISION
12- ATP   = AMERICAN TRUST PUBLICATIONS
13- AVC   = AUDIO-VISUAL CENTER
14- IBS   = ISLAMIC BOOK SERVICE
15- MBA   = MUSLIM BUSINESSMEN ASSOCIATION
16- MYNA   = MUSLIM YOUTH OF NORTH AMERICA
17- IFC   = ISNA FIQH COMMITTEE
18- IPAC   = ISNA POLITICAL AWARENESS COMMITTEE
19- IED   = ISLAMIC EDUCATION DEPARTMENT

20- MAYA   = MUSLIM ARAB YOUTH ASSOCIATION
21- MISG   = MALASIAN [sic] ISLAMIC STUDY GROUP
22- IAP   = ISLAMIC ASSOCIATION FOR PALESTINE
23- UASR   = UNITED ASSOCIATION FOR STUDIES AND RESEARCH
24- OLF   = OCCUPIED LAND FUND
25- MIA   = MERCY INTERNATIONAL ASSOCIATION

26- ISNA   = ISLAMIC CIRCLE OF NORTH AMERICA
27- BMI   = BAITUL MAL INC
28- IIIT   = INTERNATIONAL INSTITUTE FOR ISLAMIC THOUGHT
29- IIC   = ISLAMIC INFORMATION CENTER

Page 18 of 18

GLOSSARY

Note: Arabic words transliterated into English may be spelled in a variety of ways. For example, words beginning with "j" may be spelled "dj" and some words beginning with "z" may also be spelled with "dh" at the beginning. The presence or absence of a final letter "h" is another common variation.

abaya	Arab outer garment for women, a loose robe covering the whole body apart from the face, feet and hands. Called a *chador* in Iran
abrogation	see *naskh*
ahadith	see *hadith*
ahl al-kitab	"people of the book"; Christians and Jews (as opposed to Muslims or pagan polytheists)
alim	see *ulama*
amir	commander, leader, prince
ayatollah	"sign of God"; in Shi'a Islam an honorary title for the highest ranking jurists/scholars
Al-Azhar	the oldest, most authoritative and prestigious university of Sunni Islamic studies, based in Cairo
baraka	blessings and good spiritual influences sent by God, which are believed to surround the burial places of faithful Muslims (saints)
Barelwis	a strand of South Asian Islam which is very traditional and has an emphasis on Sufism, folk Islam and Muhammad veneration. The majority of South Asian Muslims in the UK are Barelwis
batini	inner, esoteric, hidden, secret

bay al-salam	payment in advance for deferred delivery of a commodity
bay al-sarf	rules on the exchange of money for money
bay bithamin ajil (BBA)	
	sale of goods on deferred payment basis, similar to *murabaha* but with the payment on a deferred basis
bil saif	*jihad* by force
burqa	Afghan outer garment for women, a loose robe with covers the whole body and face, with a mesh grille over the eyes
caliph	(*khalifa*) literally "successor" or "deputy"/ vicegerent to Muhammad and therefore the spiritual and political leader of the whole Muslim community
caliphate	(*khilafa*) "vicegerency"; the office of the caliph
chador	Iranian outer garment for women, a long loose robe covering the whole body apart from the face, feet and hands
Chishti	a Sufi order, particularly strong in the Indian subcontinent; emphasis on devotional music, dancing and mysticism
Dajjal	*al-masih ad-dajjal:* the Antichrist, pseudo-Messiah
Dar al-Harb	the House of War, where non-Muslims rule
Dar al-Islam	the House of Islam, territory under Muslim political dominion
Dar al-Kufr	the House of Unbelief (another name for *Dar al-Harb*)
darul uloom	seminary
darura	necessity
da'wa	the call or invitation to true Islam, Muslim mission to convert others to Islam
Deobandi	radical Islamic movement, very influential in South Asia and Afghanistan. Rejects all Western influences and seeks to return to classical Islam. In recent years has become militant
dhikr	see *zikr*

dhimmi	Jews, Christians and Sabeans living under an Islamic government. See pages 190–191 for details of the regulations for *dhimmi*
fard	obligatory acts, divinely commanded in the Qur'an, fulfilment of which is rewarded and neglect of which is punished; divided into individual duties (*fard 'ayn*) and collective duties (*fard kifayah*)
Fatimids	Isma'ili dynasty based in Cairo, ruling from 969 to 1171
fatwa	a religious or juridical opinion pronounced by a recognised authority (e.g. Ayatollah Khomeini on the killing of Salman Rushdie) usually written and published
fay	war booty (including land) gained without fighting
fiqh	Islamic jurisprudence, the science of applying Islamic law (*shari'a*)
fitna	sedition, strife, the breakdown of law and order, which is evil and must be subdued
Fivers	Zaydis
Folk Islam	popular Islam, with an emphasis on the supernatural, incorporating local pre-Islamic superstitions and customs
hadd	(pl. *hudud*) a punishment for a crime "against religion" whose punishment has been specified in the Qur'an (e.g. amputation for theft)
hadith	(pl. *ahadith*) a tradition which records the sayings and deeds of Muhammad (*sunna*). The *ahadith* are reports of the *sunna*. There are various collections of these traditions, some of which are considered more reliable and authoritative than others
haj	pilgrimage to Mecca
hakimiyya	God's rightful sovereignty and rule
halal	that which is permitted by Islamic law
Hanafi	a Sunni school of *shari'a*, founded by Imam abu Hanifa (died 767)
Hanbali	a Sunni school of *shari'a*, founded by Imam Ahmad ibn Hanbal (died 855)

haq mehr	financial settlements in marriage
haram	acts which are forbidden and punishable according to Islamic law (c.f. *makruh, mubah*)
hawza	a traditional Shi'a religious college for training Islamic scholars and jurists
hijab	"curtain" or "partition"; refers to the veil between God and man but has come to mean the seclusion or separation of women; practised in different ways in different countries. (In many countries women wear a scarf called the *hijab*, which covers the hair and neck.)
hijra	literally "migration". Primarily used of Muhammad's flight from Mecca to Medina on 20 June 622. This was the turning point in Muhammad's career; marks the beginning of the Muslim era and calendar. It is also used of an earlier migration of Muslims from Mecca to Abyssinia and in general of the migration of Muslims from an enemy land to a secure place for religious causes.
hudud	see *hadd*
Ibadi	see under Khariji
ijara	a leasing agreement, whereby the bank buys an item for a customer and then leases it back over a specific period
ijara-wa-iqtina	like *ijara*, except that the customer is able to buy the item at the end of the contract
ijma'	consensus; specifically, in Islamic Law, the unanimous consensus of the learned (c.f. *qiyas*)
ijtihad	a striving to understand and apply the Qur'an and *sunna* to situations not addressed in the sources
ilhad	heresy
'ilm	authoritative knowledge; encompasses all four sources of authority, knowledge of which is considered true guidance
imam	in Sunni Islam, the prayer leader and teacher in a mosque; in Shi'a Islam, the supreme ruler of the

	Muslim community (equivalent to the caliph in Sunni Islam)
Imamites	See Twelvers
iman	faith; defined as the belief of the heart and the confession of the lips of the truth of the Muslim religion
irtidad	apostasy from Islam
islahi	reformist. Used for example of a reformed type of Salafism established in 1995–1996 which rejected the use of violence and espoused peaceful oppostion to secular Muslim regimes.
Isma'ilis	a Shi'a sect, found today mainly in India, Pakistan, Syria and Yemen. Also called "Seveners" because they recognise seven Imams of the hours of 'Ali.
isnad	"supporting" – the transmissional chain, usually the first part of a *hadith,* containing the names of the persons responsible for handing down the tradition
istisna	payment in advance for goods that are manufactured and delivered at a later date
Ja'fari	Twelver Shi'a Islamic law
jahiliyya	the state of pagan ignorance and immorality in pre-Islamic Arabian society
jihad	literally "striving". The term has a variety of interpretations including (1) spiritual struggle for moral purity (2) trying to correct wrong and support right by voice and actions (3) military war against non-Muslims with the aim of spreading Islam. *Jihad* is regarded as one of the fundamentals of Islam.[467]
jilbab	loose, ankle-length coat or robe covering the entire body except hands, feet and head, worn by Arabs
jinn	a spirit created by Allah from fire. Some are good, but many are evil.
jizya	a humiliating poll-tax collected from the *dhimmi*
julus	a Sufi procession

ka'ba	the central sacred cube-shaped shrine in the great mosque at Mecca; centre of Muslim pilgrimage and the direction in which Muslims face in prayer
kafir	(pl. *kuffar*), infidel, one who does not believe in the Islamic articles of faith. This is a term of gross insult.
Khaibar	an oasis about 100km from Medina, which at the time of Muhammad was populated by Jewish tribes
khalifa	see caliph
Khalwati	a Sufi order which gained prominence in the Ottoman Empire and is now mainly found in Turkey and the Middle East
khanit	caste-like group of men who dress as women in Oman
kharaj	a tax, often used to mean specifically a land tax paid by non-Muslim residents of Islamic lands. It was imposed in addition to *jizya*.
Khariji	literally "seceders". A puritanical sect of Islam with a highly developed doctrine of sin. Sinners were considered apostates. The sect began in 657 as a result of disputes over the succession to the caliphate, and continued to rebel against the caliphate for two centuries. They survive today in a more moderate variant, the Ibadis.
khilafa	see caliphate
khimar (kumar)	woman's headdress consisting of a circle of fabric with a whole cut for the face, usually reaches to the waist
khutba	the sermon at Friday prayers
kuffar	see *kafir*
kufr	unbelief (c.f. *kafir*)
madhab	a school of Islamic law
madrassa	literally "school"; used in Islam to mean an Islamic religious school where pupils are taught mainly Islamic subjects

mahdi	the rightly guided one; the coming saviour who will establish Islam in all the earth filling it with justice
makruh	acts disapproved of but not forbidden or punishable in Islamic law (c.f. *haram, mubah*)
Maliki	a Sunni school of *shari'a*, founded by Imam Malik ibn Anas (died 795)
Maslaha	public good
mazar	shrine where a Sufi saint or *pir* is buried
millet	the system of classifying and organising religious minorities as separate and semi-autonomous communities in the Ottoman Empire
mubah	acts which are permissible, but neither rewarded nor punished in Islamic law (c.f. *haram, makruh*)
mudaraba	a specialist investment by a financial expert in which the bank and the customer share any profits
muezzin	the one who gives the call to prayer from the mosque
mufassala	separation, i.e. from unbelievers and *jahiliyya*
mufti	a Sunni scholar who is an interpreter and expounder of *shari'a*, one who is authorised to issue *fatwas*
muhajirun	the Muslims who moved from Mecca to Medina with Muhammad
mujahid	(pl. *mujahidin*) fighter engaged in *jihad*
mujtahid	senior Islamic scholar; person who engages in *ijtihad,* a mental striving to understand and correctly apply the Qur'an.
mullah	religious/mosque leader in countries from Iran eastwards, equivalent to *imam* in Arab countries
murabaha	sale at an agreed mark up over seller's costs
murid	the pupil of a *murshid, sheikh* or *pir* in Sufi Islam; expected to be docile, submissive and teachable before his guide
murshid	an alternative word for *pir*
musharaka	an investment partnership in which profit sharing terms are agreed in advance and losses re-pegged to the amount invested (similar to private equity)

mustergil	a life-long female-to-male cross-dresser in southern Iraq
Naqshbandi	a Sufi order, especially strong in Central Asia
naskh	abrogation (cancellation) of verses in the Qur'an. The normal rule is that verses revealed later in time abrogate contradictory verses on the same subject revealed earlier.
neo-Salafism	a confusing term used by different writers to convey very different meanings. As well as denoting the contemporary Salafi-Jihadi trend, it is also used to describe the Wahhabi-influenced modern Salafism as distinct from the older Egyptian-influenced Salafism of the the early to mid-twentieth century.
neo-Wahhabism	Salafism, (a more strict and puritanical movement than Wahhabism)
niqab	woman's opaque veil covering at least the lower half of the face. If it covers the whole face there is a usually a slit for the eyes.
OIC	Organisation of the Islamic Conference, an international body to which Muslim countries belong
PBUH	abbreviation for "Peace Be Upon Him", often inserted after name of Muhammad in English writings to show respect
pir	spiritual guide in Sufi orders (also *sheikh* or *murshid*)
PLO	Palestine Liberation Organisation
purdah	the general seclusion and segregation of women as practised particularly in Afghanistan and Pakistan, including the complete covering of the face and body when out in public
qadi	judge appointed by a ruler on the basis of his superior knowledge of Islamic Law, whose decisions are binding and final
Qadiri	the oldest Sufi order, very widespread

qibla	the direction of prayer, initially towards Jerusalem, later changed to Mecca
qiyas	analogical legal reasoning by a *mujtahid*. It is one of the four sources of the *shari'a,* alongside the Qur'an, *sunna,* and *ijma'.*
Quraish	the Arab tribe to which Muhammad and the first Muslims belonged
Ramadan	the name of the month in the Islamic calendar during which Muslims are obliged to fast from sunrise to sunset
rasul	apostle, messenger
riba	financial gain forbidden in the Qur'an. Some Muslims understand *riba* to be **extortionate** interest, others to mean **any** kind of interest.
ribat	strengthening the frontiers of Islam; a type of defensive *jihad*
salaf	pious ancestors
Salafism	also called *Salafiyya.* A movement for reform and revival calling for a return to the Qur'an and *sunna* and to the example of the first pious Muslims, the *salaf.* Salafis consider themselves to practise a purer form of Islam than Wahhabis do.
SAS or SAW	abbreviation for the Arabic phrase *sala Allah 'alayhi wa sallam* (God prayed over him and gave him peace), often inserted after name of Muhammad in English writings to show respect.
salat	ritual daily prayer five times a day; one of the obligatory "pillars" of Islam
sawm	general term for fasting in Islam, encompassing both the obligatory fast of Ramadan as well as other fasts
Seveners	Isma'ilis
Shadhili	a Sufi order, predominant in North Africa, which has given rise to many suborders
Shafi'i	a Sunni school of *shari'a,* founded by Imam Muhammad bin Idris ash Shafi'i (died 820)

271

shahada	the Muslim creed: "There is no god but Allah, and Muhammad is his messenger." Also called *kalimatu shahada*
shahid	literally a witness; used for a martyr, one who loses their life in God's cause
shalwar kameez	loose trousers and tunic as worn in Pakistan
shari'a	Islamic law
sheikh	literally "old man" or "elder"; this title has a range of different meanings. It can be given to heads of religious orders, Quranic scholars, jurists, those who preach and lead prayers in the mosque, and to Sufi saints. It is also used for a village elder or tribal chief.
Shi'a	the second largest branch in Islam comprising 10–20% of all Muslims; support the claim of 'Ali and his descendants to the leadership of the entire Muslim community
shirk	literally "association"; polytheism, idolatry; pagan association of other deities with Allah. This is the most serious sin in Islam.
shura	the principle of mutual consultation for the right guidance of the *umma*
Sufism	the mystical movement in Islam; permeates all branches and sects
Sufiya	Sufi spiritual leaders
sunna	"path", "way" or "manner of life"; the actions, words and way of life of Muhammad as the supreme model for Muslims to follow. (c.f. *hadith*)
Sunnis	followers of the main branch of Islam comprising some 80% of all Muslims worldwide
sura	a chapter of the Qur'an
takaful	Islamic insurance based on pooling resources to help the needy
takbir	the phrase *Allahu Akbar* (Allah is most great) that opens Muslim prayer

takfir	the legal declaration of a Muslim individual, community or institution as apostate and infidel, worthy of death, justifying *jihad* against them
taliban	students in *madrassas*. Also the movement that arose in *madrassas* in the North West Frontier Province of Pakistan composed of such students who went on to conquer and rule most of Afghanistan from 1996 until 2001
taqiyya	the practice of dissimulation in times of danger; the concealing of one's true beliefs when in danger. A doctrine which is very strong in Shi'a Islam but also present in Sunni Islam.
taqlid	blind imitation in legal interpretation; unquestioning acceptance of authority of main leaders of the schools of law
tariqa	a Sufi order or brotherhood
tawhid	unity, oneness; basic doctrine of Islam declaring the absolute oneness of Allah, which is also the essence of the *shahada*
tazkiya	purification (of an individual's life and soul); also a recommendation given by the Muslim World League
Twelvers	also called Imamites. The largest subdivision of Shi'a Islam; they recognise twelve Imams of the house of 'Ali
ulama, ulema	(sing. *alim*), learned men; scholars and religious authorities in Sunni Islam
umma	the community or nation of Islam; composed of all Muslims worldwide; the People of Allah, a nation with its basis in religious confession.
'urf	local custom accepted as Islamic law when not contradicting *shari'a*
Wahhabism	strictly puritanical form of Sunni Islam, predominant in Saudi Arabia. (c.f. neo-Wahhabism and Salafism)
waqf	a religious endowment, often a building or plot of land for religious purposes

wa'z mahfil	religious conferences
zakat	the obligatory legal alms due from every Muslim in proportion to their wealth and property; one of the obligatory pillars of Islam. The beneficiaries are the poor in the Muslim community. According to the glossary in the *Noble Qur'an* (Hilali and Khan's version), it is seen as "the major economic means for establishing social justice and leading the Muslim society to prosperity and security". The Qur'an defines the beneficiaries of Muslim charitable giving in 9:60 as follows:

> As-Sadaqat (here it means *Zakat*) are only for the *Fuqara'* (poor), and *Al-Masakin* (the poor) and those employed to collect (the funds); and to attract the hearts of those who have been inclined (towards Islam); and to free the captives; and for those in debt; and for Allah's Cause (i.e. for *Mujahidun* – those fighting in holy battle), and for the wayfarer (a traveller who is cut off from everything); a duty imposed by Allah. And Allah is All-Knower, All-Wise. [Explanatory text in brackets is added by the editors of this version.][468]

zawiya	a North African term for a small mosque or place or prayer, in particular a meeting place for Sufis, usually with some residential accommodation
Zaydis	Shi'a sect which ruled Yemen for many centuries. Also called Fivers because they recognise five Imams of the house of 'Ali
zikr	an act of devotion in Sufi Islam; the discipline of recollection; meditative repetition of certain Islamic formula with the aim of achieving a trance-like state of union with Allah

BIBLIOGRAPHY

Abbas, Tahir, "Muslims in Britain after 7/7: the problem of the few", *openDemocracy,* 14 December 2005, http://www.opendemocracy. net/conflict-terrorism/muslims_3120.jsp, viewed 14 August 2007.

"Abu Hamza faces extradition to US after arrest", *TIMES ONLINE,* 27 May 2004.

Adil, Abdul, "Muslims dismayed at Blunkett comments", *The Muslim News,* Issue 175, 28 November 2003.

El-Affendi, Abdelwahab, "Hizb al-Tahrir: the paradox of a very British party", *The Daily Star,* 2 September 2003, http://web.archive. org/web/20030904172117/ http://www.dailystar.com.lb/opinion/02_09_03_c.asp, viewed 8 August 2007.

Ahmad, Khurshid, *Economic Development in an Islamic Framework* (Leicester: The Islamic Foundation, 1979).

——, "Implementation of Shari'a", *Tarjiman Al Quran,* October 1998, www.jamaat.prg/Isharat/1998/1098.html, viewed 23 August 2005.

——, "Israel, Pakistan and the Muslim World", *Tarjuman Al Quran,* September 2003, http://www.jamaat.org/Isharat/ish0903.html, viewed 9 September 2005.

——, *Lectures on Economics: An Introductory Course* (Karachi: Institute of Chartered Accounts, 1968).

——, "Man and the Future of Civilization: An Islamic Perspective", *Tarjuman Al Quran,* April 2002, www.jamaat.org/Isharat/ ish0402.html, viewed 9 September 2005.

——, "Musharraf, Taliban and Implementation of Shariah Bill in NWFP", *Tarjuman Al Quran,* July 2003, www.jamaat.org/Isharat/ ish0703.html, viewed 23 August 2005.

——, "Muslim Ummah at the Threshold of 21st Century", *Tarjuman Al Quran*, November 1997, http://www.jamaat.org/world/twentyfirst.html, viewed 9 September 2005.

——, *Towards Monetary and Fiscal System of Islam* (Islamabad: Institute of Policy Studies, 1981).

Ahmed, Khaled, "How Islam Is Used By Us", *The Daily Times*, 5 December 2003, http://www.mail-archive.com/sacw@insaf.net/msg00060.html, viewed 8 August 2007.

——, "Reassertion of the Barelwis in Pakistan", *The Friday Times*, 8 September 2000.

Ajami, Fuad, "Tariq Ramadan", *The Wall Street Journal*, 7 September 2004.

Alam, Fareena, "A Humane Muslim Future", *openDemocracy*, 8 March 2005, http://www.opendemocracy.net/faith-europe_islam/article_2363.jsp, viewed 7 August 2007.

——, "Five principles for Islam's future", *openDemocracy*, 8 March 2005, http://www.opendemocracy.net/faith-europe_islam/article_2363.jsp, viewed 24 August 2005.

Alexiev, Alex, "Tablighi Jamaat: Jihad's Stealthy Legions", *Middle East Quarterly*, Vol. XII, No. 1, Winter 2005.

Alibhai-Brown, Yasmin "Revealed the brutal truth that hides inside the Burqa", *The Evening Standard*, 30 November 2005.

Ali, Farkhunda, "American Muslim Military Participation in the War Clarified by American Muslim Scholars", 11 October 2001, http://www.icgt.org/SpecialArticles/MuslimsInMilitary.htm, viewed 6 August 2007.

Ali, Muhammad Mumtaz, *The Muslim Community in Britain: An Historical Account* (Malaysia: Pelanduk Publications, 1996).

"Al-Qaradhawi Speaks in Favor of Suicide Operations at an Islamic Conference in Sweden", MEMRI, *Special Dispatch Series*, No. 542, 24 July 2004.

Al-Sharq Al-Awsat (19 July 2003), extracts in English translation in MEMRI, *Special Dispatch Series*, No. 542, 24 July 2003.

Amer, Mohammed, "Dressing up for your Shaikh: the Minhajul Quran Movement in London" in *Muslim Religious Authority in Western Europe*, International Institute for the Study of Modern Islam (ISIM), Leiden, 30 September–1 October 2005.

Amiel, Barbara, "Muslims have just as much to fear from militant Islam", *The Daily Telegraph*, 24 November 2003.

Annual Report and Financial Statements, 31 December 2006, Islamic Bank of Britain, http://www.islamic-bank.com/imagesupload/ IBBAnnualReport2006.pdf, viewed 12 October 2007.

Ansari, Humanyun, *Muslims in Britain*, Minorities Group International, 2002.

Antisemitic Incidents Report 2006 (London: The Community Security Trust, 2007).

"Antisemitism and Racism", Annual Reports, Country Reports United Kingdom 2005, The Stephen Roth Institute for the Study of Contemporary Antisemitism and Racism, Tel Aviv University, http://www.tau.ac.il/Anti-Semitism/asw2005/uk.htm, viewed 30 August 2007.

"Antisemitism Worldwide 2002/3", http://www.tau.ac.il/Anti-Semitism/asw2002-3/uk.htm, viewed 10 October 2005.

"A question of leadership", transcript, *Panorama*, BBC1, 21 August 2005, http://news.bbc.co.uk/1/hi/programmes/panorama/4171950. stm, viewed 6 August 2007.

Attewill, Fred, "Met orders review after Muslim refuses to guard Israeli embassy", *The Guardian*, 5 October 2006.

"Attitudes to Living in Britain: A Survey of Muslim Opinion", Growth for Knowledge (GfK) NOP Social Research, *Dispatches*, TV Channel 4, 24 April 2006, http://www.imaginate.uk.com/ MCC01_SURVEY/Site%20Download.pdf, viewed 13 August 2007.

'Azzam, Abdullah, *Defence of the Muslim Lands* (London: Ahle Sunnah Wal Jama'at, no date).

——, *Join the Caravan* (London: Azzam Publications, 1996).

Badawi, Zaki, *Islam in Britain* (London: Taha Publishers, 1981).

——, "The Concept of Jihad in Islam", transcript from recording, Council on Christian Approaches to Defence and Disarmament, Westminster Abbey, 18 April 1996.

Baker, Mike, "Why the U-turn on faith schools?" *BBC News*, 4 November 2006.

Baldwin, Tom, "Blair faces wrath of Britain's Muslims", *The Times*, 19 September 2002.

Bale, Joanna, "Killed for loving the wrong man", *The Times*, 15 July 2006.

Banglawala, Inayat, "A malicious campaign", *The Guardian*, 18 July 2007.

al-Banna, Hassan, *Five Tracts of Hasan al-Banna (1906-1949): A Selection from the Majmu'at Rasa'il al-Imam al-Shahid*, (Berkeley, California: University of California Press, 1978).

——, *Selected Writings of Hasan al-Banna Shaheed*, transl. S.A. Qureshi (New Delhi: Militant Book Centre, 1999).

Bashier, Zakaria, "A Model for Islamization", *The Muslim*, August–November 1977, text of a talk delivered at the FOSIS 14th Annual Summer Conference, http://www.salaam.co.uk/knowledge/model.php, viewed 7 August 2007.

Birt, Yahya, "Being a Real Man in Islam: Drugs, Criminality and the Problem of Masculinity", revised June 2001, http://www.islamfortoday.com/birt01.htm, viewed 14 December 2003.

Blackburn, Chris, "Jamaat-i-Islami: A threat to Bangladesh?", http://www.secularvoiceofbangladesh.org/Jamaat%20i%20Islami%20%20A%20threat%20to%20Bangladesh%20by%20Chris%20Blackburn.htm, viewed 8 January 2007.

"BMF Objectives" http://www.bmf.eu.com/bmf_obj.php, viewed 8 August 2007.

Bodi, Faisal, "Islamophobia should be as unacceptable as racism", *The Guardian*, 12 January 2004.

Bone, James, "Islam's troublemaker", *The Times*, 27 April 2004.

Brandon, James and Murray, Douglas, *How British libraries encourage Islamic extremism*, (London: Centre for Social Cohesion, 2007).

Bright, Martin, "Radical links of UK's Moderate Muslim Group", *The Guardian*, 14 August 2005.

"Britain grapples with 'honour killing' practice", *Christian Science Monitor*, 19 October 2005.

"British Muslims want Islamic law", *Hindustan Times*, 30 November 2004.

Browne, Anthony, "Time for truth about this sinister brotherhood", *The Times*, 11 August 2004.

Burke, Jason, "Muslim fights to make three wives legal", *The Observer*, 20 February 2000.

Butt, Hassam, "My plea to fellow Muslims: you must renounce terror", *The Observer,* 1 July 2007.

Caeiro, Alexander, "European Islam and Tariq Ramadan", *ISIM Newsletter,* No. 14, June 2004.

Cameron, David, "What I learnt from my stay with a Muslim family", *The Observer,* 13 May 2007.

Campbell, Duncan, "Pakistan says al-Qaida link to plot found", *The Guardian,* 17 August 2006.

Carlile, Jennifer, "Gay and 'passionate about Islam' ", *MSNBC.com,* 6 July 2006, http://www.msnbc.msn.com/id/13712248/, viewed 7 August 2007.

Casciani, Dominic, "Bin Laden is seen as a hero", *BBC News,* 4 August 2005.

——, "Minister backs new Muslim group", *BBC News,* 19 July 2006.

"Change foreign policy – top Muslims", *The Evening Standard,* 22 July 2005.

"Cleric guilty of spreading hate", *BBC News,* 24 February 2003.

Coleman, Clive, "There is a stealthy rise of Sharia courts in Britain", *The Times,* 2 December 2006.

"Conquered Land", *Encyclopaedia of Islam,* CD-ROM Edition v. 1.0, © 1999 Koninklijke Brill NV, Leiden, The Netherlands.

"Cousin accused of bride murder", *BBC News,* 6 October 2003.

Cowan, Rosie, "Most senior al-Qaida terrorist yet captured in Britain gets 40 years for plotting carnage", *The Guardian,* 8 November 2006.

Crompton, Louis, *Homosexuality and Civilization* (Cambridge, Massachusetts: Harvard University Press, 2003).

Cronem, David Garbin, "Bangladeshi diaspora in the UK: some observations on socio-cultural dynamics, religious trends and transnational politics" (draft version, June 2005), Surrey University, prepared for the Conference on Human Rights and Bangladesh, School of Oriental and African Studies, University of London, 17 June 2005.

Cummins, Will, "We must be allowed to criticise Islam", *The Daily Telegraph,* 11 July 2004.

Damrel, David, "A Sufi Apocalypse", *ISIM Newsletter,* 4 December 1999.

Darwish, Adel, "Obituary: Sheikh Abdul Aziz bin Baz", *The Independent*, 14 May 1999.

"Death before dishonour", *The Observer Magazine*, 21 November 2004.

"Debate over Female Circumcision in Egypt", MEMRI, *Special Dispatch Series*, No. 42, 3 August 1999.

Dhillon, Hardeep, "Islamic Finance Moving into the Mainstream", *Credit*, November 2005.

Dhondy, Farrukh, "Institutional inspiration", *The Guardian*, 2 July 2002.

Donohue, J.J. and Esposito, J.L. *Islam in Transition: Muslim Perspectives* (New York: Oxford University Press, 1982).

Dovkants, Keith, "Muslim extremists step up resistance", *This is London*, 22 January 2003.

Downer, Alexander, "Terrorism: Our Common Struggle", Speech to the Executive Council of Australian Jewry, Melbourne, 27 November 2006, http://www.foreignminister.gov.au/speeches/2006/061127_terrorism.html, viewed 7 August 2007.

Esposito, John L., ed., *Oxford Encyclopedia of the Modern Islamic World*, Vol. 2 (New York: Oxford University Press, 1995).

Farah, Douglas, "Hezbollah's External Support Network in West Africa and Latin America", International Assessment and Strategy Centre, 4 August 2006, http://www.strategycenter.net/research/pubID.118/pub_detail.asp#, viewed 17 January 2007.

al-Faruqi, Isma'il Raji, *Islam* (Brentwood, Maryland: International Graphics, 1984).

al-Faruqi, Lois Lamya', "Islamic Traditions and the Feminist Movement: Confrontation or Cooperation?", *Jannah.org*, http://www.jannah.org/sisters/feminism.html, viewed 30 August 2005.

Faruqi, M.H. "The promise of Turabi's release", *Impact International*, Vol. 33, Issue 10, October 2003.

"Fatwa for 'gay Jesus' writer", *BBC News*, 29 October 1999.

Ford, Richard, "Jail imams vetted by security services and Muslim books screened for code", *The Times*, 26 February 2007.

Frean, Alexandra, "Summer camps for children 'could stop racial segregation' ", *The Times*, 23 September 2005.

From dawa to jihad: The various threats from radical Islam to the democratic legal order, Ministry of the Interior and Kingdom Relations (The Hague: General Intelligence and Security Service, December 2004).

Garland, Sarah, "Cleric Turns Against Al Qaeda", *The New York Sun*, 18 September 2007.

General Intelligence and Security Service, Annual Report 2003, http://www.fas.org/irp/world/netherlands/aivd2003-eng.pdf, viewed 8 August 8, 2007.

"General Issues of Faith From the Fundamentals of the Salafee Creed", transl. and annotated by Dr Abu Ameenah Bilal Philips, http://www.bilalphilips.com/bilal_pages.php?option=com_content &task=view&id=289, viewed 17 October 2007.

Gerholm, Thomas, "Two Muslim intellectuals in the postmodern West: Akbar Ahmed and Ziauddin Sardar" in *Islam, Globalization and Postmodernity*, eds. Akbar Ahmed and Hastings Donnan (London and New York: Routledge, 1994).

"Giant mosque for 40,000 may be built at London Olympics", *The Sunday Times*, 27 November 2005.

Gillan, Audrey, "Hizbut-Tahrir, little known", *The Guardian*, 19 June 2002.

Gledhill, Ruth, Sulaiman, Tosin and Woolcock, Nicola, "Muslims shocked by anti-British protest at mosque", *The Times*, 3 April 2004, http://www.timesonline.co.uk/tol/news/uk/article1055208.ece, viewed 14 August 2007.

Glees, Anthony and Pope, Chris, *When Students Turn to Terror: Terrorist and Extremist Activity on British Campuses* (London: The Social Affairs Unit, 2005).

Godson, Dean, "They know the extent of our reach", *The Spectator*, 5 May 2007.

Goto, Shihoko, "Terror crackdown won't stop Muslim giving", 12 September 2004, http://www.islamdaily.net/EN/Contents.aspx?AID=1673, viewed 7 August 2005.

Grare, Frederic, *Political Islam in the Indian Subcontinent: The Jamaat-i-Islami* (New Dehli: Manohar, 2001).

Greaves, Ron, "Cult, Charisma, Community: The Arrival of Sufi Pirs and Their Impact on Muslims in Britain" *Journal of Muslim Minority Affairs*, Vol. 16, No. 2, July 1996.

——, "The Reproduction of Jamaat-i Islami in Britain", *Islam and Christian-Muslim Relations,* Vol. 6, No. 2, 1995.

——, *The Sufis of Britain: An Exploration of Muslim Identity* (Cardiff: Cardiff Academic Press, 2000).

Gresch, Alain, "Saudi Arabia: reality check", *Le Monde diplomatique,* February 2006.

Haddad, Yvonne Y., "Sayyid Qutb: Ideologue of Islamic Revival" in *Voices of Resurgent Islam,* ed. John Esposito (New York: Oxford University Press, 1983).

——, "The Quranic Justification for an Islamic Revolution: The View of Sayyid Qutb" in *Middle East Journal,* Vol. 37, No. 1, Winter 1983.

Al-Halawani, Ali and Mohammad, Hany, "Scholars Launch Pan-Muslim Body in London", http://www.islamonline.net/English/News/2004-07/12/article01.shtml, viewed 9 August 2007.

"Hamza was betrayed by trusted lieutenant", *TIMES ONLINE,* 30 May 2004.

Harrison, David, "Media 'contributing to rise of Islamophobia' ", *The Sunday Telegraph,* 10 September 2006.

Hauser, Albrecht, *Germany's Future – an Islamic Republic? Islam's Challenge to Church and Society in Germany and Europe*, paper presented at a conference at the Center for Lutheran Theology and Public Life, Concordia Seminary, St Louis, USA, 12 October 2007.

Helm, Toby, "Jews and Freemasons controlled war on Iraq, says No 10 adviser", *The Daily Telegraph,* 12 September 2005.

"Hezbollah", Anti-Defamation League, 29 September 2006, http://www.adl.org/main_Terrorism/hezbollah_overview.htm?Multi_page_sections=sHeading_7, viewed 17 January 2007.

"Hezbollah, Profile of the Lebanese Shiite Terrorist Organization of Global Reach Sponsored by Iran and Supported by Syria", Intelligence and Terrorism Information Center at the Center for Special Studies, http://www.terrorism-info.org.il/malam_multimedia/ENGLISH/IRAN/PDF/JUNE_03.PDF, viewed 17 January 2007 or http://www.terrorisminfo.org.il/malam_multimedia/English/eng_n/html/hezbollah.htm, viewed 9 August 2007.

al-Hilali, Muhammad Taqi-ud-Din and Khan, Muhammad Muhsin, *Interpretation of the Meanings of the Noble Qur'an*. 15th edition (Riyadh: Darussalam, December 1996).

How Europe's Muslims See Themselves at Home and in the World: Findings from Surveys in Britain, France, Germany, Spain and the Netherlands, February–June 2005. Office of Research, U.S. Department of State.

Huntington, Samuel P., *The Clash of Civilisations and the Remaking of the World Order* (New York: Simon and Schuster, 1996).

Husain, Ed, *The Islamist* (London: Penguin Books, 2007).

Hussain, Delwar, "Bangladeshis in east London: from secular politics to Islam", *openDemocracy*, 7 July 2006.

Hussain, Imtiaz Ahmed, "Migration and Settlement: A Historical Perspective of Loyalty and Belonging" in *British Muslims: Loyalty and Belonging*, Proceedings of a seminar held on 8 May 2002, eds. Mohammad Siddique Seddon, Dilwar Hussain and Nadeem Malik (Markfield: The Islamic Foundation, 2003).

Hussain, Zahid, Tendler, Stewart and McGrory, Daniel, "Al-Qaeda's 'British chief' is seized in police raids", *The Times*, 5 August 2004.

Ibn Rushd, *The Distinguished Jurist's Primer: Bidayat al-Mujtahid*, Vol. 1, transl. Imran Ahsan Nyazee (Reading: Garnet, 1994).

Ibn Sallam, *The Book of Revenue (Kitab al-Amwal)*, transl. Imran Ahsan Khan Nyazee (Reading: Garnet, 2002).

Ibn Taymiyya, Taqi al-Din Ahmad, *Majmu'at al-Fatawa li-Sheikh al-Islam Taqi al-Din Ahmad Bin Taymiyya al-Hurani*, (al-Mansourah: dar al-wafa' wal nashr wal tawzi', 1997). [English transl. Yeor, Bat, *Islam and Dhimitude: Where Civilizations Collide* (Madison, Teaneck: Farleigh Dickinson University Press and Lancaster, UK: Gazelle Book Services, 2002)].

"IHRC Advisors", *IHRC Newsletter*, Vol. 6, Issue Ramadan 1426/ October 2005, http://www.ihrc.org.uk/file/IHRC-Issue%206-2005-LOW%20RES.pdf, viewed 10 October 2005.

"Interview with Sheik Muhammad Sayyid Tantawi, Grand Imam of al-Azhar", *Almsarif Alkuwaitia (The Kuwaiti Banks)*, 1 October 2007.

"Interview with Vali Nasr", *Frontline*, http://www.pbs.org/wgbh/pages/frontline/shows/saudi/interviews/nasr.html, viewed 14 February 2007.

Iqbal, Muzaffar, "Making sense of a non-sense!", *Impact International,* Vol. 33, Issue 4, April 2003.

——, "The clash of civilisations!", *Impact International,* Vol. 33, Issue 8, August 2003.

——, "The road to freedom", *Impact International,* Vol. 33, Issue 6&7, June–July 2003.

——, "Welcome to the new empire!", *Impact International,* Vol. 33, Issue 5, May 2003.

Irfan, Ahmad, "Reporting at Camp David", *Impact International,* Vol. 33, Issue 6&7, June–July 2003.

Islam and Truth, Joint publication of Barnabas Fund and the Institute for the Study of Islam and Christianity, 2007.

"Islam Awareness Week", BBC, http://www.bbc.co.uk/religion/religions/islam/living/islamawarenessweek_1.shtml, viewed 12 October 2007.

"Islam Channel programme 'The Agenda' and Yvonne Ridley", MCB Statement, 22 June 2005, http://www.mcb.org.uk/article_detail.php?article=announcement-459, viewed 7 August 2007.

"Islamic agencies play vital role in fighting poverty – Thomas", DFID, http://www.dfid.gov.uk/news/files/pressreleases/pr-islamicagencies.asp, viewed 12 October 2005.

"Islamic Extremism In Europe", Hearing before the Subcommittee on Europe and Emerging Threats of the Committee on International Relations, US House of Representatives, One Hundred Ninth Congress, First Session, 27 April 2005, Serial No. 109–34. http://internationalrelations.house.gov/archives/109/20917.PDF, viewed 9 August 2007.

"Islamic House of Britain plc obtains FSA approval to become the first Islamic retail bank to open in any Western country", 9 August 2004, http://www.nortonrose.com/news/pre3107/news7491.aspx, viewed 9 August 2007.

"Islamic Seminaries are a problem, says Siddiqui", Press Release, The Muslim Parliament of Great Britain, 7 September 2007, http://www.muslimparliament.org.uk/seminaries.html, viewed 4 October 2007.

Islam in Britain: The British Muslim Community in February 2005, Institute for the Study of Islam and Christianity (Pewsey, Wiltshire: Isaac Publishing, 2005).

"Islamists highly active in Britain, says report", *The Peninsula On-Line,* 4 February 2007, http://www.thepeninsulaqatar.com/Display_news.asp?section=world_news&month=april2007&file=world_news2007040284144.xml, viewed 14 August 2007.

"I was a fanatic . . . I know their thinking, says former radical Islamist", *Daily Mail,* 1 July 2007.

"Jamaat-e-Islami's fatal isolationism", editorial, *Daily Times,* 8 August 2005.

Jan, Abid Ullah, "Islam, Faith and Power", *The Muslim Weekly,* 8 July 2005.

Jenkins, Philip, "Nor Shall My Sword Rest in my Hand", *Chronicles Magazine,* March 2002.

Johnson, Boris, "The Shabina Begum case never had anything to do with modesty", *The Daily Telegraph,* 23 March 2006.

Johnstone, Philip, "Radical Muslim loses his appeal against detention", *The Daily Telegraph,* 28 January 2004.

"Kano: Nigeria's ancient city-state", *BBC News,* 20 May 2004.

Katz, Rita and Kern, Michael, "Center of the Jihadist World", *National Review,* 14 July 2005.

Kelso, Paul and Vasagar, Jeevan, "Muslims reject image of separate society", *The Guardian,* 17 June 2002.

Kepel, Gilles, *Allah in the West: Islamic Movements in America and Europe* (Stanford, California: Stanford University Press, 1997).

——, *The War for Muslim Minds: Islam and the West* (Cambridge, Massachusetts and London: Belknap Press of Harvard University Press, 2004).

Kettani, M. Ali, "The Problems of Muslim Minorities and their Solutions" in *Muslim Communities in Non-Muslim States* (London: Islamic Council of Europe, 1980).

Khadduri, Majid, *War and Peace in the Law of Islam* (Baltimore: Johns Hopkins Press, 1955).

Khan, Timur, *Islam & Mammon: The Economic Predicaments of Islamism* (Princeton, NJ: Princeton University Press, 2004).

Khan, Yasmin, "Beyond the Bogeyman", *The Guardian,* 7 July 2006.

Khwaja, Maruf, "Terrorism, Islam, reform: thinking the unthinkable", *openDemocracy,* 28 July 2005, http://www.opendemocracy.net/conflict-terrorism/reform_2706.jsp, viewed 7 August.

Kite, Melissa and Hennessy, Patrick, "State seeks control of Muslim schools", *The Daily Telegraph*, 7 August 2005.

Kristianasen, Wendy, "Britain's multiculturalism falters", *Le Monde diplomatique,* November 2006.

Laffin, John, *The Dagger of Islam* (London: Sphere Books, 1979).

Laurence, Jonathan, "Managing Transnational Islam in Western Europe: The Limits of Institutional and Postnational Approaches", Department of Government, Harvard University, paper prepared for presentation at the conference "Immigration in a Cross-National Context: What Are the Implications for Europe?" organised by the EU Center at Syracuse, http://web.archive.org/web/20050206092149/http://www.lisproject.org/immigration/papers/laurence.pdf, viewed 8 August 2007.

Lawton, John, "Muslims in Europe: The Presence," January/February 1979, http://www.saudiaramcoworld.com/issue/197901/muslims.in.europe-the.presence.htm, viewed 8 August 2007.

"Leading Islamist Sheikh Yousef Al-Qaradhawi: We are Fighting in the Name of Islam...", MEMRI, *Special Dispatch Series*, No. 1102, February 28, 2006.

"Leading Sunni Sheikh Yousef al-Qaradhawi and Other Sheikhs Herald the Coming Conquest of Rome", MEMRI, *Special Dispatch Series*, No. 47, 6 December 2002.

Leville, Sandra and Muir, Hugh, "Secret report brands Muslim police corrupt", *The Guardian,* 10 June 2006.

Levitt, Matthew A., "Still With Us? Testing Britain's Counter-Terror Resolve", *National Review Online*, 5 September 2003, http://www.nationalreview.com/script/printpage.p?ref=/comment/comment-levitt090503.asp, viewed 17 January 2007.

Lewis, Bernard, "License to Kill: Usama bin Ladin's Declaration of Jihad", *Foreign Affairs,* November/December 1998.

Lewis, Philip, *Islamic Britain: Religion, Politics and Identity Among British Muslims* (London & New York: I.B. Tauris, 1994, 2002).

"Libyan leader Mu'ammar Al-Qadhafi: Europe and the U.S. Should Agree to Become Islamic or Declare War on the Muslims", MEMRI, TV Monitor Project, Clip No. 1121, 10 April 2006, http://www.MEMRItv.org/Transcript.asp?P1=1121, viewed 22 August 2006.

Lister, Sam, "Imam 'instructed British Muslims to ill infidels' ", *TIMES ONLINE*, 23 January 2003.

MacAskill, Ewen and Dodd, Vikram, "The Pakistan connection: suspicion falls on al-Qaida", *The Guardian*, 12 August 2006.

MacEoin, Denis, *The Hijacking of British Islam: How extremist literature is subverting mosques in the UK* (2007).

Maher, Shiraz, "How I escaped Islamism", *The Times*, 12 August 2007.

——, "How we can rid Britain of violent extremism", *The New Statesman*, 12 July 2007.

Malik, Kenan, "Are Muslims hated?", transcript, *30 Minutes*, TV Channel 4, broadcast 8 January, http://www.kenanmalik.com/tv/c4_islamophobia.html, viewed 10 October 2005.

Malik, Mustafa, "Muslims Pluralize the West, Resist Assimilation", *Journal of Middle East Policy Council*, Vol. XI, No. 1, Spring 2004.

Malik, Zubeida, "Polygamy law set for challenge", *BBC News*, 18 June 2000.

Manifestations of Antisemitism in the EU 2002–2003, European Monitoring Centre on Racism and Xenophobia, http://fra.europa.eu/fra/index.php?fuseaction=content.dsp_cat_content&catid=1, viewed 30 August 2007.

Manningham-Buller, Eliza "The International Terrorist Threat to the UK", Northeast Intelligence Network, 10 November 2006, http://www.homelandsecurityus.com/MI5report110906, viewed 9 August 2007.

Maréchal, Brigitte, "The Muslim Brotherhood and Religious Authority in Western Europe", *Muslim Religious Authority in Western Europe*, conference report by the International Institute for the Study of Modern Islam (ISIM), Leiden, 30 September–1 October 2005.

Marshall, Paul, "Outside encouragement sharia rules Nigeria – with the help of foreign Islamists", *National Review Online*, 5 May 2004.

Masmoudi, Radwan A., "The Silenced Majority", *Journal of Democracy*, Vol. 14, No. 2, April 2003, http://www.islam-democracy.org/art_jod_april-2003.asp, viewed 7 August 2007.

Masood, Ehsan, "A Muslim Journey", *Prospect Magazine,* Issue 113, August 2005, http://www.prospectmagazine.co.uk/article_details. php?id=6989, viewed 7 August 2007.

——, *British Muslims: Media Guide* (London: British Council, 2006).

——, "British Muslims must stop the war", *openDemocracy,* 30 August 2005, http://www.opendemocracy.net/conflict-terrorism/ british_sufis_2786.jsp, viewed 7 August 2007.

al-Mawardi, Abu'l-Hasan, *al-Ahkam as-Sultaniyyah: The Laws of Islamic Governance,* transl. Asadullah Yate (London: Ta-Ha Publishers, 1996).

——, *The Ordinances of Government: al-Ahkam al-Sultaniyya w'al-Wilyat al-Diniyya,* transl. Wafaa H. Wahba, The Centre for Muslim Contribution to Civilization (Reading: Garnet Publishing Ltd, 1996).

Mawdudi, Abu'l A'la, *Jihad fi Sabilillah (Jihad in Islam),* transl. Khurshid Ahmad, ed. Huda Khattab (U.K.I.M. Dawah Centre, January 1997).

——, *Let us be Muslims,* ed. Khurram Murad (Leicester: The Islamic Foundation, 1982).

——, *The Islamic Law and Constitution* (Lahore: Islamic Publications, 1980).

——, *The Islamic Movement: Dynamics of Values, Power and Change,* ed. Khurram Murad, (London: Islamic Foundation, 1984).

——, *The Punishment of the Apostate According to Islamic Law,* transl. and annotated by Syed Silas Husain and Ernest Hahn (Lahore: Islamic Publications, 1994).

——, *Witnesses Unto Mankind* (Birmingham: UK Islamic Mission, 1986).

Mayer, Ann Elizabeth, *Islam and Human Rights: Tradition and Politics* (Boulder, Colorado: Westview Press, 1991).

"MCB meet minister over Religious Hatred bill", *The Muslim Weekly,* Issue 87, 8–14 July 2005.

McGregory, Daniel and Ford, Richard, "Terrorist suspect flees police in mosque", *The Times,* 17 January 2007.

McGrory, Daniel, "Cleric's tape threat to destroy Rome", *The Times,* 3 April 2004.

—— and Ford, Richard, "Extremist on deportation list is linked to Islamic advice group", *The Times*, 1 September 2005.

McKenna, Terence, "The Recruiters", *The National*, June 2002.

McRoy, Anthony, "Bari is hope for British Muslims", www.naba.org. uk/content/articles/Diaspora/606_McRoy_Bari_MCB.htm, viewed 6 June 2007.

——, *From Rushdie to 7/7: The Radicalisation of Islam in Britain* (London: The Social Affairs Unit, 2006).

MEMRI The Middle East Media Research Institute, PO Box 27837, Washington DC 20038-7837, USA http:\\memri.org:

"Al-Qaradhawi Speaks in Favor of Suicide Operations at an Islamic Conference in Sweden", MEMRI, *Special Dispatch Series,* No. 542, 24 July 2004.

Al-Sharq Al-Awsat (19 July 2003), extracts in English translation in MEMRI, *Special Dispatch Series*, No. 542, 24 July 2003.

"Debate over Female Circumcision in Egypt", MEMRI, *Special Dispatch Series,* No. 42, 3 August 1999.

"Leading Islamist Sheikh Yousef Al-Qaradhawi: We are Fighting in the Name of Islam...", MEMRI, *Special Dispatch Series*, No. 1102, February 28, 2006.

"Leading Sunni Sheikh Yousef al-Qaradhawi and Other Sheikhs Herald the Coming Conquest of Rome," MEMRI, *Special Dispatch Series*, No. 47, 6 December 2002.

"Libyan leader Mu'ammar Al-Qadhafi: Europe and the U.S. Should Agree to Become Islamic or Declare War on the Muslims", MEMRI, TV Monitor Project, Clip No. 1121, 10 April 2006, http://www.MEMRItv.org/Transcript.asp?P1=1121, viewed 22 August 2006.

"Muslim Soldiers in the U.S. Armed Forces in Afghanistan: To Fight or Not to Fight?" MEMRI, *Inquiry and Analysis Series*, No. 75, 6 November 2001.

Pashut, Adam, "Dr 'Azzam Al-Tamimi: A Political-Ideological Brief", MEMRI, *Inquiry and Analysis Series*, No. 163, 19 February 2004.

"Reactions to Sheikh Al-Qaradhawi's Fatwa Calling for the Abduction and Killing of American Civilians in Iraq", MEMRI, *Special Dispatch Series*, No. 794, 6 October 2004.

"Sheik Yousuf Al-Qaradhawi: Islam's 'Conquest of Rome' Will Save Europe from Its Subjugation to Materialism and Promiscuity", MEMRI, TV Monitor Project, Clip No. 1592, 28 July 2007, http://www.memritv.org/clip_transcript/en/1592.htm, viewed 6 November 2007.

"Sheikh Yousuf Al-Qaradhawi: Resistance in Iraq is a Duty of Every Muslim", MEMRI, *Special Dispatch Series*, No. 828, 14 December 2004.

"The Prophet Muhammad as a Jihad Model", MEMRI, *Special Dispatch Series*, No. 246, 24 July 2001.

Miliband, David, Speech to the College of Europe, Bruges, 15 November 2007, http://www.publicpolitics.net/modules.php?op=modload&name=News&file=article&sid=84959, viewed 16 November 2007.

"Minister backs new Muslim group", *BBC News*, 19 July 2007.

Misra, Ashutosh, "Rise of Religious Parties in Pakistan: Causes and Prospects", http://www.ciaonet.org/olj/sa/sa_apr03/sa_apr03mia01.html, viewed 8 August 2007.

Montero, David, "British bomb plot spotlights charities", *Christian Science Monitor*, 16 August 2006.

Moore, Charles, "Stirring up racial hatred – not the medium", *The Daily Telegraph*, 11 August 2007.

Morgan, Adrian, "Leading Muslim terrorists have been educated at Britain's universities", *Family Security Matters,* 5 January 2007, http://www.familysecuritymatters.org/homeland.php?id=559672, viewed 3 July 2007.

Murad, Khurram, *Da'wah Among Non-Muslims In The West* (Leicester: The Islamic Foundation, 1986).

Murray, Stephen O. and Roscoe, Will, *Islamic Homosexualities: Culture, History and Literature* (New York and London: New York University Press, 1997).

Murtagh, Peter, "Rushdie in hiding after Ayatollah's death threat", *The Guardian,* 18 February 1989.

"Muslim Council of Britain: Much ado about nothing", *Q-News,* March–April 2002.

"Muslim Educational Centre of Oxford Annual Conference", http://www.meco.org.uk/panel.htm#karim, viewed 11 October 2005.

Muslim Religious Authority in Western Europe, International Institute for the Study of Modern Islam (ISIM), Leiden, 30 September–1 October 2005.

"Muslim school offers best added value", *The Times*, 13 January 2005.

"Muslims, Mosques & Angry Young Men! An Interview with MPACUK", http://www.mpacuk.org/content/view/1067/105/, viewed 11 October 2005 or http://www.mpacuk.org/content/view/1067/39/, viewed 7 August 2007.

"Muslim Soldiers in the U.S. Armed Forces in Afghanistan: To Fight or Not to Fight?" MEMRI, *Inquiry and Analysis Series*, No. 75, 6 November 2001.

"Muslim veil 'allowed in courts' ", *BBC News*, 24 April 2007.

"MPACUK SUCCESS", *The Muslim Weekly*, 16 May 2005.

Nasr, Seyyed Vali Reza, "Islamic Economics: Novel Perspectives" in *The Political Economy of the Middle East*, Vol. III, eds. Tim Niblock and Rodney Wilson (Cheltenham and Northampton, Massachusetts: Edward Elgar Publishing, 1999).

——, *The Vanguard of the Islamic Revolution: The Jama'at-i Islami of Pakistan* (Berkeley: University of California Press, 1994).

Nettler, Ronald, "A Modern Islamic Confession of Faith and Conception of Religion: Sayyid Qutb's Introduction to *tafsir, Fi Zilal al-Quran*" in *British Journal of Middle Eastern Studies*, Vol. 21, No. 1, 1994.

——, *Past Trials and Present Tribulations: A Muslim Fundamentalist's View of the Jews* (Oxford: Pergamon Press, 1987).

Nielsen, Jorgen, "Islamic Foundation" in *The Oxford Encyclopedia of the Modern Islamic World*, Vol. 2, ed. John L. Esposito (New York: Oxford University Press, 1995).

Noorzoy, M. Siddieq, "Islamic Laws on Riba (Interest) and their Economic Implications", *International Journal of Middle East Studies*, Vol. 14, Issue 1, 1982.

NOP Poll of British Muslims, 8 Aug 2006, http://www.ukpollingreport.co.uk/blog/archives/291, viewed 13 August 2007.

Norfolk, Andrew, "Hardline takeover of British mosques", *The Times*, 7 September 2007.

OFSTED report 2002, http://www.ofsted.gov.uk/reports/manreports/113.htm, viewed 30 November 2005 or http://www.ofsted.gov.uk/

reports/pdf/?inspectionNumber=108823&providerCategoryID=16
384&fileName=\\school\\100\\s163_100372_20061017.pdf,
viewed 9 August 2007.

"OIC summit rubberstamps western colonialist aggression in Iraq",
www.1924.org, viewed 27 April 2004; or http://www.hizb.org.uk/
hizb/ht-britain.html, viewed 14 August 2007.

O'Neill, Sean, "Britain rejects Bush's charges against charity", *The
Daily Telegraph,* 25 September 2003.

——, "British Islam colleges 'link to terrorism' ", *The Times,* 29 July
2004.

—— and Boyes, Roger, "Islamic missionary group links alleged
plotters", *The Times,* 17 August 2006.

—— and Lappin, Yaacov, "Britain's online imam declares war as he
calls young to jihad", *The Times,* 17 January 2006.

—— and McGrory, Daniel, *The Suicide Factory: Abu Hamza and the
Finsbury Park Mosque* (London: Harper Collins, 2006).

——, Rumbelow, Helen and Gledhill, Ruth, "Muslim 'task force'
criticised for being too establishment", *The Times,* 20 July 2005.

"One in 10 'backs honour killing' ", *BBC News,* 4 September 2006.

O'Sullivan, Jack, "Defender of his Faith", *The Guardian,* 15 January
2003.

Parsa, Ali, *Shariah property investment: developing an international
strategy* (London: Royal Institution of Chartered Surveyors, 2005).

Pashut, Adam, "Dr 'Azzam Al-Tamimi: A Political-Ideological Brief",
MEMRI, *Inquiry and Analysis Series,* No. 163, 19 February 2004.

Paz, Reuben, "The Coronation of the King of the Golden Path: Sheikh
Qaradawi Beomes Imam *Al-Wasatiyyah* and a School and
Movement by Itself", The Project for the Research of Islamist
Movements (PRISM), Occasional Papers, Vol. 5, No. 3, August
2007.

Peck, Sally and Henry, Emma, "Husband held over pregnant teenager's
murder", *The Daily Telegraph,* 15 May 2007.

Phillips, Melanie, "The British Inquisition (1)", 13 January 2005,
http://www.melaniephillips.com/diary/archives/000988.html,
viewed 22 January 2007.

Phillips, Sir Trevor, "Include Muslims in British History", *The Muslim
Weekly,* 28 September–4 October 2007.

"Police delve into honour killings", *BBC News*, 30 September 2003.

"Press Release: Islamic Relief nationwide appeal for Pakistan Quake", Islamic Relief, http://www.mabonline.info/english/modules.php?name=News&file=article&sid=548, viewed 12 October 2005 or http://www.reliefweb.int/rw/RWB.NSF/db900SID/ACIO-6H2TRT?OpenDocument, viewed 7 August 2007.

"Profile: Abu Hamza", *BBC News*, Friday 17 January 2003.

Purves, Libby, "Britain, spiritual home to this creed of hate", *TIMES ONLINE*, 21 January 2003.

al-Qaradawi, Yusuf, Response to "Challenging the Applicability of Shar'ia" http://www.islamonline.net/fatwa/english/FatwaDisplay.asp?hFatwaID=61551, viewed 10 August 2005.

——, *Priorities of the Islamic Movement in the Coming Phase* (Swansea: Awakening Publications, 2000).

al-Qaradawi, Yusuf et al., "Fatwa", http://www.unc.edu/~kurzman/Qaradawi_et_al.htm, viewed 6 August 2007.

"*Q-News* The Muslim Magazine", http://www.q-news.com/about.htm, viewed 5 October 2005.

Qutb, Sayyid, *Fi Zilal al-Quran*, Vol. 3 (Beirut: Dar al-Shuruq, 1987).

——, *Islam and Peace* (Cairo: Dar al-Shuruq, 1988).

——, *Milestones* (Indianapolis: American Trust Publications, 1990).

——, "Our Struggle with the Jews" in *Past Trials and Present Tribulations: A Muslim Fundamentalist's View of the Jews,* ed. Ronald L. Nettler (Oxford: Pergamon Press, 1987).

——, "Social Justice in Islam" in *Sayyid Qutb and Islmaic Activism: A Translation and Critical Analysis of 'Social Justice in Islam'*, ed. W. Shephard (Leiden: E.J. Brill, 1996).

——, *The Islamic Concept and its Characteristic* (Indianapolis: American Trust Publication, 1991).

Radical Islam In Central Asia: Responding To Hizb Ut-Tahrir, International Crisis Group, Asia Report No. 58, Brussels, 30 June 2003.

Radu, Michael, "The Problem of 'Londonistan'; Europe, Human Rights, and Terrorists", *Foreign Policy Research Institute,* 12 April 2002.

Ramachandran, Sudha, "Mixing aid with terror", *Asia Times,* 22 September 2005.

Ramadan, Tariq, "The Contradictions of the Islamic World", *Qantara.de,* http://www.qantara.de/webcom/show_article.php/_c-476/_nr-88/i.html, viewed 13 September 2005.

Raman, B., "Bangladesh: A Bengali Abbasi Lurking Somewhere?", South Asia Analysis Group, Paper No. 232, 23 April 2001, http://www.saag.org/papers3/paper232.html, viewed 17 October 2007.

"Reactions to Sheikh Al-Qaradhawi's Fatwa Calling for the Abduction and Killing of American Civilians in Iraq", MEMRI, *Special Dispatch Series*, No. 794, 6 October 2004.

"Residing in the land of Unbelievers: Three Fataawaa by Shaykh, Muhammad Ibn Saalih al'Uthaimeen", http://www.allaahuakbar.net/scholars/uthaymeen/residing_in_land_of_unbelievers.htm, viewed 17 October 2007.

Reynalds, Jeremy, "Radical Islamic Group Warns Muslims Against Helping British or American Military", *American Daily,* 10 February 2003.

Rippin, Andrew, *Muslims: Their Religious Beliefs and Practices*, Vol. 2 (London and New York: Routledge, 1993).

Roy, Amit, "British Honour for Key Muslim", *The Telegraph* (Calcutta, India), 12 June 2005.

Rufford, Nicholas and Taher, Abdul, "British Muslim says troops are fair target," *The Sunday Times*, 11 October 2004.

Rushdie, Salman, "The Right Time for An Islamic Reformation", *The Washington Post,* 7 August 2005.

Sacranie, Iqbal, "We need protection from the pedlars of religious hatred", *The Daily Telegraph,* 14 December 2004.

Saeed, Osama, "Will The State Protect Islamic Teaching?", *The Scotsman*, 18 May 2005.

Sankari, Jamal, *Fadlallah: The Making of a Radical Shi'ite Leader* (London: Saqi, 2005).

Sardar, Ziauddin, *Desperately Seeking Paradise* (London: Granta, 2004).

——, "Rethinking Islam", *Islam For Today*, June 2002, http://www.islamfortoday.com/sardar01.htm, viewed 7 August 2007.

——, "Viewpoint: The global voices reclaiming Islam", *BBC News,* 6 September 2005.

Sarwar, Ghulam, *Islam: Beliefs and Teachings,* 5th edition (London: The Muslim Educational Trust, 1998).

Sayyid, Salman, "Muslims in Britain: Towards a Political Agenda" in *British Muslims: Loyalty and Belonging,* Proceedings of a seminar held on 8 May 2002, eds. Mohammad Siddique Seddon, Dilwar Hussain and Nadeem Malik (Markfield: The Islamic Foundation, 2003).

"School wins Muslim dress appeal", *BBC News,* 22 March 2006.

Shahar, Yael and Karmon, Ely, "London-Based Islamic Group Issues Fatwa against Israel", *International Policy Institute for Counter-Terrorism,* 19 October 2000.

"Sharia Council, Terms and Conditions for Talak or Divorce", Darul Uloom London, http://www.darululoomlondon.co.uk/sharia.htm, viewed 8 January 2004.

"Sheik Yousuf Al-Qaradhawi: Islam's 'Conquest of Rome' Will Save Europe from Its Subjugation to Materialism and Promiscuity", MEMRI, TV Monitor Project, Clip No. 1592, 28 July 2007, http://www.memritv.org/clip_transcript/en/1592.htm, viewed 6 November 2007.

"Sheikh Yousuf Al-Qaradhawi: Resistance in Iraq is a Duty of Every Muslim", MEMRI, *Special Dispatch Series,* No. 828, 14 December 2004.

"Show support for Sister Yvonne Ridley", http://www.ummah.com/forum/showthread.php?t=59532, viewed 7 August 2007.

Siddiqui, Kalim, *In Pursuit of the Power of Islam: Major writings of Kalim Siddiqui,* ed. Zafar Bangash (London: The Open Press, 1996).

——, *The Muslim Manifesto: a strategy for survival* (London: Muslim Institute, 1990).

Siddiqi, Shamim A., *Methodology of Dawah Ilallah in American Perspective* (Brooklyn: The Forum for Islamic Works, 1989).

Sikand, Yoginder, *The Origins and Development of the Tablighi-Jama'at (1920-2000)* (New Delhi: Orient Longman, 2002).

"Silencing voices of dissent", *Q-News,* March–April 2002.

Simpson, Daniel, "British radicals urge Muslims to fight back", *Middle East Times,* Issue 99-13, 28 March 1999.

Slack, James, "Why race chief wants to sink our role in the Armada", *Daily Mail,* 25 September 2007.

Solihin, S.M., *Studies on Sayyid Qutb's Fi Zilal al-Quran* (unpublished thesis, Department of Theology, University of Birmingham, 1993).

Striving for Revival (Leicester: Young Muslims UK, 1993).

"Student was shot by 'Muslim Boys' gang", 6 January 2006, http://journals.aol.co.uk/kenningtonnews/KenningtonNews/entries/2006/01/07/student-was-shot-by-muslim-boys-gang/2035, viewed 30 August 2007.

Taher, Abul and Gadher, Dipesh "Islamists infiltrate four universities", *The Sunday Times*, 12 November 2006.

Tamimi, Azzam, "Concepts of Life Beyond Death: Martyrdom, Resurrection, Heaven & Hell", Institute of Islamic Political Thought, 26 March 2004, http://www.ii-pt.com/web/papers/concept.htm, viewed 8 September 2005.

——, "From Oslo, down the Road Map: No peace, more blood", *Impact International,* Vol. 33, Issue 10, October 2003.

——, "Fundamentalism and violence: an Islamic viewpoint", Islamic Institute of Political Thought, 26 March 2004, http://www.ii-pt.com/web/papers/view.htm, viewed 8 September 2005.

——, "Jewish Crusade!", Islamic Institute of Political Thought, http://www.ii-pt.com/web/articles/jewish.htm, viewed 26 March 2004.

"Tariq Ramadan Calls for Hudud Freeze", *IslamOnline,* 30 March 2005, http://www.islamonline.net/English/News/2005-03/30/article07.shtml, viewed 4 July 2007.

Taseer, Aatish, "A British jihadist", *Prospect Magazine,* 13 August 2005.

Taylor, Matthew, "Two thirds oppose state aided faith schools", *The Guardian*, 23 August 2005.

Tharoo, Sajjad, "UK Muslims launch report and campaign on anti-Muslim discrimination", http://www.muslimedia.com/archives/world00/uk-report.htm, viewed 7August 2007.

"The Biography of Sheikh Omar Bakri Muhammad", http://www.almuhajiroun.com/\default.asp.

"The Charter of Allah: The Platform of the Islamic Resistance movement (Hamas)", transl. and annotated by Raphael Israeli, Harry Truman Research Institute, The Hebrew University, Jerusalem, Israel, http://www.fas.org/irp/world/para/docs/880818.htm, viewed 6 August 2007.

The Islamic Foundation: Objectives, Activities, Projects (Markfield, no date).

The Moral Maze, BBC Radio 4, 14 July 2004, www.bbc.co.uk/radio4/religion/moralmaze.shtml, viewed 4 January 2005.

"The Muslim Law (Shariah) Council", http://www.muslimcollege.ac.uk/index.asp?id=170&type=detail, viewed 6 August 2007.

"The Network", *CBS News*, 25 March 2007.

"The Prophet Muhammad as a Jihad Model", MEMRI, *Special Dispatch Series*, No. 246, 24 July 2001.

"The Rushdie Affair – 1988–91", "http://www.salaam.co.uk/themeofthemonth/september03_index.php?l=1, viewed 8 August 2007.

"The Sacred Duty of Defending Jerusalem", 23 August 2005, http://www.islamonline.net/servlet/Satellite?pagename=IslamOnline-English-Ask_Scholar/FatwaE/FatwaE&cid=1119503543558, viewed 6 August 2007.

"The unholy past of the Muslim cleric demanding the Pope's execution", *This is London*, 19 September 2006.

"The Universal Declaration of Human Rights", Islamic Sharia Council of UK & Ireland, http://www.islamic-sharia.co.uk/preface.html, viewed 6 January 2004 or http://www.islamic-sharia.org/index.php?option=com_content&task=view&id=13&Itemid=28&limit=1&limitstart=4, viewed 9 August 2007.

"The war for Muslim minds: an interview with Gilles Kepel", *openDemocracy*, 11 November 2004, www.openDemocracy.net, viewed 24 August 2005.

"They destroy the Houses of Allah", *The Media Office of Hizb-ut-Tahrir* (Sudan), 12 May 2005, http://www.hizb-ut-tahrir.info/english/sudan/2005/may1205.htm, viewed 6 August 2007.

Thomson, Ahmad, "Incorporating Muslim Personal Law into UK Domestic Law" in *Fiqh for Today: Muslims as Minorities*, Conference Booklet, 5th Annual AMSS (UK) Conference, 21–22 February 2004, in cooperation with *The International Institute of Islamic Thought, The Muslim College, Q News Media*.

"Two-thirds of British Muslims say war on terror targets Islam", *Associated Press*, 24 December 2002, quoted in *ummahnews.com*.

"UK bombing fears now focus on enemy within", *The Times*, 4 April 2004.

"UK Muslims condemn honour killings", *BBC News,* 30 September 2003.

"UK: Persecution of converts from Islam", *Barnabas Aid,* March–April 2006.

"UK 'terror target' claim dismissed", *BBC News,* 7 January 2002.

"Undercover Mosque", *Dispatches,* TV Channel 4, 15 January 2007.

Vasagar, Jeevan, "British Muslims warn of 'conflict for generations' ", *The Guardian,* 14 January 2003.

——, "Dilemma of the Moderates", *The Guardian,* 19 June 2002.

Vidino, Lorenzo, "Aims and Methods of Europe's Muslim Brotherhood", *Current Trends in Islamist Ideology,* Vol. 4, Center on Islam, Democracy and the Future of the Muslim World, 1 November 2006.

Webb v City of Philadelphia, US District Court Case 05-5238, 27 June 2007.

Wegerif, Boudewijn, "The new Islamic Dinar", http://www.appropriate-economics.org/materials/dinar.html, viewed 14 August 2007.

Werbner, Pnina, *Imagined Diasporas Among Manchester Muslims* (Oxford: James Currey, 2002).

Wesley, Robert, "British Terrorist Dhiren Barot's Research on Radiological Weapons", *Terrorism Monitor,* Vol. 3, Issue 44, 14 November 2006.

"What is Progressive Islam?" *ISIM Newsletter,* No. 13, December 2003.

Whine, Michael, "Is Hizb ut-Tahrir Changing Strategy or Tactics?", Hudson Institute, Center for Eurasian Policy, Occasional Research Paper Series I (Hizb ut-Tahrir), No.1, http://www.hudson.org/files/publications/EurasianPaper_Aug42006.pdf, viewed 9 August 2007.

——, "The Advance of the Muslim Brotherhood in the UK" in *Current trends in Islamist Ideology,* Vol. 2, eds. Hillel Fradkin, Husain Haqqani and Eric Brown, Center on Islam, Democracy and the Future of the Muslim World, Washington DC: The Hudson Institute, 2005.

——, "The Mode of Operation of Hizb ut Tahrir in an Open Society", The Institute for Counter-Terrorism, 20 February 2004, http://web.archive.org/web/20040603033412/http://www.ict.org.il/articles/articledet.cfm?

Whitaker, Brian, "Satellite phone gives US vital evidence", *The Guardian,* 28 May 2004.

"White Fright", transcript, *Panorama, BBC1,* 7 May 2007 and *BBC News,* 25 May 2007.

"Why Islam Awareness Week", November 2007, http://www.iaw. org.uk/, viewed 12 October 2007.

"Why NGO boss was thrown out", *East African Standard,* 5 March 2004, http://www.africanewssearch.com/index.php?archive=1& month=3&day=5&year=2004, viewed 9 August 2007.

World Wide Religious News (WWRN), Europe, http://www.wwrn.org/ sparse.php?idd=8405, viewed 9 August 2007.

Yilmaz, Ihsan, "Muslim Alternative Dispute Resolution and Neo-Ijtihad in England", *Alternatives: Turkish Journal of International Relations,* Vol. 2, No. 1, Fall 2003.

——, "Law as Chameleon: The Question of Incorporation of Muslim Personal Law into the English Law", *Journal of Muslim Minority Affairs,* Vol. 1, No. 2, October 2001.

Zakaria, Yamin, "Inside the Mind of a Suicide Bomber – Targeting Civilians, Part 2", http://www.mpacuk.org/content/view/1015/103/, viewed 11 October 2005 or http://www.mpacuk.org/content/view/ 1015/39/, viewed 7 August 2007.

REFERENCES AND NOTES

Please note that material on websites is often removed after a short period, and websites themselves may also disappear.

1   Zaki Badawi, *Islam in Britain*, London: Taha Publishers, 1981, pp. 26–27.
2   Abu'l A'la Mawdudi, *Jihad fi Sabilillah (Jihad in Islam)*, translated by Khurshid Ahmad, ed. Huda Khattab, UKIM Dawah Centre, January 1997, p. 14.
3   Abul A'la Mawdudi, *Witnesses Unto Mankind*, Birmingham: UK Islamic Mission, 1986, pp. 2–3.
4   Shamim A. Siddiqi *Methodology of Dawah Ilallah in American Perspective*, Brooklyn: The Forum for Islamic Works, 1989, pp. 136–137.
5   Ministry of the Interior and Kingdom Relations, *Form dawa to jihad: The various threats from radical Islam to the democratic legal order*, The Hague: General Intelligence and Security Service, December 2004
6   Ghufran Mahmood, who attends the Madina Mosque in Keighley, made this clear in his comment in the online magazine Deenport.com dated 24 May 2007. He also asked other readers for ideas of how to attract more non-Muslims to the mosque.
7   "Why Islam Awareness Week", November 2007, http://www. iaw.org.uk/, viewed 12 October 2007; "Islam Awareness Week", BBC, http://www.bbc.co.uk/religion/religions/islam/living/islamawarenessweek_1.shtml, viewed 12 October 2007.
8   Muhammad Taqi-ud-Din al-Hilali and Muhammad Muhsin Khan, *Interpretation of the Meanings of the Noble Qur'an*. 15th edition, Riyadh: Darussalam, December 1996, pp. 845–864.

9   Office of Research, U.S. Department of State, *How Europe's Muslims See Themselves at Home and in the World: Findings from Surveys in Britain, France, Germany, Spain and the Netherlands, February–June 2005.*

10 Imtiaz Ahmed Hussain, "Migration and Settlement: A Historical Perspective of Loyalty and Belonging" in *British Muslims: Loyalty and Belonging*, Proceedings of a seminar held on 8 May 2002, ed. Mohammad Siddique Seddon, Dilwar Hussain and Nadeem Malik, Markfield: The Islamic Foundation, 2003, p. 33.

11 Salman Sayyid "Muslims in Britain: Towards a Political Agenda" in *British Muslims: Loyalty and Belonging*, Proceedings of a seminar held on 8 May 2002, ed. Mohammad Siddique Seddon, Dilwar Hussain and Nadeem Malik, Markfield: The Islamic Foundation, 2003, pp. 88–89.

12 Farkhunda Ali, "American Muslim Military Participation in the War Clarified by American Muslim Scholars", 11 October 2001, http://www.icgt.org/SpecialArticles/MuslimsInMilitary.htm, viewed 6 August 2007; "Qaradawi et al. fatwa", http://www.unc.edu/~kurzman/Qaradawi_et_al.htm, viewed 6 August 2007.

13 *Al-Sharq Al-Awsat* (London), 30 October 2001, quoted in "Muslim Soldiers in the U.S. Armed Forces in Afghanistan: To Fight or Not to Fight?", The Middle East Media Research Institute (MEMRI), Inquiry and Analysis Series, No. 75, 6 November 2001.

14 "Reactions to Sheikh Al-Qaradhawi's Fatwa Calling for the Abduction and Killing of American Civilians in Iraq", The Middle East Media Research Institute (MEMRI), Special Dispatch Series, No. 794, 6 October 2004.

15 Webb v City of Philadelphia, US District Court Case 05–5238, 27 June 2007.

16 *Dispatches*, TV Channel 4, 15 January 2007. In November 2007 Ofcom ruled that the programme had not been misleading.

17 Charles Moore, "Stirring up racial hatred – not the medium", *The Daily Telegraph*, 11 August 2007.

18 Fred Attewill, "Met orders review after Muslim refuses to guard Israeli embassy", *The Guardian*, 5 October 2006.

19 Daniel McGregory and Richard Ford, "Terrorist suspect flees police in mosque", *The Times*, 17 January 2007.

20 The author has been informed of a number of cases of the kind described in this paragraph in personal conversations by those who wish to remain anonymous.

21 For example, at least three hundred million copies of *Interpretation of the Meanings of the Noble Qur'an,* which is described and quoted on pp. 19–21.

22 The term "neo-Salafism" is one of the most confusing, since it is used by different writers to convey very different meanings. As well as denoting the contemporary Salafi-Jihadi trend, it is also used to describe the Wahhabi-influenced modern Salafism as distinct from the older Egyptian-influenced Salafism of the the early to mid-twentieth century.

23 Hasan al-Banna, *Selected Writings of Hasan al-Banna Shaheed,* translated by S.A. Qureshi, New Delhi: Militant Book Centre, 1999, pp. 31–32.

24 Lorenzo Vidino, "Aims and Methods of Europe's Muslim Brotherhood", *Current Trends in Islamist Ideology,* Vol. 4, Center on Islam, Democracy and the Future of the Muslim World, 1 November 2006.

25 "Leading Sunni Sheikh Yousef al-Qaradhawi and Other Sheikhs Herald the Coming Conquest of Rome," The Middle East Media Research Institute (MEMRI), Special Dispatch Series, No. 47, 6 December 2002.

26 Lorenzo Vidino, "Aims and Methods of Europe's Muslim Brotherhood", *Current Trends in Islamist Ideology,* Vol. 4, Center on Islam, Democracy and the Future of the Muslim World, 1 November 2006.

27 The Deobandi originally held that there was no need for a *jihad* against the British Raj since Muslims in British India were able to practise their religion freely.

28 Majid Khadduri, *War and Peace in the Law of Islam,* Baltimore: Johns Hopkins Press, 1955, pp. 51, 53.

29 Sayyid Qutb, *Milestones,* Indianapolis: American Trust Publications, 1990, p. 102.

30 Muhammad Taqi-ud-Din al-Hilali and Muhammad Muhsin Khan, *Interpretation of the Meanings of the Noble Qur'an,* 15th edition, Riyadh: Darussalam, December 1996.

31 *Fay* is war booty (including land) gained without fighting.

32 Ibn Taymiyya, *Majmu'at al-Fatawa li-Sheikh al-Islam taqi al-Din Ahmad bin Taymiyya al-Hurani*, al-Mansourah: dar al-Wafa' Wal nashr Wal Tawzi', 1997, p. 308. English translation from Bat Yeor, *Islam and Dhimitude: Where Civilizations Collide*, Madison, Teaneck: Farleigh Dickinson University Press and Lancaster, UK: Gazelle Book Services, 2002, p. 59.

33 Ibn Sallam, *The Book of Revenue (Kitab al-Amwal),* translated by Imran Ahsan Khan Nyazee, Reading: Garnet, 2002, pp. 51–58.

34 "Conquered Land", Extract from the Encyclopaedia of Islam, CD-ROM Edition v. 1.0, ©1999 Koninklijke Brill NV, Leiden, The Netherlands.

35 Majid Khadduri, *War and Peace in the Law of Islam*, Baltimore: The Johns Hopkins Press, 1955, pp. 158–160.

36 Abu'l-Hasan al-Mawardi, *al-Ahkam as-Sultaniyyah: The Laws of Islamic Governance*, translated by Asadullah Yate, London: Ta-Ha Publishers, 1996, pp. 200–201.

37 Ibn Rushd, *The Distinguished Jurist's Primer: Bidayat al-Mujtahid*, Vol. 1, translated by Imran Ahsan Nyazee, Reading: Garnet, 1994, p. 480.

38 "The Sacred Duty of Defending Jerusalem", 23 August 2005, http://www.islamonline.net/servlet/Satellite?pagename=IslamOnline-English-Ask_Scholar/FatwaE/FatwaE&cid=1119503543558, viewed 6 August 2007.

39 Yusuf al-Qaradawi, *Priorities of the Islamic Movement in the Coming Phase*, Swansea: Awakening Publications, 2000, p. 163.

40 Bernard Lewis, "License to Kill: Usama bin Ladin's Declaration of Jihad", *Foreign Affairs,* November/December 1998.

41 Isma'il Raji al-Faruqi, *Islam,* Brentwood, Maryland: International Graphics, 1984, p. 60.

42 Kalim Siddiqui, *In Pursuit of the Power of Islam: Major writings of Kalim Siddiqui,* London: The Open Press, 1996, pp. 254–255.

43 "The Charter of Allah: The Platform of the Islamic Resistance movement (Hamas)*", translated and annotated by Raphael Israeli, Harry Truman Research Institute, The Hebrew University, Jerusalem, Israel, http://www.fas.org/irp/world/para/docs/880818.htm, viewed 6 August 2007.

44 Pnina Werbner, *Imagined Diasporas among Manchester Muslims*, Oxford: James Currey, 2002, pp.116–117.

45 When the Islamic government of Sudan demolished a mosque, the extremist group Hizb ut-Tahrir denounced this vehemently as an "evil" act, arguing from the Qur'an and the *shari'a* that mosques are "not allowed to be destroyed or demolished or violated under any pretext" and that "the land [on which the mosque is built] is the land of Allah". See "They destroy the Houses of Allah", The Media Office of Hizb-ut-Tahrir in Sudan , 12 May 2005, http://www.hizb-ut-tahrir.info/english/sudan/2005/may1205.htm, viewed 6 August 2007.

46 The author has been personally told of a number of cases of intimidation or discrimination designed to force non-Muslims out of Muslim areas, but all the individuals requested anonymity so the details cannot be cited here.

47 Transcript of "White Fright", *Panorama*, *BBC1*, shown 7 May 2007, *BBC News*, 25 May 2007.

48 Seyyed Vali Reza Nasr, "Islamic Economics: Novel Perspectives" in Tim Niblock and Rodney Wilson, eds., *The Political Economy of the Middle East*, Volume III, Islamic Economics, Cheltenham and Northampton, Massachusetts: Edward Elgar Publishing, 1999, pp. 205–219.

49 M. Siddieq Noorzoy, "Islamic Laws on Riba (Interest) and their Economic Implications", *International Journal of Middle East Studies*, Vol. 14, Issue 1, 1982, pp. 3–17.

50 Timur Khan, *Islam & Mammon: The Economic Predicaments of Islamism*, Princeton, NJ: Princeton University Press, 2004, pp. 14–16.

51 This position was reaffirmed by Sheik Muhammad Sayyid Tantawi, Grand Imam of al-Azhar, in an interview published in the weekly magazine *Almsarif Alkuwaitia (The Kuwaiti Banks)*, 1 October 2007, in which he stated that a "predefined interest rate is religiously permissible in Islam and it does not count as unlawful usury".

52 Seyyed Vali Reza Nasr, "Islamic Economics: Novel Perspectives" in Tim Niblock and Rodney Wilson, eds., *The Political Economy of the Middle East*, Volume III, Islamic Economics", Cheltenham and Northampton, Massachusetts: Edward Elgar Publishing, 1999, pp. 205–219.

53   Some of Khurshid Ahmad's key works are: *Towards Monetary and Fiscal System of Islam*, Islamabad: Institute of Policy Studies, 1981; *Lectures on Economics: An Introductory Course*, Karachi: Institute of Chartered Accounts, 1968; *Economic Development in an Islamic Framework*, Leicester: The Islamic Foundation, 1979.

54   "Hardeep Dhillon, "Islamic Finance Moving into the Mainstream", *Credit*, November 2005, p. 30.

55   Wendy Kristianasen, "Britain's multiculturalism falters", *Le Monde diplomatique*, November 2006.

56   M. Ali Kettani, "Problems of Muslim Minorities" in *Muslim Communities in Non-Muslim States*, London: Islamic Council of Europe, 1980, p. 103.

57   Ibid., pp. 91–107.

58   Ehsan Masood, *British Muslims: Media Guide*, London: British Council, 2006, p. 14.

59   *Muslim Religious Authority in Western Europe*, report by the International Institute for the Study of Modern Islam (ISIM), Leiden, 30 September–1 October 2005 estimated 1,500 mosques; Ehsan Masood, *British Muslims: Media Guide*, London: British Council, 2006, p. 7, claims at least 1,600 mosques; Inayat Banglawala, A malicious campaign, *The Guardian*, 18 July 2007 gives a figure of around 1,700 mosques in the UK.

60   Humayun Ansari, *Muslims in Britain*, Minorities Group International, 2002, p. 23

61   Ihsan Yilmaz, "Muslim Alternative Dispute Resolution and Neo-Ijtihad in England", *Alternatives: Turkish Journal of International Relations*, Vol. 2, No. 1, Fall 2003, pp. 117–118.

62   Ihsan Yilmaz, "Law as Chameleon: The Question of Incorporation of Muslim Personal Law into the English Law", *Journal of Muslim Minority Affairs*, Vol. 1, No. 2, October 2001, pp. 297–308.

63   Islam has rules about how many menstrual cycles a divorced woman must have before she may remarry. The website says that if a divorcée is too young to have started menstruating, she must wait three months before re-marrying. "Sharia Council, Terms and Conditions for Talak or Divorce", Darul Uloom London, http://www.darululoomlondon.co.uk/sharia.htm , viewed 8 January 2004.

64 Clive Coleman, "There is a stealthy rise of sharia courts in Britain", *The Times*, 2 December 2006.

65 World Wide Religious News (WWRN), Europe, http://www.wwrn. org/sparse.php?idd=8405, viewed 9 August 2007.

66 Clive Coleman, "There is a stealthy rise of sharia courts in Britain", *The Times*, 2 December 2006.

67 Humayun Ansari, *Muslims in Britain*, Minority Rights Group International, 2002, p. 18.

68 Mustafa Malik, "Muslims Pluralize the West, Resist Assimilation", *Journal of Middle East Policy Council*, Vol. XI, No. 1, Spring 2004.

69 Ruth Gledhill, Tosin Sulaiman and Nicola Woolcock, "Muslims shocked by anti-British protest at mosque", *The Times*, 3 April 2004, http://www.timesonline.co.uk/tol/news/uk/article1055208.ece, viewed 14 August 2007.

70 Tahir Abbas, "Muslims in Britain after 7 / 7: the problem of the few", *openDemocracy*, 14 December 2005, http://www.opendemocracy. net/conflict-terrorism/muslims_3120.jsp, viewed 14 August 2007.

71 Dominic Casciani, "Bin Laden is seen as a hero", *BBC News*, 4 August 2005.

72 Samuel P. Huntington, *The Clash of Civilisations and the Remaking of the World Order*, New York: Simon and Schuster, 1996, pp. 118, 259–260.

73 Darryl J.J. Brock, Unpublished Research Note for PhD at University of Wales, Lampeter, 13 October 2007.

74 Richard Ford, "Jail imams vetted by security services and Muslim books screened for code", *The Times*, 26 February 2007.

75 Yahya Birt, "Being a Real Man in Islam: Drugs, Criminality and the Problem of Masculinity", revised June 2001, http://www. islamfortoday.com/birt01.htm, viewed 14 December 2003.

76 Sandra Leville and Hugh Muir, "Secret report brands Muslim police corrupt", *The Guardian*, 10 June 2006.

77 Louis Crompton, *Homosexuality and Civilization*, Cambridge, Massachusetts: Harvard University Press, 2003, p. 162.

78 Stephen O. Murray and Will Roscoe, *Islamic Homosexualities: Culture, History and Literature*, New York and London: New York University Press, 1997, p. 6.

79 Ibid., pp. 306–309.

80 Jennifer Carlile, "Gay and 'passionate about Islam' ", *MSNBC.com*, 6 July 2006, http://www.msnbc.msn.com/id/13712248/, viewed 7 August 2007.

81 James Bone, "Islam's troublemaker", *The Times*, 27 April 2004.

82 Zubeida Malik, "Polygamy law set for challenge", *BBC News*, 18 June 2000.

83 Jason Burke, "Muslim fights to make three wives legal", *The Observer*, 20 February 2000.

84 "Debate over Female Circumcision in Egypt", The Middle East Media Research Institute (MEMRI), Special Dispatch Series, No. 42, 3 August 1999.

85 Female Genital Mutilation Act 2003, chapter 31

86 "Muslim veil 'allowed in courts' ", *BBC News*, 24 April 2007.

87 "One in 10 'backs honour killing' ", *BBC News*, 4 September 2006; "Britain grapples with 'honour killing' practice", *Christian Science Monitor*, 19 October 2005.

88 "Police delve into honour killings", *BBC News*, 30 September 2003.

89 Death before dishonour", *The Observer* Magazine, 21 November 2004.

90 "Cousin accused of bride murder" *BBC News*, 6 October 2003.

91 "UK Muslims condemn honour killings", *BBC News*, 30 September 2003.

92 Joanna Bale, "Killed for loving the wrong man", *The Times*, 15 July 2006.

93 Sally Peck and Emma Henry, "Husband held over pregnant teenager's murder", *The Daily Telegraph*, 15 May 2007.

94 "Two-thirds of British Muslims say war on terror targets Islam", *Associated Press*, 24 December 2002, quoted in ummahnews.com.

95 Paul Kelso and Jeevan Vasagar, "Muslims reject image of separate society", *The Guardian*, 17 June 2002.

96 Growth for Knowledge (GfK) NOP Social Research, "Attitudes to Living in Britain: A Survey of Muslim Opinion", for TV Channel 4 Dispatches, 24 April 2006, http://www.imaginate.uk.com/MCC01_SURVEY/Site%20Download.pdf, viewed 13 August 2007; NOP Poll of British Muslims, 8 Aug 2006, http://www.ukpollingreport.co.uk/blog/archives/291, viewed 13 August 2007.

[97] *Islam in Britain: The British Muslim Community in February 2005*, report by the Institute for the Study of Islam and Christianity, Pewsey, Wiltshire: Isaac Publishing, 2005, pp. 118–119; "UK: Persecution of converts from Islam", *Barnabas Aid*, March–April 2006, p. 13.

[98] "Student was shot by 'Muslim Boys' gang", 6 January 2006, http://journals.aol.co.uk/kenningtonnews/KenningtonNews/entries/2006/01/07/student-was-shot-by-muslim-boys-gang/2035, viewed 30 August 2007.

[99] *Islam in Britain: The British Muslim Community in February 2005*, report by the Institute for the Study of Islam and Christianity, Pewsey, Wiltshire: Isaac Publishing, 2005, pp. 117–118; *Manifestations of Antisemitism in the EU 2002–2003*, a report by the European Monitoring Centre on Racism and Xenophobia, http://fra.europa.eu/fra/index.php?fuseaction=content.dsp_cat_content&catid=1, viewed 30 August 2007; *Antisemitic Incidents Report 2006*, London: The Community Security Trust, 2007; "Antisemitism and Racism", Annual Reports, Country Reports United Kingdom 2005, The Stephen Roth Institute for the Study of Contemporary Antisemitism and Racism, Tel Aviv University, http://www.tau.ac.il/Anti-Semitism/asw2005/uk.htm, viewed 30 August 2007.

[100] Jamal Sankari, *Fadlallah: The Making of a Radical Shi'ite Leader*, London: Saqi, 2005, pp. 100–108, 142, 179–180; International Crisis Group, *Radical Islam In Central Asia: Responding To Hizb Ut-Tahrir*, Asia Report No. 58, Brussels, 30 June 2003, pp. 11–15; Zafar Bangash, ed., *In Pursuit of the Power of Islam: Major Writings of Kalim Siddiqui*, London: The Open Press, 1996, pp. 253–255.

[101] Young Muslims UK, *Striving for Revival*, Leicester: Young Muslims UK, 1993, pp. 29–32.

[102] Zakaria Bashier, "A Model for Islamization", *The Muslim*, August–November 1977, text of a talk delivered at the FOSIS 14th Annual Summer Conference, http://www.salaam.co.uk/knowledge/model.php, viewed 7 August 2007.

[103] Ibid.

[104] Ibid.

[105] The strategy document is reproduced in Appendix 2.

[106] Dean Godson, "They know the extent of our reach", *The Spectator*, 5 May 2007.

107 "Islamists highly active in Britain, says report", *The Peninsula On-Line*, 4 February 2007, http://www.thepeninsulaqatar.com/Display_ news.asp?section=world_news&month=april2007&file=world_news 2007040284144.xml, viewed 14 August 2007.

108 Quoted by Alexander Downer (Australian Minister For Foreign Affairs), "Terrorism: Our Common Struggle", Speech to the Executive Council of Australian Jewry, Melbourne, 27 November 2006, http://www.foreignminister.gov.au/speeches/2006/061127_ terrorism.html, viewed 7 August 2007.

109 Denis MacEoin, *The Hijacking of British Islam: How extremist literature is subverting mosques in the UK*, 2007, especially pp. 5–6.

110 One of the most significant exceptions is Indonesia, where the progressive reformist organisation Nahdatul Ulama has around 30 million members.

111 "What is Progressive Islam?" *ISIM Newsletter*, No. 13, December 2003; Radwan A. Masmoudi, "The Silenced Majority", *Journal of Democracy*, Vol. 14, No. 2, April 2003, http://www.islam-democracy. org/art_jod_april-2003.asp, viewed 7 August 2007.

112 Ehsan Masood, "A Muslim Journey", *Prospect Magazine*, Issue 113, August 2005, http://www.prospectmagazine.co.uk/article_details. php?id=6989, viewed 7 August 2007.

113 Hassan Al-Banna, *Five Tracts of Hasan al-Banna (1906–1949): A Selection from the Majmu'at Rasa'il al-Imam al-Shahid*, Berkeley, California: University of California Press, 1978, pp. 24, 71–72.

114 Ibid., pp. 155–156.

115 Andrew Rippin, *Muslims: Their Religious Beliefs and Practices*, Vol. 2: *The Contemporary Period*, London and New York: Routledge, 1993, pp. 91–93.

116 Yvonne Y. Haddad, "Sayyid Qutb: Ideologue of Islamic Revival" in John Esposito, ed., *Voices of Resurgent Islam*, New York: Oxford University Press, 1983, pp. 85–87; Ronald Nettler, "A Modern Islamic Confession of Faith and Conception of Religion: Sayyid Qutb's Introduction to *tafsir*, *Fi Zilal al-Quran*" in *British Journal of Middle Eastern Studies*, Vol. 21, No. 1, 1994, pp. 102–104.

117 Sayyid Qutb, *Milestones*, English translation, Indianapolis: American Trust Publications, 1990, pp. 5–10, 15–17, 45–50, 66–67, 101,

123; Sayyid Qutb, *The Islamic Concept and its Characteristic*, Indianapolis: American Trust Publication, 1991, p. 12.

[118] Sayyid Qutb, *Milestones*, English translation, Indianapolis: American Trust Publications, 1990, pp. 64–68, 91–92.

[119] Yvonne Y. Haddad, "The Quranic Justification for an Islamic Revolution: The View of Sayyid Qutb" in *Middle East Journal*, Vol. 37, No. 1, Winter 1983, pp. 17–18.

[120] Nettler, "A Modern Islamic Confession of Faith and Conception of Religion: Sayyid Qutb's Introduction to *tafsir, Fi Zilal al-Quran*" in *British Journal of Middle Eastern Studies*, Vol. 21, No. 1, 1994, pp. 98–102; S.M. Solihin, *Studies on Sayyid Qutb's Fi Zilal al-Quran* (unpublished thesis, Department of Theology, University of Birmingham, 1993), p. 284.

[121] Sayyid Qutb, *Islam and Peace*, Cairo: Dar al-Shuruq, 1988, pp. 80–85; Sayyid Qutb, *Fi Zilal al-Quran*, Vol. 3, Beirut: Dar al-Shuruq, 1987, pp. 1433–1435; Sayyid Qutb, *Milestones*, English translation, Indianapolis: American Trust Publications, 1990, pp. 88–89.

[122] Sayyid Qutb, *Milestones*, English translation, Indianapolis: American Trust Publications, 1990, pp. 94–96.

[123] Sayyid Qutb, "Social Justice in Islam" in W. Shephard, ed., *Sayyid Qutb and Islamic Activism: A Translation and Critical Analysis of 'Social Justice in Islam'*, Leiden: E.J. Brill, 1996, pp. 284–288.

[124] Sayyid Qutb, *Milestones*, English translation, Indianapolis: American Trust Publications, 1990, pp. 94–96.

[125] Ronald L. Nettler, *Past Trials and Present Tribulations: A Muslim Fundamentalist's View of the Jews*, Oxford: Pergamon Press, 1987, foreword and p. x.

[126] Sayyid Qutb, "Our Struggle with the Jews" in Ronald L. Nettler, *Past Trials and Present Tribulations: A Muslim Fundamentalist's View of the Jews*, Oxford: Pergamon Press, 1987, p. 81.

[127] Ibid., p. 72.

[128] Ibid. See also Sayyid Qutb, *Milestones*, English translation, Indianapolis: American Trust Publications, 1990, pp. 94–96.

[129] Sayyid Qutb, "Our Struggle with the Jews" in Ronald L. Nettler, *Past Trials and Present Tribulations: A Muslim Fundamentalist's View of the Jews*, Oxford: Pergamon Press, 1987, pp. 75–85.

130 Abu'l A'la Mawdudi, *Jihad fi Sabilillah (Jihad in Islam)*, translated by Khurshid Ahmad, Birmingham: UK Islamic Mission, 1997, pp. 13–15.

131 Ibid., pp. 3, 8.

132 Abu'l A'la Mawdudi, *Let us be Muslims*, ed. Khurram Murad, Leicester: The Islamic Foundation, 1982, pp. 53–54.

133 Abu'l A'la Mawdudi, Jihad fi Sabilillah (Jihad in Islam), translated by Khurshid Ahmad, Birmingham: UK Islamic Mission, 1997, pp. 5, 10–11.

134 Abu'l A'la Mawdudi in J.J. Donohue and J.L. Esposito, eds., *Islam in Transition: Muslim Perspectives*, New York: Oxford University Press, 1982, pp. 94–97; Mawdudi, *Witnesses Unto Mankind*, Birmingham: UK Islamic Mission, 1986, p. 32; Abu'l A'la Mawdudi, *Jihad fi Sabilillah (Jihad in Islam)*, translated by Khurshid Ahmad, Birmingham: UK Islamic Mission, 1997, pp. 4, 12.

135 Abu'l A'la Mawdudi, *The Islamic Movement: Dynamics of Values, Power and Change*, ed. Khurram Murad, London: Islamic Foundation, 1984, p. 79.

136 Abu'l A'la Mawdudi, *Jihad fi Sabilillah (Jihad in Islam)*, translated by Khurshid Ahmad, Birmingham: UK Islamic Mission, 1997, pp. 12–13.

137 Abu'l A'la Mawdudi, *The Punishment of the Apostate According to Islamic Law*, translated and annotated by Syed Silas Husain and Ernest Hahn, Lahore: Islamic Publications, 1994, pp. 46–49.

138 Ann Elizabeth Mayer, *Islam and Human Rights: Tradition and Politics*, Boulder, Colorado: Westview Press, 1991, p. 152.

139 Adel Darwish, "Obituary: Sheikh Abdul Aziz bin Baz", *The Independent*, 14 May 1999.

140 "Residing in the land of Unbelievers: Three Fataawaa by Shaykh. Muhammad Ibn Saalih al-`Uthaimeen", http://www.allaahuakbar. net/scholars/uthaymeen/residing_in_land_of_unbelievers.htm, viewed 17 October 2007.

141 "Jamaat-e-Islami's fatal isolationism", editorial, *Daily Times*, 8 August 2005.

142 Khurshid Ahmad, "Man and the Future of Civilization: An Islamic Perspective", *Tarjuman Al Quran*, April 2002, www.jamaat.org/ Isharat/ish0402.html, viewed 9 September 2005.

[143] Khurshid Ahmad, "Musharraf, Taliban and Implementation of Shariah Bill in NWFP", *Tarjuman-ul-Quran*, July 2003, www.jamaat.org/Isharat/ish0703.html, viewed 23 August 2005.

[144] Sean O'Neill, "British Islam colleges 'link to terrorism' ", *The Times*, 29 July 2004.

[145] Khurshid Ahmad, "Musharraf, Taliban and Implementation of Shariah Bill in NWFP", *Tarjuman-ul-Quran*, July 2003, www.jamaat.org/Isharat/ish0703.html, viewed 23 August 2005.

[146] Khurshid Ahmad, "Implementation of Shari'ah", *Tarjuman Al Quran*, October 1998, www.jamaat.org/Isharat/1998/1098.html, viewed 23 August 2005.

[147] Khurshid Ahmad, "Israel, Pakistan and the Muslim World", *Tarjuman Al Quran*, September 2003, http://www.jamaat.org/Isharat/ish0903.html, viewed 9 September 2005.

[148] Khurshid Ahmad, "Muslim Ummah at the Threshold of 21st. Century", *Tarjuman Al Quran*, November 1997, http://www.jamaat.org/world/twentyfirst.html, viewed 9 September 2005.

[149] Some of Khurshid Ahmad's key works are: *Towards Monetary and Fiscal System of Islam*, Islamabad: Institute of Policy Studies, 1981; *Lectures on Economics: An Introductory Course*, Karachi: Institute of Chartered Accounts, 1968; *Economic Development in an Islamic Framework*, Leicester: The Islamic Foundation, 1979.

[150] Khurram Murad, *Da'wah Among Non-Muslims In The West*, Leicester: The Islamic Foundation, 1986, p. 12.

[151] Ibid., pp. 22–23.

[152] James Brandon and Douglas Murray, *How British libraries encourage Islamic extremism*, London: Centre for Social Cohesion, 2007, pp. 18–19.

[153] Frederic Grare, *Political Islam in the Indian Subcontinent: The Jamaat-i-Islami*, New Delhi: Manohar, 2001, notes 15, 21, pp. 85–86; B. Raman, "Bangladesh: A Bengali Abbasi Lurking Somewhere?", South Asia Analysis Group, Paper No. 232, 23 April 2001, http://www.saag.org/papers3/paper232.html, viewed 17 October 2007.

[154] James Brandon and Douglas Murray, *How British libraries encourage Islamic extremism*, London: Centre for Social Cohesion, 2007, pp. 18–19.

155 Kalim Siddiqui, *The Muslim Manifesto: a strategy for survival*, London: Muslim Institute, 1990, pp. 12, 28–30.

156 Kalim Siddiqui in Zafar Bangash, ed., *In Pursuit of the Power of Islam: Major Writings of Kalim Siddiqui*, London: The Open Press, p. 129.

157 Ibid., pp. 253–255.

158 Kalim Siddiqui, *The Muslim Manifesto: a strategy for survival*, London: Muslim Institute, 1990, pp. 11–12.

160 Ibid., p. 16.

161 Adam Pashut, "Dr 'Azzam Al-Tamimi: A Political-Ideological Brief", The Middle East Media Research Institute (MEMRI), Inquiry and Analysis Series, No. 163, 19 February 2004

162 Sean O'Neill, "British Islam colleges 'link to terrorism' ", *The Times*, 29 July 2004.

163 'Azzam al-Tamimi. "Jewish Crusade!", *Islamic Institute of Political Thought*, http://www.ii-pt.com/web/articles/jewish.htm, viewed 26 March 2004.

164 Azzam Tamimi, "Fundamentalism and violence: an Islamic viewpoint", *Islamic Institute of Political Thought*, 26 March 2004, http://www.ii-pt.com/web/papers/view.htm, viewed 8 September 2005.

165 Azzam Tamimi, "Concepts of Life Beyond Death: Martyrdom, Resurrection, Heaven & Hell", *Institute of Islamic Political Thought*, 26 March 2004, http://www.ii-pt.com/web/papers/concept.htm, viewed 8 September 2005.

166 Fuad Ajami, "Tariq Ramadan", *The Wall Street Journal*, 7 September 2004.

167 "Tariq Ramadan Calls for Hudud Freeze", *IslamOnline*, 30 March 2005, http://www.islamonline.net/English/News/2005–03/30/article07.shtml, viewed 4 July 2007.

168 Alexandre Caeiro, "European Islam and Tariq Ramadan", *ISIM Newsletter*, No. 14, June 2004.

169 "The war for Muslim minds: an interview with Gilles Kepel", *openDemocracy*, 11 November 2004, www.openDemocracy.net, viewed 24 August 2005.

170 Gilles Kepel, *The War for Muslim Minds: Islam and the West*, Cambridge, Massachusetts and London: Belknap Press of Harvard University Press, 2004, pp. 279–280.

[171] Tariq Ramadan, "The Contradictions of the Islamic World", *Qantara.de*, http://www.qantara.de/webcom/show_article.php/_c-476/_nr-88/i.html, viewed 13 September 2005.

[172] Ibid.

[173] Reuven Paz, "The Coronation of the King of the Golden Path: Sheikh Qaradawi Beomes Imam *Al-Wasatiyyah* and a School and Movement by Itself ", The Project for the Research of Islamist Movements (PRISM), Occasional Papers, Vol. 5, No. 3, August 2007.

[174] Yusuf al-Qaradawi, http://www.islamonline.net/fatwa/english/FatwaDisplay.asp?hFatwaID=61551, viewed 10 August 2005.

[175] Yusuf al-Qaradawi, *Priorities of the Islamic Movement in the Coming Phase*, Swansea: Awakening Publications, 2000, p. 34.

[176] Ibid., p. 171.

[177] "The Prophet Muhammad as a Jihad Model", The Middle East Media Research Institute (MEMRI), Special Dispatch Series, No. 246, 24 July 2001.

[178] Yusuf al-Qaradawi, *Priorities of the Islamic Movement in the Coming Phase*, Swansea: Awakening Publications, 2000, pp. 163–167.

[179] "Leading Islamist Sheikh Yousef Al-Qaradhawi: We are Fighting in the Name of Islam . . .", The Middle East Media Research Institute (MEMRI), Special Dispatch Series, No. 1102, 28 February 2006.

[180] "Sheikh Yousuf Al-Qaradhawi: Resistance in Iraq is a Duty of Every Muslim", The Middle East Media Research Institute (MEMRI), Special Dispatch Series, No. 828, 14 December 2004.

[181] *Al-Sharq Al-Awsat* (19 July 2003), extracts in English translation in The Middle East Media Research Institute (MEMRI), Special Dispatch Series No. 542, 24 July 2003.

[182] Ibid.

[183] Alain Gresch, "Saudi Arabia: reality check", *Le Monde diplomatique*, February 2006.

[184] Sarah Garland, "Cleric Turns Against Al Qaeda", *The New York Sun*, 18 September 2007.

[185] "General Issues of Faith From the Fundamentals of the Salafee Creed", translated and annotated by Dr Abu Ameenah Bilal Philips, http://www.bilalphilips.com/bilal_pages.php?option=com_content&task=view&id=289, viewed 17 October 2007.

[186] Toby Helm, "Jews and Freemasons controlled war on Iraq, says No 10 adviser", *The Daily Telegraph*, 12 September 2005.

[187] Ahmad Thomson, "Incorporating Muslim Personal Law into UK Domestic Law" in *Fiqh for Today: Muslims as Minorities*, Conference Booklet, 5th Annual AMSS (UK) Conference, 21–22 February 2004, in cooperation with The International Institute of Islamic Thought, The Muslim College, Q News Media.

[188] Peter Murtagh, "Rushdie in hiding after Ayatollah's death threat", *The Guardian*, 18 February 1989. Also quoted in Salman Rushdie, "The Right Time for An Islamic Reformation", *The Washington Post*, 7 August 2005. See also Amit Roy, "British Honour for Key Muslim", *The Telegraph* (Calcutta, India), 12 June 2005.

[189] "The Rushdie Affair – 1988–91", "http://www.salaam.co.uk/themeofthemonth/september03_index.php?l=1, viewed 1 December 2005.

[190] Jeevan Vasagar, "British Muslims warn of 'conflict for generations'", *The Guardian*, 14 January 2003.

[191] Tom Baldwin, "Blair faces wrath of Britain's Muslims", *The Times*, 19 September 2002.

[192] *The Moral Maze*, BBC Radio 4, 14 July 2004, www.bbc.co.uk/radio4/religion/moralmaze.shtml, viewed 4 January 2005.

[193] Will Cummins, "We must be allowed to criticise Islam", *The Daily Telegraph*, 11 July 2004.

[194] Iqbal Sacranie, quoted in Melanie Phillips, "The British Inquisition (1)", 13 January 2005, http://www.melaniephillips.com/diary/archives/000988.html, viewed 22 January 2007.

[195] Iqbal Sacranie, "We need protection from the pedlars of religious hatred", *The Daily Telegraph*, 14 December 2004.

[196] "MCB meet minister over Religious Hatred bill", *The Muslim Weekly*, Issue 87, 8–14 July 2005.

[197] Anthony McRoy, "Bari is hope for British Muslims", www.naba.org.uk/content/articles/Diaspora/606_McRoy_Bari_MCB.htm, viewed 6 June 2007.

[198] David Garbin Cronem, "Bangladeshi diaspora in the UK: some observations on socio-cultural dynamics, religious trends and transnational politics", (draft version – June 2005), Surrey University, prepared for the Conference on Human Rights and Bangladesh, School of Oriental and African Studies, University of London, 17 June 2005.

199 David Harrison, "Media 'contributing to rise of Islamophobia' ", *The Sunday Telegraph*, 10 September 2006.

200 Abdullah 'Azzam, *Defence of the Muslim Lands*, London: Ahle Sunnah Wal Jama'at, no date, pp. 4–6.

201 Abdullah 'Azzam, *Join the Caravan*, London: Azzam Publications, 1996, pp. 36–38.

202 Abdullah 'Azzam, *Defence of the Muslim Lands*, London: Ahle Sunnah Wal Jama'at, no date, p. 7.

203 Ibid., pp. 7–17.

204 Abdullah 'Azzam, *Join the Caravan*, London: Azzam Publications, 1996, p. 13.

205 Abdullah 'Azzam, *Defence of the Muslim Lands*, London: Ahle Sunnah Wal Jama'at, no date, pp. 7–17.

206 Ibid., pp. 29–33.

207 "The Biography of Sheikh Omar Bakri Muhammad", http://www.almuhajiroun.com/\default.asp; Keith Dovkants, "Muslim extremists step up resistance", *This is London*, 22 January 2003; Jeremy Reynalds, "Radical Islamic Group Warns Muslims Against Helping British or American Military", *American Daily*, 10 February 2003.

208 "UK bombing fears now focus on enemy within", *The Times*, 4 April 2004.

209 "Fatwa for 'gay Jesus' writer", *BBC News*, 29 October 1999.

210 Yael Shahar and Ely Karmon, "London-Based Islamic Group Issues Fatwa against Israel", *International Policy Institute for Counter-Terrorism*, 19 October 2000.

211 Jeremy Reynalds, "Radical Islamic Group Warns Muslims against Helping British or American Military", *American Daily*, 10 February 2003.

212 Sean O'Neill and Yaacov Lappin, "Britain's online imam declares war as he calls young to jihad", *The Times*, 17 January 2006.

213 Sean O'Neill, Helen Rumbelow and Ruth Gledhill, "Muslim 'task force' criticised for being too establishment", *The Times*, 20 July 2005.

214 Rita Katz and Michael Kern, "Center of the Jihadist World", *National Review*, 14 July 2005.

215 Terence McKenna, "The Recruiters", *The National*, June 2002; Philip Jenkins, "Nor Shall My Sword Rest in my Hand", *Chronicles*

Magazine, March 2002; Philip Johnstone, "Radical Muslim loses his appeal against detention", *The Daily Telegraph*, 28 January 2004.

[216] Daniel McGrory, "Cleric's tape threat to destroy Rome", *The Times*, 3 April 2004.

[217] Ibid.

[218] Daniel Simpson, "British radicals urge Muslims to fight back", *Middle East Times*, Issue 99–13, 28 March 1999.

[219] "Profile: Abu Hamza", *BBC News*, Friday 17 January 2003; Libby Purves, "Britain, spiritual home to this creed of hate", *TIMES ONLINE*, 21 January 2003; Michael Radu, "The Problem of 'Londonistan': Europe, Human Rights, and Terrorists", *Foreign Policy Research Institute*, 12 April 2002.

[220] "Abu Hamza faces extradition to US after arrest", *TIMES ONLINE*, 27 May 2004; "Hamza was betrayed by trusted lieutenant", *TIMES ONLINE*, 30 May 2004; Brian Whitaker, "Satellite phone gives US vital evidence", *The Guardian*, 28 May 2004.

[221] Sean O'Neill and Daniel McGrory, *The Suicide Factory: Abu Hamza and the Finsbury Park Mosque*, London: Harper Collins, 2006, pp. 310–311.

[222] Sam Lister, "Imam 'instructed British Muslims to ill infidels' ", *TIMES ONLINE*, 23 January 2003; "Cleric guilty of spreading hate", *BBC News*, 24 February 2003.

[223] James Brandon and Douglas Murray, *How British libraries encourage Islamic extremism*, London: Centre for Social Cohesion, 2007, pp. 21–22.

[224] "The unholy past of the Muslim cleric demanding the Pope's execution", *This is London*, 19 September 2006.

[225] Jack O'Sullivan, "Defender of his Faith", *The Guardian*, 15 January 2003.

[226] Zaki Badawi, "The Concept of Jihad in Islam", transcript from recording, Council on Christian Approaches to Defence and Disarmament, Westminster Abbey, 18 April 1996.

[227] Zaki Badawi, *Islam in Britain*, London: Taha Publishers, 1981, pp. 26–27.

[228] Jack O'Sullivan, "Defender of his Faith", *The Guardian*, 15 January 2003.

[229] Ibid.

230 Ibid.
231 Zaki Badawi, "The Concept of Jihad in Islam", transcript from recording, Council on Christian Approaches to Defence and Disarmament, Westminster Abbey, 18 April 1996.
232 Ziauddin Sardar, "Rethinking Islam", *Islam For Today*, June 2002, http://www.islamfortoday.com/sardar01.htm, viewed 7 August 2007; Thomas Gerholm, "Two Muslim intellectuals in the postmodern West: Akbar Ahmed and Ziauddin Sardar" in Akbar Ahmed and Hastings Donnan, eds., *Islam, Globalization and Postmodernity*, London and New York: Routledge, 1994.
233 Ziauddin Sardar, "Rethinking Islam", *Islam For Today*, June 2002, http://www.islamfortoday.com/sardar01.htm, viewed 7 August 2007.
234 Ibid.
235 Ibid.
236 Ibid.
237 Ibid.
238 Ibid.
239 Ibid.
240 Ziauddin Sardar, "Viewpoint: The global voices reclaiming Islam", *BBC News*, 6 September 2005.
241 Ehsan Masood, "A Muslim Journey", *Prospect Magazine*, Issue 113, August 2005,http://www.prospectmagazine.co.uk/article_details. php?id=6989, viewed 7 August 2007.
242 Fareena Alam, "A Humane Muslim Future", *openDemocracy*, 8 March 2005, http://www.opendemocracy.net/faith-europe_islam/ article_2363.jsp, viewed 7 August 2007; Fareena Alam, "Five principles for Islam's future", *openDemocracy*, 8 March 2005, http://www.opendemocracy.net/faith-europe_islam/article_2363.jsp, viewed 24 August 2005.
243 Maruf Khwaja, "Terrorism, Islam, reform: thinking the unthinkable", *openDemocracy*, 28 July 2005, http://www.opendemocracy.net/ conflict-terrorism/reform_2706.jsp, viewed 7 August 2007.
244 Ibid.
245 Ed Husain, *The Islamist*, London: Penguin Books, 2007.
246 Ibid.
247 Aatish Taseer, "A British jihadist", *Prospect Magazine*, 13 August 2005.

[248] "I was a fanatic . . . I know their thinking, says former radical Islamist", *Daily Mail*, 1 July 2007; "The Network", *CBS News*, 25 March 2007.

[249] Aatish Taseer, "A British jihadist", *Prospect Magazine*, 13 August 2005.

[250] "UK 'terror target' claim dismissed", *BBC News*, 7 January 2002; Adrian Morgan, "Leading Muslim terrorists have been educated at Britain's universities", *Family Security Matters*, 5 January 2007, http://www.familysecuritymatters.org/homeland.php?id=559672, viewed 3 July 2007.

[251] "I was a fanatic . . . I know their thinking, says former radical Islamist", *Daily Mail*, 1 July 2007; "The Network", *CBS News*, 25 March 2007.

[252] Aatish Taseer, "A British jihadist", *Prospect Magazine*, 13 August 2005.

[253] "I was a fanatic . . . I know their thinking, says former radical Islamist", *Daily Mail*, 1 July 2007; "The Network", *CBS News*, 25 March 2007.

[254] Hassan Butt, "My plea to fellow Muslims: you must renounce terror", *The Observer*, 1 July 2007.

[255] Ibid.

[256] Shiraz Maher, "How I escaped Islamism", *The Times*, 12 August 2007; Shiraz Maher, "How we can rid Britain of violent extremism", *The New Statesman*, 12 July 2007.

[257] "Minister backs new Muslim group", *BBC News*, 19 July 2007.

[258] "A question of leadership", transcript, *Panorama*, *BBC1*, 21 August 2005, http://news.bbc.co.uk/1/hi/programmes/panorama/4171950.stm, viewed 6 August 2007.

[259] "Muslim Council of Britain: Much ado about nothing", *Q-News*, March-April 2002, pp. 22–23; "Silencing voices of dissent", *Q-News*, March-April 2002, p. 26.

[260] Ehsan Masood, "British Muslims must stop the war", *openDemocracy*, 30 August 2005, http://www.opendemocracy.net/conflict-terrorism/british_sufis_2786.jsp, viewed 7 August 2007.

[261] Jeevan Vasagar, "Dilemma of the Moderates", *The Guardian*, 19 June 2002.

262 "Muslim Council of Britain: Much ado about nothing", *Q-News*, March–April 2002, pp. 22–23; "Silencing voices of dissent", *Q-News*, March–April 2002, p. 26.

263 MCB Statement, "Islam Channel programme 'The Agenda' and Yvonne Ridley", 22 June 2005, http://www.mcb.org.uk/article_detail.php?article=announcement-459, viewed 7 August 2007; "Show support for Sister Yvonne Ridley" petition, http://www.ummah.com/forum/showthread.php?t=59532, viewed 7 August 2007.

264 "Muslim Council of Britain: Much ado about nothing", *Q-News*, March–April 2002, pp. 22–23; "Silencing voices of dissent", *Q-News*, March–April 2002, p. 26.

265 Martin Bright, "Radical links of UK's Moderate Muslim Group", *The Guardian*, 14 August 2005; "A question of leadership", transcript, *Panorama*, BBC1, 21 August 2005, http://news.bbc.co.uk/1/hi/programmes/panorama/4171950.stm, viewed 6 August 2007.

266 Ehsan Masood, "British Muslims must stop the war", *openDemocracy*, 30 August 2005, http://www.opendemocracy.net/conflict-terrorism/british_sufis_2786.jsp, viewed 7 August 2007.

267 Wendy Kristianasen, "Britain's multiculturalism falters", *Le Monde diplomatique*, November 2006.

268 http://www.islamicthought.org/ks-home.html, viewed 8 August 2007; Gilles Kepel, *Allah in the West: Islamic Movements in America and Europe*, Stanford, California: Stanford University Press, 1997, pp. 139–144.

269 Kalim Siddiqui, *The Muslim Manifesto: a strategy for survival*, London: The Muslim Institute, 1990, pp. 12,28–30.

270 http://www.islamicthought.org/icit-doc.html, viewed 11 October 2007.

271 http://www.halalfoodauthority.co.uk/front.html, viewed 11 October 2007.

272 "The Rushdie Affair – 1988–91", http://www.salaam.co.uk/themeofthemonth/september03_index.php?l=1, viewed 8 August 2007.

273 http://www.fosis.org.uk/index.htm, viewed 11 October 2005 or http://web.petabox.bibalex.org/web/20030618120515/www.fosis.org.uk/about/intro_to_fosis.htm, viewed 28 August 2007.

274 "BMF Objectives" http://www.bmf.eu.com/bmf_obj.php, viewed 8 August 2007.

275 Wendy Kristianasen, "Britain's multiculturalism falters", *Le Monde diplomatique*, November 2006.

276 Dominic Casciani, "Minister backs new Muslim group", *BBC News*, 19 July 2006; Wendy Kristianasen, "Britain's multiculturalism falters", *Le Monde diplomatique*, November 2006.

277 "School wins Muslim dress appeal", *BBC News*, 22 March 2006; Boris Johnson, "The Shabina Begum case never had anything to do with modesty", *The Daily Telegraph*, 23 March 2006.

278 Ron Greaves, *The Sufis of Britain: An exploration of Muslim identity*, Cardiff: Cardiff Academic Press, 2000, pp. 82–83.

279 Ron Greaves, "Cult, Charisma, Community: The Arrival of Sufi Pirs and Their Impact on Muslims in Britain", *Journal of Muslim Minority Affairs*, Vol. 16, No. 2, July 1996, pp. 169–192 (see p. 172).

280 Ashutosh Misra, "Rise of Religious Parties in Pakistan: Causes and Prospects", http://www.ciaonet.org/olj/sa/sa_apr03/sa_apr03mia01.html, viewed 8 August 2007.

281 Khaled Ahmed, "How Islam Is Used By Us", *The Daily Times*, 5 December 2003, http://www.mail-archive.com/sacw@insaf.net/msg00060.html, viewed 8 August 2007.

282 Khaled Ahmed, "Reassertion of the Barelwis in Pakistan", *The Friday Times*, 8 September 2000.

283 David Garbin Cronem, "Bangladeshi Diaspora in the UK: Some Observations on Socio-cultural Dynamics, Religious Trends and Transnational Politics", (draft version, June 2005), Surrey University, prepared for the Conference on Human Rights and Bangladesh, School of Oriental and African Studies, University of London, 17 June 2005.

284 Philip Lewis, *Islamic Britain: Religion, Politics and Identity Among British Muslims*, London & New York: I.B. Tauris, 1994, 2002, pp. 81–89.

285 http://www.wimmauritius.org/about.html, viewed 8 August 2007.

286 Philip Lewis, *Islamic Britain: Religion, Politics and Identity Among British Muslims*, London and New York: I.B. Tauris, 1994, 2002, pp. 81–89.

287 http://www.sultani.co.uk/, viewed 8 August 2007.

288 Philip Lewis, *Islamic Britain: Religion, Politics and Identity Among British Muslims*, London and New York: I.B. Tauris, 1994, 2002, pp. 81–89.

289 Mohammed Amer, "Dressing up for your Shaikh: the Minhajul Quran Movement in London" in *Muslim Religious Authority in Western Europe*, report by the International Institute for the Study of Modern Islam (ISIM), Leiden, 30 September–1 October 2005.

290 Ron Greaves, "Cult, Charisma, Community: The Arrival of Sufi Pirs and Their Impact on Muslims in Britain" *Journal of Muslim Minority Affairs*, Vol. 16, No. 2, July 1996, pp. 169–192 (see p. 171).

291 Ibid., p. 172.

292 http://www.faizaneislam.org/about.shtml, viewed 8 August 2007.

293 Andrew Norfolk, "Hardline takeover of British mosques", *The Times*, 7 September 2007.

294 Philip Lewis, Islamic Britain: Religion, Politics and Identity Among British Muslims, London and New York: I.B. Tauris, 1994, 2002, pp. 96–101, 135–138

295 http://www.inter-islam.org/index.htm, viewed 8 August 2007.

296 Yoginder Sikand, *The Origins and Development of the Tablighi-Jama'at (1920–2000)*, New Delhi: Orient Longman, 2002, pp. 246–249.

297 Yoginder Sikand, *The Origins and Development of the Tablighi-Jama'at (1920–2000)*, New Delhi: Orient Longman, 2002, pp. 246–250; David Garbin Cronem, "Bangladeshi Diaspora in the UK: Some Observations on Socio-cultural Dynamics, Religious Trends and Transnational Politics", (draft version–June 2005), Surrey University, prepared for the Conference on Human Rights and Bangladesh, School of Oriental and African Studies, University of London, 17 June 2005.

298 Alex Alexiev, "Tablighi Jamaat: Jihad's Stealthy Legions", *Middle East Quarterly*, Vol. XII, No. 1, Winter 2005.

299 "Giant mosque for 40,000 may be built at London Olympics", *The Sunday Times*, 27 November 2005.

300 Alex Alexiev, "Tablighi Jamaat: Jihad's Stealthy Legions", *Middle East Quarterly*, Vol. XII, No. 1, Winter 2005.

301 General Intelligence and Security Service, Annual Report 2003, http://www.fas.org/irp/world/netherlands/aivd2003-eng.pdf, viewed 8 August 8, 2007.

302 Sean O'Neill and Roger Boyes, "Islamic missionary group links alleged plotters", *The Times*, 17 August 2006.

303 Ibid.

304 *TV Channel 4 Dispatches*, "Undercover Mosque", broadcast 15 January 2007.

305 http://www.ahlehadith.co.uk, viewed 14 November 2005.

306 http://www.greenlanemasjid.org/aboutus.asp, viewed 30 August 2007.

307 David Montero, "British bomb plot spotlights charities", *Christian Science Monitor*, 16 August 2006.

308 Seyyed Vali Reza Nasr, *The Vanguard of the Islamic Revolution: The Jama'at-i Islami of Pakistan*, Berkeley: University of California Press, 1994, pp. 16–17.

309 Abul A'la Mawdudi, *The Islamic Law and Constitution*, Lahore: Islamic Publications, 1980, pp. 100–101.

310 R. A. Greaves, "The Reproduction of Jamaat-i Islami in Britain", *Islam and Christian-Muslim Relations*, Vol. 6, No. 2, 1995, pp. 187–210.

311 http://www.ukim.org/DesktopDefault.aspx, viewed 8 January 2007.

312 Anthony McRoy, *From Rushdie to 7/7: The Radicalisation of Islam in Britain*, London: The Social Affairs Unit, 2006, p. 167.

313 Khurshid Ahmad, "Muslim ummah at the Threshold of 21st Century", *Tarjumanul Qur'an*, November 1997, www.jamaat.org/world/ twentyfirst.html, viewed 8 August 2007; www.islamic-foundation. org.uk/, viewed 8 August 2007; John L. Esposito, ed., *The Oxford Encyclopedia of the Modern Islamic World*, New York: Oxford University Press, 1995, Vol. 2, pp. 309–310, entry on "Islamic foundation" by Jorgen Nielsen; *The Islamic Foundation: Objectives, Activities, Projects*, Markfield, no date; Jorgen S. Nielsen, *Muslims in Western Europe*, Edinburgh: Edinburgh University Press, 1992, pp. 43–51, 134–136; Philip Lewis, *Islamic Britain: Religion, Politics and Identity Among British Muslims*, London and New York: I.B. Tauris, 1994, 2002, pp. 100–105, 198.

314 http://www.muslim-ed-trust.org.uk

315 Ghulam Sarwar, *Islam: Beliefs and Teachings*, London: The Muslim Educational Trust, 1980, 5th edition 1998, pp. 177–179.

[316] http://www.isb.org.uk; Philip Lewis, *Islamic Britain: Religion, Politics and Identity Among British Muslims*, London and New York: I.B. Tauris, 1994, 2002, pp. 112, 201, 206.

[317] http://www.ymuk.net

[318] Anthony McRoy, *From Rushdie to 7/7: The Radicalisation of Islam in Britain*, London: The Social Affairs Unit, 2006, pp. 167–168.

[319] Ibid., p. 167.

[320] http://www.islamicforumeurope.com/live/ife.php, viewed 8 August 2007; Delwar Hussain, "Bangladeshis in East London: From Secular Politics to Islam", *openDemocracy*, 7 July 2006; David Garbin Cronem, "Bangladeshi Diaspora in the UK: Some Observations on Socio-cultural Dynamics, Religious Trends and Transnational Politics", (draft version, June 2005), Surrey University, prepared for the Conference on Human Rights and Bangladesh, School of Oriental and African Studies, University of London, 17 June 2005.

[321] Muhammad Mumtaz Ali, *The Muslim Community in Britain: An Historical Account*, Kelana Jaya, Selangor Darul Ehsan, Malaysia: Pelanduk Publications, 1996, pp. 77–82; John Jawton, "Muslims in Europe: The Presence," January/February 1979, http://www.saudiaramcoworld.com/issue/197901/muslims.in.europe-the.presence.htm, viewed 8 August 2007.

[322] Michael Whine, "The Advance of the Muslim Brotherhood in the UK" in Hillel Fradkin, Husain Haqqani and Eric Brown, eds., *Current Trends in Islamist Ideology*, Vol. 2, Center on Islam, Democracy, and the Future of the Muslim World, Washington DC: The Hudson Institute, 2005, pp. 30–39; Jonathan Laurence, "Managing Transnational Islam in Western Europe: The Limits of Institutional and Postnational Approaches", Department of Government, Harvard University, paper prepared for presentation at the conference "Immigration in a Cross-National Context: What Are the Implications for Europe?" organised by the EU Center at Syracuse, http://web.archive.org/web/20050206092149/http://www.lisproject.org/immigration/papers/laurence.pdf, viewed 8 August 2007; Brigitte Maréchal, "The Muslim Brotherhood and Religious Authority in Western Europe", *Muslim Religious Authority in Western Europe*, conference report by the International Institute for the Study of Modern Islam (ISIM), Leiden, 30 September–1 October 2005.

323 www.mabonline.net, viewed 8 August 2007; Barbara Amiel, "Muslims have just as Much to fear from Militant Islam", *The Daily Telegraph*, 24 November 2003; Anthony Browne, "Time for Truth about this Sinister Brotherhood", *The Times*, 11 August 2004.

324 "Islamic Extremism In Europe", hearing before the Subcommittee on Europe and Emerging Threats of the Committee on International Relations, US House of Representatives, One Hundred Ninth Congress, First Session, 27 April 2005, Serial No. 109–34, http://internationalrelations.house.gov/archives/109/20917.PDF, viewed 9 August 2007; Anthony Browne, "Time for Truth about this Sinister Brotherhood", *The Times*, 11 August 2004.

325 Anthony McRoy, *From Rushdie to 7/7: The Radicalisation of Islam in Britain*, London: The Social Affairs Unit, 2006, p. 162.

326 www.eu-islam.com/en/templates/index_en.asp, viewed 28 September 2005.

327 Nicholas Rufford and Abdul Taher, "British Muslim says troops are fair target," *The Sunday Times*, 11 October 2004.

328 http://www.e-cfr.org/eng/ and http://www.e-cfr.org

329 "Al-Qaradhawi Speaks In Favor of Suicide Operations at an Islamic Conference in Sweden", The Middle East Media Research Institute (MEMRI), Special Dispatch Series, No. 542, 24 July 2004.

330 http://www.islamonline.net/servlet/Satellite?pagename=IslamOnline-English-Ask_Scholar/FatwaE/FatwaE&cid=1119503548186, viewed 6 December 2005.

331 Sean O'Neill, "British Islam Colleges 'Link To Terrorism' ", *The Times*, 29 July 2004.

332 Ali al Halawani and Hany Mohammad, "Scholars launch pan-Muslim body in London", http://www.islamonline.net/english/news/2004–07/12/article01.shtm, viewed 9 August 2007.

333 Michael Whine, "The Advance of the Muslim Brotherhood in the UK" in Hillel Fradkin, Husain Haqqani and Eric Brown, eds., *Current Trends in Islamist Ideology*, Vol. 2, Center on Islam, Democracy, and the Future of the Muslim World, Washington DC: The Hudson Institute, 2005, pp. 30–39.

334 "Islamic Extremism In Europe", Hearing before the Subcommittee on Europe and Emerging Threats of the Committee on International Relations, House of Representatives, One Hundred Ninth Congress,

First Session, 27 April 2005, Serial No. 109–34, http://internationalrelations.house.gov/archives/109/20917.PDF, viewed 9 August 2007.

335 http://web.archive.org/web/20060818175540/http://www.iipt.com/web/advisors.htm, viewed 9 August 2007.

336 "OIC summit rubberstamps western colonialist aggression in Iraq", www.1924.org, viewed 27 April 2004; or http://www.hizb.org.uk/hizb/ht-britain.html, viewed 14 August 2007; Audrey Gillan, "Hizbut-Tahrir, Little Known", *The Guardian*, 19 June 2002; Abdelwahab El-Affendi, "Hizb al-Tahrir: The Paradox of a very British Party", *The Daily Star*, 2 September 2003, http://web.archive.org/web/20030904172117/http://www.dailystar.com.lb/opinion/02_09_03_c.asp, viewed 8 August 2007.

337 Michael Whine, "Is Hizb ut-Tahrir Changing Strategy or Tactics?", Hudson Institute, Center for Eurasian Policy, Occasional Research Paper Series I (Hizb ut-Tahrir), No. 1. http://www.hudson.org/files/publications/EurasianPaper_Aug42006.pdf, viewed 9 August 2007.

338 Ibid.

339 Michael Whine, "The Mode of Operation of Hizb ut Tahrir in an Open Society", The Institute for Counter-Terrorism, 20 February 2004, http://web.archive.org/web/20040603033412/http://www.ict.org.il/articles/articledet.cfm?articleid=515, viewed 8 August 2007.

340 http://www.wamy.co.uk/bd_about.htm

341 http://www.islah.tv/index.php?/english/empp2/, viewed 6 December 2005 or http://www.socialcohesion.co.uk/pubs/cdlr.php, viewed 9 August 2007.

342 http://www.islah.tv/index.php?/english/about/, viewed 6 December 2005.

343 Zahid Hussain, Stewart Tendler and Daniel McGrory, "Al-Qaeda's 'British chief' is seized in police raids", *The Times*, 5 August 2004.

344 Abul Taher and Dipesh Gadher, "Islamists infiltrate four universities", *The Sunday Times*, 12 November 2006; Robert Wesley, "British Terrorist Dhiren Barot's Research on Radiological Weapons", *Terrorism Monitor*, Vol. 3, Issue 44, 14 November 2006; Rosie Cowan, "Most senior al-Qaida terrorist yet captured in Britain gets 40 years for plotting carnage", *The Guardian*, 8 November 2006.

[345] Ewen MacAskill and Vikram Dodd, "The Pakistan connection: suspicion falls on al-Qaida", *The Guardian*, 12 August 2006; Duncan Campbell, "Pakistan says al-Qaida link to plot found", *The Guardian*, 17 August 2006.

[346] Eliza Manningham-Buller, "The International Terrorist Threat to the UK", text of a speech delivered on 9 November 2006, published by Northeast Intelligence Network, 10 November 2006, http://www.homelandsecurityus.com/mi5report110906, viewed 9 August 2007.

[347] http://www.sicm.org.uk/index.php?page=about_sicm, viewed 9 August 2007.

[348] http://www.wabil.com

[349] http://www.alkhoei.org, viewed 12 September 2005.

[350] http://www.world-federation.org/AboutUs/, viewed 12 September 2005.

[351] http://www.ic-el.com/english/, viewed 12 September 2005 or http://www.ic-el.com/users/English/English/index.htm, viewed 9 August 2007.

[352] http://www.vob.org, viewed 12 September 2005.

[353] "Hezbollah, Profile of the Lebanese Shiite Terrorist Organization of Global Reach Sponsored by Iran and Supported by Syria", Intelligence and Terrorism Information Center at the Center for Special Studies, http://www.terrorism-info.org.il/malam_multimedia/english/iran/pdf/june_03.pdf, viewed 17 January 2007 or http://www.terrorism-info.org.il/malam_multimedia/English/eng_n/html/hezbollah.htm, viewed 9 August 2007. See also Douglas Farah, "Hezbollah's External Support Network in West Africa and Latin America", International Assessment and Strategy Centre, 4 August 2006, http://www.strategycenter.net/research/pubID.118/pub_detail.asp#, viewed 17 January 2007.

[354] Matthew A. Levitt, "Still With Us? Testing Britain's Counter-Terror Resolve", *National Review Online*, 5 September 2003, http://www.nationalreview.com/script/printpage.p?ref=/comment/comment-levitt090503.asp, viewed 17 January 2007.

[355] Ibid.

[356] "Hezbollah", Anti-Defamation League, 29 September 2006, http://www.adl.org/main_Terrorism/hezbollah_overview.htm?Multi_page_sections=sHeading_7, viewed 17 January 2007.

[357] http://www.iis.ac.uk/home

[358] http://www.akf.org.uk/akf.html

[359] David Damrel, "A Sufi Apocalypse", *ISIM Newsletter*, 4 December 1999.

[360] Ziauddin Sardar, *Desperately Seeking Paradise*, London: Granta, 2004, pp. 64–71.

[361] http://www.pharo.com/intelligence/swordofislam/articles/ifis15quran. asp, viewed 28 September 2005 or Boudewijn Wegerif, "The new Islamic Dinar", http://www.appropriate-economics.org/materials/ dinar.html, viewed 14 August 2007.

[362] http://www.wokingmuslim.org/about.htm, viewed 6 December 2005.

[363] Melissa Kite and Patrick Hennessy, "State seeks control of Muslim schools", *The Daily Telegraph*, 7 August 2005; Osama Saeed, "Will the State protect Islamic Teaching?", *The Scotsman*, 18 May 2005; Mike Baker, "Why the U-turn on Faith Schools?" *BBC News*, 4 November 2006.

[364] Matthew Taylor, "Two thirds oppose state aided faith schools", *The Guardian*, 23 August 2005.

[365] See "Interview with Vali Nasr", *Frontline*, http://www.pbs.org/wgbh/ pages/frontline/shows/saudi/interviews/nasr.html, viewed 14 February 2007.

[366] "Islamic Seminaries are a problem, says Siddiqui", The Muslim Parliament of Great Britain, press release, 7 September 2007, http://www.muslimparliament.org.uk/seminaries.html, viewed 4 October 2007.

[367] Anthony Glees and Chris Pope, *When Students Turn to Terror: Terrorist and Extremist Activity on British Campuses*, London: The Social Affairs Unit, 2005, pp. 49–87.

[368] For further examples and their refutation see *Islam and Truth*, a joint publication of Barnabas Fund and the Institute for the Study of Islam and Christianity, 2007, pp. 4–6.

[369] Yasmin Khan, "Beyond the Bogeyman", *The Guardian*, 7 July 2006.

[370] The suggestion is refuted by various historians in James Slack, "Why race chief wants to sink our role in the Armada", *Daily Mail*, 25 September 2007.

371 Sir Trevor Phillips, "Include Muslims in British History", *The Muslim Weekly*, 28 September–4 October 2007.

372 http://www.salaam.co.uk/education/index.php?file=./ips.php, viewed 29 November 2005; http://www.islamia-pri.brent.sch.uk/, viewed 30 November 2005.

373 OFSTED report 2002, http://www.ofsted.gov.uk/reports/manreports/ 113.htm, viewed 30 November 2005 or http://www.ofsted.gov.uk/ reports/pdf/?inspectionNumber=108823&providerCategoryID=1638 4&fileName=\\school\\100\\s163_100372_20061017.pdf, viewed 9 August 2007.

374 "Muslim school offers best added value", *The Times*, 13 January 2005.

375 http://home.btconnect.com/lia/lia.html, viewed 30 November 2005.

376 http://www.islamic-college.ac.uk/, viewed 30 November 2005.

377 http://www.hawza.org.uk/, viewed 30 November 2005.

378 http://www.mihe.org.uk/html/aboutmihe.htm, viewed 30 November 2005.

379 Ihsan Yilmaz, "Muslim Alternative Dispute Resolution and Neo-Ijtihad in England" in *Alternatives: Turkish Journal of International Relations*, Vol. 2, No. 1, Fall 2003, including note 68, pp. 119–121, 139.

380 "British Muslims want Islamic law", *Hindustan Times*, 30 November 2004.

381 "The Muslim Law (Shariah) Council", http://www.muslimcollege.ac. uk/index.asp?id=170&type=detail, viewed 6 August 2007.

382 The Fatwa Committee's web address is http://www.iccuk.org/ services/Imams/fatwas/fatwa.htm, viewed 9 August 2007.

383 World Wide Religious News (WWRN) Europe, http://www.wwrn. org/parse.php?idd=9655&c=27, viewed 6 January 2004 or http: //www.wwrn.org/sparse.php?idd=8405, viewed 9 August 2007.

384 http://www.ahlehadith.co.uk/ijbuk/index.htm, viewed 6 January 2004 or http://www.mjah.org/ContactUs/tabid/57/Default.aspx, viewed 13 August 2007.

385 http://www.darululoomlondon.co.uk/sharia.htm, viewed 6 January 2004 or http://web.archive.org/web/20040224181257/ darululoomlondon.co.uk/sharia.htm, viewed 14 August 2007.

386 http://www.shariah-institute.org/new.htm or http://web.archive.org/web/20041206220725/http://www.shariah-institute.org/new.htm, viewed 14 August 2007; http://www.shariah-institute.org/shariah. htm, viewed 6 January 2004 or http://web.archive.org/web/20050214024059/http://www.shariah-institute.org/shariah.htm, viewed 14 August 2007.

387 http://www.wamy.co.uk/fatwas/fatwa_template.html, viewed 6 January 2004 or http://www.islamonline.net/servlet/Satellite?cid= 1119503614923&pagename=IslamOnline-English-Ask_ Scholar%2FFatwaCounselorE%2FFatwaCounselorE, viewed 14 August 2007.

388 Islamic Sharia Council of UK & Ireland, "The Universal Declaration of Human Rights" http://www.islamic-sharia.co.uk/preface.html, viewed 6 January 2004 or http://www.islamic-sharia.org/index. php?option=com_content&task=view&id=13&Itemid=28&limit=1 &limitstart=4, viewed 9 August 2007.

389 http://www.aml.org.uk, viewed 2 December 2005.

390 http://www.ainakhan.com/islamiclaw.html, viewed 30 November 2005.

391 Ali Parsa, *Shariah property investment: developing an international strategy*, London: Royal Institution of Chartered Surveyors, 2005.

392 Ibid.

393 Ibid.

394 "Institute of Islamic Banking and Insurance", http://www.islamic-banking.com/institute/index.php, viewed 29 November 2005.

395 "Islamic House of Britain plc obtains FSA approval to become the first Islamic retail bank to open in any Western country", 9 August 2004, http://www.nortonrose.com/news/pre3107/news7491.aspx, viewed 9 August 2007; http://www.islamic-bank.com/islamicbanklive/ Board/1/Home/1/Home.jsp, viewed 12 October 2007; Islamic Bank of Britain, *Annual Report and Financial Statements, 31 December 2006*, http://www.islamic-bank.com/imageupload/ IBBAnnualReport2006.pdf, viewed 12 October 2007.

396 http://www.amanahfinance.hsbc.com, viewed 30 November 2005 or http://www.hsbcamanah.com/1/2/hsbc-amanah/1/2, viewed 9 August 2007.

397 http://www.muslimaid.org, viewed 30 November 2005 or http: //ramadan.muslimaid.org /, viewed 9 August 2007.

398 Shihoko Goto, "Terror crackdown won't stop Muslim giving", 12 September 2004, http://www.islamdaily.net/EN/Contents.aspx?AID= 1673, viewed 7 August 2005.

399 Charity commission, http://www.charity-commission.gov.uk/ registeredcharities/showcharity.asp?remchar=&chyno=1078489, viewed 12 October 2007.

400 Chris Blackburn , "Jamaat-i-Islami: A threat to Bangladesh?", http: //www.secularvoiceofbangladesh.org/Jamaat%20i%20Islami%20% 20A%20threat%20to%20Bangladesh%20by%20Chris%20Black burn.htm, viewed 8 January 2007.

401 http://www.islamic-relief.com, viewed 29 November 2007.

402 Charity Commission, http://www.charity-commission.gov.uk/ registeredcharities/showcharity.asp?remchar=&chyno=328158, viewed 12 October 2007.

403 Islamic Relief press release: "Press Release: Islamic Relief nationwide appeal for Pakistan Quake", http://www.mabonline.info/ english/modules.php?name=News&file=article&sid=548, viewed 12 October 2005 or http://www.reliefweb.int/rw/RWB.NSF/ db900SID/ACIO-6H2TRT?OpenDocument, viewed 7 August 2007.

404 DFID press release: "Islamic agencies play vital role in fighting poverty – Thomas", http://www.dfid.gov.uk/news/files/pressreleases/ pr-islamicagencies.asp, viewed 12 October 2005.

405 http://www.interpal.org

406 http://www.intelligence.org.il/eng/sib/12_04/interpal.htm, viewed 12 October 2005 or http://www.terrorisminfo.org.il/malam_ multimedia/html/final/eng/sib/12_04/interpal.htm, viewed 9 August 2007.

407 Sean O'Neill, "Britain rejects Bush's charges against Charity", *The Daily Telegraph*, 25 September 2003.

408 Sudha Ramachandran, "Mixing aid with terror", *Asia Times*, 22 September 2005.

409 Paul Marshall, "Outside encouragement sharia rules Nigeria – with the help of foreign Islamists", *National Review Online*, 5 May 2004; "Kano: Nigeria's ancient city-state", *BBC News*, 20 May 2004.

[410] "Why NGO boss was thrown out", *East African Standard*, 5 March 2004, http://www.africanewssearch.com/index.php?archive=1& month=3&day=5&year=2004, viewed 9 August 2007.

[411] Faisal Bodi, "Islamophobia should be as unacceptable as racism", *The Guardian*, 12 January 2004.

[412] Abdul Adil, "Muslims dismayed at Blunkett comments", *The Muslim News*, Issue 175, 28 November 2003.

[413] http://www.ihrc.org.uk

[414] Sajjad Tharoo, "UK Muslims launch report and campaign on anti-Muslim discrimination", http://www.muslimedia.com/archives/world00/uk-report.htm, viewed 7 August 2007.

[415] Anthony McRoy, *From Rushdie to 7/7: The Radicalisation of Islam in Britain*, London: The Social Affairs Unit, 2006, pp. 153–155.

[416] "IHRC Advisors", *IHRC Newsletter*, Vol. 6, Issue Ramadan 1426 /October 2005, http://www.ihrc.org.uk/file/ihrc-issue%206–2005-low%20res.pdf, viewed 10 October 2005; Daniel McGrory and Richard Ford, "Extremist on deportation list is linked to Islamic advice group", *The Times*, 1 September 2005.

[417] Daniel McGrory and Richard Ford, "Extremist on deportation list is linked to Islamic advice group", *The Times*, 1 September 2005.

[418] Anthony McRoy, *From Rushdie to 7/7: The Radicalisation of Islam in Britain*, London: The Social Affairs Unit, 2006, pp. 153–155.

[419] Kenan Malik, "Are Muslims hated?", *30 Minutes*, TV Channel 4, broadcast 8 January 2005, transcript, http://www.kenanmalik.com/tv/c4_islamophobia.html, viewed 10 October 2005.

[420] "Change foreign policy – top Muslims", *The Evening Standard*, 22 July 2005.

[421] "Antisemitism Worldwide 2002/3", http://www.tau.ac.il/Anti-Semitism/asw2002–3/uk.htm, viewed 10 October 2005.

[422] http://www.fairuk.org, viewed 7 October 2005.

[423] http://www.fairuk.org/media.htm, viewed 7 October 2005.

[424] http://www.mpacuk.org, viewed 7 October 2005.

[425] MPAC statement: "MPAC is a non-profit making organisation working with the community, helping the Muslims to help themselves" http://www.mpacuk.org/content/view/9/314/84/, viewed 7 August 2007; Faisal Bodi, "Islamophobia should be as unacceptable as racism", *The Guardian*, 12 January 2004.

426 "Muslim Educational Centre of Oxford Annual Conference", http://www.meco.org.uk/panel.htm#karim, viewed 11 October 2005.
427 "MPACUK Success", *The Muslim Weekly*, 16 May 2005.
428 "Muslims, Mosques & Angry Young Men! An Interview with MPACUK", http://www.mpacuk.org/content/view/1067/105/, viewed 11 October 2005 or http://www.mpacuk.org/content/view/1067/39/, viewed 7 August 2007.
429 Yamin Zakaria, "Inside the Mind of a Suicide Bomber – Targeting Civilians, Part 2", http://www.mpacuk.org/content/view/1015/103/, viewed 11 October 2005 or http://www.mpacuk.org/content/view/1015/39/, viewed 7 August 2007.
430 "Muslims, Mosques & Angry Young Men! An Interview with MPACUK", http://www.mpacuk.org/content/view/1067/105/, viewed 11 October 2005 or http://www.mpacuk.org/content/view/1067/39/, viewed 7 August 2007.
431 "MPACUK Success", *The Muslim Weekly*, 16 May 2005.
432 Ehsan Masood, *British Muslims: Media Guide*, London: British Council, 2006, p. 50.
433 http://www.muslimnews.co.uk/index/section.php?page=about_us, viewed 5 October 2005.
434 http://www.themuslimweekly.com
435 Abid Ullah Jan, "Islam, Faith and Power", *The Muslim Weekly*, 8 July 2005.
436 Shahid Butt quoted in "Change Foreign Policy – Top Muslims", *The Evening Standard*, 22 July 2005.
437 See entry on "Great Britain", in John L. Esposito, ed., *Oxford Encyclopedia of the Modern Islamic World*, New York: Oxford University Press, 1995, Vol. 2, p. 71.
438 Ehsan Masood, *British Muslims: Media Guide*, British Council, 2006, p. 50.
439 M.H. Faruqi, "The promise of Turabi's release", *Impact International*, Vol. 33, Issue 10, October 2003. p. 36
440 Azzam Tamimi, "From Oslo, down the Road Map: No peace, more blood", *Impact International*, Vol. 33, Issue 10, October 2003, pp. 19–21.
441 Muzaffar Iqbal, "The clash of civilisations!", *Impact International*, Vol. 33, Issue 8, August 2003, p. 6

442 Ahmad Irfan, "Reporting at Camp David", *Impact International*, Vol. 33, Issue 6&7, June–July 2003, p. 37.
443 Muzaffar Iqbal, "The road to freedom", *Impact International*, Vol. 33, Issue 6&7, June–July 2003, p. 8.
444 Muzaffar Iqbal, "Welcome to the new empire!", *Impact International*, Vol. 33, Issue 5, May 2003, p. 8.
445 Muzaffar Iqbal, "Making sense of a non-sense!", *Impact International*, Vol. 33, Issue 4, April 2003, p. 8.
446 "*Q-News* The Muslim Magazine", http://www.q-news.com/about. htm, viewed 5 October 2005.
447 Ehsan Masood, "British Muslims must stop the war", *openDemocracy*, 30 August 2005, http://www.opendemocracy.net/ articles/ViewPopUpArticle.jsp?id=2&articleId=2786, viewed 5 October 2005 or http://www.opendemocracy.net/conflict-terrorism/british_ sufis_2786.jsp, viewed 7 August 2007.
448 David Cameron, "What I learnt from my stay with a Muslim family", *The Observer*, 13 May 2007.
449 Yasmin Alibhai-Brown, "Revealed the brutal truth that hides inside the Burqa", *The Evening Standard*, 30 November 2005.
450 Farrukh Dhondy, "Institutional inspiration", *The Guardian*, 2 July 2002.
451 Abd Al-Rahman Al-Rashed, writing in *Al-Sharq Al-Awsat* (London), 14 November 2005. Partial English translation in The Middle East Media Research Institute (MEMRI), Special Dispatch Series No. 1036, 29 November 2005.
452 Quoted in Alexandra Frean, "Summer camps for children 'could stop racial segregation'", *The Times*, 23 September 2005.
453 M. Ali Kettani, "The Problems of Muslim Minorities and their Solutions" in Islamic Council of Europe, *Muslim Communities in Non-Muslim States*, London: Islamic Council of Europe, 1980, p. 105. This book comprises some of the papers given at an international seminar organised in London in July 1978 by the Islamic Council of Europe, sponsored by the Organisation of the Islamic Conference and financed by the Islamic Solidarity Fund.
454 Lois Lamya' al-Faruqi, "Islamic Traditions and the Feminist Movement: Confrontation or Cooperation?", *Jannah.org* http://www. jannah.org/sisters/feminism.html, viewed 30 August 2005.

455 Albrecht Hauser, *Germany's Future – an Islamic Republic? Islam's Challenge to Church and Society in Germany and Europe*, paper presented at a conference at the Center for Lutheran Theology and Public Life, Concordia Seminary, St Louis, USA, 12 October 2007.

456 Ayatollah Khomeini, at a press conference in Paris, February 1979, quoted in John Laffin, *The Dagger of Islam*, London: Sphere Books, 1979, p. 123.

457 Altaf Gauhar, writing in *The Guardian*, 26 February 1979, quoted in John Laffin, *The Dagger of Islam*, London: Sphere Books, 1979, p. 1.

458 Editorial in *The Guardian Weekly*, 14 April 1979.

459 Albrecht Hauser, *Germany's Future – an Islamic Republic? Islam's Challenge to Church and Society in Germany and Europe*, paper presented at a conference at the Center for Lutheran Theology and Public Life, Concordia Seminary, St Louis, USA, 12 October 2007.

460 Excerpts from a speech given by Libyan leader Mu'ammar Al-Qadhafi, aired on Al-Jazeera TV on 10 April 2006. See "Libyan leader Mu'ammar Al-Qadhafi: Europe and the U.S. Should Agree to Become Islamic or Declare War on the Muslims", The Middle East Media Research Institute (MEMRI). TV Monitor Project, Clip No. 1121, 10 April 2006, http://www.MEMRItv.org/Transcript.asp?P1=1121, viewed 22 August 2006.

461 Ibid.

462 Yusuf al-Qaradawi, excerpts from a programme aired on Qatar TV on 28 July 2007. See "Sheik Yousuf Al-Qaradhawi: Islam's 'Conquest of Rome' Will Save Europe from Its Subjugation to Materialism and Promiscuity", The Middle East Media Research Institute (MEMRI). TV Monitor Project, Clip No. 1592, 28 July 2007, http://www.memritv.org/clip_transcript/en/1592.htm, viewed 6 November 2007.

463 David Miliband's speech to the College of Europe, Bruges, 15 November 2007, http://www.publicpolitics.net/modules.php?op=modload&name=News&file=article&sid=84959, viewed 16 November 2007.

464 Ibid.

465 Abu'l Hasan al-Mawardi, *The Ordinances of Government: al-Ahkam al-Sultaniyya w'al-Wilyat al-Diniyya*, translated by Wafaa H. Wahba, The Centre for Muslim Contribution to Civilization, Reading: Garnet Publishing Ltd, 1996, pp. 152-154.

466 http://www.txnd.uscourts.gov/pdf/Notablecases/holyland/07–30–07/0030085.pdf, viewed 28 August 2007.

467 Muhammad Taqi-ud-Din al-Hilali and Muhammad Muhsin Khan, *Interpretation of the Meanings of the Noble Qur'an*, 15th edition, Riyadh: Darussalam, December 1996, pp. 845–864.

468 Ibid., Q9:60.

INDEX

Page references in bold are for glossary definitions, e.g. in the following example there is a glossary definition on page 263: *amir* 29, **263**